Becoming Foucault

INTELLECTUAL HISTORY OF THE MODERN AGE

Series Editors

Angus Burgin
Peter E. Gordon
Joel Isaac
Karuna Mantena
Samuel Moyn
Jennifer Ratner-Rosenhagen
Camille Robcis
Sophia Rosenfeld

BECOMING FOUCAULT

The Poitiers Years

Michael C. Behrent

PENN

UNIVERSITY OF PENNSYLVANIA PRESS

PHILADELPHIA

Published by
University of Pennsylvania Press
Philadelphia, Pennsylvania 19104-4112
www.upenn.edu/pennpress

Printed in the United States of America on acid-free paper
10 9 8 7 6 5 4 3 2 1

Hardcover ISBN: 978-1-5128-2514-5
eBook ISBN: 978-1-5128-2513-8

A catalogue record for this book is available
from the Library of Congress.

For my father and the memory of my mother

CONTENTS

Introduction

After his death, two ceremonies were held for Michel Foucault. Though only a few hundred kilometers separated them, they were worlds apart. The first took place on the morning of Friday, June 29, 1984. It did not bring out the thousands who, four years earlier, had poured into Paris's streets to accompany Jean-Paul Sartre's coffin to its final resting place at Montparnasse Cemetery. But Foucault's *levée du corps*, when the philosopher's body was removed from Paris's La Pitié-Salpêtrière Hospital, was undeniably an event. Several hundred attendees assembled to watch Foucault's casket being carried from the mortuary to the courtyard outside. As they did, the philosopher Gilles Deleuze, standing at a podium, read from the recently published second volume of Foucault's *History of Sexuality*. The attendees represented a cross section of French academic, cultural, and political life. The philosophers Michel Serres and Jacques Derrida could be seen in the crowd, alongside the ethnologist Georges Dumézil and the historians Paul Veyne and Jacques Le Goff. Robert Badinter, the sitting minister of justice, paid his last respects, as did the well-known acting couple Yves Montand and Simone Signoret. Other members of the audience included the publisher of *Le nouvel observateur* magazine, the director of the French National Library, and editors from the prestigious Gallimard publishing house. A brief televised news segment on the ceremony noted the presence of "former Maoists."[1]

A quite different ceremony occurred later that afternoon. Foucault's coffin was loaded into a hearse, which began a several-hour drive southwest. Its destination was the small village of Vendeuvre-du-Poitou. It was here that Foucault's mother lived, not far from Poitiers, the provincial town where Foucault had been born and raised. In the local newspaper, Foucault's mother, sister, and brother announced an "religious funeral . . . followed by a private burial in the Vendeuvre cemetery."[2] The service was held in the village's ancient church. Afterward, some fifty people gathered at a nearby cemetery, located along a country road. The local paper reported: "Before the pale wood coffin covered in wreaths [stood] a friend of the writer, a Dominican monk of the Saulchoir Abbey in Paris," whose library Foucault often visited during his final years. The monk, who had become a close friend of the philosopher, read passages from *The Archaeology of Knowledge* and *The Order of Things*. The "mortal remains of Michel Foucault were then buried at 6 P.M. in the very simple family vault, near his father, a surgeon deceased in 1959 and his maternal grandparents and great-grandparents." An excerpt from a poem by René Char was read. Then "the philosopher's mother, an 84-year-old lady, with her son and daughter on either side, threw a carnation onto the coffin."[3]

The two funeral ceremonies capture something fundamental about Foucault: the tension between the milieu in which he lived and worked as a renowned philosopher and the world into which he had been born. The Paris ceremony, attended by the famous and anonymous alike, captured the heady dynamism of Parisian intellectual and political life. The Vendeuvre ceremony, however, consisted primarily of family members and personal relations. The former ceremony was secular, occurring on the steps of an austere institution, of the kind that Foucault so frequently addressed in his writing; the latter was religious, steeped in provincial Catholicism. The former focused on Foucault the individual; the latter, while celebrating the man, also honored a family name, with accounts noting that one of the twentieth century's best-known thinkers was the son of a respected local physician.

The Parisians who attended the Vendeuvre ceremony experienced emotional whiplash when, still disoriented by their loss, they discovered their friend's provincial home. In a fictionalized account, the writer Hervé Guibert, who had been very close to the philosopher at the end of his life, recalled meeting Foucault's mother. She was "rigid, royal, and transparent, without a tear, in her hood chair beneath an eighteenth-century painting, [as] she held court, surrounded by several wives of the village's prominent citizens who had come to offer their condolences." With Foucault's brother, Guibert visited the family property: "it was very vast, [the Foucaults] were undeniably a great provincial bourgeois family, the most respected family in the village. . . . I never imagined that [Foucault] was born into so comfortable a family."[4]

Decades after his death, Foucault's work has become canonical, even if his original and often troubling perspective can still elicit controversy. Not only does he continue to be widely read and frequently referenced, but his life, too, has become a cultural touchstone. For some, he represents the ancient idea of an exemplary life in a postmodern idiom, thanks to the innovative forms of political activism he pioneered and the way he lived his sexual identity. For others, he embodies the nihilistic lifestyle resulting from the eradication of authority and social norms that his philosophy might be interpreted as championing. Yet whatever position one takes, the point of reference is typically the facet of Foucault's life on display at the Paris ceremony: the world in which he forged his intellectual and political relationships and cultivated his philosophical and academic persona.

The setting in which Foucault spent his early years is rarely discussed and far less familiar. But was it so far removed from Foucault's subsequent life as friends like Guibert implied? In the Vendeuvre cemetery, Foucault was laid to rest next to his father, Paul Foucault, who, as local reports never failed to mention, was a well-regarded Poitiers-based surgeon. Few of his son's books fail to address doctors and medical science, and some make it their explicit focus. The regional newspaper's account of the funeral alludes to the Foucault family's prominence, and Guibert described them as a "great provincial bourgeois family." Not only was Foucault self-conscious about his origins—"I lived as a child in a petit bourgeois, provincial milieu in France," he once told an interviewer—but the specific character of the bourgeois family—including its sexual dynamics—is a theme that he explicitly pondered in his work.[5] The Foucaults' home life, as these accounts suggest, was comfortable. But Foucault would have also associated it with the Second World War's darkest hours, when British bombs exploded nearby and Gestapo agents stalked the streets. The religious ceremony and the presence of a Dominican brother were also bridges between both worlds. On the one hand, Foucault's *History of Sexuality* had led him to explore the theology and ascetic practices of early Christians, compelling him to spend long hours at the library of a Dominican monastery in Paris (where the monk who spoke at the funeral resided). On the other hand, this interest harked back to Foucault's upbringing, when he was immersed in a culturally Catholic environment and taught by priests and monks. Far from being an eerie coda to the life of an avant-garde thinker, Foucault's burial in Vendeuvre evoked formative moments of the philosopher's youth.

This book explores the Foucault of the Vendeuvre funeral rather than the Parisian *levée du corps*. More precisely, it argues that Foucault's early experience decisively shaped his thought and intellectual personality. While this study will focus on Foucault's earliest years in Poitiers, it is not, strictly speaking, a biography, at least in the conventional sense. It is, rather, an inquiry into the relationship between thought and experience. Foucault's early life was the matrix of his mature thought. His youthful experiences did not rigorously determine his later theoretical positions or concepts so much as they focused his mind on a lived reality that, years later, would become the object of philosophical elaboration. While this study proposes an approach to intellectual biography and a framework for conceptualizing the intersection between individual experience and thought, it is also a book whose method is tailored to its subject. In understanding Foucault, experience matters because he was, in a very real sense, a philosopher of experience. To reflect on the experiences that shaped him is not just to identify factors that influenced his thinking. It is to grasp something crucial about his philosophical style.

Yet in what sense was Foucault a philosopher of experience? And why is it necessary to focus specifically on his earliest years? It is to these questions that we now turn.

A Philosopher of Experience

So influential has Foucault's impact been on contemporary thought that it is tempting to see his philosophy as engaged with similarly consequential interlocutors. Foucault, after all, proposed spirited critiques of phenomenology, structuralism, and deconstruction; nursed a sustained skepticism toward psychoanalysis; and probed the blind spots of liberalism and Marxism. While this perception of Foucault is broadly accurate, it overlooks crucial dimensions of his work that are hiding in plain sight. For instance, almost every book that Foucault published through the mid-1960s dealt with doctors and medicine. His early essays on mental illness (*Maladie mentale et personnalité*, 1954) and *Madness and Civilization* (1961) examined the medicalization of madness in modern times; *The Birth of the Clinic* (1963) traced the advent of the medical gaze by way of the "anatomo-clinical" method; and *The Order of Things* (1966) focused on the life sciences (along with linguistics and political economy) as a framework for understanding the changing structure of knowledge from the Renaissance to the nineteenth century. It is no coincidence that the thinker who dwelt on these matters was the son of a surgeon and descended from a long line of medical professionals on both sides of his family—a lineage of which he was acutely aware and that he occasionally mentioned. Foucault did not launch his philosophical career by polemicizing against a major philosophical system or devising one of his own. He began by wrestling with issues that were central to his—and his family's—experience. One would be hard-pressed to make a similar case, say, for Karl Marx, who as a young man embraced Hegelian philosophy rather than continuing the legal studies encouraged by his father, a Prussian bureaucrat, or for Sigmund Freud, who, for all his legendary "greed for knowledge," devoted himself to studies in neurology and physiology that had little to do with his petit bourgeois upbringing.[6] Applied to Foucault, the term "philosopher of experience" is by no means a generic claim. It captures something unique about his character as a thinker.

For Foucault, what mattered was not simply experience itself—its purity or authenticity—but the insights that experience makes possible. He was particularly intrigued by the relationship between experience, knowledge, and truth. He first articulated these interests in an unpublished thesis he wrote in 1949, while enrolled at the École Normale Supérieure, on G. W. F. Hegel's *Phenomenology of Spirit*.[7] The main conclusion that he drew from his reading of Hegel's celebrated work was that knowledge and experience are tightly intertwined—not just in the banal sense that one learns from experience, but, more profoundly, because knowledge makes experience possible and experience is saturated with knowledge. Emphasizing how Foucault's early writings drew on his upbringing in a medical family implies neither that he was sentimentally attached to medicine nor that he was engaged in an oedipal revolt against his father and the medical profession (though both these claims contain an element of truth). It is to say, rather, that Foucault believed that his experience was philosophically significant—that in the recesses of these experiences flowed epistemological currents that only a particular kind of inquiry could measure. This approach comes perilously close to biographical reductionism, as it appears to suggest that Foucault's thought was a means by which he settled his own psychological scores, rendering it of little consequence to anyone other than Foucault himself. Yet such a criticism is valid only if one accepts the claim that biography is philosophically reductive— in other words, that a philosophers' experiences have no bearing on their thought. This book argues that, at minimum, this was *not* Foucault's position—and that our understanding of his contributions to modern thought will be enriched by identifying the experiences that formed the raw material of his oeuvre.

Thus "experience" is not simply a vantage point from which Foucault's life and thought can be analyzed; it is also a Foucauldian concept—one that he employed frequently and that mattered greatly to him. Yet unquestioned assumptions about Foucault's philosophy have obscured the place of experience in his thinking. Commentators often interpret Foucault's references to the idea of experience as vestiges of his philosophical immaturity, as they are primarily found in his early writings. The young philosopher's investment in this concept is often attributed to his early interest in phenomenology, a school of thought that traces various forms of cognition back to specific states of consciousness and seeks to restore the lived experience in which intellectual activity originates. Once he had honed his archaeological method—and had thus become a mature thinker—he no longer succumbed, so the thinking goes, to the lure of a supposedly pristine level of experience existing prior to philosophical elaboration but viewed experience as entirely constructed through epistemological and linguistic frameworks. Experience, in this way, is often associated with a position that Foucault had to abandon to come into his own theoretically.[8]

It is true that Foucault attached particular importance to experience in his youth and that this position was tied to his attraction to phenomenology, which, during his student days, was at the height of its influence. Yet Foucault put the concept to work well beyond his youthful phase. It made a particularly dramatic return in his final years. Indeed, references to experience abound in Foucault's work, to the point that they become a kind of leitmotif. Clearly, Foucault believed that much was at stake in the notion of experience.

That Foucault used the term so frequently should not be surprising. "Experience" figures prominently in the lexicons of the thinkers who had the greatest impact on Foucault's early thought and who belonged to what one might call the long history of German idealism. Immanuel Kant, to whom Foucault devoted a portion of his doctoral thesis, defined philosophy's task, in *Critique of Pure Reason*, as identifying the "*a priori* principles [that] are indispensable for the possibility of experience."[9] Hegel, the subject of Foucault's 1949 thesis, saw experience (*Erfahrung*) as the process through which consciousness works its way toward true knowledge or "science." Phenomenologists like Edmund Husserl drew on the idealist tradition to argue that the study of ordinary experience in its various forms could rise to the level of rigorous science. The recurrence of "experience" in Foucault's oeuvre can be explained by his early engagement with these thinkers.

In the 1949 Hegel thesis, Foucault offers his first sustained reflection on experience. Here, Foucault wrestles with the technical question of the place of transcendentals in Hegel's thought. For Kant, who gave the term its modern meaning, transcendentals refer to the intellectual preconditions that must obtain for both experience and knowledge to be possible. Without a priori (or pre-experiential) conditions like space and time or unity and plurality, neither experience nor knowledge would be possible. But what do these claims have to do with Hegel? Because Hegel's thought is concerned with the formation of consciousness through historical processes, rather than with knowledge's preconditions, Foucault's decision to search for the very Kantian concept of transcendentals in Hegel's magnum opus is a surprising move. Yet doing so allowed Foucault to explore his understanding of experience and its philosophical significance. Whereas Kant maintained that much of what we call consciousness exists prior to experience, Hegel showed, according to Foucault, that consciousness emerges out of the rough-and-tumble of experience itself. This did not simply mean that consciousness is bombarded with sensory data. It also means that the concepts or categories that that consciousness uses to organize experience are *the outcomes* of earlier experiences. In short, according to Foucault, the study of experience demonstrates that transcendentals are not only *constituting* (in the sense that they make experience possible) but *constituted* (that is, they arise from experience itself). This striking observation—that some experiences generate the very conditions that make other experiences possible—is tied to another crucial insight that Foucault gleaned from Hegel: that experience is inseparable from knowledge, that knowledge is the energy that drives experience forward.

Anyone having some familiarity with Foucault's thought will recognize, in his Hegel thesis, a rough draft of his signature concept of the "historical a priori": the idea that knowledge at any given period is determined by mental structures that precede all specific experiences, yet which (contra Kant) vary from epoch to epoch. Insights such as these helped Foucault, at the dawn of his philosophical career, to formulate his own understanding of experience. Experience, he believed, is not just *what* we learn; it is also *how we know* and the *kind of self* we are. In other words, the categories through which we know the world and the way we understand our own subjectivity are distillations of experience. Experience is not simply the raw material of knowledge, but the medium, as it were, in which knowledge exists. To have experiences is to be a knowing being—and vice versa.

While Foucault's understanding of the concept of experience no doubt evolved, it persisted in his lexicon and, throughout his career, occupied a prominent position in his thought. In his 1954 introduction to an essay by the existential psychiatrist Ludwig Binswanger, Foucault spoke of "oneiric experience," characterizing dreams as a "specific form of experience." These experiences, he claimed, were irreducible to positivistic analysis: "Dreams, like all imaginary experiences, are thus a specific form of experience that does not allow itself to be entirely reconstituted by psychological analysis."[10] The imperative of retrieving the experience of psychological states from the distortions of scientific positivism was a recurring motif in his early writings. In his first book, published in 1954, Foucault asserted that mental illness could be understood only by those who could place themselves at the "center of this experience," grasping it "from within."[11] Around the same time, he used a Hegelian vocabulary to admonish psychiatrists to see mental illness as an "experience of . . . contradiction" and as man's "experience of his negativity."[12] In *Madness and Civilization*, the pathbreaking study he published in 1961, Foucault defined his task as the "reconstitution of [the] experience of . . . madness," through a history, not of "knowledge" but the of "rudimentary movements of an experience."[13]

In a series of essays from the 1960s, moreover, Foucault analyzed avantgarde literature in terms of the types of experiences explored by its leading proponents. Raymond Roussel probes the "marvelous and suffering experience of language." Georges Bataille inhabits a world in which the death of God has become the "constant realm of our experience," inaugurating "an experience of finitude and being, of limits and transgression." Pierre Klossowski reconnects with "Christian experience"; Marcelin Pleynet confronts his readers with the "simple experience that consists in taking a pen and writing"; and *nouveau roman* authors like Philippe Sollers are engaged in a "series of experiences" unique to "language" itself.[14]

During this early phase, "experience" was what Foucault believed he was studying—at least as much as knowledge, structures, and discourse. In his later work, despite a dramatic change in focus, the reference to experience nonetheless persists. *The Birth of the Clinic* (published in 1963) is often seen as settling Foucault's score with phenomenology and taking a decisive step toward structuralism, the social sciences paradigm that emphasized the primacy of impersonal (especially linguistic) structures in the determination of meaning. Yet even in this book, Foucault refers to the "medical experience" epitomized by the French anatomist Bichat and Freudian psychoanalysis, pairing it with the "lyrical experience" associated with poets such as Hölderlin and Rilke. The "forms of finitude" that inhere in modern medical epistemology are rooted in a shared "experience," begun in the eighteenth century and which "we have yet to escape."[15] While Foucault no longer spoke of a phenomenological recovery of experience, he doubled down on his Kantian stance, describing the book as an effort to identify "the conditions of possibility of medical experience" in modern times.[16]

While Foucault did occasionally refer to experience in the late 1960s (his late archeological period) and the 1970s (his genealogical phase), it was at the dawn of the 1980s, when his attention turned to subjectivity and sexuality, that "experience" began to resurface in his writing in a conceptually significant way. In *The Use of Pleasure*, the second volume of his history of sexuality, Foucault described the original project as a "history of sexuality as experience"—"if one understands experience," he qualified, as "the correlation, in a culture, of domains of knowledge, types of normativity, and forms of subjectivity."[17] Beginning with the second volume, however, the *History* would strike out in a new direction, downplaying power and normativity and prioritizing selfhood and the "games of truth . . . through which being is historically constituted as experience, that is, as something that can and must be thought."[18] As Foucault once again emphasized the centrality of experience to his work, he attempted to explain the difference between his earlier use of the term and the manner in which he now understood it. In an earlier draft of *The Use of Pleasure*'s introduction, Foucault connected his conception of a history of experiences to his early writings: "To study forms of experience in this way—in their history—is an idea that originated with an earlier project, in which I made use of the methods of existential analysis in the field of psychiatry and in the domain of 'mental illness.'" This approach ultimately left Foucault "unsatisfied" (for reasons beyond the scope of this project), leading him to emphasize "the domain where the formation, development, and transformation of forms of experience can situate themselves: that is, a history of thought." Yet properly understood, thought refers to a kind of action, insofar as action is always steeped in truth criteria, a particular attitude toward rules, and relationships to oneself and others. In terms that evoked his Hegel thesis, Foucault concluded that the "study of forms of experience" examines action and practices "*insofar as* they are inhabited by thought."[19]

The language Foucault used for his history carried over into his political activism. After returning from a trip to Poland in 1982, during which he observed the Communist regime's efforts to suppress the independent Solidarity trade union, Foucault observed: "in the behavior of the Poles, there was a moral and social experience that can no longer be erased."[20] Around the same time, Foucault agreed to write a retrospective essay on his oeuvre for a dictionary of philosophers (under the transparent pseudonym "Maurice

Florence," or "M.F."), in which the concept of experience was prioritized: what interested Foucault about the "discourses of mental illness, delinquency, [and] sexuality" is not that they simply impose some external and arbitrary truth on subjects, but that they "open a field of experience in which subjects and objects are each constituted only under simultaneous conditions, yet in which they are incessantly changing in relation to one another, and thus changing the field of experience itself."[21] In one of his last interviews, Foucault mused that not that much separated his most recent books from his early ones: all "revolved around the problem, which is always the same, . . . of the relations between subjects, truth, and the constitution of experience."[22]

On several occasions, Foucault described his books as autobiographies. Because his work comes across as forbidding and austere, this claim is often considered enigmatic. If, however, one considers Foucault's own writings, and specifically what he said about experience, the meaning of this peculiar claim comes into focus. While Foucault believed that experience was shaped by preexisting knowledge conditions and power structures, he also believed that experience fed back into these knowledge conditions and power structures—into what, earlier in his career, he called the "historical a priori." His own work recapitulated this transition from experience to knowledge. In 1981, Foucault explained: "Each time I had tried to do a theoretical work, it was based on elements of my own experience."[23]

In seeking to identify the early experiences that shaped Foucault's philosophy, this book provides a thick description, as it were, of his own thought process. Foucault's emphasis on the centrality of experience to thought is an invitation to unpack the experiences that informed his own philosophy.

The Young Philosopher and Experiential Matrices

Some of the most significant modern philosophers are young philosophers—that is, philosophers whose youthful work is original and distinct enough from their mature work that it is considered to have its own value and unity, while also shedding light on the thinker's oeuvre in its entirety. Because philosophers' youthful work provides opportunities to reinterpret their thought, assessments of these early stages are prone to polemic. The debate over the "young Hegel" pitted those who saw the philosopher's youthful writings as steeped in mysticism and pantheism against those who gleaned in them a trenchant critique of established religion and political economy.[24] Even more fraught has been the debate over the "young Marx," which ensued after Marx's early writings were published for the first time in the twentieth century. In these works, some found a thinker concerned with human alienation under capitalism and immersed in Hegelian concepts, and thus an alternative to the economism and historical determinism that had come to define Marxism; others dismissed Marx's youthful pronouncements as inadequately scientific and tainted by idealism.[25] More recently, the historian Edward Baring has posited the existence of a "young Derrida"— a thinker of Foucault's milieu and generation—to explore the discrepancies between the founder of deconstruction's early thought and his mature work.[26]

The problem of the "young Foucault" has been more rarely addressed, though this is likely to change in the years ahead. José Luis Moreno Pestaña made a valiant early effort to reconstruct the young Foucault's thought, focusing on a handful of early but long-available publications as well as the possible influence of his teachers. Ultimately, Moreno Pestaña is interested less in the content of Foucault's early thought than in the intellectual strategies through which Foucault managed to fashion himself as a stylishly radical thinker on the French intellectual market.[27] Recently, Stuart Elden has proposed a useful reconstruction of Foucault's early thought during this same period, drawing on the trove of manuscripts that are now available at the Bibliothèque National in Paris. Without weighing in on the interpretive positions Elden takes in his book, it is worth noting that he begins his narrative at the point at which Foucault began his studies at the École Normale Supérieure in Paris. "Foucault's childhood and early schooling," Elden explains in his introduction, "will not be discussed here."[28]

While this book is about the "young Foucault," it does not approach the topic in the same manner as Moreno Pestaña or Elden. What it means by the "young Foucault" is different. Rather than focus primarily on early writings that precede his better-known published work, this study will explore the place of experience in Foucault's thought—specifically, the way in which experiences in childhood and adolescence shaped Foucault's intellectual preoccupations and philosophical personality. Instead of presenting a chronological narrative of his youth, this book examines the primary experiential matrices of his thought. By "experiential matrices," I mean experiences that marked Foucault and that he later felt compelled to ponder and theorize. Experiential matrices constitute the nexus between biography, historical context, and intellectual production. For instance, in a 1968 interview dealing primarily with his literary style, Foucault remarked: "I am the son of a surgeon."[29] As Chapter 1 will demonstrate, this statement has a biographical dimension, relating to Foucault's father, Paul Foucault, and the long line of doctors from which he came; a historical dimension, linked to the rise of the medical profession in nineteenth-century France; and an intellectual-historical dimension, in that medicine and medical discourse were privileged objects of reflection in Foucault's work. The point is not to present Foucault's story as predetermined by his youth, but to identify the conceptual vectors passing through his thought—vectors in which early experience informs mature reflection.

The uncovering of the experiential matrices of Foucault's thought thus makes it necessary to operate on multiple temporal planes. On the one hand, Foucault's mature work and utterances provide direct and indirect clues to the formative experiences that shaped his thinking. On the other hand, it is necessary to reconstruct the historical contexts needed to fully grasp the nature of these early experiences. In this way, analyzing Foucault in terms of experiential matrices requires a method that is constantly moving back and forth between Foucault's mature work and his early years, between his considered thought and its origins in unarticulated experience.

The experiential matrices approach thus implies both a residually causal argument—certain early experiences played a decisive role in determining Foucault's interests and concerns—as well as a hermeneutic one, focused on the meaning that Foucault assigned those experiences. The method pursued in this book is, consequently, both rigorously empirical and boldly speculative. I carefully reconstruct the contexts that shed light on Foucault's early life, drawing on local and professional histories, contemporary sources, and archival materials. At the same time, I use the evidence to reflect on what it tells us about Foucault's formative experiences and, in this way, to advance claims about the origins and character of his thought. In identifying the contexts that are *relevant* to Foucault's thought (as opposed to irrelevant contexts, which, despite being concurrent with his youth, did not become matrices for his subsequent reflections), I have relied in particular on Foucault's own testimony. Unlike other major French thinkers of his generation, Foucault never wrote an autobiographical text—not even one that, like noteworthy texts by Jacques Derrida and Pierre Bourdieu, sought to reconceive the autobiographical genre in light of his theoretical positions.[30] Yet Foucault, over the course of his life, gave scores of interviews; and while he only rarely used them as occasions to reflect on his life, the instances in which he did—as well as what aspects of his past he chose to dwell on—are significant. I have considered these utterances as clues to identifying the experiential matrices of Foucault's early years. This approach is necessary because it delimits the bays and estuaries in the sea of Foucault's experience that make the contours of his thought most apparent. It may not be surprising, for instance, that Foucault referred to his provincial upbringing in Poitiers or that he was a child during the Second World War. But when he mentions the assassination of Engelbert Dollfuss in 1934 as the great political fear of his youth or invokes the fear of death he experienced during wartime bombardment, we can take these references as invitations to consider the impact of these early experiences on his later thought. In some cases, I have identified experiential matrices not by drawing on interviews, but by observing well-defined themes that recur in Foucault's writings. For example, the fact that, at various moments in his writings and teaching, Foucault repeatedly referred to forensic pathology (known in French as *l'expertise médico-légale*) and fascism has justified my decision to view them as experiential matrices, which in turns makes it necessary to do the historical research required to grasp how these themes became relevant to Foucault's early life. The experiential matrices approach thus entails its own kind of hermeneutic circle, involving an analytical back-and-forth between Foucault's mature pronouncements and a contextual reconstruction of his early years.

While this approach emphasizes the formative character of Foucault's early years on his subsequent thought, it is not strictly speaking a psychological study, and even less a psychoanalytic one. In what follows, I do not seek to provide an account of Foucault's early years that identifies a pattern of psychological motivations that informed his later work, nor do I attempt to analyze the young Foucault's childhood to reconstruct, in Freudian terms, his "family romance." This choice is, in part, pragmatic: because there are no available sources about these aspects of Foucault's early years—memoirs, letters, or diaries—such an approach would face serious obstacles. Consequently, this book's approach is less psychological than historical: it shows how many of Foucault's theoretical reflections were rooted in specific historical experiences and a distinct social environment. The stakes of this method are, moreover, not so much psychological as cognitive: it seeks to identify the root experiences, as it were, that Foucault subsequently elaborated into theoretical arguments.

This approach, moreover, provides a novel lens through which to read Foucault's work. There has been a tendency to view Foucault as a thinker

who prioritized methodology, whether by theorizing the epistemological paradigms that characterize a particular epoch, tracing shifting configurations
of power relations, or analyzing the various ways selfhood can be fashioned
through ethics. In this reading, the content addressed by Foucault exists
mainly to validate his innovative methodologies. Without denying Foucault's
status as the founder of important new paradigms in the humanities and the
social sciences, the experiential matrices approach shows how the concrete
issues he addressed were as central to his philosophical enterprise as were the
methodologies he developed to explain them. When one considers Foucault's
thought as a reckoning with his earliest formative experiences, one sees not
only a thinker who is concerned with epistemological structures and power
relations, but also one who was preoccupied, at various points in his life, with
the rise of the French medical profession, the nature of National Socialism
and the Vichy regime, the bourgeoisification of the working class, the evolving relationship between the family and the state in modern times, and the
development of forensic pathology. In this way, the experiences that prompted
Foucault to arrive at his distinctive theoretical positions are brought into focus.

In formulating this approach, I have been particularly influenced by the
work of the historian Jerrold Seigel and his conception of intellectual biography. Seigel seeks to interpret the oeuvre of philosophers, writers, and artists
by identifying recurrent themes and patterns in their work that harmonize
with and are reinforced by similar patterns in their personal lives. Thus the
"struggle between individual self-affirmation and social obligation" that is
thematized in Émile Durkheim's religious sociology mirrors the same conflict he lived out as an Alsatian Jew who excelled in the meritocratic educational system of the Third Republic.[31] Similarly, the tension between a
craving for the concrete world and the desire to capture it in the language of
philosophical abstraction is central, Seigel argues, to Karl Marx's historical
materialism as well as to the dynamics of his personal life.[32] Of his approach
Seigel writes: "Comparable contradictions, expressed in comparable patterns
of recurrence, can be found in the careers of other thinkers. . . . Nor do these
patterns constitute merely the 'background' of a theoretical system; the real
import of a thinker's propositions often remains hidden without them."[33]

This approach makes it possible to identify the interplay between Foucault's experiences, the meanings he assigned them, and his mature thought
by blending biography, contextual intellectual history, and a close reading of texts. While it aspires to elucidate Foucault's philosophical personality, this method does not rely on specific psychological theories (such as

psychoanalysis and the Oedipus complex), even when the material might appear to invite them. Rather, this approach takes its cues from the spontaneous self-interpretations offered by Foucault himself, connecting them to moments in Foucault's youth in which they initially emerged.

To interpret the young Foucault, this book will examine four broad experiential matrices and associated patterns of thought. The first was Foucault's exposure to the medical profession, thanks largely to his father, a surgeon, and the long line of doctors in his family's past. This experience accounts for Foucault's deep ambivalence toward medicine, which he saw as both an archetypal form of knowledge and a practice that can dehumanize and silence individuals deemed sick and unhealthy. The second is Foucault's familial and intimate relationships, as interpreted through the term "intensities," which he frequently used to characterize particularly close personal connections. Family ties, in Foucault's lexicon, could be stilted and apathetic, but they could also be passionate and emotionally fraught. In this way, they modeled other relationships into which individuals could be drawn. These insights provide a vantage point from which to consider Foucault's views about his own family and the meaning of his bourgeois identity, as well as the relationship between intimate connections and his self-described "personal obsession" with confinement. The third experiential matrix is the young Foucault's experience of the Second World War and the German occupation of France. It is ironic how little attention has been devoted to the twentieth century's great philosopher of power's firsthand experience with a regime that has become synonymous with totalitarian rule. A reconstruction of Foucault's wartime experience lays bare a number of formative matrices: his preoccupation with death and the philosophical significance of exposure to death; his fascination with the ways in which families are permeable to social and political forces; his insights into the instability, reversibility, and brittleness of power relations; and his understanding of fascism, which, though he devoted little sustained reflection to it, occupies a strategic place in his thought. Finally, a fourth matrix is the school system in which Foucault was educated and, in particular, his exposure to philosophy. This matrix connects Foucault's youth to the earliest discernable elements of his formal philosophical training. Examining this moment shows the conflict to which Foucault was exposed between Third Republican rationalist humanism, on the one hand, and a Catholic critique of this humanism, on the other.

When Foucault claimed, as referenced above, that his work was always grounded in "elements of my own experience," he added: "It was indeed because I thought I recognized in things that I saw, in institutions that I had to deal with, [and] in my relationships with others cracks, muffled tremors, dysfunction, that I undertook a work, a few autobiographical fragments."[34] What follows is an attempt to take Foucault at his word, to use this claim as a hermeneutic for attaining a richer understanding of his thought and the contexts that enabled it.

CHAPTER 1

Doctors

The cemetery is unremarkable: an acre or two of tombs lining a few sandy paths, shaded by haphazardly planted poplar trees. A wall separates the graveyard from the even Poitou landscape, several scattered houses, and a country road leading to the nearby village. One enters through a rusting metal gate, topped by a dark cross. Just off the main path lies a flat, horizontal, rectangular tombstone. On the gray granite, one can just make out, carved in gold lettering that is almost washed out by the gleaming surface, the words: "Paul-Michel Foucault: Professeur au Collège de France, 1926–1984." The philosopher shares his resting place with two family members. One he never knew: a maternal third great-grandfather, who died in 1848. The other he knew all his life: Anne Foucault née Malapert, his mother, who was born with the century and died in 1987, three years after her son. A pot of begonias lies at the foot of the grave; on it stands a small tablet with an image of the Virgin Mary and the word "souvenirs."

Immediately to the left lies a tomb made of darker stone, covered with a rectangular embossed cross. Of the four names engraved on the headstone, two are identified as doctors—this professional title replacing, on the slab's limited surface, any mention of a first name. Second from the bottom is "Docteur Foucault"—born 1893, died 1959—the father and husband, respectively, of the man and woman lying in the adjacent grave. At the top is "Docteur Malapert" (born 1864, died 1925): the father-in-law and colleague, at the Hôtel-Dieu in nearby Poitiers, of Dr. Foucault and the philosopher's maternal grandfather. Beneath the Poitou's rolling, oceanic clouds, the remains of the son lie a few dusty inches from those of his father, their tombs abutting yet separated amid the rural silence (Figure 1).

Silence, Foucault suggested in a rare autobiographical interview, was a quality he associated with his father, the surgeon Paul Foucault. The "speech of

Figure 1. Vendeuvre-du-
Poitou Cemetery. The tomb
on the right is that of Michel
Foucault and his mother,
Anne Foucault née Malapert.
The tomb on the left is that
of Foucault's father, Paul
Foucault, and his maternal
grandfather, Henri Malapert.
Photograph by Jean-François
Liandier.

the doctor," Foucault explained in 1968, "is extraordinarily rare."[1] This insight
was impressed on him by his upbringing: "I belong to a medical milieu, one
of those provincial medical milieus that, in relation to the rather sleepy life of
a small town is undoubtedly a relatively adaptive or, as they say, progressive
milieu."[2] Yet this world, "particularly in the provinces," remained "profoundly
conservative." It "still belonged to the nineteenth century." The hallmark of

this medical environment was its glib commitment to rationalism. "In the nineteenth century, the bourgeoisie found in medical science, in the care for the body and health, an everyday rationalism. . . . I believe that this character of the doctor, thus formed and, as it were, sacralized in the nineteenth century, who took the place of the priest, who gathered around himself in order to rationalize them all the old beliefs and credulities of eighteenth and nineteenth-century France's provinces, peasantry, and petty bourgeoisie, I believe this character has remained rather frozen, rather immobile, rather similar to himself since this time." Foucault added: "I lived in this milieu in which rationality assumed an almost magical prestige."[3]

The stature of these provincial, conservative, frozen-in-time doctors, of whom Foucault's father was evidently an example, owed much to their silence. "Indeed, the doctor—and particularly the surgeon, and I am the son of a surgeon—is not one who speaks, but one who listens." Yet the doctor's quiet does not imply a willingness to hear another's speech. For what he listens to is not words, but the inchoate rumble of organisms. The doctor "listens to the speech of others, not to take it seriously, not to understand what it means, but, through it, to track down the signs of serious illness, that is, an illness of the body, an organic illness." Words are sounds that mediate between two silences: the doctor's laconic attention, and the inarticulate sounds of the body. "The doctor listens, but in order to pass through the words of the other and reach the body's mute truth. The doctor does not speak, . . . he palpates."[4]

Though he worried about offering an "autobiography that is at once too anecdotal and too banal" to be of interest, Foucault, in his description of the archetypal surgeon, conveys impressions of his father. "The surgeon discovers the lesion in the sleeping body, he opens the body and sews it back up, he operates: all this while being utterly mute, reducing words to an absolute minimum. He names and orders, that is all."[5] For the medical mind, speech is self-indulgent verbiage; when doctors listen, it is not to grasp a speaker's meaning, but to discern a symptom, material to inform a diagnosis. When the surgeon utters his own words, silence seeps into his pronouncements, limiting his words to their strictest, most circumscribed meanings. A few years earlier, reflecting on psychoanalysis's account of family relations, Foucault suggested that this kind of truncated, orderly speech exemplified the role not of doctors, but of fathers in general: "Melanie Klein and then Lacan have shown that the father, as the third person in the Oedipal situation, is not only a hated and threatening rival, but he whose presence limits the relationship between the mother and the child, to which the fantasy of devouring gives its first anguished form. The father is thus he who separates, that is to say, he who protects when, pronouncing the Law, he ties together into a major experience space, rules, and language. Of a sudden it creates the distance all along which develops the rhythm of presences and absences, the speech the primary form of which is constraint, and the relationship between signifier and signified on the basis of which not only will language be edified, but the repressed with be rejected and symbolized."[6] The surgeon's clipped utterances and precise meaning exemplifies, in this way, the paternal function, which severs the bond uniting mother and child with the scalpel of clinical speech, instituting an orderly world that is haunted in its interstices by a chilling silence.

In his first major book, Foucault maintained that madness in modern societies had been engulfed by a similar silence—a silence that had only become more deafening as madness was construed as a medical phenomenon. In the original preface to *Madness and Civilization*, Foucault wrote: "In the midst of the serene world of mental illness, modern man no longer communicates with the madman. . . . A common language does not exist; or, rather, it no longer exists; the constitution of madness as mental illness in the late eighteenth century takes official note that the dialogue has been broken off, that separation is taken for granted, and thrusts into forgetting those imperfect, somewhat stammering words, lacking fixed syntax, in which the exchange between madness and reason took place." Modern psychiatry—the medical discourse on madness—"could only be founded on such a silence." Foucault had undertaken to write not "the history of this language," but "the archaeology of this silence."[7] Yet the weight of this medical silence could be heard only if one *listened to*—and *heard*—the confused speech to which doctors paid no heed. It was imperative, Foucault contended, to "let speak, on their own, these words, these texts that arise from beneath language, and that were not made to accede to speech." He added: "And perhaps the most important part of this work, in my eyes, is the place I have granted to the very text of the archives themselves."[8] He seems to have in mind the testimonials of the mad he had found in the Bibliothèque de l'Arsenal, which led him to wonder whether it was possible for certain words to be heard: "Is there a place in the universe of our discourse for the thousands of pages in which Thorin, a nearly illiterate servant and 'furious madman,' transcribed, in the late seventeenth century, his bolting visions and his barking terror?"[9] Whether such words could truly accede to language was a question Foucault left in doubt. Yet it was still possible to fashion a language that, rather than accepting as a *fait accompli* the silencing of madness on which psychiatry was founded, could convey the "primitive vivacity" with which reason and madness had once engaged in an "indefinite debate." The ambition of this language—and that of *Madness and Civilization* itself—was to be "*absolutely heard.*"[10] In these statements, a project is being formed: that of restoring to speech, of liberating the words that medical knowledge, in its laconic indifference, has rendered irrelevant. To pierce its stony silence with the expressive fervor of words.

Yet in the 1968 interview, Foucault curiously mused that, in the end, his own work was not so different from his father's: "I imagine that in my dip pen there is an old inheritance of the scalpel."[11] The difference was that the son sliced with the very thing that the father had seemed to discredit: language— words, that is, insofar as they had anything other than a narrow, referential purpose. This "deep, functional devaluation of speech in the old practice of clinical medicine" weighed down on him for much of his childhood. Until he was ten or twelve, speech, for him—one presumes in his family—was little more than "wind."[12] In a much later interview, Foucault referred to the same childhood impressions when he commented: "When I was a boy I never thought of becoming a writer."[13] Yet what Foucault, as a thinker, came to realize, is that the view of language he attributed to his father was itself an illusion: for language, undeniably, *exists*—it has its own consistency, its own "density," its own positivity. Far from being "wind," language is "discourse"— words that seep into the world, giving it its form and often constraining force. Foucault would make this point in *The Archaeology of Knowledge*, the book he published the following year to disabuse those of his "contemporaries" who were "victims of the same mirages as my childhood." The analysis of language needed, in this way, to become positive and scientific: "an analysis of things that are said insofar as they are *things*."[14] Foucault conceded that this had not been always his personal experience with language. He was drawn to writing because it represented the very antithesis of clinical analysis—an activity that was "extremely soft, felt-like," suffused with an "impression of velvet." This idea of "velvety writing," straddling "the affective and the perceptual," is one that constantly guided Foucault when he was writing, helping him to choose his expressions.[15] Consequently, it surprised him to hear that others found in his writing a certain "aggressiveness," a "dry and mordant" tone.[16] Despite his "conversion" to writing, Foucault concluded, upon reflection: "I must have kept from childhood, and even in my writing, a certain number of filiations that can be found."[17] He mused: "do I trace on the whiteness of paper the same aggressive signs that my father traced on the bodies of others when he operated? I have transformed the scalpel into a dip pen."[18]

As a writer, Foucault had absorbed and sublimated his father's experience in one other way as well: he was not only a surgeon, but an anatomist who performed autopsies on corpses: "A piece of paper, for me, is perhaps the bodies of other people."[19] Foucault went so far as to situate his consciousness of the connection between writing and death at a specific moment in his own life: "What is certain, what I felt immediately when, around the time I was thirty, I began to experience the pleasure of writing, is that this pleasure always communicated a little with the death of others, [and] with death in general."[20] When Foucault turned thirty in 1956, he had, of course, completed a small book and several lengthy essays. Yet this reference to the age at which he finally began to enjoy writing and connected this sensation to the "death of others" seems difficult to dissociate from a crucial event in his life: on September 14, 1959, a month before his son's thirty-third birthday, Paul Foucault died. The philosopher described his own writing as a kind of autopsy—a practice that his father had taught at the École de Médecine of Poitiers. Using images that recalled the famous cartoon of Gustave Flaubert, at the foot of an operating table, holding up Emma Bovary's dripping heart with a scalpel plunged through it, as he prepares to examine it with the magnifying glass in his other hand, Foucault observed that by speaking of the dead, he "postulate[d], in a sense, their death." He explained: "Speaking of them, I am in the situation of the anatomist who does an autopsy. With my writing, I roam around the body of others, I make incisions in it, I lift the teguments and the skin, I try to uncover the organisms and, bringing the organs to light, to make appear this site of lesions, this site of pain, this something that characterized their life, their thought, and that ultimately, in its negativity, organized all that they were. The venous heart of things and men—that is, deep down, what I have always tried to bring to light."[21]

Foucault, in short, was perpetuating a family tradition, which made him the latest in a long line of doctors and surgeons—albeit in the very idiom that the medical profession and presumably his own father had dismissed as bereft of value, as so much "wind." And his assumption of this heritage was contingent on "the death of others"—including, it would seem, that of Foucault's own father. He was often asked, Foucault told the interviewer, whether he was a philosopher, a historian, a sociologist, or something else. His answer: "I am neither, I am a doctor, or, shall we say, I am a diagnostician. I want to do a diagnosis, and my work consists in bringing to light through incisions something that is the truth of what is dead."[22] Foucault was the son his father wanted, who would take over his own practice—but only after his death, once his body had been reduced to a corpse, like the many corpses he had cut open. "I think that I am entirely faithful to my heredity, since, like my father and my grandparents, I want to make a diagnosis." The only difference, he said, was that "I want to do it on the basis of writing, I want to do it in this element of discourse that doctors, ordinarily, reduce to silence."[23]

Foucault's musings indicate that he believed that his father's profession and intellectual demeanor had informed, in ways that were at once obvious and obscure, his own philosophical concerns and style. Questions relating to doctors, medical knowledge, and the medical profession played a significant role in shaping the concerns and dispositions that eventually coalesced into his mature thought. The point is not that the young Foucault, growing up in a household organized around and financed by the medical profession, was already developing a critique of the medical mind-set that he would formulate in such later works as *The Birth of the Clinic*—though in truth, Foucault never wrote a book that did not touch on medicine, at least in passing. The claim is rather that this milieu provided him with the raw experiential material that he could later reformulate on a high theoretical plane as he acquired an increasingly sophisticated skill for philosophical argumentation in his late teens and twenties. Medicine seems to have become the template for the philosophical problems that preoccupied him most of his life—specifically, how established forms of knowledge and institutions claim to understand individuals in ways that dispossess them of their identity and ensnare them in networks of social control.

A Family of Doctors

Michel Foucault was supposed to have been a doctor. His biographers tell a version of the same story. Around the time he was sixteen, Foucault had an argument with his father, in which the elder Foucault insisted that his son go to medical school, before yielding to his wife's and Michel's objections.[24]

The medical profession is one of the crucibles of the young Foucault's development. As Foucault himself noted in the 1968 interview, his "father and ... grandparents" were all doctors. For decades, medicine had been the foundation of the livelihood and status of Foucault's family.

Foucault's mother, Anne Malapert, belonged to a long line of doctors and pharmacists that had been established in Poitiers since the early nineteenth century. Her family's medical dynasty was founded by her great-grandfather,

Pierre-Prosper Malapert (whom I shall refer to as Prosper), who was born in 1798 in Charroux, a village south of Poitiers.[25] A passion for science brought him to Paris, where he trained at the École de Pharmacie, established in 1803. Returning to Poitiers, he opened a pharmacy in 1822 that he would manage for nearly forty years. As he approached forty, he returned to school to become a *pharmacien de première classe*. This resulted in his appointment as professor of chemistry at the local medical school, the École Préparatoire de Médecine et de Pharmacie de Poitiers, making him the first of many of Foucault's relatives to be associated with that institution. Malapert thus joined the financial benefits of owning a pharmacy to the social prestige of an academic title. He was, moreover, an enthusiastic amateur scientist, who, among other discoveries, invented a way of producing ice by dissolving sodium sulfate with sulfuric acid. He regularly published his findings in the *Bulletin de la Société de Médecine de Poitiers*. Despite his wealth, recognition, and large family, his old age was disrupted by tragedy: in 1876, his son, Édouard Prosper Malapert, died suddenly at age forty-eight. He had followed in his father's footsteps, studying in Paris at the École de Pharmacie, where he defended a thesis,[26] before becoming a professor at the Poitiers medical school and, as his obituary described him, a "distinguished chemist."[27] When Prosper Malapert died over a decade later, at eighty-nine, it befell his grandson to uphold the family association with medicine. While one of Édouard Prosper's sons became a military officer and the other a philosopher (to whom we will return in the fourth chapter), his youngest son, Henri Paulin Prosper, born in 1864, followed the Malaperts' by now well-traveled path. After studying medicine and acquiring the prestige of an *internat* (or residency) at a Parisian hospital, he was appointed, like his father and grandfather before him, to the Poitiers medical school, not as a pharmacist, but as a professor of surgical pathology and operating medicine. He also had a lucrative surgical practice and served as surgeon at Poitiers's main hospital, the Hôtel-Dieu.[28]

Henri Malapert died in 1925 and thus never knew his grandson Michel Foucault, who was born the following year. But he did know Paul Foucault, Michel's father: not only was Malapert Foucault's father-in-law, but the two men were colleagues in the tight-knit world of Poitiers's medical establishment. He presumably saw his daughter Anne Malapert's marriage to Paul Foucault in 1924 as an alliance between two distinguished medical families: the Foucaults' commitment to the profession was as deep and long-standing as the Malaperts'.

Like the Malaperts, the Foucaults participated in the rise of the medical profession in the early nineteenth century. The founding father on this side of the family was Jacques-Symphorien Foucault, born in 1811. In 1835, he defended a thesis at the Paris medical faculty,[29] and immediately registered as a doctor in Nanterre, a village to the west of Paris that had yet to become the major suburb it is today.[30] With some regularity, he attended and made presentations to the Academy of Medicine in Paris. He published in Parisian medical journals. Jacques-Symphorien Foucault was particularly proud of a siphon he had invented to provide continuous irrigation of the "bladder, the urethra, the vagina, the uterus and the rectum."[31] To his Parisian colleagues, he offered insights he had gathered as a country doctor and surgeon. In 1860, he described the ordeal of delivering the child of a twenty-four-year-old woman with rickets. The mother's pelvis being unusually narrow, the child's head could not be extracted, despite his best efforts with forceps. He rejected decollating—that is, decapitating—the child, as it was a "barbarian operation, despite being authorized, recommended, and suggested by the art." He opted, instead, for a symphysiotomy, a procedure that, by splitting the pelvic symphysis, creates more room for the infant to be removed. Though the infant died, the mother was able to "return to her occupations" within two months.[32] Jacques-Symphorien Foucault may have been a country doctor, but he was not lacking in ambition.

Some of his aspirations were no doubt realized by his son. Born in Nanterre in 1844, Paul Victor Foucault studied in Paris, where he was taught by a "who's who" of the French medical elite. In medical school, he attended the lectures of the great Alfred Velpeau, the chair of clinical surgery at the Paris medical faculty and the author of important textbooks. He interned with such medical luminaries as Aristide Verneuil, Ulysse Trélat, and Henri-Louis Roger. He was drawn to the emerging field of public health. From 1869 to 1870, he interned at the Hôpital des Enfants Malades (Paris's children hospital) during a measles epidemic that resulted in a high death rate among its young patients. He wrote a study of the incident that, in 1870, was awarded the Paris medical faculty's prestigious Montyon prize.[33] Later that year, he briefly served as a doctor during the Franco-Prussian War, tending to soldiers wounded during military efforts to end the siege of Paris.[34] In 1872, he published his medical thesis, *Essay on Mixed Nerve Tumors*. In this work, Paul Victor Foucault showed—like his father before him—an interest in and familiarity with the history of medicine, prefacing his study with a discussion of nerve tumors in the works of Hippocrates, Galen, and Ambroise Paré, among others. He also referenced more recent authors, showing a notable interest in Rudolf Virchow's work on the rare form of cancer known as chordoma. Though his thesis was devoted to offering a detailed anatomical pathology of nerve tumors, dwelling extensively on several operations he had observed during his residencies, it betrayed an urbane and literary flair. Thanks to his accomplishments, he achieved a level of material comfort in addition to a solid reputation. In 1879, he married Marie-Sophie-Louise de Cuvillon, who belonged to an old aristocratic family from northern France.[35] Her father was a prominent violinist, and her paternal uncle a military doctor decorated during the Crimean War.[36] Though Paul Victor was born in modest Nanterre, he moved his family to Fontainebleau, a well-heeled town some sixty kilometers southeast of Paris. It was here that, in 1893, Paul André Foucault—the philosopher's father—was born.

"In aristocratic peoples," Tocqueville once wrote, "all generations [are] so to speak contemporaries. A man almost always knows his ancestors and respects them; he believes he already perceives his great-grandsons and he loves them."[37] The Malaperts and Foucaults were not, for the most part, aristocrats, but the epitome of the professional bourgeoisie. Yet one senses that, like the nobility, they saw themselves as belonging to a dynasty, in which honor and commitment to the medical profession weighed as much as name and title. Prosper Malapert was described in his obituary as "an *homme de bien*, honest and conscientious." His "long existence" was "so well filled." His students, the author concluded, would long remember him, and he would "serve as an example to pharmacists and would teach them to place the honor and glory of their profession above any vain demands."[38] A history of the Poitiers medical school referred to Prosper Malapert as "the eminent toxicologist, whom old Poitevins piously remember."[39] They were proud of the learned societies to which they belonged, as well as the distinctions they had earned: Paul Victor Foucault received the Montyon prize, and Henri Paulin Malapert the *Légion d'honneur*.[40] Professional status could be leveraged into political responsibilities: when Édouard Prosper Malapert died in 1876, a liberal newspaper remembered him not only as a "distinguished chemist," but also as a city councilor whose death was "a loss for the republican party, of which he had always been one of the most valiant soldiers."[41] These memories, moreover, were preserved in the family's oral traditions. Foucault's biographers have drawn on stories about his medical forefathers passed down to his siblings and cousins.[42] A scholar who researched the family's first doctor for a paper published in 1976 noted that he had benefited from the "oral tradition[s]" provided by "Madame Foucault, née Malapert, the great granddaughter of Prosper Malapert"—and the philosopher's mother.[43]

As each new generation of doctors completed its studies and prepared to join the profession, it expressed gratitude, moreover, for the role played by its predecessors in making possible the opportunities that would soon be their own. This recognition is particularly evident in the dedications they included in their medical theses. There is a ritualistic quality to these dedications, in the way they recognize exhaustive lists of mentors who, from residency to residency, guided fledgling doctors to their goal. They also testify to the powerful role that family and, in particular, the paternal example played in shaping the career choices of the sons of medical families. In 1872, Paul Victor dedicated his thesis to Jacques-Symphorien Foucault, writing: "To my father: my most certain model in the career into which I have followed him."[44] In 1923, Paul André acknowledged his father, Paul Victor Foucault, who did not live to see his son complete his training: "To the memory of my father, who will always remain for me the example of probity and professional conscientiousness."[45]

These dedications attest to the nexus between family and professional life in nineteenth-century culture. As Jerrold Seigel argues, the bourgeois family functioned as a "resource" and a "network," notably by providing children with the means, the dispositions, and the contacts required to prosper in a world in which social relations were becoming increasingly open-ended. "Webs of family connections," Seigel writes, "provided people with resources for gaining access to the more extended and powerful networks of means through which distant resources could be coordinated and directed toward particular goals."[46] It seems likely that Foucault's ancestors used their contacts (such as their memberships in professional societies) and educational pedigree to provide similar opportunities to the rising generation. Thanks to these contacts, the fact that the Malaperts were based in Poitiers, for instance, did not exclude them from the prestigious professional networks centered in the Parisian medical community. The material wealth that the medical profession increasingly provided would itself have been a significant resource for ensuring their children could undertake the time-consuming and costly expense of medical studies in Paris (where all five of Foucault's doctor forefathers discussed here studied). The "assemblages of capital, talent, and information" accumulated by nineteenth-century medical families such as the Foucaults and Malaperts served as "vehicles for inserting" their sons into "outside economic, political, or cultural linkages" that helped them in "developing their talents or fulfilling their aims and ambitions."[47]

The dedications also testify to a powerful ideal that shaped both families' images of themselves as exemplifying the honor and status of the rising
medical profession. At the nineteenth century's outset, the social standing
and professional identity of doctors was tenuous at best. They were tainted by
their association with manual labor, despite their work's nominally "liberal"
character. Financially, their situation tended to be less stable than other professions (notably owing to a persistent problem of collecting bills), and they
were only just beginning to establish themselves as a well-regulated profession. Over the course of the nineteenth century, their circumstances changed
dramatically. New legislation that defined the medical career (the law of 19
Ventôse year XI [1803] and that of November 30, 1892), the establishment of
professional associations (notably the Association Générale des Médecins de
France in 1858), and the introduction of more rigorous training in medical
schools contributed to defining the medical career as a profession and significantly raised its social status. If Paul Victor Foucault, in 1872, could see his
father as his "most certain model in the career" in which he followed him, it
was because the career itself was increasingly well defined. Since medicine
rests its authority on knowledge, moreover, professionalization also entailed
a certain politics of truth, as evidenced in the crusade against charlatanism.
The "probity" Paul André Foucault admired in his father may refer, at least in
part, to his ongoing concern with this problem.

Doctors in this period came to think of themselves as answering a calling,
as fulfilling a quasi-religious mission to society that entailed altruism and
sacrifice. In the homage they paid to their fathers, the Foucaults and Malaperts made the professional values of nineteenth-century doctors a family
ideal. This ideal was one that Michel Foucault would interrogate in his work,
particularly when he pondered the changing status of the medical profession and its implication for medical knowledge. He liked to refer to the fact
that "in the nineteenth century, health replaced salvation" and the doctor has
"taken over from the priest."[48] This remark was not simply a comment on
medical knowledge's discursive authority, but a direct reference to the profession's own self-understanding. The notion that the medical profession
was a *sacerdoce*—a priesthood, of sorts—was a commonplace in nineteenth-
century medical literature. One of the first authors to write about medical
ethics in France described the doctor's role as a "moral apostolate" and spoke
of the "perilous priesthood" to which the medical profession was called.[49]
Foucault's claim that doctors had acquired a quasi-priestly status in modern
times was an insight that was not only scholarly, but experiential: it showed

an awareness of the terms in which doctors—the family profession of the
Foucaults and Malaperts—had asserted their professional ascendency over
the century proceeding his birth.

An Excellent Knife

As a father, it was incumbent on Paul Foucault to provide his own children
with the same resources that had made his own career possible, and to pass
onto them the same professional ethos. Foucault's father remains, however,
a somewhat elusive character. His extensive writings are mostly purged of
autobiographical hints; testimonials from his friends and colleagues are few
and far between. His writing lacks the refinement and teasing wit of his own
father's prose. He might, perhaps, have shared his father's opinion, stated in a
study from 1872, that doctors who write must let the facts speak for themselves
and erase their own personalities: "The author has effaced himself as much as
possible, and is content to bring to the stage numbers and facts, genuinely
tragi-comic characters, and to make them play the roles they must assume,
depending on their absolute value and monotonous eloquence; hence a uni-
formity in [this book's] exposition [and] a dryness of style that truly leaves one
in despair."[50] Michel Foucault's famous reflections on the obsolescence of the
"author function" in scientific discourse, written nearly a century later, largely
mirror those of his own grandfather: beginning in the seventeenth or eighteenth century, he observed, scientific discourse began to be received "on its
own terms, in the anonymity of a truth that had been established or that could
always be demonstrated anew"; scientific discourse found its validity in its
internal coherence, "not because it referred to the individual who produced"
it.[51] The doctor, as Foucault had earlier observed, is he who "reduc[es] words
to an absolute minimum"; he "names and orders, that is all."
     Paul André Foucault was born in Fontainebleau on July 21, 1893. Follow-
ing the trail blazed by his father, and assisted, one imagines, by the wealth
of his aristocratic mother, he went to Paris to study medicine. In March
1914, at the age of twenty, he passed the *externat*, a competitive examination
that qualified him for a residency in Paris. His studies were interrupted by
the First World War, during which he served as an auxiliary doctor on the
Serbian front. He was decorated on several occasions (a point that will be
addressed in Chapter 3).[52] After returning from the front, he passed the *internat*—the second and highly prestigious exam that qualified medical students

for the next round of residencies. The leading historian of the French medical profession described the "aristocracy consisting of the interns of Paris hospitals" as an "extreme minority and a privileged elite" that "crowned the student world": only a fraction of the 350 to 400 students who took the *internat* each year qualified for one of the coveted available seats (generally between fifteen and sixty).[53] To be an "ancien interne des hôpitaux de Paris" was a lifelong distinction. Paul Foucault did the latter part of his residency at the Hôpital Saint-Antoine, founded during the French Revolution, located in the Faubourg Saint-Antoine, the working-class neighborhood that was the site of much revolutionary tumult during the nineteenth century. His mentors at Saint-Antoine, which according to some had the best surgery ward in the capital, included Joseph Arrou (1861–1938) and especially Félix Lejars (1863–1932), whom a contemporary described as "one of the most distinguished surgeons in Paris."[54] Lejars directed Paul Foucault's thesis, *Occlusions intestinales et coudures iléales* (Intestinal obstructions and ileal kinks), which he defended in Paris in January 1924 (Figure 2).[55]

The very month he became a doctor, he also married Anne Malapert in Poitiers. It is uncertain how the couple met. Clearly, Paul André Foucault had professional contacts with his future father-in-law prior to the wedding, as he thanks "Monsieur le docteur P. Malapert" in his thesis. Though the ceremony was held in Poitiers, the couple's status was sufficiently prominent to earn them mention in *Le Figaro*, one of the leading Parisian newspapers. Of the four doctors present at the wedding, Placide Mauclaire, a witness for the groom, was undoubtedly the most prestigious: in addition to being a prolific scholar and *chef de service* at the Pitié-Salpêtrière hospital in Paris, he was also, at the time of Paul Foucault's wedding, the sitting president of the Académie Nationale de Chirurgie, France's leading surgical society. In his writings, Mauclaire had referenced Paul Foucault's father as well as grandfather.[56] Paul Foucault also thanked Mauclaire in his thesis. The fact that a doctor who occupied such a preeminent place in his field attended a young doctor's wedding—in Poitiers, no less—is indicative of the young Foucault couple's social standing.

After his marriage, Paul Foucault permanently left Paris for Poitiers, where, with the help of his father-in-law, he made his medical career. Around the time he settled there, Poitiers had roughly twenty-four thousand inhabitants, including thirty-four doctors, and seventeen pharmacists.[57] Paul Foucault's professional life was based on three pillars. First, he had a position at the town's main hospital, the Hôtel-Dieu, where, in 1924, he was appointed an assistant surgeon (under his father-in-law). Second, he was also appointed

Figure 2. Paul Foucault (standing, second from right) during his residency at the Hôpital Bretonneau in Paris during the early 1920s. BIU Santé médecine–Université Paris Cité.

to the faculty of Poitiers's École de Médecine et de Pharmacie, which was located in the same complex as and overlapped considerably with the Hôtel-Dieu. Paul Foucault became the head of the school's surgery clinic, in addition to teaching the practical courses on anatomy and physiology. Because hospitals in France were, until 1945, reserved primarily for the poor, the most important of his professional pillars was the third: his work as a surgeon in two private clinics. The first was the Clinique du Pont-Achard, on Rue Georges-Guynemer, on Poitiers's west side; the second was the Clinique des Sœurs Hospitalières, on Rue Jean Jaurès in the town center, close to the school Michel Foucault attended.[58] Consistent with the tradition of la médecine libérale, he worked essentially as a private businessman, selling his talents as surgeon and obstetrician to the local population. Though he worked through these clinics, some of his work was run directly out of the home: located at 10, Rue de la Visitation—later renamed Rue Arthur Ranc—it had been built by Henri Malapert in 1903 and was just around the corner from the latter's home on the Rue des Écossais. This elegant three-story house was situated at the top of the steep cliffs that rise some forty meters above the Boivre River and the Poitiers train station, on the western side of the old city. With his two cars and a driver who could double as an anesthesiologist, Paul Foucault traveled through Poitiers and the surrounding countryside, bringing in considerable income while working long hours. Anne Foucault helped to run the business from their home, with the assistance of a hired secretary. Their income allowed them to live a comfortable life, which included a retinue of servants in their home and a country house, also inherited from the Malaperts, fifteen kilometers away in the village of Vendeuvre-du-Poitou. Their first child, Francine, was born in Poitiers in 1925. On October 15 of the following year, she was followed by Paul-Michel.[59]

The little we know about Paul Foucault's personality is gleaned from distant and fragmentary memories related to his work. When he began his career in Poitiers as a *chef de clinique* at the medical school, his father-in-law (and neighbor) was a full professor of surgical pathology and operating medicine. In January of his first year in Poitiers, however, Henri Malapert died.[60] By 1938, Paul Foucault was an associate surgeon at the hospital, and the following year, he was appointed to the chair of anatomy.[61] It was as a surgeon that Foucault's father left his mark. Those who knew him described him as an *"excellent couteau"*—an excellent knife. His wit, if contemporaries are to be believed, could also be cutting. One anecdote concerns his apparent rivalry with a younger colleague, a surgeon named Jacques Quivy. "It is said that while visiting the sick, questioning a patient in a very poor state, [Paul Foucault] asked in front of his students: 'Who is taking care of you, *mon ami*?' 'Doctor Quivy,' the other replied, and, turning toward his students, Paul Foucault archly—or was it mischievously?—observed: *'Docteur Quivy, malade qui meurt'*—roughly, "the doctor lives, the patient dies" (playing on the fact that "Quivy" sounds identical to *"qui vit,"* "who lives").[62]

Though recollections about Paul Foucault are rare, they tend to gravitate around the themes of surgery, his caustic sense of humor, and death. David Macey recounts how, shortly after the war, the surrealist painter André Masson, who briefly lived in the countryside near Poitiers, was treated by Foucault's father. In "a rather macabre gesture of friendship," Paul Foucault "showed him the corpse of a stillborn child with a rare lesion that exposed parts of the brain membrane." It became a subject of a "strange, swirling drawing" that Masson gave the doctor—and which, subsequently, long remained on the philosopher's work desk.[63] Moreover, in a short story à clef published shortly after Michel Foucault's death, his lover and confidant Hervé Guibert describes a dying philosopher who recalls how, as a child, he was "taken by his father, who was a surgeon, into one of the rooms in the Poitiers hospital, where a man was having his leg amputated—this is how one burnishes a boy's virility."[64] While there exist few assessments of Paul Foucault's character, his numerous writings at least partially confirm his strong identification with surgery in some of its more gruesome forms. They also suggest a dry and rather dark sense of humor. Some of his papers convey an almost comic assessment of the human body's weakness and vulnerability.

Paul Foucault, it is worth noting, wrote extensively (as shall be discussed below). In addition to publishing papers in national and regional medical journals (particularly, but not exclusively at the beginning of his career), he also presented multiple papers each year to the local medical society, the Société de Médecine de la Vienne, which met at the medical school and whose deliberations (including the text of papers) were routinely published in the Poitiers medical school's journal, the Revue médicale du Centre-Ouest, which Paul Foucault and several of his colleagues had helped to launch. Between 1929 and 1947 (excepting the years at the height of the war, when publication was interrupted), Paul Foucault published dozens of papers in this journal. Most describe unusual or exceptional circumstances he encountered in his surgical practice. For this reason, it is difficult, moreover, to discern dispositions and motives in these papers: they simply present, after all, cases that came the doctor's way.

Even so, Paul Foucault's writing is permeated with references to reproductive and excretory organs, gynecology, pregnancy, and the physiological aspects of sexual abnormality. On several occasions, for instance, Paul Foucault reported on how he had handled the presence of "foreign bodies" that women had inadvertently introduced into their lower orifices. In November 1938, an elderly woman suffering from vomiting and severe pain showed up at his clinic, explaining that the day before, she had pushed a thermometer into her urethra so deeply that it had slipped away from her, vanishing inside her body. Based on a diagnosis of the symptoms (an x-ray machine was not available), the doctor was able to surmise that the object had lodged in her bladder. A brief incision allowed him to locate and extract it.[65] In a paper given in November 1947, Paul Foucault mentioned four instances in which foreign objects had been introduced in vaginas: one was a pessary, and two involved attempted abortions (one with parsley). He dwelt longest on the

final case: "The fourth observation . . . relates to a drinking glass that a peasant woman of around forty had slid inside her for an unmentionable purpose.
Her husband awkwardly attempted to remove the glass with pliers and broke
the edge, which resulted in deep vaginal cuts and significant hemorrhaging."[66]
A vaginal incision was necessary to remove the glass.

Paul Foucault also reported on several cases of genital malformation. In
1938, he presented the case of Mademoiselle D., age forty-eight, who had never
had her period. On inspection, it was discovered that she had "no vagina, and
that the vulvar region was represented by a depression that was closed shut
by a solid membrane."[67] A year earlier, he described a similar case, that of
Madame B., a thirty-six-year-old woman who had never menstruated and
who experienced difficulties having intercourse in the first months of marriage. Examination of her vulva revealed that she, too, lacked a vagina, which
was no more than a "depression covered by a highly resistant epidermized
mucous membrane," while her urinary meatus was sufficiently open that it
easily admitted the tip of a thumb or two to three centimeters of the finger.
These measurements were presumably more than just a manner of speaking:
a photograph included in the article shows a close-up of the patient's vulva,
with fingers from two older, seemingly male hands pulling it from either side
to display the oversized meatus. What most interested Paul Foucault was the
way in which the couple had, despite Madame B.'s physical defect, overcome
a significant obstacle to sex by using her meatus for intercourse—a "truly
abnormal modality of coitus," as he put it. "One does not know," he concluded
wryly, "whom one should admire more: the woman's patience and her submission to an act that must have been, at the beginning, particularly painful
and, subsequently, relatively bothersome, or the man's obstinacy and his con-
stancy in seeking, then creating an orifice of sufficient dimensions to practice
a semblance of copulation."[68]

Each year, the *Revue médicale du Centre-Ouest*, of which Paul Foucault
was a leading figure and an editor in his capacity as a faculty member of the
Poitiers medical school, chose an epigraph for its cover. For 1937, it was a
quote from Bossuet: "Of all the passions of the human mind, one of the most
violent is the desire to know [*le désir de savoir*]."[69] Though we cannot know
if Paul Foucault chose this quotation, it seems representative of the approach
to knowledge that his acquaintances associated with him. Paul Foucault was
a surgeon, whose work, literally and figuratively, consisted in cutting open
bodies and penetrating their depths. His daily life entailed a penetrative relationship to human bodies. He pierced through tissues and organs, hunted

down "foreign bodies" that had themselves penetrated the body's orifices, and preoccupied himself with the penetration to which sexual and excretory organs are naturally (or not so naturally) prone. This literal penetration of the body's outer contours dovetailed with a metaphorical penetration of its secrets, thanks to the scalpel-like precision of his "desire to know."

This "desire to know" would be the exact locus of Michel Foucault's deep ambivalence toward the medical profession and the pursuit of knowledge in general, and his father in particular. In many respects, his own work partook in Paul Foucault's "desire to know"; at times, the philosopher suggested that he, in his own thinking (thanks to Nietzsche's decisive example), pursuing a second-order and hence superior "desire to know," insofar as what he sought to know was the meaning and purpose of knowledge itself. Yet at the same time, and for this very reason, Foucault's thought was a furious protest against the "desire to know." As he explained in his 1971 lectures, the deceit lying at the Western pursuit of knowledge since Aristotle—who famously said that "all men by nature desire to know"—was its failure to take seriously the idea of knowledge *as* desire. As *philo sophia*—love of wisdom—philosophy exemplified this "desire to know" while circumventing its meaning—as if "it were sufficient to make it the epigraph of its own discourse to justify its existence and to show that it is—suddenly—necessary and natural: all men by nature desire to know." Foucault's project, by contrast, was to shine a glaring light on this sleight of hand—to reveal the "elision of the desire to know that is nonetheless named [by the term] philosophy to explain and justify its existence."[70] From this perspective, one sees that the "desire to know" is, first of all, a *desire*: how else is one to explain the persistence with which Paul Foucault, throughout his life, ran his hands over and inside human bodies, his incessant *touchers rectaux* and *vaginaux* (rectal and vaginal examinations), justified in the name of knowledge at its most puritanically objective? The "desire to know" is, moreover, *violent* and *cruel*—in the incisions with which the surgeon opens the body, as well as, perhaps, the patronizing tone with which he mocks the masturbatory and mating habits of old women and peasants. The point is not that Paul Foucault was, as Guibert's short story suggested, a sadist, a father who forced his young son to witness amputations to teach him to be a man. It is, rather, that Foucault's father came to exemplify, in his son's eyes, the fact that medicine harbored an inherently sadistic dimension, a certain pleasure taken in the cutting and penetration of bodies that cast the entire enterprise of the "desire to know" in a new and troubling light. "Knowledge," Foucault once commented, "is not made for understanding; it is made for cutting."[71] In this remark from one of Foucault's best-known essays, the echo of Paul Foucault's Poitiers clinics and lecture halls makes itself heard.

Paul Foucault and His Kinks

The connection between knowledge and surgery—and, by extension, cutting—is one that Foucault's father explored not only in his medical practice, but in his extensive scholarly writings. In 1926, he published his *Titres et travaux*, a comprehensive summary of his articles and papers that came to over two hundred pages.[72] If Paul Foucault impressed on his son the ethos of the medical profession, he was also his earliest model of a scholar. Yet on this front, Foucault's father does not seem to have always appeared as all powerful and all knowing. Despite his intellect and proficiency as a surgeon, Paul Foucault, over the course of his career, embraced several medical theories that were subsequently revealed to be irrefutably false. His unflinching professionalism notwithstanding, a whiff of charlatanism pervades some of his work.

This is notably the case of Paul Foucault's 1924 thesis, *Occlusions intestinales et coudures iléales* (Intestinal obstructions and ileal kinks). His study built on the work of French and especially British doctors who tried to connect intestinal disorders to a wide range of medical conditions, including psychological afflictions, as well as to various social and cultural problems. The key figure in this movement was the British surgeon Arbuthnot Lane (1856–1943), who taught and practiced at Guy's Hospital in London. Lane, who was considered one of the finest surgeons of his day, became aware of the stress placed on the body by the colon in its non-evacuated state. The human intestinal system, he concluded, had evolved to serve the needs of a four-legged creature; once humans began to stand upright, the body had to support the colon's gravitational pull with only two legs. The better to harness the colon, the human body developed a series of adhesive bands. These, in turn, distorted the colon, leading it to develop "kinks" (*coudures*, in French). In propping up the colon, in other words, the body blocked its own waste evacuation system: the result was constipation, or, as Lane called it, "chronic intestinal stasis." Modern civilization only made matters worse: toilets and bed mattresses, not to mention the modern diet, exacerbated the problem of sagging colons. As one scholar puts it, adult life consisted, for Lane, in a "vicious downward spiral of tightening of the intestine and retention of waste matter in the body."[73]

The problem of chronic intestinal stasis went beyond mere discomfort. The colon, for Lane, was little more than a "sewage system" and a "cesspool": the maintenance of waste in the body due to the colon's kinking exposed it to dangerous toxins. Bipedalism led to constipation, which resulted, in turn, in what Lane called "autointoxication." Such was modern man's plight. Autointoxication was not, according to this theory, confined to physical ailments. Lane saw autointoxication as "the cause of all the chronic diseases of civilization,"[74] including the psychological illnesses that obsessed his contemporaries. He believed that violence and suicidal dispositions often resulted from self-intoxicating colons and, further, maintained that "the mental condition which is brought about by auto-intoxication" is one that "medical men are very fond of calling . . . neurasthenia."[75] To treat these conditions, Lane and his followers advocated invasive surgery. Several present-day doctors observe: "Lane was convinced that neurasthenia was almost always a matter of colonic toxemia. Beyond lifestyle interventions and internal disinfectants for mild or early-stage colonic stasis, a chronic state, in Lane's view, could only be resolved by surgery, typically a colectomy or complete colon bypass (so-called short circuit)."[76] In the first decades of the twentieth century, colectomies and similar procedures were all the rage. Lane himself was a superb surgeon whose patients rarely died in operation. Yet even at his own hospital, the total number of colectomies performed each year (about forty) resulted in the relatively high mortality rate of 16.5 percent. A colleague of Lane's was shocked at "how light-heartedly colectomy has been recommended for comparatively trivial symptoms."[77] The most horrific application of the ideas to which Lane had lent credibility occurred in the United States. Henry Cotton, a psychiatrist who served as the medical director at the New Jersey State Hospital from 1907 to 1930 and who had studied under Emil Kraepelin in Germany, launched an aggressive program of "surgical bacteriology" that sought to cure his inmates of mental illness by removing "fecal infections." He began by extracting teeth but increasingly targeted colons. The many colectomies he performed—without surgical training—at his facility had an extraordinarily high mortality rate: 33.3 percent, according to his own reckoning.[78] A report on the hospital concluded that mortality was indeed the main consequence of these methods, but Cotton's closeness to the medical establishment—particularly his mentor, the psychiatrist Adolf Meyer of Johns Hopkins—shielded him, at least initially, from public rebuke. By the 1920s, Lane's ideas, and their disastrous consequences in the hands of doctors like Cotton, had been largely discredited.

It was at the tail end of the Lane fad that Foucault's father defended a thesis that took the British surgeon's theories as its foundation. The thesis focused on *occlusions intestinales*, the French translation of Lane's idea of "intestinal stasis," when caused by kinks in the ileum, the final tract of the small intestine before it connects to the colon (or large intestine). Ileal kinks or *coudures iléales* were so closely associated with Lane's theory that they were often dubbed, as Paul Foucault noted, "*coudures de Lane*"—"Lane's bands" or "Lane's kinks." As Lane put it in a paper published in the *Lancet*, the ileum contained "the first and last kinks"—the first kink to develop in childhood, and the last in the intestinal tract. It was thus critical to his theory, as well as to surgical remedies. Lane wrote: "The fuller recognition of the function of this kink, the lowest in position, has helped me to understand the physiology of the large bowel both in the savage and civilised communities. It has also enabled me to deal surgically with the conditions of defective drainage of the intestine more effectually and at less risk to the life of the individual than I was previously able to do."[79] In his thesis, Paul Foucault referred extensively to Lane's work, citing more papers by Lane in his bibliography than those of any other doctor. Foucault's interest in this topic was presumably inspired in part by the fact that his thesis director, Félix Lejars, was one of the main French surgeons working on intestinal stasis. Lane's influence was also evident in Paul Foucault's observation that one of the symptoms evident in intestinal blockage associated with ileal kinks was a "predominance of phenomena of auto-intoxication."[80]

Paul Foucault's thesis was more than just a regurgitation of Lane's arguments. Rather than focusing on the way bands in the intestine and colon created obstructions, Foucault was interested in ileal kinks resulting from inflammations and infections that were associated with various forms of appendicitis as well as bacillary lesions. Yet what made them problematic was still the fact that they resulted in intestinal obstructions. Moreover, as Foucault noted, "certain facts tend to prove" that intestinal obstruction resulting from ileal kinks "can occur in the course of chronic intestinal stasis."[81] Finally, like Lane, Foucault advocated surgery as the means for removing these obstructions. Foucault's interest in Lane was not limited to his thesis work. He referenced Lane in a 1924 paper devoted to cecal volvulus (a form of intestinal obstruction that occurs when the caecum, located between the small bowel and colon, becomes disconnected from the abdominal wall and screws around on itself), noting Lane's observation that kinks situated near colic flexures, exacerbated by the weight and dilation of the ascending colon, can result in complete obstruction or acute or chronic volvulus.[82]

Lane's work on intestinal obstruction and its discontents played, in short, a significant role in Paul Foucault's intellectual development as a surgeon. It is difficult to know exactly what to make of this influence. Paul Foucault's writing is always precise and cautiously clinical. He never seems to have explicitly endorsed the cultural criticism to which Lane was prone. And other than passing references to "auto-intoxication," he does not seem to have been interested in the implications of Lane's ideas for explaining mental illness. Yet Paul Foucault did hitch his medical star, however briefly, to a figure whose credibility was in rapid decline at the very moment when own career was taking off. Lane was not, as one modern scholar notes, a charlatan. His error lay in "stacking assumption upon assumption"; his theory was "internally consistent and plausible, but its application was tragic."[83]

Another otherwise unrelated incident suggests that Paul Foucault's skills as a doctor were not above reproach. Jean Piel, who became a significant literary figure in postwar France, notably when he succeeded Georges Bataille (to whom he was related by marriage) as the editor of the journal *Critique*, arrived in Poitiers in April 1946. At the time, he worked for the new civil service that had been created after the Liberation to promote economic reconstruction. While driving to Paris, he was seriously injured when his car slid off the road and hit a tree. David Macey, who interviewed Piel, identifies Paul Foucault as one of the surgeons who operated on him.[84] In his memoirs, Piel recalled the incident, without mentioning the surgeon by name: "Due to an error on the part of the first surgeon, who operated on my tibia without concerning himself with the state of my hip, and despite several successive operations, I was to remain crippled all my life because of this accident."[85] It is unclear if Paul Foucault was the "first surgeon" or a subsequent one.[86] Piel described the accident as a dramatic turning point in his life, an "ordeal that [he] had to surmount, whatever the cost." But he also adds that the incident struck him because he had been "the victim of a power that was then and still is, to a considerable extent, uncontrolled and unsanctioned: the power of the doctor." He added that this was a "serious problem," one that is "not resolved by improvised reforms, far from it."[87] Macey suggests that Piel knew the Foucault family as well as the young philosopher, though the latter would, at this time, have been studying in Paris. In any case, sixteen years later, when Piel became editor of *Critique*, he asked Michel Foucault to serve on its editorial board.[88] The first article Foucault wrote for Piel's journal was an essay on psychoanalytic interpretations of the German poet Friedrich Hölderlin—entitled, it so happened, "The Father's 'No.'"

Foucault would later come to be known as one of the great modern critics of science—specifically, as a thinker who would challenge scientists' self-
image, by identifying the many ways science's truth effects rested on distinctly
nonscientific grounds (such as discourse and power). Yet the true object of
Foucault's critique was always discourses that purported to be scientific,
rather than established or hard sciences. His targets were invariably sciences
of dubious scientific credibility. In 1978, Foucault told an interviewer: "if you
tell physicists about the worst horrors in the history of physics, the disgusting
behavior in which physics [or] chemistry are born, they would laugh, they
would be fine with it. . . . If you tell [the same thing] to a psychanalyst, . . . a
psychiatrist, [or] . . . a sociologist . . . they will be hurt. These sciences do not
have the same relationship to their history." A science that "feels hurt" when
confronted with its own history is not, he reasoned, "a science in the manner
of mathematics."[89] The strange career of Paul Foucault may well have been
the experiential background to Foucault's insights into the frailty of scientific
argumentation. Whether or not the elder Foucault was hurt by his brushes
with charlatanism, it seems that his son was acutely aware of the troubling
light his own family's history shed on medicine's scientific status.

The Family Medical Tradition as Experiential Matrix

Foucault's mature work points to a number of ways in which the medical
milieu of his youth provided the experiences and shaped the dispositions that
would inform his understanding of medicine and related issues in later years.
Three experiential matrices of particular importance were the professionalization and institutionalization of medicine; the "perverse implantation"
through which medicine sexualized knowledge; and the positivism inherent
in clinical practice.

Before continuing, a methodological point is in order. Strictly speaking,
all that can be identified with certainty are the medical themes that Foucault
addressed in his mature work, on the one hand, and the role that these same
themes played in his own family history, on the other. Yet the regularity with
which these themes recur indicates that Foucault was constantly trying to
make sense of his family's medical past, by redescribing the words, practices,
and events that had marked his childhood—either directly or through secondhand accounts—in the distinctive idiom he had developed as a philosopher. Because in most cases we do not know the exact way in which family

traditions were passed down, our claims about the experiential basis of Foucault's interest in medicine have a necessarily speculative dimension. This speculation can be partially offset, however, by rigorous historical research. While it cannot be known what Paul Foucault shared with his son about his medical practice and beliefs, or what Anne Foucault recounted about the Malaperts, there is still much that can be learned about the family's role in the medical profession. What follows consists of attempts to reconstruct the aspects of his family history relating to medicine that seem to have elicited Foucault's intellectual interest. Because this effort to reconstruct the past relies on documents of which Foucault may have been only dimly aware (if he knew of them at all), the resulting analysis has a sharpness of resolution, as it were, that almost certainly stands in sharp contract with the murkier but existentially compelling circumstances in which he would have learned about his family's past.

The Professionalization of Medicine and the Medicalization of Society

Foucault's family history charts the course of the professionalization and institutionalization of medicine from the early nineteenth to the twentieth century. An essay in which Foucault traced the evolution of the medical profession over the eighteenth century describes, in many respects, the world in which, during the following century, his ancestors plied their trade. "Quantitatively," this period witnessed "an increasing number of doctors, the founding of new hospitals, the opening of new clinics, and, generally speaking, a greater consumption of medical care by all classes of society."[90] Foucault's grandfathers and great-grandfathers contributed to the expanding ranks of doctors in nineteenth-century France. While the Hôtel-Dieu, Poitiers's main hospital, had existed since the seventeenth century, the French revolutionary government transferred the old hospital from a chaplaincy to the Hôtel Pinet, which had previously housed a grand seminary. It was in this building that Foucault's father would later work.[91] Together, Foucault's forefathers participated in the growing consumption of medical care in French society, from Jacques-Symphorien Foucault's medical practice in rural Nanterre in the mid-nineteenth century to the surgical practices of Paul Foucault and Henri Malapert, by way of Prosper and Édouard Malapert's management of the family pharmacy in central Poitiers.

"Qualitatively," Foucault continues, in the same essay, the medical profession experienced "more standardized training," "a more pronounced connection between their practices and the development of medical knowledge,"
and "a little more confidence attributed to their knowledge and efficiency," at
the same time that "traditional 'cures'" saw their relative value subside.[92] Two
of Foucault's ancestors trained at the École de Pharmacie in Paris, four at the
Paris medical faculty; and four of them trained future doctors and pharmacists, in turn, at the Poitiers medical school. Most of the doctors in Foucault's
family linked their practices to medical knowledge by publishing in scholarly
journals and participating in learned societies, such as the Société de Chirurgie de Paris, the Société Internationale de Chirurgie, and the Société Médicale de la Vienne. Foucault's great-great-grandfather Prosper Malapert seems
to have been particularly concerned, as a trained pharmacist, with what his
obituary called "the most contemptible charlatanism and the most shameless
puffisme [deception]."[93] In these ways, Foucault concluded, the doctor, "little
by little, detached himself more clearly from other caregivers; he began to
occupy in the social body a more extensive and more valorized place."[94] The
Légions d'honneur and *croix de guerre* that the Foucault and Malapert doctors
had received, their role in civic organizations (Édouard Malapert had been a
municipal councilor), and the bourgeois houses they owned in Poitiers testified to their increasingly prominent status.

The family's fate was particularly tied to the development of Poitiers's primary hospital, the Hôtel-Dieu. Until 1945, French hospitals were primarily
institutions aimed at assisting the indigent, as well as soldiers and travel-
ers. Consequently, Paul Foucault and Henri Malapert held positions at the
Hôtel-Dieu (to which their teaching responsibility at the medical school were
tied) while also maintaining private practices as surgeons, in keeping with
the tradition of "liberal medicine." Foucault recognized this arrangement as
central to society's steady medicalization over the eighteenth and nineteenth
centuries—a process consisting of "private, 'liberal' medicine, called forth by
individual initiative and subject to the mechanisms of supply and demand"
and, "alongside it, and perhaps opposite it, a management of medicine determined by the authorities, supported by the administrative apparatus, regulated by strict legislative structures, and addressing the entire collectivity."[95]
In short, "one universally valuable [model of] medicine of, but with two distinct domains: the hospital for the poor classes, [and] liberal and competitive
[medical] practices for the rich."[96]

The story of Poitiers's Hôtel-Dieu follows that of the continuing medicalization of French society—an issue that Foucault would later reflect on, specifically in his work on public health as well as, more generally, his work on madness, the advent of the clinic, and sexuality. The hospital was closely tied to Poitiers's status as a garrison town. In the 1790s, it had treated the wounded of the Vendée campaign. Yet its primary focus was on tending to the poor. Consequently, the hospital's upkeep was frequently neglected, and it became increasingly unhygienic. Foucault remarked that the eighteenth-century hospital was "a fragment of space that was closed in on itself, a place for the internment of men and the sick, an architecture that was solemn but awkward, which multiplied problems inside without preventing it from spreading to the outside."[97] This remark also describes the Hôtel-Dieu's condition in the late nineteenth century. A local official remembered how a new health commission, created by the public health law of 1879, found Poitiers's hospitals in "a lamentable state of dilapidation, deprived of any maintenance for many years, with finances that were hardly satisfactory and a poorly balanced budget."[98] As a result of such problems, hospitals were reorganized, as Foucault later explained: it became necessary to "arrange the hospital's interior space, in such a way that it became medically efficient: no longer a place for assistance, but a place for therapeutic activity."[99] In the late nineteenth century, the Hôtel-Dieu reorganized itself along these lines. Detached, specialized wings were built: one for the military, another for children, a third for contagious diseases. A little later, radiography and ophthalmology departments were opened.[100] The hospital became structured, in this way, around an "intensive therapeutic strategy."[101] Doctors increasingly occupied the upper reaches of the Hôtel-Dieu's hierarchy, participating in its administrative organization and the arrangement of space. In this way, they reflected the principle of what Foucault called "uninterrupted presence and hierarchical privilege of doctors."[102] Hospitals strove to be more hygienic, reducing the risk that they would spread rather than cure disease, by improving ventilation and (as Foucault put it) tending to the "problem of changing, cleaning, and transporting the linen."[103] Indeed, the *lingerie* (or linen service) of the Hôtel-Dieu, in the late nineteenth century, "still left much to be desired"; by the 1930s, internal regulations were in effect that made hospital supervisors responsible for the cleanliness of their services, including that of its linen.[104] Over the same period, the hospital also introduced sterilizers and running water into the operating rooms. As the institution that he came to know thanks to the preeminent role that his father occupied in it, the Hôtel-Dieu was the matrix for Foucault's intense interest in hospitals—their organization, hygienic practices, and therapeutic function.

In ways that Foucault would identify as characteristic of hospitals in general, the Hôtel-Dieu contributed to the medicalization of society. By the 1930s, when Foucault's father was employed there as a surgeon, the hospital had more than 600 beds at its disposal: 99 in general medicine, 87 in general surgery, 24 in special surgery, 26 in the isolation ward, 68 in infant care, 200 that were reserved for families that could pay, and 100 for the military.[105] The process of medicalization, Foucault observed, was administered through a "medical corps [that was] spread widely through society and [that was] in a position to offer care that was either completely free or, in any case, as cheap as possible."[106] In 1888, the medical staff of the Hôtel-Dieu consisted, as had long been the case, of two doctors and two surgeons. Much of the practical responsibilities of caregiving were still in the hands of the sisters of the religious congregation with which the hospital was historically associated. By the 1930s, however, there were seven doctors (one *médecin des hôpitaux* and six *adjoints*) and three surgeons—two *chirurgiens des hôpitaux*, and one *adjoint*, Paul Foucault. Other doctors ran the ophthalmology, venerology, and radiography services, and the hospital also had a head pharmacist and dentist.[107] Reflecting these trends, the Hôtel-Dieu, at the beginning of the century, provided free consultations to the public every day except Sunday between 8 and 11 A.M. Foucault's grandfather Henri Malapert served in this capacity as a consulting surgeon.[108] The hospital also offered consultations about venereal disease and opened a major serology laboratory. Thus despite the fact that some of its doctors, such as Paul Foucault, continued to have their own private practices, the Hôtel-Dieu was, in the first decades of the twentieth century, expanding its resources, personnel, and forms of medical intervention in a way that made it the nexus of a project of improving the health of the surrounding population and, by the same token, making the medical profession a significant contributor to the community's well-being.

A key moment in the transformation of the Hôtel-Dieu into a genuinely therapeutic institution was the closure in 1927—a year after Foucault was born—of Poitiers's Hôpital Général. The Hôpital Général was the subject of Foucault's first major analysis of an institution, in a crucial chapter in *Madness and Civilization*. In that book, he analyzed the opening of the Hôpital Général in Paris in 1656, as a turning point in Western society's relationship to madness: the Middle Ages' willingness to listen to madness, insofar as it was seen as offering privileged insight into the fallen nature of the human condition, transformed itself into a kind of muzzling, as madness came to be seen as one example among others of a broader problem of "unreason"—which explained why, according to Foucault, the early modern monarchy lumped together, in these newly created "general hospitals," the mad and other groups seen as threats to the social order, such as the poor, prostitutes, and petty criminals (in a strange twist of fate, the Hôpital Général—once it had been transformed into Paris's Salpêtrière Hospital—was the institution where Foucault later died). The Hôpital Général interested Foucault because it showed that modern caregiving originated in institutions of social control: the Hôpital Général, he observed, was "not a medical establishment," but "a strange power that the king had established between the police and the judicial system, at the boundaries of the law."[109] The Poitiers Hôpital Général was established in 1657, just a year after its counterpart in Paris. Like its sister institution, its purpose was to lock up "thieves, purse-cutters, and the destitute," who "through their rubbish, filth, and drunkenness, infect the air and cause sickness,"[110] as the initial regulations put it. Though located in Poitiers, this institution, as one historian observes, "participated in a process that was national in scope, which aimed to suppress poverty and begging throughout the kingdom of France." Located at the "town's limits," the hospital was a "border zone in the spatial as well as the social sense of the term," with its own "semi-autarkic life."[111] A nineteenth-century guidebook cautioned visitors to avoid this austere building, located on Place Montierneuf: "This hospice, which is immense in the extent of its buildings, constructed pell-mell, without taste and with no deliberate plan, offers nothing to excite your curiosity."[112] Perhaps it aroused the curiosity of the young Foucault: it was presumably the first of these institutions he knew of, and its history was tied to that of his family's profession.

That hospitals had ceased to be an enclosed institution for sheltering the poor and transformed themselves into what Foucault later called a "*machine à guérir*"—a healing machine—is evident in its institutional and architectural organization of Poitiers's medical institution around the time of Paul Foucault's appointment. The Hôtel-Dieu, with its imposing edifice located near the city center, was the main establishment for treating the sick. It included a military ward; a general surgery ward, with operating rooms and x-ray equipment; a general medicine ward, with a clinical laboratory; a tuberculosis ward; a pediatric ward (in a special wing); a day-care center; an ophthalmology and otorhinolaryngology ward; a radiography center offering physiotherapeutic treatments such as ultraviolet, diathermia, and electrotherapy; a bacteriology and medical chemistry laboratory; a stomatology ward; and a "completely modern" ward for the prevention of cutaneous and syphilitic diseases. The *Maternité*, or maternity ward, located in a neighboring building, had seventy-nine beds in addition to a midwifery school. On the other side of the Cain, a third institution was located. It had been founded in the mid-eighteenth century as the Hôpital des Incurables, which treated the incurably sick, who were denied entry at the Hôpital Général. In the 1920s, it became the Hôpital Pasteur, Poitiers's psychiatric hospital (to be discussed in the following chapter). The other wards served, according to a contemporary account, "idiots, epileptics, the elderly, . . . children, venereal patients, [and] cancer patients."[113] Hospitals thus became, as Foucault subsequently explained, "essential element[s] in medical technology: not only a place where one can heal, but also an instrument that, in a number of serious cases, makes healing possible."[114] These claims acquired special significance for Foucault because of the special role that hospitals played in his family history.

The development of hospitals was significant not only for their therapeutic effects, but also for their contribution to science. Hospitals, Foucault maintained, became nodal points in the articulation of "medical knowledge and therapeutic efficiency." Their impact thus went well beyond the patients they directly treated, as their role as institutions of medical research and training influenced even doctors in private practice. Foucault noted that "the hospital as a place for accumulating and developing knowledge [made possible] the training of doctors whose practice took the form of a private clientele." The coupling that occurred in Edinburgh between the Medical School and the Edinburgh Infirmary became the template of medical education. Growing up, Foucault would have experienced this trend firsthand, since his father, like most of the doctors in his family, combined a lucrative private practice and a position at the Hôtel-Dieu with an appointment at Poitiers's École de Médecine et de Pharmacie. The school prided itself on its ancient origins, which extended back to 1432, though it had been shut down during the Revolution. Since 1841, it had been an *école préparatoire*, providing medical students with their first three years of training, the remainder of which had to be completed at another institution. Yet even in this capacity, the school strove to offer a state-of-the-art medical education. Dr. Maurice-Paul Veluet, a colleague and neighbor of Paul Foucault, noted in 1933 that the school had followed the progress of modern science, first emphasizing Pasteur's germ theory before turning to biochemistry as the key to understanding disease.[115] As a preparatory school, special emphasis was given to anatomy, the subject taught by Paul Foucault. In teaching clinical observation, the medical school's close proximity to the Hôtel-Dieu proved particularly important: "All the elements necessary for *clinical teaching in medicine and surgery* and *mandatory hospital internships* can be found on the premises of the Hôtel-Dieu, which is directly connected to the premises of the School."[116] It featured an anatomical theater, where Paul Foucault presumably performed autopsies. Dr. Veluet also noted that, since the early twentieth century, a new field known as "social medicine" had emerged, which studies "the applications and role of medicine in laws and regulations [relating to] public assistance and hygiene," as well as in "social insurance, health monitoring, and the search for psychophysical aptitude for career selection."[117] The Poitiers facility sought to impact this growing field. Years later, Michel Foucault observed: "The hospital, a therapeutic instrument for those who stayed there, contributed through clinical teaching and a high level of medical knowledge, to increasing the health level of the population."[118] In this and many other respects, the rise of the medical profession and its role in the broader medicalization of society was intimately woven into the story of Foucault's family and its social circles.

Nineteenth-Century Medicine and the "Perverse Implantation"

The second experiential matrix that Foucault's upbringing provided for his subsequent development lies in nineteenth-century medical discourse and its penchant for what he called "perversity." In the first volume of his *History of Sexuality*, Foucault challenged the view that bourgeois society was founded primarily on sexual repression. Because this society had in fact expanded and enriched what could be said and known about sex, it deserved, rather, to be described as "perverse." Of the forces propelling the "discursive explosion" of sexual discourse in the eighteenth and nineteenth century, we must list "medicine first."[119] "Medicine," he continues, "made a forceful entry into the pleasures of the couple," inventing new pathologies and forms of pleasure that it undertook to manage.[120] Foucault concludes: "'Nineteenth-century 'bourgeois' society—ours, too, undoubtedly—is a society of shattering and shattered perversion."[121]

The experiential matrix for these later insights can be found, once again, in the medical environment in which Foucault was raised. The "perverse implantation" that he made a particular point of attributing to nineteenth-century medicine was an enterprise in which his family and family connections had played an active and energetic role. Their activities and writings contributed to the "sexual saturation" that Foucault saw as so characteristic of nineteenth-century culture and the long shadow it cast.[122] When combined with the relatively austere environment in which he grew up, this sexualized discourse became emblematic of the situations that preoccupied Foucault as a mature thinker: those in which apparently repressive attitudes merged with discourse that made sexuality a constant and seemingly unavoidable feature of everyday life. For the Foucaults, perversity began at home.

The medical community to which the Foucaults belonged organized, in a sense, the "perverse implantation." One almost has the impression that the references and footnotes in Foucault's later work consists, at times, in a series of sly commentaries on his family connections. In his thesis, Foucault's father thanked "M. le docteur Arrou," "in testimony to his gratitude and deep veneration." Joseph Arrou (1861–1938) was a prominent surgeon and anatomist who was long associated at the Hôpital Saint-Antoine (where Paul Foucault had done his residency) and whose area of specialty was the testicle and testicular pathologies (Figure 3).[123] In 1901, he published a treatise entitled *Surgery of the Genital Apparatus in Men*. Foucault wrote that the new forms of power centered on sexuality that emerged in the nineteenth century required "insistent examinations and observations" and a "physical approach and a play of intense sensations," of which the "medicalization of the sexually unusual was both the effect and the instrument." "Sexual oddities," "lodged in the body," attributed to "the deep character of individuals," "participated in a technology of health and pathology," at the same time that evidence of sexual behavior became analyzable as "lesions, dysfunctions, and symptoms."[124] Though Arrou wrote in a clipped, clinical style, his treatise instantiated the interrogation of sexual peculiarities through an exhaustive but curiously intimate examination of the male reproductive organ that, by the same token, obliquely explored human sexuality. In an extended chapter on varicoceles (an enlargement of the scrotum's veins), Arrou describes an exchange with a "vigorous" worker "of average size" who asked him "why the relations he entertained with his wife were almost immediately followed by violent pain felt in his balls [*bourses*] when he practiced sexual pleasure in the morning," despite the fact that nothing of the kind occurred when such relations occurred at night (Arrou found the answer by identifying a small varicocele in his testicles).[125] Arrou recognized that abnormalities in the penis could be tied to what Foucault would call the "deep character of individuals." Arrou noted, for instance, that many who are afflicted with varicoceles are neurasthenics, and that it is in the "psychic

Figure 3. Paul Foucault next to Doctor Joseph Arrou (whose name is misspelled) at the Hôpital de la Pitié during Foucault's residency in the 1920s. BIU Santé méde-cine–Université Paris Cité.

sphere" that the condition's most serious consequences occur, particularly among the most "educated subjects" (workers being far less affected). "Some *varicocéleux*," Arrou observed, "are agitated, impulsive, hypochondriacal. The infirmity, which they carefully hide, constantly occupies their minds; they believe themselves to be incomplete beings, and, consequently, fear the society of women and marriage." In extreme cases, these conditions can result in suicide.[126] In a section on castration, he noted that in cases in which both testicles were removed, "disturbances of the mental state are to be feared" and may result in "nervous afflictions that are still poorly known, which follow the excision of glands the internal secretions of which are indispensable to the organism's proper functioning."[127] With Arrou, like with many of his contemporaries, the anatomical analysis and surgical intervention became occasions for an "implantation" of sexuality into the body and individual.

Similar tendencies were evident in the writings of Foucault's father. In 1924, he published an article entitled "Torsions of the Testicles and the Spermatic Cord." His account of this condition, in which blood is cut off from the testicles because of unnatural twists in the spermatic cord from which they are suspended, was characteristically measured in tone. Yet when considering the causes of this affliction, he listed, alongside various kinds of congenital malformations, "traumatisms, muscular exertions, [and] especially masturbation."[128] In support of his claim, he references an article from a decade earlier by Louis Ombrédanne (1871–1956), a leading pediatric surgeon, which cited masturbation as a major cause of orchitis (inflammation of the testicles). Ombrédanne cites several authorities who "observed orchites

incontestably caused by excesses of masturbation that resulted in testicular atrophy."[129] Michel Foucault later described the way in which childhood
sexuality became one of the strategic focal points through which power and
knowledge seized hold of the newly discovered realm of sexuality, notably
by way of the "war against onanism that lasted, in the West, nearly two centuries."[130] Paul Foucault's article considered a surgical solution to testicular
torsions that would become inseparable, albeit in a less literal register, from
the emerging language of psychoanalysis. He described a three-year-old child
brought to the hospital in 1921 who was vomiting and agitated, with a "scrotum that was red, edematous, and painful"; an incision revealed "a blackish
testicle with, in some areas, livid spots." After several unfruitful operations,
the inevitable conclusion was reached: "It was . . . decided to practice castration."[131] Indeed, this was the heart of the question raised by such conditions,
leading Paul Foucault to ask, Hamlet-like: "Must one castrate or, to the contrary, be conservative? Everything depends on the state of the testicle."[132]

Among the most striking of Paul Foucault's articles is one that he published in 1938 with Raymond-Noël Darget (1888–1980), a colleague from
Bordeaux, entitled "On the Conduct to Adopt When Confronted with Sexual
Impotence in a Man." The article is intriguing for obvious reasons. It is a piece
in which Foucault's father, rather than discussing castration, turned to matter
of decisive interest to the question of fatherhood—virility and its shortfalls.
Published when Foucault was nearing his twelfth birthday, the article specifically discusses medical interventions aimed at impotent adolescents. More
generally, the article exemplified and practically acknowledged the way that,
according to Foucault, the *dispositif* of sexuality assembled the concept of sex
out of "anatomical components, biological functions, behaviors, sensations,
[and] pleasures," thus creating an "artificial" or "fictitious unity."[133] Far from
referring to an unambiguous clinical condition, Paul Foucault explained,
impotence brings into play "congenital malformations, remainders of venereal illnesses, glandular deficiencies, troubles of the psyche, moral and other
kinds of considerations, which can at times be masked by feelings of modesty or voluntary reticence."[134] Given that impotence presented itself, in this
way, as a complex problem, Paul Foucault found it peculiarly necessary to
remind his readers of what was involved in the "normal sexual act." Noting
that it was "pointless to expand upon" the details of this act—a classic instance
of what his son later called "very loquacious advice" counseling "discretion
and modesty"—he proceeded to do precisely that.[135] "The sexual act," he
explained, "can only take place in an individual endowed with genital instinct,

with *eroticization"*—a term, which he attributed to the Austrian endocrinol-
ogist Eugen Steinach (1861–1944), that refers to the "origins of subconscious
sexual impulses." The first phase of the sexual act begins with *"precopulatory
excitation,"* characterized in women by urethrorrhea, triggered by the "excitation of periureteral glands," and in men by a *"psycho-genetic erection,* caused
by purely cerebral incitement." Phase two begins with *"penetration,"* which
"strengthens and extends the *dermo-sensorial erection* through peripheral
incitements." The third phase marks the appearance of "voluptuous sensations," which culminates in an "acme, the *orgasm,* which coincides with *ejaculation."* The last phase is one of a "depletion," a "refractory period in which
coitus is impossible for a shorter or longer time."[136] This detailed account of the
sexual act typified the "insistent and indiscrete medical practice" that Foucault
associated with the onset of the science of sexuality.[137] Paul Foucault focused
on the most likely causes of impotence for different categories of patients.
Impotence in adolescence often resulted from malformations, which were best
dealt with immediately through surgery. In adults, impotence was often tied
to venereal disease (an affliction to which Poitiers's Hôtel-Dieu had reserved
an entire clinic). For the elderly, the final category, fewer therapeutic cures
were available. Intriguingly for a physician who was so adamantly positivistic,
Paul Foucault implicitly referred in this article to the lessons of psychoanalysis.
He notes that some adults are prone to "psychic impotence." Sometimes it
involves a "hyperemotive" person, or an "anxious" one, who, under the impact
of an "initial shock, be it sensory or mental," finds him- or herself overcome by
an "obsessive idea," "inhibiting the sexual act" partially or entirely, particularly
during the precopulatory phase. At other times, these psychic impotents can
be "depressive" patients, "neurasthenics," whose impotence encompasses the
entire sexual act and who experience "diminutions in libido."[138] He later notes
that advanced hyperthyroid conditions can result in a situation in which "the
libido is in deficit."[139] He also appears to speak positively of "psychotherapy,"
which, he claims, it would be "pointless . . . to neglect."[140] We have, of course,
no way of knowing if Foucault was aware of his father's article, either when it
was published or subsequently. But whatever its merits, the article embodied
the prying, intrusive way in which, in Foucault's mature opinion, the medical
profession sexualized the body, organized it around principles of normality
and abnormality, and used sexuality to enhance its susceptibility to medical
intervention.

   In his articles on testicular torsions and on impotence, Paul Foucault provides suggestive hints about his ideas concerning masculinity and, implicitly,

homosexuality. In both papers, he refers to testicular implants—*greffes testicu-laires*. He concludes his study of testicular torsions by asking: "Must resulting testicular atrophy be treated by testicular implants? Only the future can tell us."[141] Oddly, the later essay ends on the same note, with Paul Foucault observing that senile men afflicted with "total impotency" should resort to "testicular implants."[142] This interest in testicular implants in two papers published fourteen years apart suggests an ongoing interest on Paul Foucault's part in a theory concerning the connection between the testicles and masculinity and the role that surgery could play in enhancing the latter that flourished in the 1920s before being discredited. In the late nineteenth and early twentieth centuries, historians of medicine teach us, "common opinion held that the loss of sperm caused a debilitation of the entire organism, especially of the nervous system."[143] These theories became bound up with the belief that the testes had medical qualities that could rejuvenate the organism. The nineteenth-century physiologist Charles-Édouard Brown-Séquard (1817–94) was notorious for advocating the subcutaneous injection of monkey testicle extracts, a cure that proved commercially popular. Though Brown-Séquard's ideas always smacked of quackery, the development of endocrinology sought to place intuitions about the role of testicles and particularly testicular secretions in male health on a scientific footing. Around 1912–13, the first successful testicular implants occurred, typically to replace testicles that had been lost or damaged by injury or disease-related castration. From the outset, the purpose of these operations was to restore male sexual potency: to ensure that men could have erections, intercourse, and wives. These operations proved instrumental to the Austrian physiologist Eugen Steinach's development of endocrinology and the hormone concept. One historian notes: "On the basis of his castration and transplantation experiments, . . . Steinach postulated between 1910 and 1916 that the sex-specific build and behavior of animals were determined by the internal secretion component of their respective reproductive glands, or 'puberty glands.'"[144]

Yet even after Steinach had shown that the testicles functioned through the secretion of the hormone testosterone, older ideas about the connection between the testicles, rejuvenation, and virility persisted. This resulted in a popular fad for testicular implants, which was particularly associated with the surgeon Serge Voronoff (1866–1951). A Russian émigré who made his career in France, Voronoff developed, in the early 1920s, a technique for implanting thin layers of baboon and chimpanzee testicles into the scrotums of his patients. Not only did Voronoff become a celebrity, but he also grew wealthy as result of his testicle implant business. By 1926, he boasted of having performed over a thousand such operations.[145] His work earned him considerable cultural notoriety: Voronoff is often seen as the inspiration for the character of Professor Preobrazhensky in Mikhail Bulgakov's *Heart of a Dog*, while e. e. cummings, in a volume published in 1926, alluded to him, speaking of a "famous doctor who inserts monkeyglands in millionaires."[146] His success, however, was short-lived: by the decade's end, his practice was viewed with increasing skepticism and ultimately ridicule.

It is thus particularly surprising that, as late as 1938, Foucault's father would refer to Voronoff by name and express interest in his work. While acknowledging the technical difficulties involved in transplanting monkey testicles onto human ones, he stated that his interest lay exclusively in "the interpretation of the results." "According to Voronoff," Paul Foucault wrote, "one observes in the several days that follow the operation strong sexual and psychic excitement. For the following two to three months, favorable sentiments improve, the patient sinks back into fatigue and apathy; this is the phase of discouragement and disillusionment." Yet, he adds, "in a third phase, physical and psychic improvement gradually appears: well-being, euphoria, [and] a juvenile allure coincide with a diminution of signs of senescence; the reproductive functions start up again, sexual appetite [and] erections become possible; the patient feels rejuvenated and reinvigorated." Paul Foucault says that these results "seem well established," noting that Voronoff claimed, of 375 cases tracked following an implant, a success rate 90 percent for functional impotence and 57 percent for organic impotence. He acknowledges that "opinion is very divided" concerning Voronoff's studies and concedes that most of the operation's effects disappear after five years, making further operations necessary.[147] What is striking is that Paul Foucault seems to have given considerable weight to the idea that testicular transplants could not only rejuvenate, but also remasculinize patients—and that he did so in 1938, when Voronoff had already been written off as a quack.

Not only did Paul Foucault endorse Voronoff's ideas on the ability of testicular transplants to enhance men's virility in general; he also took seriously the idea that such operations could cure homosexuality—an assumption that itself was based on the view that homosexuals lacked sufficiently masculine attributes. In this context, Paul Foucault referred specifically to the work of Louis Dartigues (1869–1940), a surgeon and Voronoff's occasional collaborator. In his article on impotence, Paul Foucault writes: "Dartigues has obtained wonderful results for *sexual inversion*, which leads one to think that it could

be due to a deficiency of androgen hormones in the testicle."[148] The reference
to sexual inversion suggests Paul Foucault had read Dartigues's 1928 study *The
Renewal of the Organism*, which devotes a chapter to "surgical endocrinother-
apy and sexual inversion." Dartigues describes sexual inversion as "this perversion that consists of desires individuals have for individuals of the same sex,
a deviation, a defect, call it what you will" and "which was so widespread in
the decadent civilizations of Antiquity [and] which, at present, is so frequently
found in large capital cities."[149] Yet while it was commonly thought that inversion, whether "pederasty" or "Sapphism," was due to psychological afflictions,
the possibility must also be entertained that it might have resulted from dis-
cord in "the great concert of endocrinal glands that govern the organism."[150]
While some pederasts seem to embrace their condition, others "know they
are abnormal and . . . want to be normal," to find "the straight path," "to truly
be men, to start a family, to have children, [and] to possess an honorable and
happy household."[151] Dartigues claims to have met "inverted" men who, while
being anatomically normal, in the sense of having an apparently healthy penis
and testicles, sensed they were physiologically abnormal, as their reproductive
organs produced insufficient male hormones. These "males by configuration"
were, consequently, "females by interiorization."[152] As for the substance of
these claims, Dartigues simply expressed hope that these matters might be the
subject of further research. Yet the fact that these theories were unverified had
not prevented him from performing testicular transplants on gay men who
had sought his services. He tells of a thirty-three-year-old man, a "Hamlet of
erroneous passion,"[153] on whom he operated in 1925. A few months later, he
wrote Dartigues an effusive letter, thanking the doctor for curing him of his
shameful perversion. Not only did he, after the procedure, lose his interest
in men he had previously considered beautiful, but he had (according to the
letter that Dartigues quoted at length) "erotic dreams in which women were
front and center, and which provoked erections, the last dream having excited
[him] to the point of ejaculation."[154] Proof of his apparent cure came with the
news that he had married and started a family. The lesson that Dartigues drew
from this experience—though he admitted that it was only a hypothesis—was
that endocrinal theory showed that the testicles had, in addition to a sperm-
producing and ejaculatory function, a role in preserving an internal hormonal
equilibrium in the organism. This meant that, when deficiencies occurred,
testicles might be "functionally . . . more feminine than masculine, more ovar-
ian." These needed to be "virilized in order to return to physico-mental sexual
equilibrium," a goal that could be achieved notably by testicular implants.[155]

Though Dartigues admitted to having performed this operation on only three homosexuals, these remarks were presumably the basis for the admiration Paul Foucault expressed for his "wonderful results" in curing sexual inversion.

The idea that hormone theory provided clues for enhancing virility and curing homosexuality was not, it is worth remembering, embraced solely by problematic figures such as Voronoff and Dartigues, but also by scientifically well-regarded figures, notably Eugen Steinach, endocrinology's founder. His name was associated with the so-called Steinach operation, a partial vasectomy that Steinach believed would shift the testicles from sperm production to hormone production, thus offsetting the effects of aging and enhancing men's vigor and sexual potency. W. B. Yeats was among the more prominent public figures to receive such an operation. Paul Foucault spoke favorably of the effects of Steinach operations on male virility, noting that after they have been performed, "desires and erections reappear" (though he emphasized that they were a preventative rather than curative therapy).[156] Steinach also believed that endocrinology had important implications for understanding homosexuality. His theory explained that through sex-specific hormones, the nervous system is "eroticized"—a term that Paul Foucault used in his paper, attributing it to Steinach[157]—in either a male or feminine direction. Homosexuality occurs when eroticization is incomplete, leaving the body suspended between the poles of masculinity and femininity. It represents what he called "mental hermaphroditism."[158] Steinach became concerned with the psychological stress that this condition imposed on homosexuals, evident in what he saw as their tendency toward self-castration and suicide. During the First World War, Steinach and his colleague Robert Lictenstern had, to this end, performed testicular grafts from heterosexual to homosexual men. As they explained in a scientific paper, their goals was to get to the bottom of "a situation that was embarrassing and also dangerous for the individuals concerned as well as for human society."[159] Through interventions such as testicular transplants—the *greffes testiculaires* that intrigued Paul Foucault—their intention was not "to resolve the conflicts arising from homosexuality," but, rather, "to eliminate homosexuality itself, which was understood as a purely biological problem."[160]

One wonders if the words Foucault chose to describe nineteenth-century medicine's fascination with abnormal sexualities—*l'implantation perverse*—is entirely coincidental. Though the interests in surgery that defined the professional interests of his father and his family connections meant that they tended to view perversity in physiological terms, their interest in the organic basis of sexual conduct and dispositions exemplifies what Foucault later called "a multiple implantation of 'perversions.'"[161] Foucault, as we have seen, expressed anxiety about the incapacity of doctors to truly listen, to hear discourse and personal testimony when they were busy palpating the body. What would come to disturb him about nineteenth-century medicine, however, was how willing it was to *listen* to confessions of perversity. Doctors became intrigued by the "*petit peuple*" (or community) of perversion, dwelling in the "interstices of society." What one now "interrogated" was "the sexuality of children" and "the pleasure of those who do not like the other sex"[162]—subjects that Foucault's father specifically considered in his medical papers. Precisely what was demanded of them was that they speak: "It was incumbent on all these figures, who once were barely seen, to now step forward and take the floor and make the difficult confession of what they are. Undoubtedly, they are no less condemned. But *one listens to them.*"[163] While listening might seem precisely that to which speech aspires, it can, when it takes the form of confession, become ominous and troubling, a means by which the speaker becomes dispossessed of his being and even his own words. The notion that perversity is precisely something that can reveal itself through confession is indicative of the way that perversion refers less to actions (which could be recognized from a purely external perspective) than to an identity, a personality. Medical attitudes toward homosexuality exemplify this trend: "the psychological, psychiatric, [and] medical category of homosexuality" was constituted "less through a type of sexual relations than through a certain quality of sexual sensibility, by a certain way of *inverting in oneself the masculine and the feminine.*" Homosexuality ceased to be associated primarily with "the practice of sodomy" and became conceived of as "an internal androgyny, a hermaphroditism of the soul."[164] Foucault's insights echo what his father had referred to as "sexual inversion," as well as Steinach's notion of "mental hermaphroditism" and Dartigues's of "females by interiorization." However indirectly, Paul Foucault's interest in testicular grafts implanted into his son's consciousness a set of concerns that he subsequently conceptualized as *l'implantation perverse.*

Forensic Pathology and Medical Knowledge

The third way in which the Foucault family's medical tradition constituted an experiential matrix for Foucault's thought was through the development of forensic pathology or, as it known in France, *l'expertise médico-légale.* Though the question of how medical arguments could be used to establish insanity and thus internment was an important theme in *Madness and Civilization*, forensic pathology narrowly construed became one of Foucault's primary concerns from roughly 1971 to 1975. Specifically, he was interested in the way in which medicine in general and psychiatry in particular invoked the authority of truth discourses to challenge and often substitute itself for the authority of legal judgments in court cases in which the accused were deemed mentally ill or "abnormal." The most important legacy of his interest in Foucault's oeuvre is *I, Pierre Rivière, Having Slaughtered My Mother, My Sister, and My Brother: A Case of Parricide in the Nineteenth Century*. This book, published in 1973, is a collection of documents relating to a criminal case from 1835. It concerns a young Norman peasant who murdered his family, resulting in a trial in which forensic pathologists played a significant role. The Pierre Rivière case was the topic of the research seminar that Foucault directed at the Collège de France in 1971–72 and 1972–73 (this seminar being distinct from the lectures courses Foucault delivered at that institution). In his 1972 summary of the seminar's activities, he explained that the study of the Rivière case was part of a broader study of "medico-legal practices and concepts from the nineteenth century."[165] The following year's seminar was devoted entirely to preparing the Rivière book,[166] while in 1973 it focused, among other topics, on "forensic pathology [*l'expertise médico-légale*] in psychiatric questions since 1820."[167] Foucault's 1975 lecture course, *Abnormal*, includes his most complete and definitive statement on forensic pathology. The way in which psychiatrists and medical authorities, in their newfound legal responsibilities, turned the character and behavior of the accused (rather than the crime itself) into a heuristic for determining guilt marked the advent, Foucault maintained, of a new form of social control, the "power of normalization." He even noted that, after the first lecture, a member of the audience had asked him if *les expertises médico-légales* (forensic pathology reports) were not the true topic of the year's course, rather than abnormality. To which Foucault replied: "it is not exactly the same thing, but you will see that, via the problem of *l'expertise médico-légale*, I will come to the problem of the abnormal."[168] The same year, he told an interviewer that he was even preparing a book of documents (presumably in the same format as the Pierre Rivière volume) on "forensic psychiatry [*les expertises psychiatriques*] in penal matters."[169] Thus for at least five years, the quite narrow questions of forensic medicine and psychiatry lay at the center of Foucault's preoccupations.

While there are clearly abundant contextual reasons for Foucault's interest in this particular form of medical-legal power in the early 1970s, forensic pathology simultaneously constitutes one of the experiential matrices from which his preoccupations emerged, owing to his family's close ties to this medical practice. In addition to being a prominent pharmacist, Prosper Malapert, Foucault's great-great-grandfather, was a pioneer of forensic medicine in its heyday—the age of Pierre Rivière. As a pharmacist, Malapert was summoned before courts on numerous occasions to author *expertises médico-légales*—a term that appears in his obituary.[170] Malapert was, moreover, trained by and close to Mathieu Orfila (1787–1853), the Parisian doctor and medical professor who founded toxicology and was a major figure in early forensic pathology. In addition to being a professor of legal medicine at the Paris medical faculty and serving on the inaugural editorial board of the *Annales d'hygiène publique et de médecine légale*, Orfila carved out a role for physicians in legal proceedings thanks to the fame he acquired while serving as an expert witness in a series of trials in the 1830s—"a period that was perceived as suffering from an epidemic of poisoning crimes."[171] In this way, Orfila's career exemplifies "the overlapping sites of chemistry, medicine, and law in nineteenth-century France."[172]

Foucault was well aware of Orfila's central role in the boundary between law and medicine, as the forensic pathologist played a role in the Pierre Rivière trial with which Foucault was so preoccupied in the early 1970s. Specifically, Orfila was one of seven doctors (one other being Esquirol, the prominent psychiatrist) who signed an expert opinion that was requested of the Cour de Cassation in 1835 when the Rivière case went to appeals: Orfila and his cosigners declared, in their brief statement, that the evidence overwhelmingly suggested that Rivière was insane and thus could not be guilty of murder under the penal code.[173] Interventions like this—all the more striking in Orfila's case, given that he was a chemist by training, not a psychiatrist— are precisely what worried Foucault about forensic pathology: the way it identified a deviant personality lurking beneath criminal acts (even if, in this instance, it resulted in Rivière's acquittal). In his contribution to the volume, sociologist Robert Castel—one of Foucault's frequent collaborators during this period—analyzed the role played by these Parisian doctors in asserting the legal relevance of the medical perspective at this crucial moment in the appeals process, describing Orfila in these terms: "Orfila, the authority in legal medicine with his *Traité de médecine légale* [Treatise on legal medicine] in four volumes, member of the Royal Council on Public Instruction and the General Council on Hospices, departmental councilman for the Seine, and dean of the Medical Faculty."[174] Foucault himself specifically mentioned

Orfila in his 1972 report on his Collège de France teaching, in which, while discussing the activities of the research seminar, he noted the role in the Rivière case of Esquirol and Orfila, whom he described (not entirely accurately) as "great Parisian psychiatrists of the period."[175]

Given Orfila's role as a supporting actor in the Rivière drama, it is all the more striking that this key figure in the history of legal medicine played a significant role in Foucault's family history through his association with Prosper Malapert. Foucault's great-great-grandfather met Orfila on his first trip to Paris in 1820. Orfila seems to have traveled to Poitiers on several occasions, notably to report on individuals practicing medicine illegally. It was Orfila who encouraged Malapert, in 1838, to resume his studies and pursue his own field of pharmacy by focusing on toxicology. Orfila's pioneering role in the use of medicine and specifically toxicology seems to have made an impression on Malapert. The local historian who studied Foucault's ancestor notes: "According to a family tradition, Malapert was at Orfila's side, in 1840, at the famous trial of Madame Lafarge."[176] The historian's source for this claim was Anne Foucault (Née Malapert), the philosopher's mother, which suggests that Foucault, while growing up, likely heard about his ancestor's association with Orfila. The Lafarge case was a cause célèbre in July Monarchy France. It involved an unhappy wife accused of poisoning her husband with arsenic. The affair was discussed extensively in the French press, in addition to being passionately debated in Parisian salons. Orfila's role in it was complex, but directly tied to his authority as a toxicologist. The trial, which took place at Tulle, hinged on the results of a recently developed procedure for detecting arsenic known as the Marsh test. The lawyer defending Madame Lafarge asked Orfila to evaluate the way the test had been administered by local doctors; he responded with an affidavit declaring the results worthless. When Orfila eventually showed up at the trial and conducted tests himself, he concluded, despite having been called by the defense, that traces of arsenic could—so long as the tests were properly administered—be detected in the dead husband's body. Madame Lafarge was subsequently found guilty. While the historian mentioned previously concludes that Prosper Malapert was not one of Orfila's collaborators in this trial, he does maintain that Foucault's great-great-grandfather witnessed it as a member of the audience.

In any case, Malapert clearly followed in his teacher's footsteps, as he was frequently charged with being a medical expert in trials from the 1840s through the 1860s. Perhaps Malapert's most famous case was in the Meilleraye trial of 1867, in which the widow of a member of the landowning Poitevin bourgeoisie was accused of poisoning her husband. As a now well-known pharmacist and professor at the nearby Poitiers medical faculty, Malapert was hired as a court expert. Specifically, he rejected the prosecution's misleading suggestion that the poison used in the murder had been mercury salts, establishing that it was in fact arsenic.[177] The episode shows the extent to which forensic pathologists were seen, by contemporaries, as champions of truth in the service of justice, as embodiments of the belief that science could reveal guilt and innocence. During the trial, the defense attorney declared: "M. Malapert is a man who brings too much care and conscientiousness into his activities for us to have any remarks to make."[178] Speaking of Malapert's legal work, the author of his obituary observed: "The search for the complete absolute truth was his sole preoccupation. He neglected no task, no care, and no pain to make it appear before the eyes of the court and members of the jury."[179] At one trial, Malapert himself declared: "I am the expert not of the prosecution, nor of the defense, but the expert of truth."[180] Few statements could have summed up as pithily the anxieties that Malapert's great-great-grandson, Michel Foucault, would express concerning the legal role of doctors.

Foucault's family background and connections were also bound up with what was arguably the most insidious use of l'expertise médico-légale: the role it gave doctors in determining legal definitions of sexual normality and deviance. A particularly intriguing figure from this perspective is Maurice Laugier (1842–1915). Paul Foucault dedicated his thesis to, among others, "the memory of Docteur Maurice Laugier." He was, in the first place, his mother's first cousin, and he attended Paul Foucault and Anne Malapert's wedding.[181] Laugier taught clinical surgery at the Hôtel-Dieu in Paris and had served as chief surgeon at the poor house (or maison départementale) in Nanterre, the same Paris suburb where Paul Foucault's grandfather had practiced medicine. But Laugier was, most importantly, a leading figure in the development of forensic pathology. He served as the president of the Société de Médecine Légale[182] (Society of Legal Medicine) and was also a collaborator of perhaps the most influential French forensic pathologist of the nineteenth century, and someone to whom Foucault refers with some frequency in his work: Ambroise Tardieu (1818–79).

Tardieu occupies an ambivalent place in the history of medicine: he is seen by some as a brave witness to nineteenth-century society's dark truths, and by others as the epitome of this period's pathologization of sexual difference. In addition to being a professor of legal medicine, president of the Academy of Medicine in Paris, and dean of the Paris medical faculty, Tardieu was the author of often disturbing studies of the illicit underworld of nineteenth-century Parisian life, which he wrote to demonstrate how medicine could shed light on criminal cases. In 1860, for instance, he published a study of assault on minors, "Medico-Legal Study of the Abuse and Mistreatment of Children." One author has maintained that Tardieu's study of child abuse—which was frequently sexual, even if he described it in allusive terms—was a direct influence on Sigmund Freud's notorious "seduction hypothesis." Freud had, while studying under Charcot in Paris in the 1880s, attended autopsies performed by Paul Brouardel, Tardieu's student and his successor in the chair of legal medicine. He also owned a copy of Tardieu's *Medico-Legal Study of Indecent Assault* (*Étude médico-légale sur les attentats aux moeurs*).[183] Yet the latter book is grist for the mill of those who see Tardieu as having pathologized and criminalized certain forms of "deviant" sexual behavior, notably homosexuality. In addition to providing medical insights into investigating rape and assault, Tardieu's treatise also suggests approaches to examining "pederasty and sodomy," terms that he used almost interchangeably. Though the French Revolution had decriminalized sodomy, the Napoleonic Code had, through the crime known as "public offense against decency" (*attentat public aux moeurs*), made homosexual acts punishable when they occurred in the liminal spaces between private and public spheres. Tardieu's goal was to "pursue and extirpate, if possible, [the] shameful vice" of pederasty. Doing so required a distinct form of knowledge that merged medical observation with forensic categories, through which it would be possible to discern the "precise and certain declaration of the signs which can make pederasts recognizable." "Through positive facts and multiple observations," Tardieu maintained, it can be established that "the vice of pederasty leaves material traces on the forms of organs which are much more numerous and much more significant than was believed until now, and the knowledge of which will permit the forensic doctor, in the great majority of cases, to direct with sureness the pursuits which involve public morality to such a high degree." Tardieu is most notorious for having defined a typology of signs through which pederasts could be medically identified, depending on whether they were "passive" or "active." The six "characteristic signs" of the "passive" pederast consisted of "excessive development of the buttocks; funnel-shaped deformation of the anus; relaxation of the sphincter; the effacement of the folds, the crests, and the wattles at the circumference of the anus; extreme dilation of the anal orifice; and ulcerations, hemorrhoids, [and] fistulas." The less common "active" pederast could be recognized by his deformed penis and a glans that narrowed like "the snout of certain animals."[184] In the first volume of his *History of Sexuality*, Foucault quoted Tardieu's *Medico-Legal Study*, confining the author's name to his footnotes.[185] Tardieu's work—the way he brought medical knowledge into the service of legal judgments, and his participation in nineteenth-century medicine's "implantation of perversity"—was a subterranean theme of Foucault's oeuvre and an experiential matrice that, however indirectly, shaped Foucault's mature thought.

Tardieu was a direct influence, moreover, on Paul Foucault's mentor and relative Maurice Laugier, whose memory he honored in his thesis. Specifically, Laugier drew on Tardieu's *Medico-Legal Study* in his examination of acts of public indecency. One of Laugier's better-known papers sought to apply the insights of forensic medicine to gay cruising in public toilets. Grasping the nature of individual instances of such perversity was crucial to understanding the nature of the individuals who committed to them, which was the forensic pathologist's ultimate concern. They fell, Laugier maintained, into "two distinct groups." "In the first," he explained, "we place all actions committed by individuals in a state of drunkenness or in a state of more or less complete derangement of their mental faculties," such as "satisfying a need in public, . . . leaving one's home in a more or less complete state of nudity, etc." "The second, which is far more numerous . . . consists exclusively of facts relating to pederasty and onanism." But this category required a further distinction. It could include "individuals of ill repute, often ex-convicts, arrested due to their very special attitude, their incessant comings and goings from certain places that we need not mention, their provocative gestures and looks, despite the fact that they have in reality committed no public indecency other than that of displaying by their dress and conventional signs their shameful profession." At other times, however, this category consists of "individuals lacking any judicial antecedents, whose appearance and dress is in no way suspicious, and who were nevertheless surprised, either in certain places frequented by crowds or in public urinals well known to and surveilled by the police, in attitudes such that agents who are accustomed to these sad spectacles felt authorized to harbor no doubt that [these actions] were flagrant delicto."[186] Foucault's father's mentor sought, in this way, not only to categorize a particular class of perversities, but to propose a semiology of deviance, whereby behavior and appearance were seen as constitutive of an individual's underlying sexual identity.

Finally, both Tardieu and Laugier were key figures in another issue that Foucault wrestled with in the early 1970s: forensic medicine's role in determining the "true sex" of hermaphrodites. It was to Tardieu that Foucault owed

his discovery of the centerpiece of one of his document collections: the memoirs of the nineteenth-century hermaphrodite Herculine Barbin (also known
as Alexina B.), which Foucault published in 1978. It had first appeared in the
second part of Tardieu's notorious 1874 study *The Medico-Legal Question of
Identity in Relation to the Vices of Conformation of Sexual Organs* (*Question
médico-légale de l'identité dans ses rapports avec les vices de conformation des
organes sexuels*). Barbin, a hermaphrodite raised as a woman in a convent
before being declared a man, committed suicide in a Latin Quarter attic in
1868. Her memoirs, found by the coroner and police inspector who discovered her body, were handed over to Tardieu, who included them in his book.[187]
Foucault was taken by the human story lurking behind this disturbing con-
spiracy of doctors and lawyers to define an individual's truth—an individual
"whom medicine and law in the nineteenth century relentlessly questioned
about their genuine sexual identity."[188] In his studies of hermaphroditism, one
of Tardieu's key collaborators was Laugier. For volume 17 of the *Nouveau dictionnaire de médecine et de chirurgie pratiques* (New dictionary of practical
medicine and surgery), published in 1873, Laugier wrote the entry on hermaphroditism considered from an anatomical and physiological perspective,
while he coauthored with Tardieu the subsequent entry, on hermaphroditism
from the standpoint of forensic medicine. The first article is structured around
the distinction between "apparent" hermaphroditism, in which an individual
has both male and female attributes but in which the reproductive organs are
sufficiently developed for the true sex to be determined, and "true" hermaphroditism, in which anatomical examinations reveal male and female organs
in a way that renders determining sexual identity problematic. Even here,
though, Laugier insists that the term "true" is misleading when applied to hermaphroditism, as "there is not properly speaking a *true* hermaphroditism,"
in the sense of one in which an individual is "doubly fertile": such conditions
exist only in the vegetal realm.[189] It is an "anatomical truth" that "bisexual
hermaphroditism can never be perfect among animals," as "nature has destined them to possess different sexes." Yet as the article Laugier coauthored
with Tardieu makes clear, any lingering considerations about the possibility of
true hermaphroditism that might exist from an anatomic perspective must be
completely ruled out when one adopts a legal-medical perspective. Hermaphroditism is, Laugier and Tardieu contend, one of "the most serious medico-
legal questions" because medical doctors have to pronounce themselves on
such questions as the validity of marriages: since a marriage can, by definition,
be only between a man and woman, forensic doctors must reach "certitude

concerning identity."[190] Uncertainty can result in mischaracterizations of individuals' basic civil identity, and specifically in "false inscriptions on the *état
civil*," as the French refer to the system of civil registration that has been mandatory since the monarchy introduced it in the sixteenth century. Fortunately,
they maintain, the "medico-legal question of identity . . . is in reality far more
simple than the anatomical-physiological question of hermaphroditism."[191]
Not only did the issue hinge on the identification of reproductive organs, but,
for all practical purposes, serious hermaphrodite cases only ever involved
anatomically male individuals who had some external female attributes. The
forensic question of hermaphroditism was, in short, about correctly identifying men who claimed to be women. This is why, Laugier and Tardieu write,
the "search for testicles must, in any case, be the object of particular attention
on the part of the expert doctor [i.e., the forensic doctor]. The palpation of
supra- and subpubic inguinal areas [and] rectal touching will quite often make
it possible to find the penis' head, which one will recognize by its shape and
particularly by the painful sensation that one provokes by compressing it."[192]
By collaborating with the legal system and by mobilizing medical truth in the
service of legal notions of truth, forensic medicine has, according to Laugier
and Tardieu, a decisive role to play in determining an individual's "true sex."[193]

"Do we *truly* need a *true* sex?"[194] Foucault asked this question in 1978, at
the tail end of a period in which he had brought to bear his examination of the
relationship between power and knowledge on the study of the emergence of
forensic pathology over the nineteenth century. The study of forensic medicine had allowed Foucault to bring into dramatic relief his concerns about the
very idea of truth: in this practice, the juridical, even prosecutorial use of truth
to formulate verdicts reinforced the strict positivism of the clinical-anatomical
approach to medicine. Yet forensic pathology was also an experiential matrix
in which Foucault's thought gestated: it was a practice, a way of knowing, and
a scientific and professional concern that played a significant role in his family
history. The intrusive quest for the testicles of apparently female hermaphrodites through the palpation of the groin, as advocated by Laugier and Tardieu,
echoes Foucault's observation about his father: "The doctor does not speak, . . .
he palpates." The medico-legal pursuit for true sexual identity also makes
much of the importance of determining individuals' proper legal or civic registration, their *état civil*. In this way, it evokes one of the best known if most
elusive passages in Foucault's corpus: the gnomic dialogue that concludes the
first chapter of *The Archaeology of Knowledge*. An unspecific interrogator asks
"Foucault" if, as he prepares to lay bare the method he had followed in his

previous books, he is not on the verge of "changing again," if his whole work is not in a sense a ruse to cover his tracks, before he surprises his readers by suddenly reemerging from some new vantage point. In reply, "Foucault" answers: "Do not ask who I am and do not tell me to remain the same: this is a morality of civil registration;"—*une morale d'état-civil*—"it governs our papers."[195] Though it would no doubt be an exaggeration to suggest that Foucault's concerns about identity originate in the medical-legal obsession with "true sex," this preoccupation nonetheless seems to haunt this famous remark. Moreover, in the same passage, Foucault contrasts this positivistic and prosecutorial concern with writing. "What," he asks, "do you imagine that I would take such pain and such pleasure in writing" if he were not preparing a labyrinth in which he could confound all efforts to identify him? And he follows his denunciation of the morality of civil registration by concluding: "Let it leave us alone when what matters is writing [*Qu'elle nous laisse libres quand il s'agit d'écrire*]."[196] Writing—the felt-like, velvety writing he described in the 1968 interview—thus presents itself as a liberating alternative to the inquisitorial demands of a form of knowledge that discounts language in favor of rigid positivism. *The Archaeology of Knowledge*, in this way, still bears the trace of Foucault's surgeon father and his family's medical heritage.

Words and Things

In the 1968 interview discussed above, Foucault acknowledged that, in his own way, he had continued the family tradition. True, he did not become a doctor: that professional lineage was preserved, rather, by his younger brother, Denys, who completed his residency in Paris in 1959 and defended his medical thesis in 1963.[197] Yet there was, the philosopher sensed, something about his intellectual temperament, something about the way he diagnosed discourse and ideas that made him a Foucault and Malapert.

Yet even as their career paths forked, there was one specific point at which the interests of the philosopher son and those of his surgeon father crossed. Foucault's work is known for its often intensely pictorial quality. He was prone to explain his ideas by invoking striking visual set pieces, such as ships of fools sailing down medieval Germany's rivers, which opens *Madness and Civilization*, and the gruesome account of Damien's drawing and quartering that lures readers into *Discipline and Punish*. Foucault, at times, extended this visual dimension to commentaries on actual paintings: *The Order of Things* begins with the virtuosic analysis of Velázquez's *Las Meninas*; he also wrote extended studies of Manet and Magritte. Foucault's fascination with painting and visual representation throws into relief one of his father's more surprising talents: Paul Foucault was a doctor, but he was also an artist.

To be sure, Paul Foucault was an artist *because* he was a doctor: his drawings and paintings, consisting entirely (as far as we know) of anatomical illustrations, were a pursuit of surgery by other means. Clearly, he put considerable effort into them, and his focus on this work reflected a conscious choice on his part to cultivate a talent he sensed within himself. Though his own sketches occasionally illustrated some of his medical journal articles, his most accomplished work of art was a set of fourteen colored anatomical plates he published in 1946 with the Librairie des Sciences et des Arts, based on Paris's Left Bank.[198] A review of Paul Foucault's plates in the *Gazette des hôpitaux* noted that they had been "printed with great care" based on "the drawings, most of which are original, by P. Foucault, professor of anatomy at the School of Poitiers."[199] The fourteen plates illustrate the anatomy of the upper limbs, essentially the arms. The review announces subsequent plates representing the lower limbs, the torso, and the head, though there is no record that these were ever published. The first plates represent individual bones, such as the scapula or shoulder blade and the humerus (Figure 4). Paul Foucault portrays the contours of these bones realistically, with pronounced, well-defined lines, and some shading and color modulation to suggest depth. His pictures become more complex as his subject matter does: his portrayals of muscles and nerve systems in the arms create an impression of kinetic activity, comprising rhythmic arabesques and luminous pastels. A plate devoted to the pectoralis minor muscle is a kaleidoscope of gray-white bones, burnt-orange muscles, burgundy veins, yellow ligaments, and blue-green nerves. The clearly demarcated anatomical features, each of which is identified in carefully handwritten block letters, achieves the plates' pedagogical purpose. Anatomic plates have always been popular, the *Gazette des hôpitaux* review noted; "a good drawing secures acquired concepts and clarifies details that are often missed when interpreting drawings drawn from photographic documents." Paul Foucault's plates are "easy to read and their hues bring out the constitutive parts [of different anatomical regions]."[200] Though their purpose may have been didactic, Paul Foucault signed them as an artist: at the base of several plates, one finds his initials— at times creatively merged, the curve of the "P" and the two horizontal lines of the "F" crossing the same vertical line (Figure 5).

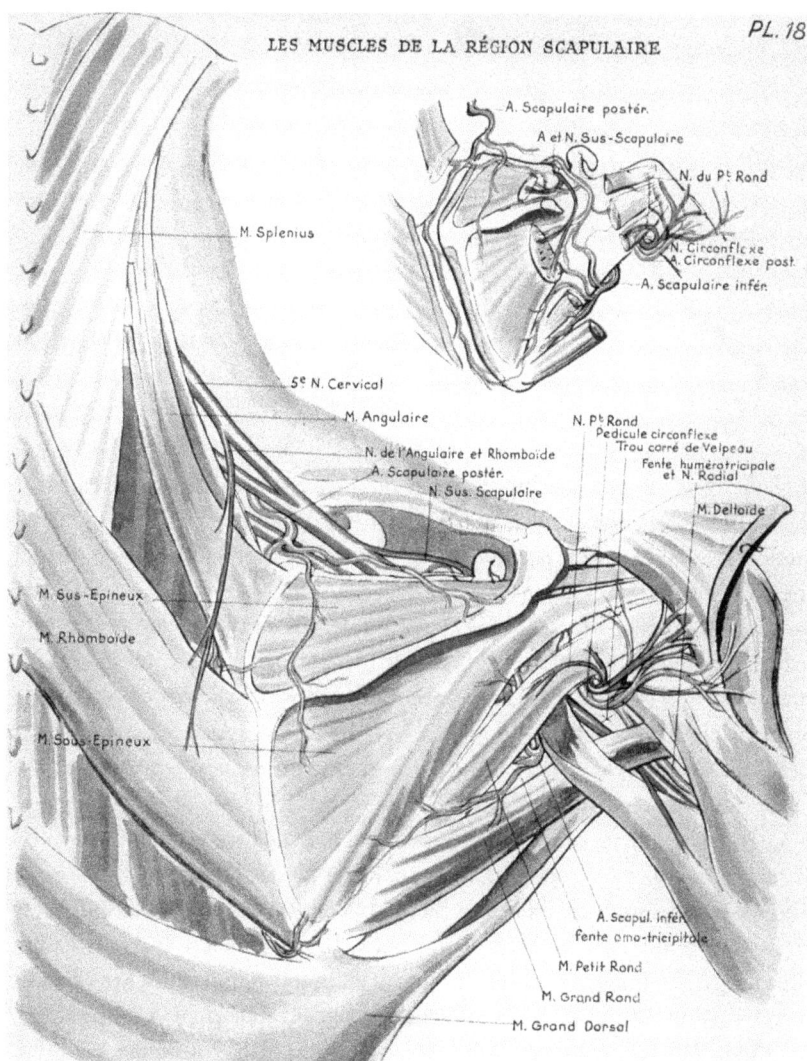

Figure 4. Paul Foucault, *Planches coloriées d'anatomie: Membre supérieur; Deuxième série*, plate 18.

Paul Foucault's plates are remarkable for their precision, as evidenced in the drawings' meticulous contours and the careful labeling of each feature. The relation between images and text is, moreover, a theme that Foucault frequently pursued in his own reflections on art. His interest in René Magritte's painting *The Treachery of Images* lay precisely in the unsettling way that

Figure 5. Paul Foucault's signature,
*Planches coloriées d'anatomie: Membre
supérieur; Deuxième série*, plate 40.

it challenged the relationship between pictures and words. Magritte's painting—a simple, realistic image of a pipe hovering above the phrase, written in
cursive letters, *Ceci n'est pas une pipe* ("This is not a pipe," the title by which
the painting is often known) is as simple, Foucault observed in a 1968 essay,
"as a page borrowed from a botany textbook: an image [*une figure*] and the
text that names it" (Figure 6).[201] It stands in a curious relationship to the two
principles that governed Western painting—and which are expressed, in representation that operate in different ways—are always separated. It may be, as
in his father's drawings, that a line connects the green tube representing cervical spinal nerve 7 with the words "7eme N. cervical" (*septième nerf cervical,*
or cervical spinal nerve 7). But the essential, Foucault writes, "is that that the
verbal sign and visual representation are never given at the same time." Some
kind of plane always establishes a hierarchy between them.[202] Second, Western art is premised on an equivalency between resemblance and affirmation:
the fact that an image resembles a thing is all that is required for an "obvious,
banal, . . . and yet nonetheless almost always silent statement" to slip into the
painting: "What you see is this."[203] An anatomical plate, for instance, implicitly declares: "This *is* a shoulder blade." What fascinated Foucault about Magritte's work, particularly *The Treachery of Images*, was the way it confounded
these principles. The "little white space" that surrounds the words and images
of an illustrated page—that creates a common space in which it is possible to
clearly distinguish a picture from its caption—becomes fluid and ambiguous
in Magritte's painting, in which the words are every bit as part of the painting
as the pipe. In a space in which linguistic signs seemed "excluded" and condemned to "roam from a distance around the image," it became evident that

Figure 6. René Magritte, *The Treachery of Images (This Is Not a Pipe)* (*La trahison des images [Ceci n'est pas une pipe]*) 1929. © 2022 C. Herscovici / Artists Rights Society (ARS), New York.

they were "surreptitiously" infiltrating the painting's plastic core: these words introduce into "the plenitude of the image, into its meticulous resemblance, a disorder"—an "order," that is, "that belongs only to them."[204]

The antonymy that Foucault posits between Western painting (as exemplified, perhaps, by a "botany textbook") and Magritte is strikingly parallel to the contrast that Foucault identified, in the interview discussed at this chapter's outset, between his love of language and the mute positivism he associated with his father (and perhaps, by extension, with his many doctor ancestors). We know nothing about what Foucault knew or thought of his father's anatomical plates, but his obvious concern with creating exact likenesses of anatomical features and his careful labeling of them clearly evoke Foucault's analyses of how representation traditionally functioned in European art. The affirmation Foucault maintained was implicit in classical representation—"what you see is this"—is, he says, "silent," much in the same way that Foucault said that his father, as a surgeon, "[did] not speak": to order and name, whether in clinical medicine or classical representation (or, a fortiori, in the intersection between the two that might occur in anatomical plates) is to devalue language, to reduce it to its purely representative function, to deny that it "exists."[205] By the same token, it implies a certain deafness and even blindness—an inability to hear utterances, a refusal to see letters except insofar as they refer to some thing. By painting words, by allowing them to erupt into the space of plastic representation, Magritte, Foucault believed, was saying that we must grasp the reality of words, to see that discourse is not a "transparent film through which one sees things," but has its own reality, its "own consistency, thickness, density"[206]—that it is carved into "the form of things."[207] Magritte allowed Foucault to articulate what he had come to see as the main difference separating him from his father and grandfathers: that unlike a doctor, he wanted to understand "things that are said insofar as they are things."[208] In challenging classical representation, Foucault was calling into question an entire family tradition.

And yet in choosing Magritte as his champion, Foucault self-consciously did not choose Klee or Kandinsky (both of whom he discussed in that essay). Magritte's contestation of classical representation takes the form of a subtle (if somewhat mischievous) homage to it. "No one, it would seem, is further removed from Kandinsky and Klee than Magritte. [His] painting is more than any other attached to the exactness of resemblances.... [His] painting is more than any other attached to carefully, cruelly separating the graphic element from the plastic element."[209] Perhaps Paul Foucault would not have felt completely lost in Magritte's world—disoriented, perhaps, but not lost. As a lifelong critic of medical positivism who nonetheless described himself as, "like [his] father and [his] grandparents," a "diagnostician," Foucault perhaps entertained the fantasy that his father would not be completely lost in his own philosophical universe, either.

On September 14, 1959, after several months of illness, Paul Foucault died at age sixty-six. Poitiers paid homage to its much-admired citizen. *Centre Presse*, the local newspaper, reported that despite his poor health, he had continued to work and stopped operating only a week before he died. The paper noted that since his arrival in Poitiers in 1924, he had "quickly won general esteem."[210] The article included a picture of Dr. Foucault in front of a blackboard displaying an anatomical drawing, presumably by his own hand. Later that week, a service was held at the Saint-Porchaire church (where Paul Foucault had been married). "All of Poitiers Attends the Funeral of Doctor Foucault," declared *Centre Presse*. Indeed, the long list of local dignitaries testified to his reputation: Poitiers's mayor and senator, the district's member of parliament, representatives from the prefect's office, the medical school faculty, the "entire medical corps of Poitiers," and a long list of judges, civil servants, and educators. The newspaper apologized for not being able to name all those who attended, since "one should name everyone, for the sympathy surrounding Doctor Foucault was so great and extended to every milieu, that all of Poitiers was present or represented at his funeral."

There was, however, one notable absence, if one is to take the newspaper account at its word. "The mourning," it noted, "was led by the son and son-in-law of Doctor Foucault."[211] Paul Foucault, of course, had two sons. Denys was studying medicine in Paris at the time. Michel was working for French cultural services in Warsaw, soon to be transferred to Hamburg. It seems possible the young philosopher may have missed his father's funeral.[212]

Nearly thirty years later, on November 11, 1987, it was the turn of Anne Foucault, the philosopher's mother, to die. By this point, the reputation of her son, who had passed away three years earlier, was stratospheric. In this heyday of "French theory," Foucault's books and ideas seemed, especially in the English-speaking world, ubiquitous. In the Poitiers newspaper, Anne Foucault's obituary referred to her celebrity status: she was "the widow of Doctor Paul Foucault, the eminent Poitevin surgeon, whose memory and reputation remains present in the recollections of many, so appreciated were his competence, his sense of duty, and his humanism." After mentioning Anne Foucault's active role in the senior citizens' club in Vendeuvre, the obituary noted, almost as an afterthought: "She was the mother of the philosopher Michel Foucault, also deceased."[213]

In an exchange in the 1970s, Foucault quizzed a young man of twenty about his relationship with his father. In passing, Foucault offered a brief but telling reference to his own father. He recalled "relations that were conflictual on precise points, but which represented a field of interest from which one was unable to detach oneself."[214] In his authority, latent violence, discreet perversity, and clinical approach to knowledge, Paul Foucault was the template of all his son came to reject. Yet insofar as he became the experiential context in which Foucault discovered medicine and the work of doctors—their concern with the body, its intensities, its pleasures, its pain, its malleability, their investment in life and their proximity to death—Foucault's father partook in a "field of interests" from which his son was never fully detached.

CHAPTER 2

Intensities

From his birth in 1926 until 1945, when, at the age of eighteen, he left to study in Paris, Foucault lived in the family home at 10, Rue Arthur Ranc in Poitiers with his mother, father, older sister, and—later—younger brother (Figure 7). While Foucault never spoke at great lengths about his upbringing, those aspects of his early life that he did occasionally dwell on testify to the importance of this period for his development and personality. In 1983, he reflected on the household in which he was raised, evoking the same themes of speech and silence that he had used when discussing his family's medical lineage in the interview discussed in the previous chapter. Foucault recalled: "I lived as a child in a petit bourgeois, provincial milieu in France, and the obligation of speaking, of making conversation with visitors, was for me something both very strange and very boring. I often wondered why people had to speak." Reflecting on the significance of this experience, he observed: "I think that any child who has been educated in a Catholic milieu just before or during the Second World War had the experience that there were many different ways of speaking as well as many forms of silence."[1] Foucault's brother, Denys, who was six years his junior, was once asked to respond to these very recollections. "The circle of family relations was very narrow," he explained, "and society conversations always revolved around the same topics. But, indeed, a certain type of conversation did not exist: personal conversations."[2] In the 1968 interview, Foucault had associated his father and the medical profession with the devaluation of speech. Here, Foucault extended this association to family life as such, or at least to his family's social interactions: in both cases, speech is presented as insubstantial, meaningless, incommunicative—"wind," as Foucault put in the earlier exchange. In this instance, however, speech is cheapened not by a doctor's truth pronouncements, but by the obligations and proprieties of social interaction. As Foucault and his

Figure 7. The Foucault family home, 10, Rue Arthur Ranc (formerly Rue de la Visitation), at the intersection of Boulevard de Verdun. Photograph by Jean-François Liandier.

brother recall them, these conversations hardly seem to be the kind in which one might be "*absolutely* heard."[3] They also evoke the philosopher's insight that power often consists less in reducing individuals to silence than in obligating them to speak.

Some thirty years after leaving the family home, Foucault found himself in a relationship that was the mirror image of the stultifying sociability he experienced in Poitiers. In this instance, too, a young man interacted with his elders. Yet the exchange was characterized not by the obligation to speak and make conversation, but by free and open dialogue and the intensity with which the older participant encouraged his young interlocutor to speak his mind. It began in the summer of 1975, with a twenty-year-old hitchhiker named Thierry Voeltzel holding a sign marked "CAEN" (the town in Normandy) as he sought a ride at the Porte de Saint-Cloud, on the outskirts of Paris. A small white car stopped, and the driver, a "bald man" with "a very elegant, unusual jacket" asked him to get in. Voeltzel believed he had a knack for making quick judgments about the men who offered him rides, but in this case, he was stumped. The driver's appearance was striking—his "glasses circled in steel," his "large-checked jacket" and "crewnecked polo shirt"—but, most importantly, he expressed a "constant interest in everything [Voeltzel] said": "My trip to Canada, the United States, my ideas, the family home to which I was headed, my friends, my readings—nothing left him indifferent."[4] Even the way the older man listened was "not ordinary": "he asked follow-up questions, wanted details." When it came to discussing what Voeltzel read, the driver's curiosity grew "almost greedy." His eyes lit up when the young man told him that, during a recent visit to a bookstore, he had flipped through a new volume about a nineteenth-century parricide named Pierre Rivière. At this point, something clicked. Voeltzel asked: "You wouldn't happen to be Michel Foucault?" After arriving in Normandy—Foucault was there to meet René Allio, the director who was making a film version of *Pierre Rivière,* in which Foucault played a judge—the philosopher offered to pick Voeltzel up the next day, when both were returning to Paris. On the trip home, the hitchhiker remembers, "everything I said enthralled him." When they got back, Foucault offered his new friend dinner; Voeltzel reminded the philosopher that he had been promised hashish. They went to Foucault's flat on the Rue de Vaugirard. They smoked a joint, then made love. The next morning, Foucault dropped him off at his parents' home in the posh sixteenth arrondissement. Finding the apartment completely empty, Voeltzel recalls sitting down on a bed and holding his head in his hands, "not knowing quite what to think": "my lover was the same age as my father." When his actual father, with whom Voeltzel had a strained relationship, learned that Foucault was gay, he asked the young man if this "bothered" (*ennuyé*) him. Voeltzel replied: "not at all." Recollecting the incident, he added: "nothing about Michel was boring" (*ennuyeux*).[5]

Foucault's memories of social occasions at his Poitiers home and his much later relationship with Voeltzel represent two poles that he was inclined to invoke when thinking about intimate relationships. One pole was associated with a hollow obligation to speak and sterile, lifeless interactions; the other was based on intense communication and proximity, a hunger for dialogue, a deep commitment to listening, and relationships that could never be described as "indifferent" or "boring." Often, Foucault sensed a kind of overlap or parallel between family relationships on the one hand, and romantic and sexual relationships on the other. One word that frequently recurs in his musings on both types of relationship is "intensity." In the conversations between Foucault and Voeltzel that were published in 1978 (from which any direct reference to Foucault was purged), the philosopher on several occasions uses the word as he questions the young man about his family life. Did Voeltzel, Foucault wanted to know, have "intense feelings" for his parents? Did he have "intense connections" with his mother?[6] In 1981, in an interview with *Gai pied* (France's first popular gay magazine), Foucault asserted that what made homosexuality subversive was not that it involved unnatural acts or forbidden pleasures. Cruising and easy sex, he contended, presented a "neat and tidy" image of homosexuality, one that was fully compatible with contemporary society's obsession with desire. Far more unsettling was gay love. "That individuals start to love one another," he observed, "that is a problem. Institutions are thrown off balance; affective intensities cross through them, they both support [the institutions] and upset them." "Institutional codes," he added, "cannot validate these relationships of multiple intensities."[7] In a discussion at Berkeley in 1983, Foucault argued that ancient practices of sexual renunciation and modern practices of sexual debauchery shared a similar goal: they were seeking lives with "greater intensity."[8]

This chapter will examine how family and relationships—both social and intimate—became another experiential matrix of Foucault's thought. Relationships not only were important to Foucault's emotional life, his character, and the practical opportunities they afforded him. They also inspired his thinking and came to occupy a significant place in his philosophical project. He reflected on social class, the nature of families, romantic and sexual relations, and the way in which relationships could be tied to phenomena such as confinement. Foucault, moreover, often saw relationships as susceptible to variable charges of intensity, ranging from ardor to apathy. The character and intensity of relationships is a recurring motif in Foucault's thought—and one that his formative years helps to elucidate.

A *Bourgeois* Family

In stating that he was raised "in a petit bourgeois, provincial milieu," Foucault was—characteristically, one is tempted to say—being misleading. By any stretch of the imagination, it strains credulity to describe Foucault's family as "petty bourgeois": in terms of wealth, property ownership, educational achievement, and professional and civic status, Foucault can be safely said to belong to a considerably higher social stratum. Yet the fact that he described his family in these terms is revealing for two reasons. First, it shows the extent to which Foucault was, in the term's most objective sense, "class conscious." Second, it draws attention to and compels us to consider Foucault's distinctive and original thinking about the bourgeoisie and its historical role.

Historians who have studied the French bourgeoisie in modern times have tended to dwell on two key facts: that the nineteenth century was the period when the bourgeoisie rose to social dominance, and that the French bourgeoisie was notable for the wide variety of strata that made it up. In her classic study, Adeline Daumard contended that the Parisian bourgeoisie (to which Foucault was connected) was divided into several recognizable categories: the finance aristocracy, which prevailed after 1830; the upper or *haute* bourgeoisie, characterized by substantial and stable wealth; the *bonne bourgeoisie*, endowed with significant fortune and tied to state service and the professions; a middling bourgeoisie, comprising clerks and shopkeepers; and a popular bourgeoisie that was barely distinguishable from the working classes. Yet while economic and even political interests frequently placed these different strata at odds with one another, they nevertheless shared several core values, particularly a belief in the importance of work and a desire to succeed, as well as a certain style of life, centered on family, *aisance* (comfort), education, and public service.[9]

Daumard notes that a key feature of "bourgeois psychology" is "the need for social climbing" (*ascension sociale*).[10] This concern is evident in Foucault's ancestors and shaped his own life opportunities. It brings to light, moreover, aspects of his background that are not entirely captured by its anchoring in the medical profession. The philosopher's great-grandfather Jacques-Symphorien Foucault, was born to a family of merchants in Angers in 1811.[11] Like an ambitious provincial in a Balzac novel, he set out to make a name for himself in Paris, where, in 1835, he became a doctor. By 1841, he and his wife were living on the main street of Nanterre, at the time a small village several miles to the west of Paris.[12] His son, Paul Victor Foucault, who was born in Nanterre in 1844, would also study in Paris and become a doctor. Yet Paul Victor, in addition to his professional success, benefited from a prestigious marriage. In June 1879, at the town hall of Paris's eighth arrondissement (one of the city's most well-heeled neighborhoods), he married Marie-Sophie-Louise de Cuvillon, the daughter of a family of Paris-based aristocrats.[13] On the family's other side, Foucault's great-great-grandfather Pierre-Prosper Malapert displayed similar energy in improving his situation. Born in 1798 in the small village of Charroux, some fifty kilometers south of Poitiers, he worked as a boy in his brother's law practice in a neighboring village. According to his obituary, after "a few years, tired of dossiers, aspiring for a more active life and drawn by his taste for the physical and natural sciences, he entered as an apprentice" at a pharmacy. Over the next six years, he studied in Poitiers, Saint-Quentin, and Versailles, before deciding to *monter à Paris*—"go up to Paris"—to study pharmacy. Though he was too poor to remain in the capital for long, he studied long enough to become a *pharmacien deuxième classe* (pharmacist second class), which allowed him to buy and run the Pharmacie Hélion in central Poitiers from 1822 until 1860.[14] As Daumard observes, the "bourgeois is a privileged person, but a privileged person who achieves and preserves his privilege through continuous effort."[15] The wealth and comfort Foucault enjoyed as a boy thus originated with the effort and ambition of his ancestors, who were almost textbook examples of ambitious, upwardly mobile nineteenth-century strivers.

The hard work of men like Jacques-Symphorien Foucault and Pierre-Prosper Malapert provided Foucault's ancestors with two other, closely related features of bourgeois life: property and material comfort. After being raised in working-class Nanterre, Paul Victor Foucault and his aristocratic bride established themselves in a comfortable house at 8, Rue Marrier in the Parisian suburb of Fontainebleau. Foucault's father, Paul André, was raised there with his parents, three older sisters, and two servants—a chambermaid and a cook, according to one set of records.[16] In Poitiers, the Malaperts, their fortune enhanced through work and marriage, acceded to a comparable level of material well-being. From the 1830s on, Prosper Malapert lived with his wife and four children at a house in central Poitiers located at 11, Rue Saint-Porchaire (near the eponymous church where Foucault's parents would marry and Foucault served as an *enfant de chœur* or altar boy).[17] They had between two to three servants and typically housed several students as well.[18] They were a short walk from the family pharmacy, located on the Rue de la Mairie (now Rue Gambetta).[19] In 1894, Henri Paulin Malapert, Prosper's grandson—and Foucault's grandfather—married Marie Henriette Rayneau, who came from a family of landowners and tax collectors in the village of Vendeuvre-du-Poitou, about twenty kilometers north of Poitiers. Through this marriage, the family acquired the property known as Le Piroir, which included a large rural home and surrounding gardens. In addition to visiting it frequently during his childhood, it was here that Foucault, throughout his life, would spend Augusts with his mother (who moved there following her husband's death). Soon, Henri Paulin Malapert and his new wife moved into a house in

Poitiers located at 1, Rue des Écossais, where they had two servants.[20] Foucault's mother, Anne Malapert, was born there in 1900. Three years later, they moved to the considerably larger house that Henri Paulin Malapert had built nearby at 10, Rue de la Visitation, on the western edge of the city center, near the cliffs overlooking the Boivre valley.[21] In 1911, the household consisted of Anne, her parents, a brother, and three servants.[22] After she married in 1924, Dr. Malapert would give this three-story white stone house to his daughter and her husband, Paul Foucault. Though the street named had changed—in the age of the radical republic, the Rue de la Visitation, named after a monastery, was renamed Rue Arthur Ranc, after a journalist and politician who had been a *communard* and Dreyfusard—Anne Foucault gave birth to Michel Foucault and his two siblings in the house in which she had grown up. The family's wealth and ease impressed members of less elevated social strata with whom they interacted. Louis Girard, Foucault's philosophy tutor during the war, recalls that, after his own marriage, he and his new wife were invited to the Foucault's "beautiful house" in Vendeuvre: "I was very impressed with this bourgeois family, me, the son of a little carpenter . . . born in a hovel."[23]

A final way Foucault's family exemplified modern bourgeois life was in their sense of civic duty. As doctors and professors, of course, the Foucaults and Malaperts inhabited the public sphere, whether boldly, as when Prosper Malapert testified as an expert in widely reported trials, or more discreetly, through participation in professional societies. Some took the step of assuming civic or political responsibilities. Jacques-Symphorien Foucault was a prominent public figure in Nanterre, not only for his medical work, but also for his leading role in founding the first municipal library in 1872 and the first town child-care center in 1876.[24] When he died in 1897 at his son's home in Fontainebleau, the town of Nanterre had not forgotten him. The municipal council sent a funeral wreath, while the local newspaper led with an obituary that declared: "After such a long medical career filled with the greatest self-sacrifice, he receives the unanimous regrets of all the patients he cured, the entire population of our town, and especially the working class for which he sacrificed himself so naturally and which will remain eternally grateful." The piece was signed: "A Worker."[25] A year later, the Nanterre municipal council voted to name a street "Rue du Docteur Foucault" in recognition of his service to the city.[26] On the other side, all three sons of Édouard Malapert—Foucault's grandfather and two great-uncles—were made chevaliers of the *Légion d'honneur*, France's highest civic distinction. Henri Paulin Malapert received it for his medical services during the First World War, Roger Malapert, a colonel in the French army, for his military service (which earned him the highest rank, that of *commandeur*), and Paulin Malapert, a philosophy professor in Paris, for his contributions to education.[27] Foucault's father was also made chevalier of the *Légion d'honneur* for his wartime medical service. Daumard observes: "All bourgeois want to have influence, many want to lead [and] dominate in professional as in private and public life. Titles [and] responsibilities were sought after."[28] In their quest for civic recognition, Foucault's family members epitomized bourgeois life and values.

The term "bourgeois" was important to Foucault both as a category of self-description and as a concept of historical and philosophical analysis. His use of the term is noteworthy, first of all, in light of his fraught relationship with Marxism. For much of his career, Foucault was a staunch critic of communism and a methodological skeptic toward Marxism, while remaining broadly sympathetic to the writings of Karl Marx himself (even if this meant, at times, reading Marx against communism and Marxism). Yet despite the distance separating his thought from Marxism, Foucault frequently made claims about European history that bore a family resemblance to Marxism's tenets, notably its emphasis on the historical role of the bourgeoisie as a class. *Madness and Civilization* and *Discipline and Punish* refer respectfully to the thesis that the bourgeoisie rose to prominence in the early modern era and achieved hegemony in the nineteenth century.

The high-water mark of Foucault's use of arguments about bourgeois rule was the first half of the 1970s, when he was also at his most politically active. During these years, Foucault was particularly concerned with the way in which the bourgeoisie used the law to defend its property and establish hegemony over other social classes. In a 1973 interview, Foucault argued that the power system that operated under the old regime depended on the exploitation of "illegalisms"—exemptions from the law that, in practice, were as structured and commonplace as legal behavior itself. During this period, Foucault notes, "the bourgeoisie" played this game as much as anyone else: to pursue its economic interest, it played fast and loose with the customs system, corporate privileges, commercial practices, and business ethics. Under this system, illegalities played off of and complemented one another: the bourgeoisie benefited from certain forms of working-class illegality, notably hostility to taxes, which the bourgeoisie shared. Thus a modus vivendi based on overlapping illegalities existed between the bourgeoisie and the working classes.

This changed dramatically, however, when, as Foucault put it, "the bourgeoisie seized political power" and was able "to adapt the structures for exercising

power to its economic interests." At this point, the nature of bourgeois property was beginning to change: as "bourgeois wealth" became invested in an
industrial-scale economy, so that it now consisted of machinery, factories, raw
materials, and stocks, "the bourgeoisie literally placed its wealth in the hands
of the lower strata." The "bourgeoisie became far more intolerant" of working-
class illegalism.[29] In a 1975 interview, Foucault indicated that this preoccupation with reducing illegalities was particularly tied to the nineteenth-century
bourgeoisie's "attachment to property": ownership in the sense of physical
possession and real estate is what made the illegal behavior of employees hired
to work on it unacceptable. Yet in recent times, Foucault began to argue, more
tolerant attitudes toward illegalism had begun to emerge—to delinquency
and petty crime, for instance. The reason was that property was "no longer
what one possesses, but that from which one profits." He added: "The accel-
eration in the flow of wealth, its greater and greater ability to circulate, the
abandonment of hoarding, practices of indebtedness, [and] the diminution in
the share of real estate in wealth mean that theft appears to people as no more
scandalous than swindles or tax fraud."[30] In making these claims, Foucault
was, at least indirectly, referring to the demise of the bourgeoisie in which he
had grown up: a class that was focused on financial responsibility, the steady
accumulation of wealth and property, and a preference for real estate. While
Foucault had no direct connection to the factory-owning bourgeoisie that
was concerned with working-class delinquency, his medical forefathers had
aligned their profession with the law in their effort to repress charlatanism
(an issue that had particularly preoccupied Prosper Malapert). When Foucault
reflected on the bourgeoisie's historic role and on the political consequences
of the bourgeoisie's concern with property, he was speaking, of course, as a
historian, but also from personal experience.

    Foucault's insistence that he came from the petty bourgeoisie is also
revealing of his distinct and nuanced form of class consciousness. He used
the phrase on several occasions: in addition to the interview from 1983 cited
at the beginning of this chapter, Foucault, in a 1975 interview, observed that
he was born in "the petty bourgeoisie of the provinces."[31] During this period,
Foucault seems to have subscribed to the idea that the petty bourgeoisie was
experiencing a decline in status and power in relation to the *grande bourgeoisie*. In an interview conducted during his trip to New York in 1970, Foucault analyzed the university crisis as arising from a conflict between the
petite and *grande bourgeoisie*: the *grande bourgeoisie* was increasingly using
universities to recruit technicians and engineers—reflecting its ever greater

need for "science and knowledge"—and a *petite bourgeoisie* that, because of its dependence on science and technology, was threatened with proletarianization.[32] In France, Foucault added, university professors were civil servants whose purpose was to perpetuate knowledge as defined by "the government, that is, the bourgeois class." The position of professors, he maintained, had become "untenable," like that of the petty bourgeoisie. And what are professors, he asked, if not "the most striking product of that class that, in the twentieth century, managed, at least in France, to be delegated by the *haute bourgeoisie* the right to exercise power?" The Third Republic, he noted, was known as the "the republic of professors" because it "recruited its political cadres from representatives of the teaching function, or from professions of the same kind"—including lawyers, and, significantly, "doctors." Now, in a very different kind of republic, "the petty bourgeoisie in France [was] losing all control over the state apparatus," forcing it to choose between joining the students in their revolutionary struggles or trying once again to seduce an *haute bourgeoisie* that no longer wants to subcontract its power, except through technical employment.[33] The point is not that Foucault was, in these remarks, speaking from a strictly autobiographical point of view. It is, rather, that he had a well-defined sense of where his family fit into the story of class relations in France, as can be seen by his use, in the early to mid-1970s, of the term "petty bourgeois" both to refer to his own social identity and to analyze contemporary events. Foucault did not use the term "petty bourgeoisie" in the more traditional sociological sense, to refer to small property owners, particularly shopkeepers. Rather, he understood the term to refer to professional and educated classes that had acquired positions of respectability and authority during the nineteenth century thanks to their willingness to support the social hegemony of a class—the *haute bourgeoisie*—that this lower class identified with yet did not belong to, owing to its relative lack of wealth. In describing himself as *petit bourgeois*, Foucault acknowledged that his social background made him simultaneously privileged and subaltern: that he belonged to a class blessed with money, prestige, and power, yet whose status was contingent on the legitimacy it bestowed on more elevated social and political forces. Something about the post-1968 crisis of French society and institutions made Foucault acutely conscious, it would seem, of his own class identity. This is evident when, in 1974, an interviewer observed that Foucault, unlike most intellectuals, rarely criticized the petty bourgeoisie. He replied: "You are right. This attitude of intellectuals, I would connect it to the Baudelairian tradition: it is the dandyism inherent in every

intellectual. It is completely abhorrent. It is easier to go after the petty bourgeoisie in its forms of existence and its ideas than after more important and
more serious enemies."[34]

Yet while welcoming this opportunity to distance himself from the petty
bourgeoisie's detractors, Foucault nonetheless engaged quite liberally in such
criticism, in the name of the critique of bourgeois values. Indeed, one evident
legacy of his upbringing was the eagerness with which, particularly in the early
1970s, he attacked "bourgeois values" and "bourgeois morality." The values
inculcated by modern society are, he contended in 1972, "an instrument of
power held by the bourgeoise." "When you are told that it is bad to steal, you are
given a certain definition of property, it is given the value that the bourgeoisie
gives it. When you are taught not to like violence, to be in favor of peace, to not
want vengeance, to prefer justice to struggle, what are you being taught? You
are being taught to prefer bourgeois justice over social struggle." Intellectuals,
teachers, and social workers who articulated these beliefs were simply doing
the bourgeoisie's bidding.[35] Foucault was, during this period, particularly concerned with the way in which the bourgeoisie wielded power by imposing
its values on subordinate groups, specifically the working class. "The bourgeoisie," he argued in 1972, has sought "to impose on the proletariat, through
penal legislation, prisons, as well as through newspapers [and] 'literature' certain categories of so-called 'universal' morality that will serve as ideological
barriers" between it and the nonproletarianized populace (which Foucault,
at this time, called "the plebe"). The proletariat, in this way, allied itself with
"the moral ideology of the bourgeoisie,"[36] accepting its "moral puritanism" or
"moral rigorism."[37] He described it as an "ideology of order, of virtue, of the
acceptance of laws, of what is and is not appropriate."[38] The proletariat had
ceased to be a revolutionary class because it has internalized bourgeois values.
Particularly as far as morality and legality were concerned, the proletariat were
"completely impregnated by bourgeois ideology." This was especially true of
the proletariat's leaders: to endow the revolutionary cause with respectability,
working-class leaders began adopting practices that betrayed a "cultural and
ideological affinity with the bourgeoisie." "Family morality," which had previously not extended to society's lower depths, was embraced in the nineteenth
century by the self-respecting laborer. The proletariat adopted such bourgeois
ideas as "popular virtue, the good worker, the good father, the good husband,
respectful of the legal order."[39] In this way, the proletariat was weaned off its
prior proclivity for insurrection and its tendency to conflate the legal system
with bourgeois rule.

Foucault's remarks in this vein provide some particularly revealing clues into his deep-seated anticommunism. "The Communist Party," he explained in 1971, "accepts and perpetuates most bourgeois values (in art, the family, sexuality, [and] daily life, in general). We must free ourselves from this cultural conservatism, just as we must free ourselves from political conservatism." He even went so far as to tell an American interviewer that the U.S. government, in repressing communists, had done a good thing: it had nipped in the bud an essentially conservative movement, indirectly allowing a more authentically revolutionary cause to flourish.[40] These were the reasons why, Foucault argued, the rejection of bourgeois values had to become the revolutionary project's primary goal. Bourgeois "puritanism" was a revolutionary handicap. There are many in contemporary society who embraced a wholesale rejection of the "bourgeois moral order." "How can we join them in political battles," he asked, "if we do not rid ourselves of our moral prejudices?"[41] Even the denunciation of bourgeois morality had to be undertaken without making concessions to bourgeois values. The critique had to be made in a playful and joyful spirit. It was necessary to show that "it is good to be dirty and bearded, to wear one's hair long, to look like a girl when one is a boy (and vice versa). One must put 'into play,' exhibit, transform and reverse the systems that peacefully shape us. For my part, this is what I try to do in my work."[42]

Examining Foucault's political pronouncements from the early 1970s thus helps to elucidate what Foucault meant by the term "bourgeois" and the problems he associated with the "bourgeoisie" when, during the same period, he used the term to describe his family. He saw himself as belonging to the *petite bourgeoisie* not in the traditional sense of shopkeepers or small property owners, but in the sense that his family, through education and professional qualifications, had been delegated political, social, and cultural authority by a hegemonic *haute bourgeoisie*, despite the fact that they were neither factory owners nor financiers. Most importantly, to be bourgeois was, for Foucault, to embrace a distinct if not always explicit set of values: ideas of moral purity, respect for the law, orderliness, and so on. Despite his criticism of the "Baudelairian" tradition of *épater le bourgeois*, Foucault's own conception of the bourgeoisie was as close to Baudelaire's as to Marx's: the bourgeoisie referred to a particular way of life that, in the name of morality, denied all primal and instinctive desires—including, as Foucault insisted in the 1970s, the desire for violence and insurgency. Yet even as he condemned the bourgeoisie, Foucault nonetheless expressed a grudging respect for its cunning. In a 1975 interview, he observed: "One would have to be as naïve as Baudelaire to believe that the bourgeoise is foolish and prudish. It is intelligent and cyni-cal."[43] Foucault made this point in nearly identical terms on at least two other occasions during these years.[44]

The terms in which Foucault discussed his family's social status and those in which he formulated a critique of French society in the early 1970s were thus interwoven in complex ways. He identified his family as belonging to the *petite bourgeoisie* while also describing the power struggles in post-1968 France as resulting, in part, from the changing relationship between the upper and the petty bourgeoisie. He spoke as one who understood the bourgeoi-sie and its cynical ways, even as he associated himself with a sector of it that occupied a subaltern position within the dominant class. Most importantly, he sought to challenge the bourgeois values and morality that he had been raised to respect and obey. In these ways, his family's social status and the fledgling class consciousness that his upbringing afforded him constituted an experien-tial matrix for at least some aspects of Foucault's subsequent social thought.

A Bourgeois *Family*

Like the bourgeoisie, family was also an experiential matrix of Foucault's thought. Indeed, the two terms were, for him, closely intertwined. Though he had on several occasions reflected on the historical development of family life in his work, it became a matter of particular concern for him when he began to plan his *History of Sexuality*. In the first volume—*La volonté de savoir*, pub-lished in 1976—Foucault devoted nearly forty pages to the historical role of the modern and specifically bourgeois family. He articulated his views about the family while expanding on his concept of the *dispositif de sexualité* (the "deployment of sexuality"). This passage was one of the most provocative hypotheses advanced in the book and counts among Foucault's most boldly speculative writings. The modern family, Foucault argued, lay at the intersec-tions of two mechanisms (*dispositifs*) that have historically governed sexual relations: a mechanism of alliances (*dispositif d'alliance*), which has existed in every society, and a mechanism of sexuality (*dispositif de sexualité*), which emerged in Western societies in the eighteenth century.[45] The mechanism of alliance regulates marriage, kinship, and the transmission of property. It is closely tied to economic relations and depends to a significant degree on the law. It regulates "the connection between partners with a defined status." Above all, it seeks to control and manage the business of reproduction. The mechanism of sexuality applies to sexual relations, but in a very different way. Its concerns are "the sensations of the body" and "the quality of pleasures." This mechanism is also harnessed to economic relations, less through property and lineage than through the body itself: its raison d'être is not to ensure reproduction, but "to proliferate, innovate, annex, invent, [and] penetrate the body in an ever more detailed way." From its onset, the *dispositif de sexualité* has sought an "intensification of the body"—its "valorization as an object of knowledge and as an element in power relations."[46] Yet while sexual relations were initially governed by this system of alliances—that is, marriage and family lineages—they increasingly became the target of an emerging mechanism of sexuality. The "family unit" (*cellule familiale*) that came to be valued in the eighteenth century resulted in the development of this mechanism along its "two principal dimensions": "the husband-wife axis and the parent-children axis."[47] The family is thus not a social or economic structure intended to limit sexuality; to the contrary, the family's role, Foucault maintains, is to "anchor" sexuality and to become its permanent "prop" (*support*). "The family is the exchanger of sexuality and the alliance: it transports the law and the legal dimension into the mechanism of sexuality; and it carries the economy of pleasure and the intensity of sensations into the regime of alliances."[48] Though this passage is cryptic, its conclusion is striking: though the family has historically been a means for regulating the production of offspring to ensure the transmission of property, it has become, in more recent times, the primary milieu in which sexuality developed—through the attention given to the female body, the preoccupation with masturbation, the regulation of birth, and the identification of perverse behavior. The family lies at the crossroads between economic calculation and the cultivation of affects and "intensities."

Foucault's family bears many of the hallmarks of the mechanism of alliance, which, despite its ancient character, overlapped significantly with what he described elsewhere as "bourgeois morality." The marriage between Foucault's parents was, literally, an "alliance" between two prestigious and prominent bourgeois families. The wedding itself was announced in *Le Figaro*, the prominent Parisian daily, in January 1924. The brief article announced the recent marriage at the Église Saint-Porchaire—the parish church in the neighborhood where they would reside—"of Mlle. Anne Malapert, daughter of Dr. Malapert, professor at the School of Medicine, and of madame [Malapert], née Rayneau, and of Dr. Paul Foucault, former resident of the hospitals of Paris, son of Dr. Foucault, deceased, and of madame [Foucault], née de Cuvillon." The brides' witnesses were her paternal uncle, Colonel Roger Malapert, an officer with a distinguished record during the First World War, and Dr. René Morichau-Beauchant, a colleague of her father's at the Poitiers medical school (to whom we shall return shortly). The witnesses appearing on the groom's behalf were his maternal uncle, Louis Robert de Cuvillon, a successful Parisian artist who bore the name of the aristocratic side of Paul Foucault's family, and Dr. Placide Mauclaire, an eminent Parisian doctor (discussed in the previous chapter).[49] Martine Segalen, an authority on the history of the family, observes that, into the modern era, the "model of bourgeois marriage continued to be, in the full sense of the word, an alliance between two family groups."[50] In uniting two quite wealthy families with established professional reputations, Foucault's parents instantiated the mechanism of alliance.

The Foucault household itself also exemplified a form of bourgeois life that remained, in many ways, rooted in this older ideal. Though it was to his own father that he owed his inroads into the medical profession, Paul Foucault, to a considerable extent, owed his status and income in Poitiers to his father-in-law, Henri Malapert. The Foucault-Malapert marriage was, in this way, strongly patrimonial. As Segalen writes, "one of the functions of marriage seen as an alliance between two lines was the transmission of patrimonies. The best way to protect this was to make sure that one's spouse was from a similar social background."[51] From his wife's father, Paul Foucault obtained not only the family home at 10, Rue Arthur Ranc and the country house in Vendeuvre, but his father-in-law's surgical practice as well.[52] Moreover, Henri Malapert presumably played a role in helping his son-in-law acquire his positions at the Poitiers medical school and hospital. While we do not know the exact amount of Paul Foucault's income, records indicate that in 1948 he earned, as a tenured anatomy professor (*professeur titularisé d'anatomie*), a monthly salary of 63,000 francs, which, in 2022, comes to around 2,450,52 euros a year (about $2,673). This was a half-time salary.[53] The average annual income of male upper managers (*cadres supérieurs*) in 1950 was around 11,380,15, in 2022 euros (about $12,414), which was nearly five times Paul Foucault's teaching income [54] But given that this income was a relatively small part of Paul Foucault's salary—he also had a fixed income from his position at the hospital and the much more extensive income from his clinics—it seems likely that he belonged to the higher income brackets of this period. David Macey observes: "For a surgeon, the accumulation of income from a variety of sources and jealously guarded positions was the key to success, and Paul Foucault was successful."[55] In practice, as Macey notes, this meant that Paul Foucault worked long days. Frequently, he made rural calls, for which he used the two automobiles he owned (the driver of which could apparently double as an anesthetist).

Another patrimonial strategy—albeit a symbolic one—is the passing down of names. Foucault's father was "Paul André," and his father was "Paul Victor." Like other Malaperts, one of Foucault's maternal grandfather's Christian names was "Paulin." In keeping with family tradition, the name given to Foucault was "Paul Michel." Administrative documents referred to the young Foucault as "Paul" or "Paul Michel." Many relatives called him by this name most of his life. For his part, Foucault, rejecting this birthright, never used "Paul"— his father's name—for his publications or professional work. Yet it was always his name—at least as far as the *état civil* and his mother were concerned. His official death record, the funeral announcement issued by his family, and his tombstone all identify him as "Paul Michel Foucault."[56]

The idea of marriage as an "alliance," a system for uniting families of similar economic standing, consolidating wealth and social capital, and ensuring the transmission of property and the family name to offspring were clearly operative in the Foucault household. The Foucaults instantiated this model of family life in other ways as well. They were, for instance, at least nominally Catholic. One of Foucault's mother's Christian names was Radegonde, in honor of Poitiers's patron saint. The family had close connections to the parish church, the Église Saint-Porchaire, which was a short walk from their home. The Foucault children regularly attended mass, though they were often accompanied by their maternal grandmother rather than their mother.[57] Foucault's brother recalled that this grandmother "went to mass almost every day."[58] The young Foucault served as an altar boy at Saint-Porchaire, and, until he went to Paris, he was continuously educated in Catholic schools. Though Foucault's mother allegedly had a Voltairian streak (the Malaperts had connections to freemasonry and republicanism), they accepted Catholicism as an institution that validated family status and regulated the basic rituals of social life, such as marriage, baptism, and death.

The conception of marriage as alliance extended to the Foucault children as well. On December 22, 1945, Foucault's sister, Francine, married, in Poitiers, a young man named Henri Fruchaud (1921–2008). Though Fruchaud had studied law—as had Francine—he, too, came from a medical family. His father, Henri Fruchaud (1894–1960), was a close friend of Paul Foucault's and a prominent doctor from Angers. In 1945, Henri Fruchaud was something of a hero: in 1940, following Charles de Gaulle's appeal to the French to resist German occupation, Fruchaud became one of the leading doctors in the Free French movement, cementing this reputation through his role in the North African and Middle Eastern campaign.

Yet Dr. Fruchaud had another claim to fame—or, rather, infamy: within the extended Foucault family, he was the one bona fide murderer. Years earlier, in 1914, when he was twenty and completing his military service in Angers, his father, a doctor in the nearby village of Saint-Mathurin-sur-Loire, asked him for assistance. The elder Fruchaud had been having an affair with one of his patients, and her husband, a miller, had promised to kill him. Having already hired a bodyguard, Fruchaud now asked his son to protect him. In May, the jealous husband, accompanied by a friend, forced the elder Fruchaud's car off the road. After a chase in which the bodyguard was immobilized, the younger Fruchaud turned to face the assailants. With his service pistol, he shot them. Days later, both men died. The younger Fruchaud was court-martialed but received a light sentence. The war soon rendered it moot. The village denounced the light sentence the members of this bourgeois family had received as a travesty of justice. After the First World War—when Paul Foucault presumably met him, while both were studying in Paris—Fruchaud was formally pardoned. When Paul Foucault died in 1959, Fruchaud made a serious effort to acquire the position his friend had left vacant in Poitiers. Fruchaud registered with the local professional organization, the Conseil de l'Ordre des Médecins de la Vienne, for this express purpose—though his sudden death in 1960 brought this project to an abrupt end. Thus Paul Foucault, at least indirectly, seems to have orchestrated another marriage of alliance: to a doctor and, perhaps less intentionally, to what his son would later call an "infamous man."[59]

Yet while the Foucault family seemed immersed in the tradition of alliance, they were beginning, in other ways, to diverge from it. His penchant for traditionalism notwithstanding, Paul Foucault embodied one of the new social forces transforming family life in the early twentieth century: as an obstetrician, he represented science's incursion into the inner sanctum of the family home. As seen in the last chapter, Paul Foucault's scientific interests had significant implications for the government of families, notably his interest in young boys' masturbation, male impotence, and virility. In his essay on impotence, Paul Foucault specifically referred to situations in which parents brought to a doctor a child whose sexual organs were presumed to be abnormal. "Adolescents [and] sometimes children," he wrote, "are brought [to the doctor] by their parents, who are worried about a malformation noticed at birth, but, with age and the development of genital organs, takes on an importance the true significance of which they are often unable to determine."[60] The assumption underlying this remark is that parents have a specific interest in the sexual normalcy of their children, and that doctors have the scientific knowledge to assist with these problems that parents themselves may lack. Paul Foucault's assertion illustrates what his son later called the "the pedagogization of the child's sex," whereby "parents, families, educators, doctors, and later psychologists must take responsibility for this precious and perilous, dangerous and endangered sexual seed." Paul Foucault's interest in masturbation's impact on testicular torsions is another example of this trend. Moreover, as an obstetrician, Paul Foucault participated in the sexualization of the female body, another feature of what his son called the deployment of sexuality. In 1925, Paul Foucault published a paper on vaginal cysts that demonstrated how the female body, grasped notably through its reproductive characteristics, had become a target of medical intervention. According to Paul Foucault, such cysts, which were typically found in adult women, were caused neither by coitus nor childbirth, but by pregnancy, which, "by impressing an excess of activity on the entire genital apparatus, increases the cyst's size.[61] Because cysts are generally painless, their symptoms can be identified only through medical examination—a process that Paul Foucault proceeded to describe in matter-of-fact detail. After "pushing aside the vulva," one sees "the lower end of the cyst, which lifts up the vagina's antero-lateral wall." "By touching," he continues, "one realizes that the cyst extends to the back of the vaginal dome." Its upper end can be difficult to locate; this is why, Paul Foucault notes, "rectal touching, combined with vaginal touching, can sometimes provide information on this matter."[62] Though these insights relate, of course, to Paul Foucault's professional life, they illustrate the way in which new preoccupations with sexuality were transforming the relationship between doctors and families, creating possibilities for medical intervention in domestic relationships and tracking a concomitant sexualization of certain aspects of these relations. Paul Foucault was, in this way, a fairly typical bourgeois father and husband of the *alliance* mold who, at the same time, participated in sexuality's deployment.

Anne Foucault (née Malapert) would also seem, in many respects, to exemplify a bourgeois mother of her day—traditional in some respects, modern in others. She ran the household at 10, Rue Arthur Ranc, where she herself had grown up. She was responsible for raising the children: Francine, born in 1925; Michel, born in 1926; and Denys, born in 1933. Yet as was typical of bourgeois households, she was assisted by a "household of servants,"[63] including a British nurse who taught the children some English.[64] She was

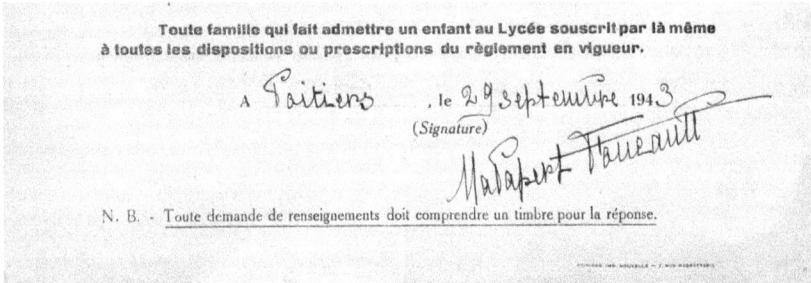

Figure 8. Foucault's inscription sheet for the Poitiers Lycée from February 1943, filled in and signed in by his mother, Anne Foucault. She signs it: "Malapert Foucault." Archives Départementales des Deux-Sèvres et de la Vienne.

especially active in tending to her children's education (Figure 8), particularly Michel's: she personally sought to find a replacement when his school's prominent philosophy teacher was arrested by the Gestapo, in addition to contacting the dean of the University of Poitiers to find a suitable philosophy tutor for her son (points to which we will return in the final chapter). Yet she was also deeply involved in her husband's work. With the assistance of a secretary, she ran the business side of his surgical practice from the family home. Indeed, coming from such a long line of distinguished Poitevin doctors, she "always regretted," according to Foucault's partner Daniel Defert, "being born too early for it to be suitable that a woman study medicine."[65] She had a reputation for knowing her mind and having her way.[66] As Didier Eribon recounts, she made her father's maxim her own: "What matters is governing oneself."[67] This adage, which would seem to epitomize bourgeois individualism and self-discipline, also evokes the Greek and Roman practices of selfhood to which Foucault devoted his final books.

Yet while he said little about his parents, the evidence we have concerning his attitude toward his parents suggests that, for Foucault, the household on Rue Arthur Ranc was suffused in emotional intensity and "saturated," as he would later put it, with an implicit yet pervasive sexuality. In his exchange with Voeltzel, he inquired whether the young man had "intense feelings, either hatred or affection" for his parents and, in general, whether his relations with them were characterized by "intensity."[68] Foucault, we know, spoke at times of his hatred of his father. Conversely, he remained, all his life, close to his mother, spending most Augusts of his adult life with her at Vendeuvre, even bringing his friends to visit her. When Voeltzel mentioned his mother, Foucault inquired whether he had "intense relations" with her.[69] Foucault's experience of family life seems to have been the crucible for one of the most striking claims of his *History of Sexuality*: that the deployment of sexuality had "intensified affective relations, the corporeal proximities between parents and children," creating a "permanent incitement to incest in the bourgeois family."[70] Foucault's use of the term incest here is replete with ambiguity: while at times it suggest sexual contact between family members, it seems, more generally, to imply any family relationship charged with emotional intensity. The bourgeois family was, for Foucault, a kind of hothouse of intimacy and concentrated affect.

Yet Foucault was careful not to adopt the standpoint of psychoanalysis, which saw the relations between parents and children as the primary circuit of incestuous sexuality. Freud's gambit, Foucault believed, was to give legitimacy to incestuous desire within the context of the bourgeois family at the very moment when incest among the lower classes was being aggressively persecuted (as with the 1889 and 1898 laws instating *la déchéance paternelle*, the loss of paternal rights resulting from incestuous and other forms of behavior).[71] Foucault summarized this argument in his conversation with Voeltzel: "what is striking, after all, in Freud . . . is that when he speaks of incest, he always speaks of it in the parent-children, children-parent direction, according to the ascending axis"—at which point Voeltzel interjects "That never interested me"—"whereas I think that's just a way of attaching children to their parents, and that, in fact, desire is far more horizontal, it connects people who are close to one another, and, of course, in this horizontal progression, what you encounter are brothers and sisters."[72] When Voeltzel reflects on the desire he has felt for a younger brother and the sexual dreams he has had about him, Foucault asks him if he should not "absolutely" have sex with him. When Voeltzel demurs, Foucault asks: "But that is, after all, the absolute dream—no?"[73]

Throughout his life, Foucault had a close relationship with his siblings: his sister, Francine, who was fifteen months older than him, and his brother, Denys, who was six years younger. One biographer observes: "The three children bore a striking likeness to one another, and all had the same fair hair, the rather prominent nose and the bright-blue eyes that were to stare from the rimless glasses Foucault wore in so many photographs."[74] The fact that the house on Rue Arthur Ranc was comfortable enough for each child to have a room did not prevent an intense sense of closeness. In particular, Foucault and his sister, Francine, were, as children, inseparable. Foucault's mother would recall the story of when, in 1930, she enrolled Francine in elementary school at the Lycée de Poitiers: Foucault, quite simply, refused to be separated from his sister. Foucault's mother—in an effort characteristic of the efforts she made on behalf of her son's education and desires—explained the problem to the schoolteacher, who, despite the fact that he was not yet four (and six was the normal registration age) agreed to let the boy sit with his colored pencils at the back of the classroom.[75]

This "horizontal" intensity seems to have remained one that Foucault felt, at least to a degree, his whole life. In the early 1950s, Foucault lived with his brother, Denys—then a medical student—on the Rue Monge in the Latin Quarter. When Foucault moved into his apartment on the Rue de Vaugirard in the fifteenth arrondissement, he found himself a short walk from his sister and her family, who lived on Avenue de Suffren. Foucault saw his sister as well as his nieces and nephews regularly at the family home in Vendeuvre. As their uncle, he did what he could to help their careers.[76]

As Foucault lay dying in the Pitié-Salpêtrière Hospital in the spring of 1984, Hervé Guibert recalls, in his diary, a visit from Francine. "His sister arrives, she offers him fruit jellies, he doesn't want any, I have one, a green one. She watches television with us. Then the television goes off, and we hear a general exclamation outside: an outage has occurred. His sister opens the window: he's too warm, she observes that the window opens the wrong way in relation to the patient's bed. She knows that in the morning he endured very painful examinations, including a lumbar puncture, which were not finished and would start over in the morning. A nurse enters to give him an injection, I leave, his sister stays. When I return there's a bandage on his arm. His sister rummages through the trash to find the name of the medicine injected into him, but the wrapper isn't there. In a container, I see his blood. His sister presses on his chest to show him how he should spit, she leaves, she'll come back tomorrow, I shake her hand."[77] Like a play by Beckett, the scene combines the pathos of imminent death with deadpan humor. At its heart lies Francine's unspoken sorrow and her nervous familiarity with her brother. The lover watches as the siblings discreetly replay their childhood—the candy, the absent presence of their doctor-father—and interact in ways that seem both tritely routine and steeped in intimacy. After his death, Francine and Denys became ferocious guardians of Foucault's estate, vigorously enforcing, however inconsistently, the philosopher's ban on posthumous publications.

There is no way of knowing, of course, whether Foucault ever realized what he called the "absolute dream." In a sense, this is not the point. What seems certain is that the family was an experiential matrix of Foucault's thought. It was, moreover, an experience steeped in ambiguities. The family was defined both

by the pragmatic preoccupations of "alliance"—law, property, inheritance—
and by the emotional-corporeal intensities of "sexuality." Paul Foucault's status
as a prominent local figure turned his household, at times, into an extension
of his social authority. One biographer observes that the dinners Foucault's
father gave "for colleagues and local *notables* were effectively business meetings. Although the children were expected to make polite conversation with
visitors, they were also required to remain silent at dinner." Yet he also notes
that for Foucault and siblings, "very formal dinners were preferable; on such
occasions, they ate separately and in much more relaxed circumstances, safe
from the demands and conventions of adult society."[78] Emotional intensity
and intoxicating proximity were, for Foucault, the intriguing flip side of the
bourgeois concern with status and wealth. The "privileged point of sexuality's
hatching is the family," and "for this reason, it is born 'incestuous.'" Yet this
incest is "constantly solicited and refused, an obsessive fear and invitation, a
dreaded secret and an indispensable link." The family-as-alliance has every
reason to fear incest's consequences, even as the family-as-sexuality must permanently incite incestuous desire and foster "the affective intensification of
the familial space."[79]

Foucault would use the same language he employed when discussing
incestuous relations to another practice he associated with the deployment
of sexuality in the bourgeois household: masturbation. "Everyone knows very
well," he once observed, "that it is impossible to prevent a child from masturbating." He coyly added that onanism was "the only pleasure that really harms
nobody." What distinguishes the place masturbation occupied in bourgeois
homes—presumably, such as his own—is not simply the fact that it was pro-
hibited and pursued, but the fact that, by virtue of this prohibition, the act
itself was intensified—for all involved. Masturbation was forbidden, he argues,
not because of prudishness, but because of the way prohibition intensified the
excitement invested in the act itself: its interdiction has endured because of
"this pleasure and anxiety and all the emotional network around it." Concerns about children's sexuality, Foucault maintained, persisted not because
they were well founded, but because *parents enjoy* dealing with them. "To take
care of the sexuality of their children was not only a question of morality for
the parents but also a question of pleasure"—specifically, "sexual excitement
and sexual satisfaction," which he went so far as to call a "systematization of
rape": "To intervene in this personal, secret activity, which masturbation was,
does not represent something neutral for the parents. It is not only a matter of power, or authority, or ethics; it's also a pleasure." He pursued: "there is

enjoyment in intervening. The fact that masturbation was so strictly forbidden for children was naturally the cause of anxiety. It was also a reason for the *intensification* of this activity, for mutual masturbation and for the pleasure of secret communication between children around this theme. All this has given a certain shape to family life, to the relationship between children and parents, and to the relations between children. All that has, as a result, not only repression but an intensification both of anxieties and of pleasures."[80] An echo of the parental preoccupation can be heard in Paul Foucault's concern with masturbation's impact on testicular torsions in young boys, and in his interest in the pediatric surgeon Louis Ombrédanne's work on the connection between masturbation and testicular inflammation. These later views confirm how Foucault saw the bourgeois family not simply as an institution of repression, but as a breeding ground of emotional and corporeal intensities. It further suggests that Foucault imagined family life as structured around two axes, that reconfigure Freud's primal horde: a horizontal axis of sibling incest and "mutual masturbation," crossed by a vertical axis of sadistic parental interdiction—itself steeped in pleasure, though perhaps of more dubious legitimacy.

Foucault often seemed to want to turn away from his family. "Breaking with one's family, I think that has been done as long as the world has existed," he once remarked, with a laugh.[81] Yet he also retained a curious and quite deep loyalty to it—at least to his mother and siblings—in addition to holding family and even "incestuous" relationships as a kind of model of human relationships founded on emotional intensity. André Gide defined his distinctive form of modern aesthetic and sexual freedom when he declared: "Families, I hate you! Shut-in homes, closed doors, jealous possessions of happiness." Foucault concurred, in many ways, while also declaring, in a kind of rejoinder to André Gide's antifamily manifesto: "Families, I desire you—and you make me desire. Shut-in homes, closed doors, jealous possessions of happiness: what are these, if not desire's native home, vectors of heightened intensity?"[82]

The Normal and the Pathological

Perhaps the most important forms of "intense relationships" that Foucault pursued and cultivated throughout his life were those with other men. In 1981, he explained: "As far back as I can remember, desiring boys meant desiring relationships with boys. It was always something important to me. Not necessarily in the form of a couple, but as a question of existence: how is it possible for men to be together? To live together, to share their time, their meals, their bedrooms, their leisure time, their sorrows, their knowledge, their confidences?"[83] In his mature years, at a time when these issues were at last being discussed publicly, Foucault famously challenged the very idea of homo-sexual identity—of "being homosexual." To be "gay"—a term he came to pre-fer to "homosexual"—Foucault contended, was not to harbor some deep inner truth, but to engage in relationships of a particular kind—sex, to be sure, but also and perhaps especially friendship, patterns of sociability, ways of sharing one's life. Needless to say, this conception of the gay "mode of existence" was the fruit of an entire life reflecting on these questions. There is no reason, and even less evidence, to believe that he espoused such views at a young age.

What is striking, however, is that the language Foucault used for describ-ing family relations was similar to the kind he employed when discussing rela-tions between men. As we saw previously, Foucault described relations with parents and siblings, particularly in the modern bourgeois household, as sus-ceptible to "intensities." Late in life, he described homosexuality as generating "affective intensities" and "relations with multiple intensities,"[84] "relations" that are "intense and satisfying."[85] Foucault believed that family relations and rela-tions with men could be infused with a surplus charge, an emotional jolt that could transform physical proximity and social connectedness into heightened forms of existence. The risk, in this quest for intensities, was that relation-ships would fail to reach their full potential and sink into apathy: Foucault's fascination with incest among siblings was closely tied to his fears about the ultimate sterility inherent in certain relationships between parents and their children—the kind found in the family conceived as an "alliance," in which self-interested, utilitarian preoccupations prevailed. Yet it seems that these affective intensities were, in Foucault's view, exposed to an additional threat: the entropy that could result from experiencing these emotional discharges as rising from within an individual, and—worse still—from individual character and nature, rather than from potentialities arising from the relationship itself.

Virtually nothing is known about Foucault's sexual experiences during his time in Poitiers. Reflecting on the impact of the sexual revolution, he mused: "For previous generations, the discovery that one was homosexual was always a solemn moment in life, a kind of illumination and a rupture at the same time, it was a kind of enchantment, the day when one realized that this is what pleasure is, and at the same time, the feeling that one was marked, that one was the black sheep, that until the end of the days that's how it would be."[86] We do not know when this "solemn moment" occurred for

Foucault. But while his move to Paris in 1945 presumably gave him concrete opportunities to explore this "illumination" for the first time, one suspects he must have had intuitions long before. According to Didier Eribon, a crystallizing experience of gay identity is what he calls the "shock of the insult."[87] Foucault never spoke of having been called a *pédé*—a "fag" or "queer." Yet elements of his biography suggest moments when he might have felt his desires and longings disparaged in ways that Eribon argues are formative of young gay people. One senses that Foucault is speaking from personal experience when he speaks of "teachers who for years, for centuries explained to children that homosexuality was unacceptable," and wonders about the "damages" such lessons might have caused.[88] Louis Girard, Foucault's philosophy tutor during the war years, speculated: "Perhaps he . . . suffered from his homosexuality. But he never spoke to me about it." He recalls one incident in particular: "When I married, in 1947, I told [Foucault]: 'It's your turn now!' He went all red. That's when I understood."[89] Despite Girard's admiration of Foucault, such remarks—and, even more so, the genre of anecdote Girard recounts—could easily be interpreted as a more subtle form of the "insults" that can be constitutive of gay identity. And though it was not specifically directed against his son, Paul Foucault's medical work was suffused with assumptions about "sexual inversion"—to the point, as we have seen, of imagining the graft of monkey testicles on homosexuals as a solution to deficient virility.

Though Foucault's early sexual experiences and thoughts are a historical black hole, one intriguing family connection gives us some understanding of how the people Foucault knew in Poitiers might have perceived homosexuality and how Foucault might have begun to acquire a vocabulary for thinking about it. The Foucault family was closely connected to one René Morichau-Beauchant, a leading figure in the early reception of psychoanalysis in France. Morichau-Beauchant was born in Vivonne, south of Poitiers, in 1873. He was the grandson of a prominent physician who served as the director of the Poitiers medical school from 1820 to 1832; though he would never hold this position, both his son and grandson would.[90] After studying in nearby Poitiers, he eventually attended medical school in Paris (specializing in gastroenterology). Upon completing his degree, he returned to Poitiers in 1903, where he worked as a doctor at the Hôtel-Dieu and as professor at the medical school. He had a solid record of publications in his field.[91] He lived in Poitiers until his death in 1952.[92]

What makes Morichau-Beauchant's career remarkable—and somewhat unexpected of a provincial doctor, however erudite—is the fact that he became an early exponent of Freudian psychoanalysis in France. Morichau-Beauchant had long been drawn to progressive causes: he had joined Marc Sangnier's liberal Catholic movement Le Sillon, in addition to writing for a Poitiers-based literary journal called L'effort, edited by the socialist writer (and later communist politician) Jean-Richard Bloch. In L'effort's first issue, which appeared in June 1910, Morichau-Beauchant published an article presenting Freud's ideas on the role of the unconscious in ensuring the individual's psychological defense.[93] Shortly thereafter, Morichau-Beauchant wrote to Freud personally. We know this because on December 3, 1910, the founder of psychoanalysis contacted Carl Jung, explaining: "Our movement seems indeed to be spreading vigorously. Not long ago I received a first letter from France (!) from a Dr. Morichau-Beauchant, professor of medicine at Poitiers, who reads psychoanalysis, works at it, and is convinced." He then quoted—in French—Morichau-Beauchant's letter, which said: "This letter will show that you also have disciples in France who are passionately following you work."[94] Freud mentioned the example of Morichau-Beauchant as evidence of psychoanalysis' steady advance to other associates as well: in 1911, Freud recommended that Sándor Ferenczi read a paper recently sent to him by "our Frenchman in Poitiers."[95] Freud also discussed Morichau-Beauchant in an exchange with Ernest Jones, who observed that the French doctor showed a "good understanding" of Freud's theories.[96] On January 2, 1912, it was to Karl Abraham that Freud wrote: "The latest favorable signs, strangely enough, have come from France. We have gained a vigorous helpmate in Morichau-Beauchant in Poitiers."[97] In his history of the psychoanalytic movement, Freud complained that France had "so far shown herself the least receptive towards psychoanalysis," while noting that the "first indications of interest came from provincial France," where "Moricheau-Beauchant [sic] (Poitiers) was the first Frenchman who openly accepted psychoanalysis."[98]

At least one letter that Morichau-Beauchant wrote to Freud has been saved. On December 3, 1913, the French doctor thanked Freud for regularly sending him his publications, while expressing regret that his medical practice had prevented him from writing more about psychoanalysis (by this point, he had published four significant articles on the topic in medical or psychoanalytic journals). He announced forthcoming articles on the "infantile complex" in neurotics and on the novelist Romain Rolland considered from a psychoanalytic point of view, as well as a history of psychoanalysis in France that he had promised Sándor Ferenczi (none of these articles seems to have been written). Morichau-Beauchant also expressed frustration at his countrymen's aversion to Freud's ideas: "It is truly curious to see how a people that more than any other, through its literature and its mores, should be able to understand it, the study of psychoanalysis struggles to see the light of day. I will strive, for my feeble part, to overcome these resistances."[99] Thus despite the fact that his efforts ultimately had little impact on Freudianism's fate in France, Morichau-Beauchant was, at least for a time, deeply engaged with the psychoanalytic movement, took its ideas very seriously, and was seen as a possible beachhead for the movement in France, in addition to being recognized by Freud and his disciples for his impressive command of psychoanalytic theory.

It is for these reasons that Morichau-Beauchant's connections to Foucault and his family are so fascinating. He is, literally, the missing link between Freud and Foucault, the single degree of separation between them. Morichau-Beauchant's ties to the Foucault family were close. Well before Paul Foucault moved to Poitiers, Morichau-Beauchant was a colleague of his father-in-law-to-be, Henri Malapert, at the Poitiers medical school and at the Hôtel-Dieu. The bonds between these families were intimate enough that when Morichau-Beauchant's daughter was born in 1905, Malapert served as a witness for her civil registration.[100] These connections presumably explain why the Malaperts chose Morichau-Beauchant to be the bride's witness when Foucault's parents were married in Poitiers in 1924.[101] Paul Foucault and Morichau-Beauchant then became colleagues—at the medical school and the hospital—ensuring that their professional lives would remain deeply intertwined. Morichau-Beauchant published papers with Foucault's grandfather as well as his father. In 1904, he and Henri coauthored a paper on breast angiomas in the prestigious *Revue de chirurgie*.[102] In December 1936, Morichau-Beauchant and Paul Foucault presented a paper together to the Société de Médecine de la Vienne, the local medical society. It was based on the diagnosis of a patient that the older doctor had referred to his younger colleague.[103] The fact that a no-nonsense surgeon like Paul Foucault could, in some of his papers, refer to the "libido" and speculate on the role neuroses might play in conditions like impotence suggests that his colleague Morichau-Beauchant's brush with psychoanalysis may have rubbed off on him as well.[104]

While evidence for the connection between Morichau-Beauchant and Paul Foucault is quite abundant, what we know about the former's relationship with Michel Foucault hinges entirely on a single anecdote. According to Foucault's partner Daniel Defert, Morichau-Beauchant made a gift of his collection of early psychoanalytical journals to Foucault in October 1951, the year before the older man died.[105] Didier Eribon speculates that this friend of the family might have provided the young Foucault, when he was growing up, with appealing "extra-curricular" reading.[106] Despite the age difference—Morichau-Beauchant was fifty-three years older than Foucault—it thus seems that both family connections and recognition of the young man's budding interest in philosophy and psychology might have made the Poitiers Freudian an early intellectual influence on Foucault.

The only way to speculate about this influence is to consider Morichau-Beauchant's essays, which Foucault may have been familiar with and perhaps even read. What, in these writings, might have stood out to a young man of Foucault's disposition? At a basic level, Morichau-Beauchant fully understood that psychoanalysis sought to unveil the deep layers of sexuality that motivated many interactions, particularly in family situations, yet that remained almost completely unacknowledged by ordinary language. Sexuality and even perversity, his writings showed, were ubiquitous. In the first place, this meant acknowledging that, as he put it, "sexuality knows no age": "its manifestations are completely evident, even among normal children, and continue, acknowledged or disguised, into the most advanced ages."[107] He observed that children's incipiently sexual feelings could be directed at not only their parents, but also "other family members living in the child's immediate entourage, particularly brothers and sisters."[108] He also noted that "sexual assaults" and "the exaggerated caresses" that some parents bestow on their children can contribute to a child's sexual awakening and, at times, to pathologies.[109] With Freud, Morichau-Beauchant concludes, "not only . . . did children lose their privilege of innocence in sexual matters . . . but one discovered in them the seed of all perversions."[110]

If a being that had been considered innocent by nature is revealed to be "the seed of all perversions," then it was clear, Morichau-Beauchant demonstrated, that the traditional distinction between normality and abnormality had to be significantly reconsidered. His interest in Freud's insights into the child's polymorphous perversity, for instance, spurred him to recognize how common it was for children to find sexual gratification in erogenous zones beyond the genital areas. Morichau-Beauchant was particularly interested in Freud's observations about how the anus became, for children, a source of sexual pleasure, which could be achieved either by controlling their bowels or evacuating them.[111] His own personal observations of such cases in Poitiers inspired an entire article devoted to the topic, entitled "False Incontinence of the Sphincter among Children."[112] "Direct masturbation of the anus with the finger," he explained, "is . . . not exceptional among children."[113]

Morichau-Beauchant recognized, furthermore, that Freud's insights into childhood sexuality challenged the notion that homosexuality was inherently abnormal. Freud has shown, he wrote, that "children before puberty fix their desires as much on persons of the same sex as on that of the opposite sex." In other words, "there exists—and even in the normal state—in infantile sexuality a homosexual element."[114] As literary evidence, he cited Romain Rolland's novel *Jean Christophe.* Elsewhere, Morichau-Beauchant claimed that it was "normal" for children to go through a phase of "hermaphrodism."[115] In explaining Freud's concept of transference (*Übertragung*), which he translated as *rapport affectif,* Morichau-Beauchant observed that it was common for doctors to become the targets of "the homosexual tendencies that are common to all psychoneurotics."[116] He also recognized the psychoanalytic significance of sadism and masochism, which Freud had discussed in his studies of childhood development. Morichau-Beauchant noticed that boys who torture animals and are violent towards weaker classmates achieve, through this behavior, "a certain sexual satisfaction," while others "experience sexual excitement in letting themselves be mistreated, whipped, etc."[117] In patients who developed strong feelings for their doctor, Morichau-Beauchant detected a "need to be dominated by a stronger will, to let oneself be guided and directed in the most futile of life's circumstances." "This need to humiliate oneself, to submit to all a loved one demands," Morichau-Beauchant asked, "does it not recall those pathological cases in which suffering becomes an exquisite pleasure when inflicted by a loved one?"[118] While sadism and masochism, "when pushed to extremes," could constitute "pathologies of love" and "sexual perversions," the fact remains, he contended, "that one finds them more or less delineated as normal features of love."[119] With his keen understanding of early psychoanalytic theory, Morichau-Beauchant did not shy away from Freud's conclusions, which suggested a far more fluid relationship between normality and abnormality than many of his contemporaries would have been prepared to recognize. "Freud's great merit," he concluded, "was to show that in sexual matters, just as in other realms, the normal and the pathological differ from one another only through imperceptible transitions."[120]

The question of homosexuality interested Morichau-Beauchant beyond its relevance to infantile sexuality and psychological development. Not only was he aware of homosexual tendencies within his social circle in Poitiers, but he also drew on psychoanalytic theory to understand them. This was the subject of a paper he published in 1912 in the movement's leading journal *Zentralblatt für Pyschanalyse,* entitled "Homosexualität und Paranoïa"

(Homosexuality and Paranoia). In November 1911, he sent the piece to Freud, who mentions it in his letter to Jones. Otto Rank translated it into German. The brief article consists almost entirely of a personal anecdote about a forty-seven-year-old acquaintance of Morichau-Beauchant's, a teacher, it would seem, in Poitiers. Though *Monsieur X* (as the article identified him) was of strong moral character, religious, and a dedicated teacher, his temperament, Morichau-Beauchant noticed, had recently become morose. During an unrelated medical consultation, Morichau-Beauchant pressed *Monsieur X* for an explanation of his altered mood. By way of a reply, the patient offered the following story: the previous year, he had, while traveling, been obliged to share a bed at an inn with his sixteen-year-old son. During the night, he ejaculated. In disgust, he did his best to clean the soiled bed sheets lest the inn's staff question his morals. Sometime afterward, *Monsieur X* and his two sons went for a walk, to pick mushrooms, in the environs of Poitiers. A passerby gave him a curious look. *Monsieur X* immediately became consumed with the idea that the man suspected him of "immoral acts" with his boys. He was haunted by "continuous angst." When a local newspaper reported that a man who had committed sexual offenses against children was being sought, he was convinced it was about him. He believed that people in the street were giving him funny looks. He was alarmed when his class reacted to his proposal for a country outing with terrified refusal. He persuaded himself that a coalition of trade unionists and freethinkers would question his morals to attack his political and religious ideas, and that they would either bring him to court or have him killed, along with his children, in the depths of the forest. He began carrying a gun. He tried to get Morichau-Beauchant to serve as a witness to his character, even as the doctor did his best to prove that these beliefs were baseless.

The meaning of *Monsieur X's* conduct dawned on Morichau-Beauchant when, a few weeks later, he read Freud's "Doctor Schreber" essay ("Psycho-Analytic Notes on an Autobiographical Account of a Case of Paranoia [Dementia Paranoides]")[121] and Ferenczi's "On the Part Played by Homosexuality in the Pathogenesis of Paranoia."[122] Though his patient had previously showed no indication of "repressed homosexual tendencies," once they had manifested themselves, they became "unbearable" to him, as a man of high morals and deep religious conviction. Consequently, he projected them outward in the form of deliria, imagining accusations on the part of others that were not entirely "without reason" since they matched up with his own "self-reproaches" concerning the "perverse desires" repressed in his unconscious.[123]

Though we can only speculate about the influence that Morichau-Beauchant might have had on the young Foucault, it is difficult to imagine that he could have been completely indifferent to his thought. Through his family's social and professional connections, he was in touch with psychoanalysis's first French enthusiast and a correspondent of Freud, Rank, and Ferenczi. Morichau-Beauchant also makes clear that the Poitiers medical community harbored genuine progressive tendencies, in contrast to the tendency of Foucault's biographers to emphasize his upbringing in a closed, provincial setting. While late nineteenth and early twentieth-century doctors (as seen in the last chapter) frequently addressed homosexuality and "sexual inversion," Morichau-Beauchant's psychoanalytic research employed a different vocabulary for discussing it, in which behavior often described in contemporary medical discourse as "abnormal" or "perverse" could be characterized as appropriate to developmental stages and, even more importantly, as having a nature that was not fundamentally different from so-called normal conduct.

There are two other ways in which Morichau-Beauchant's work intersected with the later interests of the young Foucault, suggesting a possible influence. First, Morichau-Beauchant's son recalled that his father "often repeated to me that he saw in psychoanalysis the first attempt at an approach to personality, and this semiology fascinated him."[124] The young Foucault was also intrigued by the problem of the psychological status of "personality," which he would address in his first (and later disavowed) book, *Mental Illness and Personality.* Second, Morichau-Beauchant was closely connected to Alphonse Maeder (1882–1971), a Swiss psychoanalyst whom Freud had made responsible for the movement's French outreach. Maeder broke with Freud, joining forces with another Swiss dissident, Carl Jung, to establish a new psychoanalytic circle based in Zurich. Morichau-Beauchant seems to ultimately have favored this current over Freudian orthodoxy. One figure who was involved in the Zurich circle was Ludwig Binswanger, who fascinated the young Foucault and was the subject of his first important essay.

Yet Morichau-Beauchant's work also contained many of the problems Foucault would associate with psychoanalysis. The Poitiers doctor believed that Freud's discoveries could serve the progressive mission of nineteenth-century science: by making the unconscious conscious, psychoanalysis, he maintained, had made it possible for human beings to reform and improve their very personalities.[125] Furthermore, while Morichau-Beauchant saw homosexuality, sadism, and masochism as normal tendencies in human psychological development, he believed they were mainly characteristic of the polymorphous affects of childhood: when they persisted into adulthood, they could reasonably be described as perverse. Epileptics, Morichau-Beauchant argued in one essay, are inclined to sexual perversity because they remain, as adults, locked into the polymorphism of "infantile tendencies": rather than bring them into intimate relations with other people, their sexuality pursues "multiples ends," perhaps, he speculated, as a result of "the precociousness of [their] sexual instincts and the intensity of its manifestations." For such individuals, perversity can lead to deviance. Many epileptics, he noted, citing Cesare Lombroso, are inclined to theft, murder, and arson.[126] Morichau-Beauchant's lesson was thus an ambivalent one, minimizing moral and scientific norms in some respects, while reinforcing them in others. To this must be added the fact that Morichau-Beauchant, for all the promise and brilliance of his early engagement with psychoanalysis, eventually abandoned it. He broke with Freud and remained a provincial doctor, albeit a prominent one. He never became the founder of the French school of psychoanalysis.

A Personal Obsession

As important as it must have been to him, Foucault's homosexuality was never a topic on which he dwelled much in public. Yet he did maintain that one of his lifelong intellectual concerns was rooted in experiences that were intensely personal and occurred early on: the question of confinement—that is, of what brings some human beings to enclose and lock up others. As Foucault wryly observed in 1978: "What preoccupied me for years and years, undoubtedly due to a personal obsession that could be [psycho]analyzed, what interested me was this practice of confinement, of internment as a juridical solution, a medical solution, a social solution to an entire array of problems."[127] A few years earlier, he had emphasized that this problem of gens enfermés—locked-up people—was not simply a theoretical question for him, but one rooted in his own experience: "It so happens," he explained, "that for biographical reasons, . . . I became aware of what an asylum is, and I heard those voices"—the cries of the mad—"just as anyone can, and I was overwhelmed by those voices." The first significant time Foucault spent in an asylum was likely when he interned at Sainte-Anne psychiatric hospital in Paris in the 1950s. Yet the way Foucault described this experience leaves little doubt that it also resonated with emotions that marked his childhood. "Anyone" can hear these voices, he added, except for doctors and psychiatrists—a

point that he made "not at all out of aggressivity toward them," but simply
to show that "their statutory function so filters out the dimension of the
scream in the speech of the mad that they [can] no longer hear [anything]
but the intelligible or unintelligible part of their discourse."[128] These were, of
course, the same misgivings Foucault had expressed about his father in the
1968 interview discussed in the last chapter. In this way, Foucault posited a
kind of intuitive connection between confinement and family life, between
the inchoate rage of the mad and criminals when they are put away and the
peculiar deafness of the positivistic rationality he associated with his father.

The connection between confinement and family life was the explicit
theme of a volume he published in 1982 with the historian Arlette Farge,
The Disorder of Families. In this collection of documents from the archives
of the Bastille (found, like some of the key documents that inspired *Madness
and Civilization*, at the Bibliothèque de l'Arsenal), Foucault and Farge examine the use in the eighteenth century of *lettres de cachet*, showing how these
legal documents, usually assumed to be a device whereby French kings could
arbitrarily imprison their enemies, were far more commonly requested by
ordinary families dealing with problematic relatives. The key to understanding *lettres de cachet* is not, in short, arbitrary power, but "family relations": the
documents show "the requests for confinement emanating either from a husband or a wife directed at their spouse, or from parents directed at their children."[129] It is also significant that while Foucault certainly spoke, at times, of
liberating the mad and criminals from confinement, he arguably placed even
greater emphasis on allowing them to speak. His stated intention in *Madness
and Civilization* was to recover the voice of madness that modern medical
and psychiatric discourse has silenced. Similarly, the slogan of the Groupe
Information Prisons (Prison Information Group, or GIP) in the 1970s was, as
Foucault once put it, "La parole aux détenus!"—"Let the prisoners speak!"[130]

Finally, when discussing confinement, Foucault was inclined to describe
it as "enigmatic" (a term he also applied to the problem of punishment),
insisting on how difficult it was to fathom—a comment that further suggests
that confinement was a problem with which he had long been grappling.[131]
Foucault's emphasis on the personal and—for him—ongoing character of the
question of confinement, as well as the implicit connections he drew between
confinement and (his) family life, makes it worth examining what experiential matrices might have spurred his interest in this problem during his childhood in Poitiers. Several such experiences merit consideration.

The Sequestrated Woman of Poitiers

The first experience concerns a *fait divers*—the French term for a sensational news story—that occurred in Poitiers shortly after the turn of the century. In 1988, Hervé Guibert, the writer and photographer who was close to Foucault at the end of the life, published a brief short story, "The Secrets of a Man," consisting of a thinly fictionalized account of his friend's death. In the story, a surgeon cuts open a dying philosopher's brain, where he discovers "child-hood memories" buried so deep that they could elude "the imbecility of inter-pretations." One of these "two or three images" revealed "an ordinary inner courtyard, before which the little philosopher walked by, now glorified by the shudders tied to a *fait divers*: it was here, on a straw mattress, in a kind of garage, that, for decades, had lived the one that newspapers had called the *séquestrée de Poitiers"*—the sequestrated woman of Poitiers.[132] The story Guib-ert is referring to is that of Blanche Monnier, a middle-aged woman from Poitiers whom police discovered, on May 23, 1901, living in unspeakable filth in a shuttered room in her family's bourgeois home. It was soon ascertained that, for some twenty-five years, she had been effectively imprisoned by her mother, who lived in the same house, with the knowledge of her brother, who resided across the street.

While the event occurred twenty-five years before Foucault's birth, he was connected to this strange tale in one very direct way: the building where Mon-nier was held was located a few doors down from the house where Foucault grew up. The Monniers lived at 21, Rue de la Visitation; the Foucault house was located a few doors down, at number 10 (the street was later renamed "Rue Arthur Ranc"). Each time he walked to central Poitiers or to school, the "the little philosopher" would indeed have passed by this home. Foucault's brother, Denys, recalled: "The house of the *séquestrée* was across from the Post Office [at the corner of Rue Arthur Ranc and Rue des Écossais]. Passing in front of it, we sometimes said: 'It was there.'"[133]

Beyond the fact that the street on which he grew up was closely associated with this notorious incident, other aspects of the affair resonate with the issues that came to obsesses Foucault. While the story was a staple of the turn-of-the-century popular press and *colportage* literature, it received new attention, early in Foucault's life, when, in 1930, the novelist André Gide published a collection of documents relating to the story under the title *La séquestrée de Poitiers.* In addition to being one of France's greatest living authors, Gide was also among the earliest literary figures in France to proclaim his homosexuality in public. The volume was the first to appear in a book series that Gide founded at the *Nouvelle revue française* called *"Ne jugez pas"* (Don't Judge), the goal of which was to examine "'affairs' that were not necessarily criminal, the motives of which remain mysterious, escape the rules of traditional psychology, and disturb human justice."[134] Gide's terse narrative consists mostly of excerpts from newspapers and court documents. His book is, in this way, surprisingly similar to the document collections that Foucault would later publish relating to Pierre Rivière, Herculine Barbin, and the *lettres de cachet*.

Yet as Guibert's testament suggests, one must assume that it was Blanche Monnier's story, and not simply the form Gide gave it, that made a powerful impression on the young Foucault. Hers was a tale in which confinement, madness, and the claustrophobic intensity of family life closely overlapped. What made the incident scandalous was the fact that Monnier had been imprisoned. Poitiers's leading newspaper used the term *"séquestrée"* in its initial story about the affair. Within days, it had dubbed Monnier the *"séquestrée de Poitiers."*[135] Press narratives emphasized that the police, acting on an anonymous tip from a former servant, had freed Blanche from imprisonment. When they finally gained access to 21, Rue de la Visitation, they entered a room in which the shutters had been padlocked for years. The police found a room shrouded in impenetrable darkness and pervaded by an unbearable stench. Once they had forced open the window, they discovered a woman—whom Marcel Monnier identified as his sister—"spread out on the bed, the body and the head under a cover that was repulsively dirty." "The unfortunate woman," the prosecuting magistrate later reported, "was lying naked on a rotten straw mattress. All around her had formed a kind of crust, consisting of excrement, [and] bits and pieces of putrefied meat, vegetables, fish, and bread. We also saw oyster shells, [and] creatures running over [Monnier's bed]. The latter was covered with vermin." Monnier was "frighteningly" thin; her hair formed a "thick *natte*, that had not been combed and untangled for ages" (Figure 9).[136]

The abominable physical conditions in which Monnier had been kept were exacerbated by her mental condition. By most accounts, the *séquestrée* was mad, and madness was key to her story. Monnier's mother and brother, as well as their defenders, insisted that Blanche had been restricted to her home because she was mentally ill. Though her confinement seems to have begun in the aftermath of a love affair of which the mother disapproved, the family argued that Blanche's mental state made it impossible for her to appear in public. They claimed that Monnier had an irrepressible compulsion to

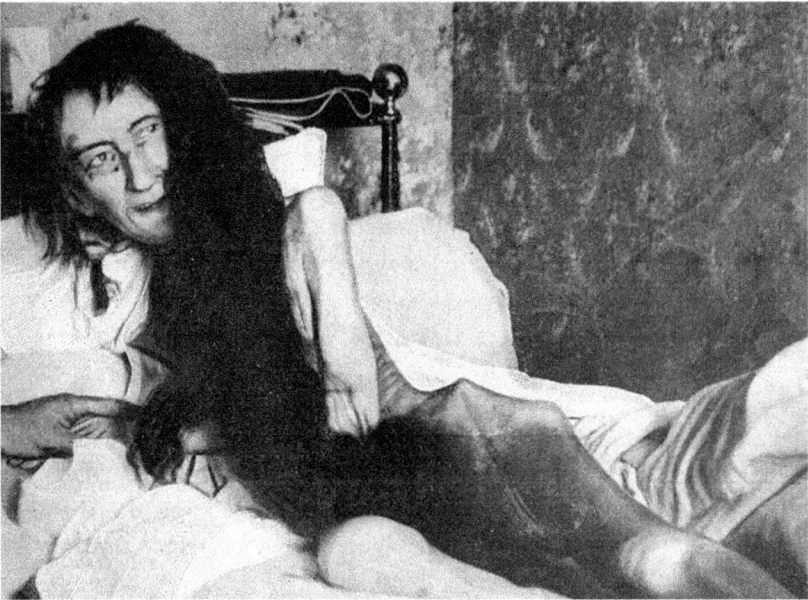

Figure 9. Blanche Monnier, in 1901, shortly after she was discovered, at Poitiers's Hôtel-Dieu.

undress herself and speak in profanities. The question of Monnier's sanity soon became a major stake in the public debate over the affair, as well as the subsequent trial. Dr. Louis Charles Eugène Lagrange, who directed the Poitiers asylum, observed: Monnier "was not in possession of all her faculties; she says things that are extravagant and disconnected; we have concluded that she is intellectually feeble. She is mad [*une aliénée*], there is no doubt."[137] Not everyone agreed. One servant said that Monnier "was not absolutely mad; sometimes she said things that made sense, but she did not want to be cleaned, and always covered her head."[138] Moreover, the chaplain of the Poitiers hospital, the Abbé de Mondion, publicly challenged the arguments that Monnier was insane because he understood they were being used by defenders of her brother and mother to excuse their actions. "I would like to be clear on one point," the chaplain wrote in the *Journal de l'Ouest*:

In order to exonerate the guilty, it has been said that [Mlle. Blanche] was mad, and that she was obsessed with uncovering herself. She has been with us for nine days, and we have noticed that she is obsessed

with covering herself... In short, one would do better to let the judicial system have its say than to exonerate an awful crime. I have said,
and I repeat it, that those who left a stranger, a daughter, or a sister in
the pitiful state in which [Mlle. Blanche] found herself upon entering the hospital are criminals, particularly since the victim is gentle,
calm, and well behaved. The windows are open, and she has never
shown the slightest sign of ill-humored or dangerous madness...
That she finds herself in a state of physical and intellectual depression is in no way surprising, given that for years she was without air,
without light, and almost without food.[139]

The chaplain's arguments also called attention to the scandal's political
stakes: Marcel Monnier (the brother), a law professor at the University of
Poitiers, was close to aristocratic and Catholic circles, at a time when the
political cleavages that manifested themselves with the Dreyfus Affair were
still deep. According to the town's republican newspaper, the clerical party
launched a petition drive to defend him, threatening business owners who
refused to sign with retaliation.[140] The paper claimed: "The upper clergy and
nobility—those who still believe in the value of titles of nobility—are banding
together to ensure the task of just reparation fails"—and this solely because
Marcel Monnier supported their agenda and because he "was one of the fervent participants in the ceremonies of St. Porchaire"—the parish church
where Foucault served as an altar boy and his parents were married—"where
each Sunday he piously took communion."[141] The question of the séquestrée's
madness thus became central to the debate over whether her confinement
had been justified, all the more so as differences of opinions closely followed
the era's political battle lines.

Not only was the affair's center of gravity the street on which Foucault grew
up; it also unfolded at one of the institutions with which his family was most
closely identified: Poitiers's hospital, the Hôtel-Dieu. Monnier was taken there
immediately after the police discovered her on May 23, where she was cleaned,
her head was shaved, and she was kept under close supervision in a hospital room. Though there is no record of Henri Malapert, Foucault's maternal
grandfather, being assigned to her, she was looked after by several of his colleagues. Dr. Maurice Léger, the director of the Poitiers medical school's bacteriology laboratory, analyzed the sample of insects the police had collected from
Monnier's mattress.[142] More importantly, the court assigned three doctors as

médecin-légistes, to undertake a forensic examination of the patient. One was Dr. Lagrange, the director of Poitier's asylum; the others were Dr. Jules Brossard and Dr. Jean Jablonski. Later, Jablonski would succeed Malapert as the president of the Société de Médecine de la Vienne. It seems likely, then, that in addition to stories associated with the affair's physical proximity to their home, the Foucault family would have memories passed down about the scandal resulting from their deep roots in Poitiers's medical community, which could also have impressed on Foucault medicine's ambivalent relationship to confinement.

Perhaps the most disturbing dimension of the *séquestrée* affair was the fact that the motivations and emotions that had resulted in Monnier's twenty-five-year confinement were all rooted in family relations. She had not, of course, been confined by a *lettre de cachet*. But as was often the case with the latter, as Foucault would explain much later, her imprisonment was an instance of a parent deciding that her child should be deprived of liberty.[143] Monnier's captivity was the tragic outcome of the tense and twisted relations between the members of family condemned to deal with one another even as they seemed incapable of getting along. In her twenties, Monnier appears to have fallen in love with an older man. Her mother disapproved; soon thereafter, Monnier disappeared from public view. Those who knew the family described the mother as "capricious, hard and imperious, as well as despotic."[144] Servants recalled that Monnier, at this time, was in full possession of her faculties, but prone to violent outbursts toward her mother and—more unusually—inclined to undress or refuse clothes, as a kind of extreme protest against her family's disorder. After the death of the father, the dean of Poitiers's university's faculty of letters, the situation worsened, as the period of genuine imprisonment began. Marcel Monnier was close to his sister and seems to have despised his mother, yet too frightened of her to challenge the arrangement she had imposed, and too concerned with social appearances to criticize her in public. Many newspapers presented the story as a tale of bourgeois hypocrisy, of sadistic cruelty and base motivations lurking beneath a shallow veneer of respectability.

Gide was fascinated with the way the stomach-turning state of Monnier's room seemed related to the family's fondness for filth. He refers to accounts that Marcel Monnier kept his own chamber pot in the middle of his bedroom, forbidding that it be emptied until it was completely full. No wonder, Gide concludes, that far from being "bothered by the foul odor of his sister's straw mattress and hair," he "took pleasure in it."[145] Interestingly, Gide ultimately concludes that Monnier's confinement was, all things considered, "largely voluntary," that it was less a case of "sequestration" than "seclusion." The sad tale was more the result of family members being under the sway of "outdated ideas" than a conscious effort to deprive an individual of her free- dom.[146] Gide's injunction to "not judge" was in many ways a plea for greater empathy for the choices made by Monnier's mother and brother. The outlook of *The Fruits of the Earth* (1897), in which Gide boldly declared "family, I hate you," has given way to a more nuanced sensibility: while still seeing families as constraints on individual freedom, he became more inclined to see them as force fields of disruptive emotion with potentially tragic consequences.

One of the most compelling aspects of Gide's account concerns Blanche Monnier's voice. While it is difficult to doubt, based on his narrative, that she was mad in some sense, the words attributed to her are consistent with the tradition of the wisdom of fools—with the idea that, from the depths of her tragic life, she was able to articulate some authentic vision of herself and her world. In her room, the police discovered inscriptions on the wall. One read: "Make beauty, nothing of love and freedom. Solitude forever. One must live and die in the dungeon one's entire life."[147] At the Hôtel-Dieu, her speech was naive and full of childlike wonder, though often uttered in patois, interspersed with obscenities. Her most notable verbal tic was preceding every noun with the words "*mon cher petit*" (my dear little). She was also obsessed with think- ing of the room where she had been confined as her "cave" (*grotte*). When the police first appeared, she allegedly cried: "Whatever you want, but don't take me from my dear little cave."[148] Blanche Monnier, in these ways, anticipated Ellen West and Thorin, Pierre Rivière and Herculine Barbin—figures who fas- cinated Foucault for their ability to wrest a distinctive voice from the very forces that attempted to silence them, and to use language to craft a world of meaning more intense and alive than the tawdry, oppressive realities to which they were condemned. In madness as well as in confinement, Foucault would later argue, a kind of radical subjectivity is possible. "The consciousness that the sick person has of his sickness is rigorously original," he argued in his first book, suggesting that in madness, as in dreams, self and world belong to a seamless fabric. Inhabiting this private world of subjective imagination could, however, lead one to lose one's foothold in the world, to become flotsam in the stream of existence: illness was, in this sense, "simultaneously a retreat into the worst of subjectivities and a descent into the worst of objectivities."[149] The chilling tale of confinement that haunted the Rue de la Visitation and the patient rooms of Poitiers Hôtel-Dieu prefigures these later insights.

Souls in Prison

Though the story of the *séquestrée* may have been the most dramatic memory of confinement that Foucault would associate with Poitiers, it was not the only one. Another possible matrix for this personal obsession was the Institution de Larnay, an establishment for the deaf and the blind located in Biard, just outside of Poitiers. Larnay acquired an international reputation during the early twentieth century due to its role in the extraordinary education of a deaf, dumb, and blind girl named Marie Heurtin (1885–1921) and her sister Marthe (1902–78). Foucault's brother, Denys, recalled: "I remember that we went to see Marthe Heurtin, a deaf, dumb, and blind woman at the Larnay Institute whom a nun had taught to answer all kinds of questions by different means. She was exhibited as a phenomenon. My brother [Michel] seemed fascinated."[150]

When Marie was brought to the Institution de Larnay, where the Sœurs de la Sagesse religious order had provided education to deaf-mute (and later blind) girls, the ten-year-old, according to someone who knew her, "had a bestial physiognomy that denoted a savage nature." "It was not a girl of ten years of age who entered Notre-Dame de Larnay," this account continued, "but a furious monster."[151] For these reasons, her family had been initially advised to commit her to an asylum.[152] Viewed as mad and monstrous, communing with the kind of animality that, he would later argue, typified certain experience of madness and abnormality, the stories Foucault heard about her might have suggested kinship with Blanche Monnier, as well as many of the marginalized people he would subsequently address in his work.

The individual who contributed the most to popularizing the theme that the Heurtins's sensory deprivation amounted to a form of captivity was also the person who probably brought the Foucaults to Larnay: Louis Arnould (1864–1949), a literature professor at the University of Poitiers. Arnould wrote an account of Heurtin's life and education entitled *Une âme en prison*— an "imprisoned soul," as English-language publications referred to it at the time. Arnould's book was so popular that it went through at least twenty-six editions over nearly five decades. Marthe Heurtin—Larnay's main draw, after Marie's death in 1921—writes in her memoirs: "From time to time, we used to get a visit from *monsieur* and *madame* Arnould. . . . They would bring us their friends as they were interested in us; it was always wonderful to see them, they were so good, so simple! I would play a game of checkers with the visitors, and almost always I won."[153] Perhaps it was under these circumstances that Foucault met Marthe Heurtin.

Arnould's oft-repeated description of Heurtin as a "soul in prison" echoes a crucial passage in Foucault's work. Foucault did not, like his fellow Poitevin, see the soul as imprisoned by the body but famously asserted that the soul *is* "the body's prison." Foucault was, of course, talking about something different than Arnould—to a degree, in any case. Arnould had wanted to show how Sister Marguerite had reached through the bars of Heurtin's physical impairment to reach her mind and her soul, thus freeing her from the mental confinement to which she had hitherto been condemned. Foucault, when writing *Discipline and Punish*, was interested in showing how the meticulous control of bodily functions and gestures had emerged as a new power form in the seventeenth century. In practice, however, Foucault's idea was related to Arnould's. Stories like this could indeed serve as evidence to Foucault's contention that the soul (contra the nineteenth-century materialists) was indeed real, but that it "it exists, it has a reality, that it is incessantly produced, around, along the surface, inside of the body through the operations of a power exercised on those who are punished—more generally, on those who are supervised [*ceux qu'on surveille*], who are trained and corrected, on the mad, on children, on pupils, on the colonized, on those who are attached to a production apparatus and who are controlled throughout their entire lives."[154] Whatever Foucault's assessment of his visit to Larnay at the time, it shows how these questions were woven into experiences that shaped his early years.

The Hôpital Pasteur: Poitiers's Asylum

As we have seen, Foucault recalled that "for biographical reasons" he had become "aware of what an asylum is" and "heard those voices" and was "overwhelmed" by them. While Foucault's most immediate experience with psychiatric hospitals seems to have occurred during his internship at Sainte-Anne's Hospital in Paris, Poitiers, too, had a well-developed infrastructure for treating—and confining—the mad with which Foucault would have been familiar, at the very least through his family's involvement in the local medical community. As discussed in the previous chapter, Poitiers had participated fully in what Foucault would call the "Great Confinement" of the seventeenth century, with the creation of its own Hôpital Général in 1657, a year after the first was founded in Paris. Located in a sprawling complex on the northern side of the town center, Poitiers's Hôpital Général was essentially a poor house, though the mad were also assigned to it, along with others who were seen as threatening the urban social order. In 1818, as new ideas about confinement (and which constitute the grim climax of *Madness and Civilization*) began to spread, the Hôpital Général was reorganized. The mad were now kept in a special ward, apart from the other detainees, thus instantiating the new visibility madness acquired thanks to the "birth of the asylum." Poitiers did not establish an asylum as such, but rather a "quartier d'aliénés" (i.e., a ward for the mad) within the Hôpital Général. In 1829, the prominent psychiatrist Jean-Étienne Dominique Esquirol (1772–1840), the disciple of Philippe Pinel—both of whom Foucault discussed in his thesis—visited the Poitiers establishment. The passage of the law of June 30, 1838, requiring each department to establish an asylum, triggered a debate over whether Poitiers's *quartier d'aliénés* should be transferred to an existing institution at Loudun. The head doctor, Jolly, and his colleagues at the Poitiers medical faculty lobbied actively to block this decision. On July 25, 1845, several professors signed a motion opposing this transfer: one of them was Prosper Malapert, Foucault's great-great-grandfather.[155] The disorderliness and disrepair of the Hôpital Général did lead to periodic calls over the nineteenth century to transfer the psychiatric patients elsewhere. This became possible when a new establishment, the Hôpital Louis-Pasteur, was founded in 1922. The new hospital encompassed the site of what had been, since the eighteenth century, one of the city's main medical facilities, alongside the Hôtel-Dieu and the Hôpital Général: the Hôpital des Incurables (the Hospital of the Incurables), which cared for poor people afflicted with diseases such as scrofula and tumors. Because of fear of contagion, the Hospital of the Incurables was located beyond the town walls, on the southeastern bank of the Clain, one of the rivers circling Poitiers. Taking over some of the buildings of the Hospital of the Incurables, the Hôpital Pasteur received, in 1926, the mad who had formally been assigned to the Hôpital Général, which was finally shut down in 1927.[156] Louis Charles Eugène Lagrange, the doctor who was appointed a forensic pathologist on the Blanche Monnier case, was one of the first directors of the new ward for mentally ill patients. Following the new language required by a government decree, the institution became, in 1937, a "psychiatric hospital."

Thus Foucault grew up in relative proximity to the Hôpital Pasteur, to which his family also had important professional connections. The 1920s and 1930s were a period of considerable transition in French psychiatry, when new and more progressive approaches to treating the mentally ill were being developed and promoted, even as most institutions clung to nineteenth-century practices. This is evident even in the discussion about these issues that occurred in Poitiers itself. Foucault's father was, we have seen, a key figure in launching the local medical journal the *Revue médicale du centre-ouest*. In four issues appearing in 1929, the journal's inaugural year, the *Revue* published a series of articles by Pierre Amouroux (c. 1873–1933), the head doctor for the psychiatric ward at the Hôpital Pasteur.[157] In addition to participating in a journal with which Paul Foucault was closely involved, Amouroux also seems to have been a next-door neighbor of the Foucault family.[158] Amouroux rejected the idea that mental illness was no more than obtuseness, a refusal to use one's capacity to reason. "It would be a prejudice today to believe that the mind is free to regulate itself by its own reason. This sovereign faculty never, as it were, determines us."[159] Yet he maintained, by the same token, that mental illness was characterized by the exaggerated share that "subjectivity" assumed in mental life, making the task of "'desubjectifying' [*désubjectiver*] the patient" psychiatry's primary task.[160]

While noting that mental illnesses frequently had organic causes and that it was heavily conditioned by heredity (in 80 percent of cases, he claimed),[161] Amouroux also emphasized that contemporary research had identified many such illnesses as partly or purely psychological. This was particularly true of the "neurosis of angst," to which he devoted a short article in the Poitiers journal. He referred to work on this topic by Freud, as well as by two French proponents of Freud's work, Paul Hartenberg, the author of *La névrose d'angoisse* (the neurosis of angst), and Francis Heckel, who wrote a study entitled *La névrose d'angoisse et les états d'émotivité anxieuse* (the neurosis of angst and states of anxious emotivity).[162] Amouroux regretted that the concept of angst had yet to be accepted by the medical community as a pathology. Its significance, he believed, lay in the fact that it showed the impact of purely psychic functions on the organism: as experiments that stimulate the cerebral cortex have shown, no bodily function escapes the brain's influence. This is what Amouroux seems to have found appealing about psychoanalysis: it demonstrated that because sicknesses like angst were frequently psychological in origin, they could only be treated by psychological means. In what seems to be a direct reference to Freud's ideas, he observed that once a doctor had determined that a patient's symptoms lack an organic basis, "one must discover the recent emotional cause, [which is] often banal and never expressed by the patient, who attaches no importance [to it]." Because "troubles always start here," "their healing depends primarily on psychological means."[163] While he remained steeped in an evolutionary paradigm and unquestioningly employed the distinction between normality and abnormality, Amouroux espoused the notion that mental illness should in many cases be treated by psychotherapy, through which the burden of hereditary dispositions could be resisted. How far he was able to put these ideas about treating mental illness into practice in his work as the director of Poitiers's psychiatric hospital is unclear; but it seems likely that his views would have had some practical impact, and the fact that he held this position is indicative of a shift in prevailing psychiatric orthodoxies. Amouroux was, moreover, a second person in the Foucault family circle, in addition to Morichau-Beauchant, to have read Freud, taken him seriously, and subscribed to many of his theories at a moment when psychoanalysis was viewed, particularly in France, with considerable suspicion.

Yet while new ideas were, in the psychiatric world, in the air, the past still weighed down heavily on the way psychiatric institutions were run. Conversations about "no restraint" approaches to treating the mentally ill were in full swing by the early twentieth century. But in 1926, when patients were transferred from Poitiers's old Hôpital Général to the new Hôpital Pasteur, it was still customary, for instance, for these institutions to hire *"guardiens de fous"*: these "watchmen of the mad" were often physically imposing, lived in the same quarters as their charges, frequently illiterate, and prone to violence and alcoholism.[164] Recourse to straightjackets was still commonplace, as one particularly chilling anecdote from the period indicates. On the night of August 21, 1931, two women, both "raving lunatics," as the Poitiers newspaper described them, were put to bed, as usual, in straightjackets in the room they shared at the Hôpital Pasteur. When a nun opened the room the following morning, one of the women ran toward her, crying, in a state of intense agitation: "I killed her! . . . If you had been she, I would have done the same to you!" During the night, she had managed to release herself from her bonds, and to strangle her still bound roommate, who belonged to an "honorable" local family.[165] *L'aliéniste français,* a journal for French psychiatrists, cited this "tragic" story, which was widely covered in the French press, as evidence of the deplorable way in which the "mentally ill are 'cared for' in some hospital wards." Unlike the Poitiers newspaper, the journal pointed out that the patients were kept not only in straightjackets, but also in "chains." It observed: "This painful event does not particularly surprise us, though it does reveal that one hundred and forty years after Pinel, the mentally ill are placed in chains."[166] Pinel's liberation of the mad from their chains would become, for Foucault, the ironic climax of *Madness and Civilization,* precisely because he saw it as a false liberation—a freedom to move that was embedded, in fact, in a far more subtle and insidious form of confinement, which pathologized madness as "mental illness." Yet in Poitiers in the 1930s, Pinel represented not "the birth of the asylum," but the unrealized promise of psychiatric reform. The *Aliéniste français* called on the French health minister to heed their appeal to make the reform of psychiatric institutions an urgent priority, and to appoint a more appropriate doctor to run the Poitiers asylum—an indication that, despite his progressive thinking, Amouroux's administration of the Hôpital Pasteur left something to be desired.

The reformist trend in psychiatry accelerated after the Second World War. Foucault's first writings—particularly *Madness and Civilization*—constituted a bitter critique of what he saw as the reformers' misguided project. Yet even as psychiatric hospitals undertook to end the tradition of confinement that had long defined them, the Hôpital Pasteur could still be cited as evidence of the quasi-medieval conditions prevailing in such establishments. In 1955 (at which point Foucault had been living in Paris for a decade), the French newsmagazine *Réalités* published a report on the state of the nation's psychiatric hospitals. The article was written by the novelist Hervé Bazin (1911–96), who had called attention, in a proto-Foucauldian vein, to the oppressive character of psychiatric hospitals (and their use by families to punish wayward offspring) in his 1949 novel *La tête contre les murs* (Head against the walls). With the magazine's celebrated photographer Jean-Philippe Charbonnier, Bazin visited the Hôpital Pasteur—and was unsparing in his assessment. In such institutions, he wrote, "there is in the first place the ghastly. If you don't believe me, go see Poitiers-Pasteur. . . . I know of nothing more repugnant than [its] dark and oozing old cloistered garden, where eighty prematurely demented patients, in their bare feet, trample the slimy paving stones and which one barely dares to cross, so suffocating is its horror and pestilence."[167] Charbonnier's sober black-and-white photographs captured the closed world that the Hôpital Pasteur's patients inhabited. At the very moment when Foucault was absorbed with his own studies of mental illness and confinement, Bazin proved that Foucault's hometown exemplified the tragic conditions against which both men revolted. It is difficult to overstate the irony of the fact that, after reorganizing the Hôpital Pasteur complex around 2011 and reconverting one of the old wards into student housing, Poitiers's municipal government, in a grotesque act of boosterism, decided to name it after one of its more famous citizens. Henceforth, it is called the Cité Universitaire Internationale Michel Foucault.

Foucault thought about relationships in terms of degrees of intensity. Intensity, he implied, was the essence of romantic relationships, but it was a possibility inherent in family relationships as well. The problem of the modern bourgeois family was, for Foucault, that it created opportunities for particularly intense relationships—through the close, often claustrophobic quarters of the bourgeois household, proximity between siblings, and affective bonds with parents—while also denying and downgrading these very opportunities. The basic perversity of the bourgeoisie, for Foucault, lay in the way that it constantly incited desires that it subsequently condemned (or at least circumscribed), that it gave with one libidinous hand what it took away with another. Perversity often—always?—was a family affair, and "familial" in the bourgeois sense. As Morichau-Beauchant recognized, desire was usually nurtured in the clammy culture of the childhood home, in a polymorphous idiom that only forked into normal and abnormal sexuality as maturity beckoned. Confinement itself was closely tied, in Foucault's mind, to family relations. As part of the disorder toward which they tend, confinement is something that families do to one another.

Lurking within this preoccupation with family bonds and their levels of intensity, one detects several incipient anxieties. The modern social order—most notably the bourgeois family—did not always live up to the intensities it made possible: medical discourse, concerns about property, the preoccupation—mitigated much of the family's potential for intensity, so that these relationships were dulled to a suffocating silence. And while confinement, at times, was simply the passion of family relations brought to a terrifying climax—few families were as close as the infamous Monniers of the Rue de la Visitation—it could also result in a complete severance of relationships—with other people, but also with the world itself. Blanche Monnier, Marie and Marthe Heurtin, and even the straightjacketed patients at the Hôpital Pasteur were not simply locked up, but relegated to a blackened world of sensory deprivation and immobility. They were not merely imprisoned; they were denied a world. How can one live the promise of intensity proffered by family relations—being with others, whether in conversation or in silence, but *being with* them—without having this intensity wane into indifferent verbiage or an imposed autism?

CHAPTER 3

War

Around 4 A.M. one night in late 1980, Michael Denneny, a New York editor, received a call from a friend, a young graduate student. "Michel Foucault is on a bad trip at Man's Country baths," the latter explained, "and we have to go down there to rescue him. He's forgotten all his English and the only thing he could remember was my phone number." The caller was Mark Blasius, a student in political philosophy at Princeton, whose dissertation Foucault would direct.[1] Denneny and Blasius took a taxi to West Fifteenth Street. When they arrived at Man's Country, one of the better-known New York bathhouses of the era, they "went from room to room" looking for Foucault. The establishment was organized around a "maze": a sequence of connecting hallways and rooms extending over ten stories, some leading to private areas, others available for public sex. Foucault once described such venues as "laboratories of sexual experimentation."[2] A patron who visited Man's Country in 1979 was amazed at "the number of naked men on the make."[3] Another remembered "a setup on the top floor" that included a "fake jail cell, so you could act out fantasies in a very clean, pristine environment."[4]

The writer Edmund White—to whom we owe the story—describes what the two men finally found: "a ball of a naked French philosopher, crazed and hissing, in the corner of a cubicle." They took Foucault back to Denneny's apartment, gave him tranquilizers, and looked after him for fourteen hours. As Foucault came down, he spoke to his friends about a matter that had been obsessing him: Ronald Reagan's election as president several weeks earlier. White, who first met the philosopher earlier that year, says that Reagan's victory "sent Foucault into a panic." Foucault, he recalls, "interpreted Reagan's victory as a return to fascism."[5]

Whatever one makes of White's secondhand story, it is safe to say that the idea of a *return* to fascism would have resonated with Foucault. Between the ages of thirteen and seventeen, he lived directly under Nazi rule. His adolescent years correspond almost exactly to the period between the fall of France and the Liberation. Between 1940 and 1944, Foucault resided a few blocks from the Gestapo headquarters, heard Occupation forces speaking German, imbibed Vichy propaganda, and witnessed the rough justice that Resistance forces inflicted on erstwhile collaborators. He also faced the same existential threat as many of his compatriots: the real possibility that he might die. Located a short distance from Poitiers's strategically important train station, Foucault's family home was threatened with destruction on several occasions, most notably by British bombers a week after D-Day. Though his house was damaged, it miraculously escaped the devastation that befell its immediate neighborhood. Death's shadow loomed over Foucault's adolescent years in other ways, too: in 1940, a Parisian doctor fleeing advancing German troops died in the family home; Foucault's father operated on a notorious Vichy propagandist after he had been stabbed and shot by a local Resistance group; and Jews detained in the local concentration camp began their march to extermination at the nearby train station. Even Foucault's education (a theme to be considered at length in the next chapter) was interrupted by death: his high school's respected philosophy teacher was arrested and later executed after the Gestapo learned of his involvement in a local Resistance network. Death, one of Foucault's lifelong obsessions, was, during the war years, a constant danger and an unshakeable concern.[6]

Though Foucault spoke little about this period, what he did say emphasized the formative role of the war in shaping his outlook. In his recollections, he evoked the anxiety, insecurity, and fear of death he experienced during those years. "I think that boys and girls of this generation had their childhood formed by these great historical events," he observed in 1982. "The menace of war was our background, our framework of existence. Then the war arrived. Much more than the activities of family life, it was these events concerning the world which are the substance of our memory. I say 'our' because I am nearly sure that most boys and girls in France at this moment had the same experience. Our private life was really threatened. Maybe that is the reason why I am fascinated by history and the relationship between personal experience and those events of which we are a part. I think that is the nucleus of my theoretical desires."[7]

When situated within the context of wartime Poitiers, these remarks help us to understand the decisive role that the web of experiences and memories associated with the Second World War played in the development of

Foucault's intellectual identity and "theoretical desires." The war constituted an experiential matrix for Foucault's thinking in several respects. First, the war contributed to making the theme of the exposure to death one of Foucault's major concerns, particularly in his youthful work. Specifically, Foucault was intrigued by how mortality had become, in modern times, a prism for understanding the human condition and epistemology. While his surgeon father's professional engagement with matters of life and death was the crucible for this disposition, Foucault's wartime experience firmly placed death at the center of his intellectual preoccupations. In his early work, through the 1960s, Foucault explored the argument, which he successively rearticulated in evermore sophisticated forms, that modern claims to knowledge were underwritten by an acceptance of death's finality, a *danse macabre* between truth and finitude that Foucault sought, in his work, to render visible. At a personal level, Foucault found death to be both terrifying and strangely alluring, an outlook that expressed itself in his suicide attempts of the 1940s and his account of a near-death experience being hit by a car in 1978.

Furthermore, the war seems to have confirmed Foucault's belief that families are permeable to social and political forces and traversed by power relations. In the 1982 interview, Foucault stated that his memories of this period consisted of "events concerning the world" rather than scenes from "family life," adding that "our private life was really threatened." He also remarked, when asked by the interviewer if he had "any fond memories of growing up in Poitiers in the 1930s and 40s," that his recollections from this time were, if "not exactly . . . strange," at least striking in that most of his "great emotional memories" were "related to the political situation."[8] Historical events had, in short, threatened the mythic security of family life. The expectation that the modern family—and especially the bourgeois family—should provide children with a basic sense of security by shielding them from external danger did not obtain, Foucault suggests, during his childhood. His later insight that families are nodes in networks of power relations—an aspect of his broader argument about the role played by "micropowers" in the social circulation of power—was rooted in his wartime experience.

The war was also the backdrop to Foucault's understanding of fascism. Fascism occupies a peculiar place in Foucault's thought, in that it was both tangential to his historical interests and central to his theoretical positions. The great theorist of power said precious little about the twentieth century's most distinctive political system. When he did speak about it, it was primarily to emphasize fascism's exceptional and anachronistic nature, as a power form that harked back to monarchical ideas of sovereignty and the connection between authority and the death penalty. Yet at other times, Foucault saw fascism as constitutive of the concept of power as such, insofar as fascism lays bare the eroticism from which power can rarely be dissociated. In the 1970s, Foucault spoke of the fascism that inhabits most people, the "fascism *that causes us to love power*" and "desire the very thing that dominates and exploits us."[9] Fascism shows that power is something we desire—an insight that, at least for Foucault, does not so much make power palatable as render desire suspect. Put differently, fascism suggests that we are all, to a degree, sadomasochists: we take pleasure in having the power to inflict suffering, even as we long to be subjected to strength surpassing our own. To Foucault, fascism was not an abstract term. He witnessed German troops marching into Poitiers in June 1944 and imposing their authority on its citizens. He was also exposed to French collaborators who embraced fascist and *fascisant* ideologies, from Pétainist doctors to the thugs of the Milice française. In these forms, fascism was undoubtedly terrifying, but it also satisfied a desire for power and a need to identify with authority figures that, in the confusion and disorientation following France's collapse, would have been particularly acute—especially for a teenage boy. It is precisely because fascism reveals power to be desirable that, Foucault would later conclude, it had to be overcome. To be a genuine and self-conscious antifascist, one must have an intuitive understanding of fascism's erotics. This is the pathos of White's anecdote: Foucault feared that Reagan had tapped into a popular inclination to "desire the very thing that dominates and exploits us," one that condemned and threatened Foucault's ability to go to Man's Country—a parodic fascist name if ever there was one—to be deliberately dominated and exploited. For Foucault, the wartime years crystallized the attraction and repulsion to power that historical fascism exemplifies.

Finally, the experience of war and occupation provided instructive lessons in the instability, reversibility, and brittleness of power relations. Between 1940 and 1944, local figures of authority in Poitiers came and went with unsettling swiftness. The political system grounded in the institutions of the Third Republic was replaced by multiple layers of German military authority and French collaborators of various kinds, ranging from bureaucrats to political activists. In 1944, German rule was, in turn, replaced by a sometimes fraught alliance between Resistance forces and de Gaulle's provisional government. In addition to being volatile, the power relations Foucault witnessed seemed symbiotically connected to resistance. A crucial feature of Foucault's mature thought is his thesis that "where there is power, there is resistance."[10] This claim was almost

literally borne out by what Foucault witnessed during the war. German efforts
to secure their control over the town were met with acts of resistance that Foucault would certainly have heard of, as when guards facilitated the escape of
concentration camp detainees being treated at the hospital where Foucault's
father worked, and when local medical students assassinated a notorious fascist journalist. The liberation of Poitiers in September 1944, when popular
forces overthrew what remained of the collaborationist regime, was probably
the closest Foucault ever came to experiencing a revolution firsthand—at least
until his time in Tunisia and Iran years later. Yet despite the multiple blows dealt
to political authority, despite the constant rerouting of chains of command, the
mechanisms of political power proved, during this period, remarkably resil-
ient. German occupation forces governed by harnessing French administrative structures; in 1944, revolutionary violence briefly unsettled the status quo
before the Resistance and the energies it had unleashed were absorbed by the
postwar state. Though the question of power—unlike that of death—was never
one of the young Foucault's explicit concerns, it became the focus of his mature
work, in ways that drew on intuitions gleaned from earlier experiences.

The Second World War is an elusive matrix for Foucault's thought, but
a decisive one. By reconstructing how the war was experienced in Poitiers,
the specific ways it impacted Foucault and his family, and Foucault's later
references to the war and related topics, it becomes evident that Foucault's
thought and concerns bear the distinctive imprint of an era—specifically, that
of German-occupied France. The war did not rigorously determine Foucault's
philosophical positions so much as shape his affective life, cultivate his worldview, and provide him with intuitions and materials that would leave an indel-
ible mark on his philosophical enterprise.

The Presence of Death and Affective
Intensity: The First World War

Though Foucault experienced the Second World War firsthand, war had long
played a significant role in his family's history. Indeed, military experience
was second only to medicine as a hallmark of the Foucaults' identity. Born
only eight years after the end of the great national culling that was the First
World War, Foucault was raised amid men who had fought under the colors.

Of these, the most important was his own father. The tensions between
Europe's two rival alliance systems came to a head as Paul Foucault was

immersed in his medical studies. In 1913, he received a student deferment. But on August 11, 1914, a little over a week after Germany had declared war on France, Paul Foucault, at the age of twenty-one, enlisted in the army as a *soldat de seconde classe* (i.e., a private) in the fifth section of military nurses. On June 11, 1915, he was named an auxiliary doctor.[11] Later that year, he was serving with the Forty-Fifth Infantry Regiment, which deployed to Salonika to participate in French efforts to defend Serbia. Already threatened by Austria, the Serbian kingdom's situation became even more serious when, in October 1915, Bulgaria invaded it after entering the war on the side of the Central Powers. Under General Maurice Sarrail, French forces sought to strengthen Serbia's position by advancing along the Vardar River, only to encounter robust Bulgarian resistance. The French retreated to Salonika, where they remained for much of the following year.[12]

Though the French failed in their efforts to protect Serbia from the Central Powers, Paul Foucault himself seems to have served with valor. His heroism was part of the rationale for awarding him, years later, the *Légion d'honneur*. Paul Foucault, according to the citation, demonstrated "the most absolute selflessness in his service as battalion doctor, as much in the course of the operations of the first fortnight of December 1915"—when fighting with the Bulgarians was particularly intense—as during an unspecified period "when morbidity reached a particularly high rate." He "accepted to be evacuated only when his strength had abandoned him." In 1918, while still on the Serbian front, but now serving with the 241st Artillery Regiment of the 122nd Infantry Division, Paul Foucault's conduct was again hailed as exemplary: he "did not hesitate to immediately go to the location of a bombarded unit to give first aid to the gravely wounded and to evacuate them." He "remained until the end of the bombardment, prepared to provide all necessary aid."[13]

While Paul Foucault seems to have been strongly committed to the military—he remained a member of the reserves for most of his life—only briefly was it his primary occupation. Another relative Foucault knew as a child, his maternal great uncle, devoted his entire career to the army. Paulin Louis Prosper Roger Malapert, the older brother of Foucault's grandfather, was born in Poitiers in 1861. He attended the École Spéciale Militaire de Saint-Cyr, France's most prestigious military academy.[14] In August 1914, after a sleepy career punctuated by steady promotions, he suddenly found himself, at the age of fifty-three, preparing to lead troops into battle. He spent most of the war commanding the 320th Infantry Regiment, which fought at the First Battle of the Marne and then at Verdun.[15] Like Paul Foucault, Colonel Malapert's bravery was commended by his superiors. At Verdun, General Robert Nivelle praised Malapert for his "energy" and "bravery," noting that when Malapert's troops were exposed to "the most violent of bombardments," he kept their morale high through his "courage, his spirit, and his good humor."[16] After the war, Malapert sought to honor his men's sacrifice by helping launch Poitiers's chapter of the Union Nationale des Combattants (UNC, or National Combatants Union), the leading veterans' organization. Following his death in 1933, an article in the UNC newspaper celebrated Malapert's character and humanity. For Malapert, "the old *Poilus* of the trenches were not beasts of burden or cannon fodder, nor even instruments of glory and victory: they were, more than anything, men, whose life was infinitely precious, and to whose sons, wives, and mothers he was accountable."[17] Similar sentiments were expressed at his funeral, which was attended by many of Poitiers's leading citizens. Gathering around his casket were his brother, the philosopher Paulin Malapert, and "Doctor Paul Foucault."[18] Perhaps the latter's six-year-old son was also present.

Colonel Malapert gave more to the war effort than his energy and leadership ability: he also lost a son. Born in 1888, Prosper Jules François Roger Malapert was serving as a *sous-lieutenant* in the Thirty-Second Infantry Regiment when hostilities broke out. After attacking Lorraine as part of Plan XVII and holding the line at the Marne, his regiment fought the Germans at Ypres during the Race to the Sea. During this engagement, on November 3, 1914, the younger Malapert was killed by the enemy at Zonnebrecke, Belgium. He was twenty-six.[19]

What did Foucault think of his family's military experiences? The only clues come from reflections made much later in his career. While Foucault had much to say about military strategy as a model for power relations and the connection between total war and biopolitics, his most intimate thoughts on soldiers' experiences during the Great War appeared in a 1981 interview with *Gai pied*, the newly founded gay magazine. Foucault raised the experiences of First World War soldiers at a surprising juncture: when the conversation turned to the "relational and affective virtualities" (as he put it) that can exist between members of the same sex. Foucault was not making the trite claim that military life fostered homoeroticism. His point, rather, was that war created an opportunity for men to develop relationships of a kind they were usually denied in conventional society, at least in modern Europe. This perspective was rooted in Foucault's view, which came to the fore of his thinking in the early 1980s, that cultivating and experimenting with relationships was far more interesting, creative, and liberating than the pursuit of sex and sexuality. The relative tolerance from which relations between women have benefited is instructive, Foucault argued, less for the resulting sexual connections than for the relational intensities they made possible—relationships of "love" and "affection," which could be alternatively "dense, wonderful, and sunny" and "very sad" and "very dark." Men have traditionally been denied access to such relationships: "men's bodies were forbidden to men" in a "drastic" way.[20] The one exception to this prohibition, Foucault argued, was war. "You have soldiers, young officers, who . . . spent months, years together," Foucault explained. "During the First World War, men fully lived together, on top of each other."

Yet this opportunity for men to cultivate passionate relationships with one another was predicated and justified on one condition: that their lives be in danger. The close proximity in which men lived during the war was permitted only because "death was present": "ultimately, giving oneself [*dévouement*] to one another [and] serving others was sanctioned by the interplay of life and death." These novel occasions for male connectedness were tinged—and perhaps enhanced—by mortality and finitude. Foucault mused: "Except for a few remarks about camaraderie, the brotherhood of souls, of a few very fragmentary testimonials, what do we know of the affective whirlwinds, the tempests of the heart that may have occurred in such moments? And one can ask what made it possible, in these absurd, grotesque wars, in these infernal massacres, that people nonetheless got by." The best explanation, he concluded, was an "affective fabric."[21]

In his accounts of family relations, Foucault was uninclined to describe the relationship between children and their fathers as "intense." Such relationships were to be found, in his thinking, between siblings and lovers, perhaps between children and their mothers. But the silence and deafness he associated with his father's medical persona seemed bereft of the affective charge that Foucault sought in relationships. This perspective brings Foucault's comments about the First World War into clearer relief: *only* in an ordeal such as the Great War, he implies, could his father and other men in his family experience relational intensity. Foucault's references to the "*dévouement*" and "camaraderie" of soldiers during this war not only draws on the language of affective intensity but also evokes the terms in which his father's and great uncle's military records were praised. Yet Foucault was not saying "that it was because [soldiers] were in love with one another that they continued to fight." He expressed his aversion for the kind of reasoning that, when analyzing such situations, declares: 'Ah, *voilà* homosexuality!'" What intrigued Foucault was

not that soldiers might be tempted to experiment with same-sex relationships, but rather that their exposure to imminent death justified male friendships and heightened their intensity. He explained: "honor, courage, not
losing face, sacrifice, leaving the trench with one's pal, ahead of one's pal . . .
implied a very intense affective knot." These relationships were inseparable
from what Foucault later called the "already-thereness of death (*le déjà-là de
la mort*),"[22] which pervaded existence on the front. They "made possible this
infernal life in which, for weeks, guys trudged in mud, dead bodies, [and]
shit, starved, [and] got drunk in the morning for the attack."[23]

It is unlikely that Foucault could have uttered these words without his
own family's experiences in mind. Yet what is most striking is the way Foucault makes no secret of the fact that he is expressing a fantasy—how he *imagines* the experience of front soldiers to have been. He is engaging in a kind
of family romance: the father who rushed to the assistance of his fallen com-
rades amid the roar of battle belongs to an entirely different affective register
than the hushed, cold, palpating physician. It was perhaps only as a *poilou*
fighting Europe's most senseless war that he could imagine a father susceptible to intensity.

The Execution of Dollfuss

If intensity was in short supply in his family relations, it was abundantly
available in European politics in the era in which Foucault grew up. As he
explained in 1983, "nearly all [his] great emotional memories" from the 1930s
and 1940s were "related to the political situation." The subdued and slightly
stultifying sociability in his parents' household stood in stark contrast with the
high drama of interwar politics. In the same interview, Foucault recalled one
event that had a particular impact on him as a child: "I experienced one of my
first great frights when Chancellor Dollfuss was assassinated by the Nazis in,
I think, 1934. It is something very far from us now. I remember very well that
I was really scared by that. I think it was my first strong fright about death."[24]

Foucault remembered correctly: Austrian chancellor Engelbert Dollfuss
was assassinated—though "murdered" is the better word—on July 25, 1934.
At the time, Foucault was about three months shy of his eighth birthday. And
while well known to historians, Dollfuss's assassination is not one of the better
remembered events of the "age of extremes." A member of the conservative
Christian Social Party, Engelbert Dollfuss had assumed the chancellorship of

Austria in 1932, at a time of economic crisis and political unrest. After Hitler came to power in Germany in January 1933, Dollfuss feared that Austrian Nazis might try to overthrow his government. In March 1933, he effectively disbanded the parliament and established a personal dictatorship based on Catholic corporatist principles. As he grew increasingly hostile to Nazism, Dollfuss turned to Benito Mussolini for protection from Germany. Despite his aversion to Nazism, Dollfuss epitomized the authoritarian and militaristic politics of the era: he used a private militia to crush Austrian socialists in Vienna, going so far as to order that artillery shells be fired at housing projects where socialist sympathizers were known to live.[25]

Dollfuss's assassination captured international public opinion because it provided irrefutable evidence of the brutality that Nazis were prepared to employ to achieve their political aims. But what would it have meant to an eight-year-old boy in a provincial French town? Though we obviously cannot know, we can grasp something about the meaning in which the event was enshrouded by considering how it was reported in Poitiers's leading newspaper, *L'avenir de la Vienne*. On July 27, 1934, the headline read: "A 'Hitlerian' Putsch in Vienna: Chancellor Dollfuss Assassinated by the Nazis." The article describes how, during the attempted takeover, "terrorists" seized control of the local radio station while roughing up the announcer and marched through Vienna's streets toting machine guns. The story's focal point was the Austrian Nazis' seizure of the chancery, where Dollfuss lived. Disguised as a pro-Dollfuss militia, a dozen Nazis were allowed into the building. Upon finding Dollfuss, they shot him twice, wounding him in the chest and neck. *L'avenir de la Vienne* recounted what happened next: "The chancellor covered his face with both hands, called for help, and collapsed onto his back. The servant who was present was expelled from the room; the chancellor remained alone in the room with his murderers." While the hour of his death was unclear, it was known, the article explained, "that the insurgents refused him any medical help and any religious assistance, despite the desires expressed by the dying man. Chancellor Dollfuss died in solitude. His last breath was heard only by his enemies."[26]

The next day, *L'avenir de la Vienne* again led with news from Vienna. Alongside stories on the assassination's political and diplomatic fallout, further information about the murder was provided. The chancellor had died a "long and painful" death. When he made an attempt to leave the room in which he was being held, one of the Nazis shot him again, this time in the neck: "this wound . . . was fatal."[27] The following day, *L'avenir de la Vienne*

reported that "by a tragic coincidence, the only witness to Chancellor Dollfuss's agony and final moments has gone mad and lost his memory."[28] The
newspaper's account of Dollfuss's state funeral in Vienna was sympathetic
and melodramatic. It reported that Austria's president hailed the slayed chancellor as a "martyr" and that the archbishop declared that Dollfuss's "blood"
would be "the ransom of Austria's pacification."[29] L'avenir de la Vienne gave
particular attention to the ceremony's religious, almost mystical quality.

Reflecting on how children of his generation experienced the war, Foucault (as we have seen) observed: "Our private life was really threatened."[30]
This anxiety seems closely connected to the fear that Dollfuss's assassination
elicited in Foucault. Dollfuss was killed not in a public assassination, but in a
home invasion: Nazi "terrorists" broke into his private quarters, threatening
his "private life" in the most terrifying way imaginable. The story of a man—
especially one as powerful and famous as Dollfuss—for whom home provided no security from a gang of cruel, violent murderers could easily have
dealt a severe blow to a child's sense of safety, leading him to question his parents' ability to provide protection. The assassination encapsulated, moreover,
the pervasive sense of insecurity and brutality that characterized this period.
As contemporaries noted, Dollfuss's killing occurred less than a month after
Hitler's purge of the Sturmabteilung (SA)—the Night of the Long Knives—
and seemed to confirm Nazism's association with generalized killing. Nazism,
Foucault later contended, consists in "the most complete unleashing of the
power to murder" in which "the power to kill, the power of life and death is
given not only to the state, but to an entire series of individuals."[31] Dollfuss's
assassination was, furthermore, distinctly macabre. His ordeal was drawn
out over several hours and involved multiple gunshot wounds. Arguably, it
amounted to a form of supplice or torture. And the refusal of last rites to a
leader known for his staunch Catholicism had a particularly sadistic quality.
In his final hours, Dollfuss was denied the care of both doctors and priests, a
position that may have been both horrifying—yet also strangely alluring—to
a young man raised in a Catholic medical family.

Despite their apparent differences, Foucault's remarks about World War
I soldiers and his memories of the Dollfuss assassination revolve around
a common set of historical, emotional, and psychological themes. In both
cases, Foucault was reflecting about dimensions of contemporary reality in
which individuals were exposed to death. And death, in both cases, had a
gruesome, painful, and humiliating quality, in which bodies were reduced to
their most helpless, biological characteristics. Both stories, moreover, were

interwoven with concerns about affective and intimate relationships: the former allowed Foucault to reflect on how men in his family might relate to one another outside the home, while through the latter, he contemplated the nightmare of a home overtaken by hostile and threatening forces. Death and the tenuousness of intimate relationships were bound up, for Foucault, with his ambivalent feelings about security.

Security, Territory, Population: The Eve of War

Though his memories may in this respect have a retroactive character, Foucault seems to have sensed a change in the tenor of daily life in the 1930s. In addition to the cruelty of the Dollfuss assassination, he recalled the arrival in Poitiers of refugees from the Spanish Civil War, as well as debates with classmates about Mussolini's Ethiopian campaign. As the war clouds gathered, his father, who had remained a reserve officer in Poitiers since being discharged from active duty in 1918, was summoned to participate in training exercises. For a week in mid-November 1938, Paul Foucault participated, without pay, in a program of "obligatory instruction" organized by the military's Ninth Region. Then, on September 3, 1939—the day that France declared war on Germany, following its invasion of Poland—Paul Foucault was called back to active duty and assigned to the St. Joseph Hospital in Poitiers as head doctor.[32]

In his fleeting recollections, Foucault described the fear and uncertainty he felt as war loomed. Nothing brought home this insecurity like aerial warfare and the fact that, for the first time, civilian populations found themselves exposed to bombs released from enemy planes sweeping over them. Following Germany's invasion of Poland on September 1, 1939, the French press detailed the effects of the Luftwaffe's devastating bombing of Polish territory. After France declared war on Germany, popular anxieties at the prospect of air raids against the French interior intensified. In Poitiers, newspapers described the steps being taken to prepare for impending hostilities. Local authorities were particularly eager to impress on Poitiers's citizens how much airplane technology had advanced since 1918, making civilian preparedness essential. In early September, *L'avenir de la Vienne* explained that bombers could now fly at four hundred kilometers an hour, carrying payloads of one to two thousand kilograms. Bombs, it warned, could be explosive, incendiary, or poisonous (including bacteriological agents). While their goal was to destroy infrastructure, they were also designed to have a "demoralizing" effect on civilians and troops.³³ Like towns throughout France, Poitiers also put into effect the government-mandated program of civil defense, known as *Défense passive* (Passive Defense). Once war was declared, authorities went through considerable lengths to ensure that the local population understood that enemy bomb raids would be devastating and that only deliberate planning could offer protection. One newspaper article warned: "The public . . . must not imagine that it will shield itself from dangers from the air at the last minute through good luck. The characteristic of this danger is its *suddenness*, one must not count on, to protect oneself from it, the virtues of the '*système D*' [i.e., *système débrouillard*, or thinking quickly on one's feet]."³⁴ In early September, Poitevins were woken up at 3:30 A.M. by sirens announcing an imminent attack. Though it did not transpire, *L'avenir de la Vienne* noted with concern that many citizens failed to take the warning seriously: the population needed to understand that "an alert does not mean chatting on the Place d'Armes"—Poitiers's central square—"or on balconies."³⁵ Howling air-raid sirens became part of daily life, even before the invasion. The *Défense passive* service also organized a system of air-raid shelters, based on a *quadrillage*-like division of the city into sectors consisting of multiple islets (*îlots*). These shelters were intended to provide protection from small incendiary bombs and explosions, and citizens were encouraged to ensure they were equipped with benches, flashlights, and water. The Foucault household belonged to the islet 2 of sector 4, whose leader, a *Monsieur* Texier, lived several doors down at 17, Rue Arthur Ranc.³⁶ Preparations such as these may well have contributed the sense of insecurity and terror that Foucault recalls experiencing.

The worsening international situation also resulted in the influx of thousands of refugees into Poitiers. Foucault specifically recalled the arrival of refugees from Spain following Franco's victory over the Republicans in 1939. But Poitiers became a destination point for refugees from within France as well. When war broke out in September 1939, the French government ordered the evacuation of areas that were believed to be most exposed to German invasion, particularly communities that were in front of the Maginot Line. Much of this population, particularly the inhabitants of the Moselle (in Lorraine) were advised by authorities to relocate to Poitiers and surrounding areas. In the first ten days, some forty thousand Lorrains fled to the environs of Poitiers. Many spent several days traveling in cattle cars in the heavy summer heat. Foucault may have witnessed the appearance of this mass of humanity firsthand as they arrived at the train station near his home. Close by, a reception center was set up, where at one point, some fourteen hundred refugees slept on mattresses and under tents.[37] To supervise the refugees' arrival in the region, the government chose an up-and-coming member of parliament for the Moselle named Robert Schuman, who would later serve as prime minister and play a major role in founding the European Union. Commenting to the local newspaper on the reception of his constituents in Poitiers, Schuman regretted that "in some localities, they were not always very understanding of the misfortune of others" but praised the hospitality of Poitiers's citizens: "As soon as I arrived, I had the impression that everyone did the utmost to receive these unfortunates well, to mitigate the sadness and pain of such a rapid evacuation."[38] Yet though the city government had issued directives encouraging locals to welcome their less fortunate compatriots, not all Poitevins were hospitable. The local newspaper told the story of a "regrettable incident" in which a truck full of workers and peasants from the Moselle arrived on Poitiers's main square, the Place d'Armes. When they tried to get their bearings using poor French—presumably they were native German speakers—someone in the gathering crowd denounced them as spies and demanded their arrest. Despite appeals to national solidarity in a time of war, similar incidents involving outsiders were frequent, only intensifying after France's defeat.[39]

The outbreak of war in 1939 profoundly destabilized the world in which Foucault had been raised. The relative safety of his early years gave way to a period of pervasive insecurity. The exposure of his city and home to enemy air raids constituted an existential threat, while the arrival of refugees presented him with a vicarious experience of insecurity—the insecurity of others—even as this influx of new populations upset his conventional bearings. Both forms of insecurity were tied to anxieties about mortality: death from the sky, in one instance, and the existential dangers faced by being a stranger in an unfamiliar land, in the other. Later, Foucault would reflect on the unique kind of insecurity faced by refugees, closely linking population movements to the risk of death. The experience of the twentieth century, he argued in 1979, shows that "population migrations necessarily become painful and tragic and can only be accompanied by death and murder."[40] The problem of migration and refugee populations provided, moreover, a disturbing example of the expansive claims that modern states make on their populations. In the late 1970s, Foucault asserted: "The state must not exercise an unconditional right of life and death, whether on its people or those of another country. Refusing the state this right of life and death meant opposing the bombing of Vietnam by the United States, and, at present, it means helping refugees."[41] Though the problem of refugees might seem to be the opposite of that of confinement—excessive mobility, in one instance, extreme confinement, in the other—their meaning, as experiential matrices, seem to have overlapped in Foucault's outlook: in both instances, bodies are exposed and existentially threatened by power at its most naked and arbitrary.

Poitiers, Open City

After the false sense of security instilled by the phony war (the period between September 1939 and May 1940, when virtually no hostilities occurred between France and Germany), France found itself facing a real and present danger when Hitler launched his offensive against Belgium and the Netherlands on May 10, 1940. Within days, German Panzer divisions had pierced through the French front, isolating French and British divisions in the north from the rest of the country. By early June, German forces were preparing their final assault against Paris.

These events left much of the French population uncertain and confused. French newspapers ran brazenly propagandistic stories, praising the performance of French troops on the battlefield, despite the fact that the conflict had quickly turned to the country's disadvantage. Even as the French military position became increasingly precarious, the main newspaper in Foucault's hometown, *L'avenir de la Vienne*, ran headlines such as "Our Positions Have Consolidated at the Somme" (May 25)[42] or "On the Somme Front: Local Actions Have Turned to Our Advantage" (May 26).[43] Its masthead ran patriotic slogans, such as "Confidence!" or "Let us be worthy of our patriotic soldiers!"[44] In an attempt to address the mood in which many citizens found themselves, one article run by *L'avenir de la Vienne* in late May pointed out that nervous disorders no longer affected a small group of people, but the entire population, as their emotions vacillated between "joy and hope" and "fear and sadness." It asked: "How is one to maintain a certain intellectual and emotional balance in a body that each day is shaken and shoved around by the violence and frenzy of opposing winds?" (The answer: a good night's sleep, no strong medicine, and mild food).[45] Amid the confusion, terrifying and disorienting stories circulated. In mid-June, as a stunned population was coming to terms with defeat and occupation, the rumor spread in Poitiers that children below the age of twenty should immediately make their way to Bordeaux, where they would be shipped off to Canada. Noting that many young people had begun the journey by car, bicycle, or foot, *L'avenir de la Vienne* instructed its readers that it had been ordered by the gendarmerie to denounce these rumors and that residents should return to Poitiers as soon as possible.[46]

The resumption and intensification of the war in May 1940 further dramatized the problem of refugees. Hitler's military offensive led to a further influx of people displaced by the conflict into the interior, including Poitiers. In May, L'avenir de la Vienne admonished its readers: "Let Us Help the Refugees." Noting that they had no intention of settling in Poitiers, the article described their plight: "These refugees, who are in this way passing through Poitiers—by car, and even by bicycle—have in most cases left their country several days ago. This gives one an idea of the fatigued condition in which most find themselves. Those who arrive, in the evening, in our town find it absolutely impossible to find a hotel room. All the hotels are packed and have exceeded the very limits of their lodging possibilities." The article called on Poitevins to offer spare rooms to homeless refugees, for a modest price.[47]

The newspaper even provided a thorough description of Belgian uniforms so that Poitevins could tell friends—i.e., Belgians—from enemies.[48] After Belgium capitulated to the Germans on May 28, Poitiers briefly became the seat of Belgium's government in exile. This decision was all the more dramatic in that it raised an important question of legitimacy: King Leopold had requested terms because he believed the battle against Germany to be unwinnable, but his prime minister, Hubert Pierlot, along with Paul Raynaud, his French counterpart, had explicitly denounced the king's decision. From late May to mid-June, Poitiers was briefly the de facto capital of Belgium. The Belgian prime minister's office set up camp in the town center, in the Hôtel Gilbert and Hôtel de France, while the interior ministry was housed at Poitiers's law faculty.[49] The church Foucault attended, the Église Saint-Porchaire, arranged for a special mass for the Belgians by a Belgian, on Sunday, May 26.[50] Meanwhile, L'avenir de la Vienne used its pages to serve as a kind of bulletin board for Belgians located in France to communicate with one another.[51] The fate of Poitiers's Belgians exemplified the disorientation, danger, and vulnerability to which the war exposed so many uprooted peoples.

A far more existential threat to the Foucault family was soon to come. For the first time in centuries, Poitiers became the target of a direct military attack. On the morning of June 19, a wave of Luftwaffe planes descended on the city, releasing their bombs. A second attack occurred that afternoon. Two days later, Poitiers was hit again. The purpose of this bombing seems to have been to disrupt the strategic railroad line that passed through the city. The Foucault home was located several dozen meters above the main train station, atop the promontory on which central Poitiers rests. The German attack struck two munition trains located on the railroad line, as well as a military convoy. One of the munitions trains exploded, exacerbating casualties. According to an account by Gaston Dez, a local historian (and later Foucault's teacher), a troop train was saved from destruction by this initial explosion thanks to a quick-thinking lieutenant.[52] Much of the damage was located along Boulevard du Pont Achard and Boulevard du Grand Cerf, two roads running parallel to the train tracks—that is, immediately below the Foucault home. Many of the victims seem to have been soldiers and refugees, as both had reasons to be near the train station. The official death count for the air raids was 131.[53]

Meanwhile, French military resistance was crumbling in the face of the German onslaught. On June 20, French forces abandoned the defense of the Loire and retreated south, as the French government, now in Bordeaux, opened negotiations with the Germans. In the Vienne department, some twenty-five hundred to three thousand French troops held their ground, though their orders by this point were simply to improve France's negotiation position in armistice talks. The armistice with Germany was declared on June 22. On Sunday, June 23, Poitiers was declared an "open city," and, by ten that morning, the Wehrmacht's Fifth Panzer Division was rolling through its streets.[54] A flag bearing the swastika was flown from town hall. The German occupation had begun.

We know very little about how Foucault experienced France's fall and Poitiers's occupation. Clearly, he associated the memories of this period with a very real taste of death—Dollfuss's assassination, the terror of aerial bombing. But death also entered the family home—another way in which his "private life" was threatened by the outside world. Shortly after France's capitulation, on July 8, 1940, *L'avenir de la Vienne* ran a funeral announcement: "We have been asked to announce the death of M[onsieur] le Professeur Mauclaire, member of the Academy of Medicine, surgeon of the Paris hospitals." He had died with church sacraments two days earlier at 10, Rue Arthur Ranc—the Foucault household. Placide Mauclaire was, as we saw in the first chapter, a prominent Parisian doctor who had been a mentor to Paul Foucault and attended his marriage. The funeral occurred at Saint-Porchaire, the same church where the wedding had occurred fourteen years earlier.[55]

What chain of events led Paul Foucault's prestigious Parisian colleague to perish in his student's provincial home? None of his obituaries provide an explanation. But it seems possible that, like many Parisians, Mauclaire may have fled the capital as the Germans closed in, joining the throng of

Frenchmen fleeing south, perhaps with the intention of seeking refuge with his protégé in Poitiers. At the time of his death, he was seventy-seven. Perhaps he was already ill; perhaps the stress, heat, and discomfort of his flight damaged his health irreparably. Not only had the war brought death and destruction to his doorstep, but its effects were most likely impressed on the thirteen-year-old Foucault by the presence, in his own home, of the corpse of his father's friend.

The Links of Power: German Occupation

The immediate effect of France's fall was that power changed hands: while much of the country's bureaucratic apparatus remained in place, it now took orders from new authorities. In the early summer of 1940, Poitiers's citizens witnessed the deployment of a new power apparatus—a political "diagram" for governing the city and surrounding areas.[56]

A central feature of the new political reality in which France found itself after its defeat was the division of the country into two zones, the occupied zone (in the north and along the Atlantic coastline) and the unoccupied zone (in the south), which, as of July 10, was governed by the Vichy regime. The Vienne was in the unusual situation of being one of thirteen departments that were split in two by the demarcation line or *Demarkationslinie*, a twelve-hundred-kilometer frontier, studded with markers and checkpoints, extending from the Spanish to the Swiss borders. The existence of this arbitrary boundary was dictated by German military goals: dividing France into two zones, in one of which German military presence was limited and essentially subcontracted to cooperating French authorities, allowed the Germans to husband their military resources for impending offensives against Great Britain and the Soviet Union. In the Vienne, thirty-three surveillance posts were placed along the demarcation line, five of which were official passing points. The nearest was approximately twenty-five kilometers from Poitiers.

The practical consequences of this deliberately artificial boundary were particularly felt by those who lived close to it. Those in the occupied zone were directly under the authority of the Militärbefehlshaber in Frankreich, the Paris-based headquarters of German occupation authorities. This had important consequences for daily life. In the occupied zone, clocks were set an hour forward so the territory would be on "German time." It was also subject to German curfews and a ban on driving cars at nighttime—a restriction that would affect Paul Foucault's medical practice, given his dependence on his car to provide surgical services throughout the region. The free zone could be accessed only from the occupied zone if one was granted a pass or *Ausweis*, which could be difficult to obtain. Paul Foucault's work may have justified such documentation, though there is no evidence he was granted it. The *Demarkationslinie* was a striking example of how administrative fiat could significantly impact ordinary life and social interactions.[57]

Even as the Germans were carving up France administratively to achieve their military goals, they were also establishing a new chain of command in Poitiers. Soon after securing the city, they established the local military command, Feldkommandantur 677, at the Hôtel du Palais on Rue Boncenne, a few blocks to the northeast of Foucault's home. A building used by the German general staff was located on Rue Jean-Jaurès, near where Foucault attended school for much of the Occupation and close to one of his father's clinics. In the summer of 1942, the Germans established the headquarters of the Sicherheitspolizei-Sicherheitsdienst (SiPo-SD, the Security Police and Security Service) and the Gestapo around the block from the street on which the Foucault's resided (Rue Arthur Ranc), at 13, Rue des Écossais. The twenty or so Germans in these services, which belonged to the SS, were under the command of one Hermann Herold from 1942 until 1944.[58] The SiPo-SD was focused primarily on gathering intelligence concerning the regime's enemies, while the Gestapo was directly involved in police work. Its sections included Jewish affairs, counterterrorism, intelligence, and "undesirables."[59] The seat of German power, at least regionally, was thus physically close to the Foucault home throughout the Occupation. The net the German forces cast over Poitiers extended directly over the space inhabited by Foucault and his family.

The Occupation was, in this sense, an informative lesson in what it means to "take power." No more than in the rest of France, the German capture of Poitiers did not mean that power magically changed hands from one day to the next. Rather, taking power involved a complex assortment of activities: laying claim to existing relationships of subordination, rerouting them to new authorities, determining what could be controlled directly and what could be left in local hands, defining priorities, divvying up responsibilities. The first step of establishing German rule in Poitiers consisted in encouraging the town to resume its normal activities and allowing established chains of authority to be reformed, even as the Germans placed themselves at the apex of the command structure. On June 24, *L'avenir de la Vienne* published an "Appeal to the Population" by Poitiers mayor Léon Bouchet—a professor of pharmacy and colleague of Paul Foucault at the medical school—that defined the basic features of the new power dispensation. The appeal began by making clear that municipal government was now subject to German military authority: "By order of the Kommandantur, the mayor of the town of Poitiers brings to the attention of the population the following instructions, which must be *rigorously respected.*" Some rules imposed entirely new restrictions. For instance, all firearms had to be handed over to the town hall; cafés, restaurants, and other public places were required to close at 9:30 P.M. (German time); and the population was forbidden from circulating through town between ten at night and six in the morning. Significantly, as far as the Foucault family was concerned, an exception was made for doctors and midwives, who were allowed out after curfew, provided they were in possession of "special legitimation cards written in German and French" issued by the Feldkommandantur. A next set of orders required citizens to return to their customary lives. Workers and employees were ordered to report to work and stores to open at their regular hours. Alongside these sticks, an occasional carrot was waved: for instance, "German soldiers will show no hostility to the civilian population." Still, sticks prevailed, particularly when dealing with challenges to German authority: the Feldkommandantur warned that citizens who chose to engage in "passive or active resistance" to these measures would face "arrest" and "retribution."[60]

The enterprise known as "collaboration" can be understood as an attempt to render German authority more economical by delegating responsibilities to the French, and as an attempt by certain French constituencies to preserve a degree of autonomy and even to advance their own agendas by cooperating with the new powers that be. Central to this task was the reorganization of regional government, specifically departmental "prefectures." Since 1800, Poitiers, as the *chef-lieu* (or capital) of the Vienne department, had been home to a *préfecture*, the bureaucracy run by a prefect, an idiosyncratically French administrative position. This office was conceived during the French Revolution and first implemented by Napoleon, as a way of ensuring that a representative of the central government was present in each of the country's administrative subdivisions. Prefects would report to the government on local affairs and oversee the state's primary concerns, namely security and the well-being of the population. Foucault was well aware of the distinctive character of France's prefectoral system. The elegant building housing the Vienne Prefecture was located several hundred meters from Foucault's home. During his well-known debate with Noam Chomsky in 1971, Foucault cited, as an example of the subordinate and localized institutions that, according to the traditional conception of the state, exercise power in a top-down way, *"l'administration"*—that is, state bureaucracy. He quickly added (in an aside that most transcriptions leave out): "in France, we call it *préfectoral*." He conceded: "I don't know what they call it"—prefectoral bureaucracy—"elsewhere."[61]

During the war, the prefectoral system was instrumental to placing France under German rule and rendering collaboration effective. Critics of the republican model had never warmed to departments, which they saw as soulless administrative units, in contrast to the provinces of the old regime, which they believed were endowed with authenticity and distinctiveness. Pétain announced the return of the provinces, each of which would be run by a governor, as a way of making the state bureaucracy both "concentrated and decentralized."[62] These new provinces would group together the old departments, and—in theory—assume some of the authority previously monopolized by the state, the fulcrum of republican power. In practice, however, Pétain limited himself simply to creating a new administrative position: a regional prefect, who presided over the prefects of several departments. On June 30, 1941, the region of Poitiers was officially created, with a regional prefect based in the Vienne Prefecture. The official appointed to this position was Louis Bourgain, who served as prefect both of the Poitiers region (which included five departments) and the Vienne department. Bourgain was a distinguished military officer who, despite being based in the occupied zone, staunchly supported Pétain's "national revolution," in part because he feared that a German defeat would result in Bolshevism's international triumph. Bourgain played a key role in the reconfiguration of regional chains of command. To harmonize policies, he held regular meetings of departmental prefects, issued regional memos, and toured the territory under his purview.

Yet even as Bourgain sought to bring the region of Poitiers under the authority of Pétain's new regime, he constantly experienced the basic dilemma of collaborationism: the only way he could claim to serve French interests was to be sure that he never ran afoul of German authorities. He was responsible for ensuring that his region provided the Germans with food and other resources. He assisted the Germans with police actions. He was the key figure in ensuring the enforcement of the Service de Travail Obligatoire (Obligatory Labor Service), requiring French citizens to enlist to serve as workers in Germany. He participated directly in the dismantling of Resistance groups and, at German orders, rounding up local Jews. Yet at the same time, he also had to rein in the efforts of some of the most extreme Nazi sympathizers, even arresting some members of Vichy's Jewish affairs bureau when their work clashed with what he regarded as more pressing administrative priorities.[63]

Though Foucault would not, of course, begin to think seriously about the problem of power until the 1970s, his hometown's experiences during the Occupation prefigured and provided context for his later ideas about power. Foucault later insisted on the heterogeneity of power—that it is almost always mistaken to see power as a uniform will emanating from a central authority that imposes, more or less equally, on all subjects under its control. For Foucault, power is always defined, rather, by its multiplicity: as he at times suggested, what we call "power" is nothing more than the sum of all power relationships (which are nothing other than all relationships *tout court*). He explained: "A society is not unitary body in which one power and only one power is exercised, but it is, in reality, a juxtaposition, a connection, a coordination, a hierarchy, too, of different powers, which nevertheless persist in their specificity."[64] The establishment of wartime administration, whether it be the German military command in Poitiers or the attempt by Bourgain to organize a new center of regional authority that would serve the collaborationist cause, illustrated this claim in slow motion: what they undertook to do was to connect, hierarchize, and juxtapose power relations that already existed in order to forge a new power configuration, with its own priorities and imperatives. Indeed, these wartime authorities simultaneously validated this truth and illustrated the tendency of government officials to ignore it: even as they were constantly negotiating with and tapping into existing power networks, they nonetheless seemed to believe that it was possible to establish, over and above them, a unitary font of sovereignty—that would, in Vichy's terms, be both "decentralized" and still, somehow, "concentrated." It is no coincidence that Bourgain aspired to be "emperor in his region."[65]

Another feature of power that intrigued Foucault, and that was closely bound up with his claim about power's heterogeneity, was its locality. Indeed, it is at the local level—at its closest proximity to individual relationships—that power is most concrete and "honest": the "rationality of power" lies in "tactics that are often very explicit at the limited level at which they are inscribed." Foucault called this "the local cynicism of power."[66] These localized power relations can become intertwined, drawing on their respective strengths and expanding their scope, eventually forming more far-flung structures or, as Foucault called them, "comprehensive mechanisms" (*dispostifs d'ensemble*). Hence the paradox of the "anonymous, almost mute" character of the "great anonymous strategies" that seem to direct power at its most general echelons—say, at the level of the state—but which do so only by coordinating the "loquacious tactics" of local actors whose "'inventors' are often lacking in hypocrisy."[67] The clarity of what the Germans and collaborationists were doing at the local level—their attempt to seize control of the civil service and police forces, to support the German war machine, to preempt Resistance activities that could undermine Franco-German relations—served as a telling lesson, in short, that all power is ultimately local and that the "great anonymous strategies"—such as "Vichy" or even "the Third Reich"—exist only insofar as they can connect into these regional networks.

If the war years constituted the experiential matrix for Foucault's theory of power, it was only insofar as the insights provided by these experiences were reactivated at a later point. The basis of this claim is Foucault's assertion that during the Second World War, politics and historical events assumed an importance for him exceeded its impact on his family. In the interview from the early 1980s referred to at this chapter's outset, Foucault, when asked if he had "fond memories of growing up in Poitiers in the 30s and 40s," shifts the question back to the war. His recollections are not exactly "strange," he explains, but what stands out to him is that nearly all his "great emotional memories . . . related to the political situation."[68] The war made politics—who marched in Poitiers's streets, who controlled its administration and police, where boundaries were drawn, what battles were fought—more significant than family. The security that a child might seek and expect from its family— and particularly a bourgeois family—was, to a considerable degree, shattered by the trauma of war. Though the Foucaults sought to protect their children from the most menacing episodes of combat, the vulnerability of the family home to air raids, the German conquest of Poitiers, the close proximity of German command posts, and an increased exposure to death all rendered any notion of the family as a bulwark against a threatening outside world a dangerous illusion. These experiences also laid bare the porous boundaries between family life and politics. Such insights informed Foucault's view that the state should not be conceived as an independent institution, but one that exists only insofar as it is plugged into local networks: the state, he observed in 1973, can function "only if enmeshed with, [if] connected to powers distributed in families (paternal authority)" and other social institutions.[69] The point, Foucault insisted, is not "whether it is the family that reproduces the state or it is the reverse." What matters is that the "family and the state function in relation to one another, by leaning on one another, and possibly even confronting one another."[70] The idea that power as well as violence could penetrate all relations, even family ones, seems to have been intimately tied to Foucault's childhood experience of the war.

The Carceral Archipelago

As we have seen, Foucault recognized that the issue of confinement, as a solution to a range of juridical, medical, or social problems, was, for him, something of a "personal obsession."[71] While the practice of confinement was present in the world in which he was raised, particularly in the medical and psychiatric fields to which his medical family was connected, it expanded and became even more conspicuous during the Second World War. Concentration and internment camps were established in Poitiers of which Foucault was undoubtedly aware and which impacted the texture of wartime life.

In 1983, Foucault recalled: "I . . . remember refugees from Spain arriving in Poitiers."[72] This memory refers to events that took place in Poitiers between 1938 and 1940. After Hitler's seizure of power in 1933 and his annexation of Austria in 1938, France had been overwhelmed with refugees from central Europe. Then, as Franco gained the upper hand in Spain's civil war, particularly after the Battle of the Ebro in 1938, a stream of Spanish Republicans crossing the Pyrenees joined the burgeoning ranks of foreign exiles in France. In early 1939, the Vienne welcomed some twenty-two hundred Spanish refugees, two-thirds of whom were housed in Poitiers.[73] As L'avenir de la Vienne's headlines chronicled the rout of the Spanish republicans in Catalonia in February 1939, a local news story reported the arrival in Poitiers's train station of a convoy of 1,248 refugees from the Spanish conflict, after another thousand had arrived the week before. The special train's passengers had been enclosed for twenty-four hours. As local officials stood on the platform, the passengers placed signs on compartment doors announcing their medical conditions. The hospital director was one of the officials present; some refugees were immediately transferred to the hospital. The remainder of the refugees were transferred to the shelter (*centre d'hébergement*) located on Rue Jean Macé. To house the refugees, the city had decided to reopen the buildings of the old Hôpital Général, which had been shut down over a decade before when its psychiatric patients were transferred to the new Hôpital Pasteur.[74] The use of the Hôpital Général as a refugee shelter was an indirect acknowledgment of that peculiar institution's original purpose, well before it was charged with tending to the mentally ill: its goal, as Foucault later wrote, was to impose order—specifically, bourgeois order—on a population that was "strangely mixed and confused."[75] The fact that Spanish refugees were greeted both by Poitiers's prefect and by its hospital director suggests that the purpose of the internment center, like that of the Hôpital Général, was as much to ensure public order as it was to tend to the sick.

Measures implemented by the Third Republic to address security concerns arising from the arrival of foreigners—such as the Spanish refugees—on French soil laid the groundwork for the internment system that developed under Vichy. On November 12, 1938, Édouard Daladier's government issued a decree that required administrative internment for foreigners with criminal records or whose activities were "dangerous for national security." Previously, foreigners had been placed under house arrest, but the government now concluded that this measure was dangerously liberal. It was necessary, Daladier explained, to distinguish "good elements" from "undesirables," who, in order to be "excluded from our territory, could not be integrated into the French collectivity." Consequently, it called for the creation of "special centers" that would be subject to "permanent surveillance." [76] This "overtly xenophobic"[77] measure resulted in the creation of dozens of internment camps throughout the country. In Poitiers, the first such camp was opened in September 1939, in a twenty-one-hundred-square-meter plot of land situated immediately outside the city, along the main road leading to Limoges. Though its official names changed over the years, it was always referred to as the "Limoges Road camp"—*le camp de la route de Limoges*. It was initially set up as the Center for Surveilled Residency (Centre de Séjour Surveillé), which would bring together in a single location the Spanish refugees who had previous been dispersed throughout Poitiers and surrounding areas.

After France's fall, the Vichy regime preserved the camp apparatus established by the Third Republic, while using it to detain new populations. The Germans had requested that certain undesirables, notably gypsies, be moved from the Atlantic coast to the interior, including the Vienne. In December 1940, the Vienne's prefect decided that the facility best suited for interning them was the Limoges Road camp, which until this point had housed only Spanish refugees.[78] The visible presence of this legendary people in the region clearly made an impression on the Poitevins. Some gave voice to long-standing prejudices, which aligned seamlessly with occupation ideology. On December 6, a writer for *L'avenir de la Vienne*—which had become openly collaborationist—expressed his "profound disgust" at the arrival of a "miserable caravan" of gypsies, after the city had already borne the costs of lodging

Spanish communists, even as it grappled with its losses in the Battle of France. One wonders, the article concluded, if "peaceful Poitiers, hard-working Poitiers," is not seen as "the mandatory garbage dump of all the parasites that it is our weakness to receive on our soil."[79] Others were fascinated with this wandering, free-spirited people, almost romanticizing them. A woman who taught the gypsies at the Limoges Road camp recalled how, upon entering it, she found children "enervated by internment, uneducated and wild," with "evidently no idea of discipline and obedience." Once education and structure brought some order to the lives of the young gypsies, they were rewarded with temporary authorizations to leave the camp, resulting in scenes that may have confirmed, for better or worse, popular prejudices against gypsies. The schoolteacher recounts: "It was a fine sight to see these poor emaciated little rascals, barefoot and in rags, setting off, two by two, and singing as they marched along the black road."[80] By evening, they were expected to cross back through the camp's barbed-wire fence.

By early 1941, the "nomads' camp" (as it was now called, in reference to its new inhabitants) was home to over four hundred gypsies.[81] Whereas previous attempts to seal the camp were largely symbolic, the authorities were now intent to prevent the internees from escaping: they surrounded it with barbed wire and built two surveillance towers. The internees were housed in fifteen wooden barracks aligned along the road, each of which could accommodate sixty-seven people (though they were frequently filled beyond capacity).[82] Measures were also taken to repress the gypsies' allegedly antisocial behavior—laziness, theft, and drunkenness. When the German head of the Feldkommandantur Von Alemann inspected the camp, he complained about the detainees' laziness and warned that its "demoralizing effects" were potentially greater than they would be for "normal men." He ordered: "laziness must be punished with very severe disciplinary sanctions."[83]

In its final incarnation, the Limoges Road camp became a holding pen for Jews. Before the war, Poitiers's Jewish population was small. This changed in 1939, with the arrival of the evacuees from the Moselle, many of whom were Jewish. One recalled upon arriving in Poitiers: "Prior to the influx of Jews from the East, there were only three or four Jewish families living with its predominantly Catholic community. The people didn't even know what a Jew looked like, and they were surprised, I think, to discover that we didn't have horns and tails. They were warm and friendly, though, and did all they could to welcome us."[84] With the German occupation, however, these Jewish inhabitants found themselves in an increasingly precarious position. In October 1940, Jews in the occupied zone were required to register with the authorities. More restrictive measures aimed at Jewish commercial activities and employment followed. Between July 15, 1941 and July 17, 1942, some seven hundred Jews, a majority of whom were French, were arrested and interned at the Limoges Road camp, where they joined the gypsy population.[85] The following year, on July 18, 1942, a first contingent of 158 Jews was transferred to the Drancy camp outside of Paris, from whence many would be sent on to the death camps in the east. Thirteen hundred were deported to Drancy in 1942 alone.[86] The Limoges Road camp had completed its transformation from a Third Republic camp for "undesirables" to an "antechamber of deportation and the Shoah."[87] The Poitiers camp was, moreover, unusual in being "one of the few mixed camps of France that confined more than one persecuted group."[88] This was reflected in the camp's architecture: by the end of 1941, it consisted of distinct, fenced-in compounds for Spaniards, Gypsies, and Jews.[89]

Inhabitants of Poitiers like the Foucault family would have been familiar with the goings-on at the camp—the arrests and roundups, changes in the camp population that reflected Occupation policies, the deportations. Many civilians interacted with the camp population, as administrators, guards, and service providers. But one relatively direct way in which Foucault would have known about the camp was through its interactions with Poitiers's medical facilities. While there is no evidence that Paul Foucault ever visited the Limoges Road camp or treated its patients, the camp played a significant role in the lives of the local medical community during the Occupation. Local doctors and eventually the hospital were responsible for providing medical assistance to the internees and monitoring the camp's hygiene. In late 1940, when the gypsies were arriving, a physician identified in the local records as "Doctor Henri B." had been requisitioned to serve as camp inspector.[90] Though the documents do not identify his full last name, he may well have been Henri Bourdeau, a young intern who would subsequently make his career in Poitiers. He brought to the attention of the authorities—the prefect and the Feldkommandantur—that health conditions at the camp were poor, noting that "corporeal hygiene at the Limoges Road camp leaves much to be desired."[91] The camp lacked showers; water and sewage was defective; the soil on which the barracks were built became a sea of mud in bad weather; and rats were common. In addition to providing medical assistance at the camp itself, Doctor B. also arranged regular visits of internees to the Hôtel-Dieu (including twenty-four who went to the hospital each week for a bath).[92] Doctor B.'s activities eventually ran afoul of the German authorities. In late 1942, the Sipo-SD requested his dismissal, on the grounds that he had "admitted into the Hôtel-Dieu Jews who are lacking practically nothing." He was also accused of being "discourteous" to German soldiers at the camp and getting along poorly with the camp's guards, in part because he refused to explain his reasons for entering and leaving the camp at all hours of the day and night.[93] What these anecdotes reveal is both that the camp was closely connected to the Hôtel-Dieu and that at least some members of the medical community engaged in passive resistance to German occupation policies.

The relationship between Poitiers's camps and its hospital was strained to a crisis point when German authorities began to suspect that these connections were being exploited to help internees escape. Prefect Bourgain reminded camp and hospital authorities that internees at the Limoges Road camp—as well as the political prisoners held at the Rouillé camp to Poitiers's west—could be transferred to local hospitals only if it would be a "danger for their existence" to be treated at the camp infirmaries.[94] Yet a number of figures in the medical establishment seem to have deliberately exploited loopholes in this rule while professing to honor it. For instance, 1941, Doctor Henri B. hospitalized several Jews whose conditions were not life-threatening on the grounds that the camp's infirmary was not functional.[95] In December 1943, the health inspector of the Vienne prefecture acknowledged, in a letter to the prefect, the ambiguity of the regulations: the criterion that hospitalization should be reserved only for those for whom camp conditions posed a "danger for their existence" could, he explained, be "interpreted in different ways." It could refer to an imminent danger of death, or to the fact that deprivation of medical assistance might pose a "danger over a more or less long period."[96] The rules became a bone of contention between the authorities and doctors because, like elsewhere in France, hospitalization provided camp internees with favorable opportunities for escape. The prefecture, the police, and the Feldkommandantur insisted that authorities at the Hôtel-Dieu (where most internees were hospitalized by early 1942) take measures to prevent escape, such as placing metal bars over windows or grouping camp internees in "secure rooms." Meanwhile, doctors politely but firmly insisted that such police measures vitiated the hospital's medical priorities: rigidly monitoring tuberculosis patients or grouping them together with other internees, for instance, posed risks of contagion. A memo from the National Police noted that "quite a few doctors find it repugnant to assist the police service" for reasons of "a moral or practical nature."[97] Yet the effect of this dispute was that hospitalized internees regularly escaped, to the point that French and German authorities began to lose patience. On March 12, 1942, after several escapes from the Hôtel-Dieu, Merdsche, a German officer responsible for administration at the Feldkommandantur, asked the prefect to investigate what "surveillance measures aimed at preventing similar escape initiatives" had been taken at the hospital, warning that if this pattern continued, he reserved the right "to arrest the personnel in charge of surveillance and to punish them for complicity."[98] In 1943 and 1944, a steady stream of memos between the prefecture and the German authorities addressed the periodic escapes of internees (particularly from the Rouillé camp) from the Hôtel-Dieu. On May 27, 1943, SS Untersturmführer Zwick of the Poitiers unit of the SiPo-SD wrote to the prefect, complaining that the recent escape from the hospital of two Jews from the Limoges Road camp had occurred because "the surveillance exercised by the personnel of the Hôtel-Dieu was not done in a serious way."[99]

German and prefectoral suspicion of the hospital's complicity in escapes was not, ultimately, entirely unfounded. The Hôtel-Dieu was staffed by several active members of the Resistance. Dr. Jacques Quivy—whom medical students remembered as the butt of Paul Foucault's caustic wit (as seen in Chapter 1)—was arrested for Resistance activities and held by the Germans as a hostage.[100] In a dramatic turn of events, on June 6, 1944, just as the Allies were invading Normandy, the man who had been the director of Poitiers's hospitals for most of the war, Joseph Garnier, was discovered by the Germans to be a member of the Resistance movement Libération Nord. Blocking off every entry into the Hôtel-Dieu, they attempted to arrest him; thanks to a resourceful midwife in the maternity ward, he was able to escape to a neighboring private residence.[101] Though there is no evidence he was involved in these activities, Paul Foucault's position at the Hôtel-Dieu would have acquainted him and his family with the conditions in Poitiers's concentration camps, as well as the microphysical power struggle over internees between the French and German authorities on the one hand and the hospitals' doctors on the other.

The specific character of wartime internment in Poitiers thus seems to have constituted a further experiential matrix for the development of Foucault's thought. The Limoges Road camp was, even before it became a tool of occupation and collaboration, founded under the Third Republic as a mechanism for dealing with individuals who, according to the Daladier government, were "dangerous for national security." During his activist period in the 1970s, the idea of the "dangerous man"—*l'homme dangereux*—came to obsess Foucault, particularly for the way it served to justify security policies aimed at imprisonment. What interested—and outraged—Foucault about the term "dangerous" was the way it became a legal rationale for punishment and imprisonment, even when no evidence of a crime existed. In 1977, he observed that in "penal law, whether it be of an Anglo-Saxon or Napoleonic type, danger has never constituted an offense. Being dangerous is not an offense. Being a danger is not a sickness." Yet by asking psychiatrists whether an individual is "dangerous," judges can transform this idea that is neither legal nor medical into a penal concept.[102] In an opinion piece published in 1978 entitled "Attention: Danger," he reflected on the oddity of the term "dangerous," which judges had begun to invoke: it refers not to what someone "has done," but to what "he is" and even "what one suspects he could be or become."[103] Spanish republicans were interned in 1939 precisely because the French government feared, based on their political backgrounds, what they "could be or become." Though Foucault emphasized the—entirely irrelevant, in his view—medical and psychiatric character of the discussion around danger in the 1970s, the use of the rhetoric of social danger—"society must be defended," as he entitled his 1976 lecture series on the topic— as a justification of internment is rooted in his childhood experiences in wartime Poitiers.

Foucault was, moreover, interested in the way that, in modern times, "vagabondage" and "nomadism" became viewed with suspicion and conflated with an illicit, undisciplined, and immoral way of life. After the fall of France, the rootless and wandering lifestyle of the gypsies led the Germans to request their removal from the coastal areas and internment further inland. As we have seen, some citizens of Poitiers reacted to the arrival of the gypsy "caravan" with disgust, worrying that they would bring theft and petty crime. When, in the 1970s, Foucault's growing interest in the problem of discipline led him to investigate various forms of "illegalism"[104]—conduct that was illegal in principle but tolerated in practice—he referred to what he called "nomadism." He defined it as a way of refusing to allow one's body to become a disciplined production machine. Common forms of this "illegalism" included "absenteeism, lateness, laziness, parties [fêtes], debauchery, [and] nomadism—in short, . . . whatever consists in irregularity [and] mobility in space."[105] This litany evokes the traits that Poitiers's inhabitants associated with the gypsies interned at what they called the camp des nomades, as well as the German commander's irritation at their refusal to engage in disciplined and productive work. Perhaps the imagination of the young Foucault was captured by the stories of the gypsies who had recently arrived in the community; perhaps he saw them firsthand, when the children were given permission to leave the camp or their parents received authorization to work in town. A local historian notes that in 1942, German authorities allowed "four nomads" living at the camp to be employed by a local construction company. It was located on Rue Arthur Ranc—the street on which Foucault lived.[106]

Finally, though Foucault said relatively little about the concentration camps of the Second World War, what he did say made it clear that he saw them as integral to the broader history of internment and confinement. Specifically, Foucault was intrigued by what he saw as one of the main alternatives any internment system must face: should one lump all internees together, or categorize them and confine them accordingly? An important part of the story of *Madness and Civilization* was the shift from the Hôpital Général, which confined to a single institution disorderly individuals of all kinds, to the asylum, premised on the notion that the mad should be confined to an institution reserved for them alone. As he began his work on prisons in the wake of police repression of the post-1968 student movement, Foucault observed to an interviewer that what struck him was that the older model of internment—general internment, that is, locking up a motley assortment of troublesome individuals in a single place—was returning. He proceeded to compare the contemporary situation in France to the wartime period: "Today, for reasons that I still do not understand well, we are returning to a kind of general, undifferentiated confinement. Nazi concentration camps brought attention to the bloody, violent, inhumane variation on this new kind of confinement— Jews, homosexuals, communists, vagabonds, gypsies, political agitators, all in the same camp."[107] What makes this comment striking is the fact that it is not entirely true: *not* all German camps were this mixed. Some camps were reserved more for political prisoners, others for gypsies; the camps used to exterminate the Jews were quite unique. Yet this grouping together of different populations—albeit at successive times—was a distinctive trait of the Limoges Road camp. Foucault's assessment points to the formative role that his own wartime experiences seem to have played in focusing the concerns that he explored at the apex of his career.

Society Must Be Defended: Medical Pétainism

Though Foucault and his family never faced internment in Poitiers's camps, they were nonetheless subject to a new regime that professed an ideology dramatically different from the late Third Republic's. Poitiers was situated in the occupied zone, but Vichy's shadow loomed over it. Local institutions were subject to Vichy's directives, and the regime's reactionary, conservative politics seeped into the town's public discourse, as it did throughout much of France. Foucault recalled how the rhetoric of Marshal Philippe Pétain, Vichy's leader, pervaded his teenage years. In 1983, Foucault commented on the remarks of a socialist politician connected to the recently elected government, who had called for replacing the existing "egoist, individualist, bourgeois cultural model" with a new cultural model based on "solidarity and sacrifice." Foucault observed: "I was not very old when Pétain came to power in France, but this year I recognized in the words of this socialist the very tones which lulled my childhood."[108]

Foucault would have heard such words, in the first place, at the Collège Saint-Stanislas, a Catholic school run by the Frères des Écoles Chrétiennes, which he began attending in fall of 1940, when he was thirteen. During the Battle of France, the school, located in central Poitiers at the intersection of Rue Jean-Jaurès and Rue de l'Ancienne Comédie, had served as a military hospital, which the Germans shut down after France's fall, allowing it to return to teaching. Saint-Stanislas seems to have hewed closely to Vichy policies. One former student remembers that the Vichy government distributed vitamin biscuits, required the raising and lowering of the national flag, and organized students into teams with their own leaders and mottos. Students were expected to sing the new anthem professing allegiance to Pétain, "Maréchal, nous voilà" (Maréchal, here we are!). When Vichy's National Delegate for Youth visited the school, students sang it for him.[109] Some of Foucault's teachers were hostile to Vichy and became active in anti-German resistance. Father Georges Duret, the school's legendary philosophy teacher (who will be considered in the next chapter), vigorously rejected Vichy's Catholic nationalist ideology. He also opposed the Legion of French Volunteers against Bolshevism, as well as the "Athlete's Oath," which the regime demanded of participants in sporting events. According to another anecdote, Duret immediately left his classroom when he noticed that Pétain's portrait had been placed above the crucifix.[110] Vichy, in these ways, permeated the climate in which Foucault was educated.

Foucault likely learned about Vichy's political ambitions from his father. The new regime found willing collaborators in the local medical establishment and assigned sympathetic doctors important roles in the *révolution nationale* or national revolution—the name Pétain gave to his project of turning France's defeat into an opportunity for national renewal on antirepublican and ultraconservative principles. Dr. Pierre Barnsby, a longtime colleague of

Paul Foucault's at the medical school and the Hôtel-Dieu, became a leading figure in medical collaboration as vice president of the Administrative Commission of Poitiers's Hospitals. On November 1, 1941, Barnsby delivered a speech to hospital personnel, which Paul Foucault likely heard in person (or at least heard about). The speech made a case for what one might call medical Pétainism. It is also a perfect example of the Vichy rhetoric that, according to Foucault, "lulled his childhood." France, Barnsby explained, had been "painfully wounded" and wanted "to stand up and live." But this could occur only if every French citizen was willing to be a "good worker in the great task of NATIONAL RENOVATION" to which "the MARSHAL, who has made a gift of his person to the Common Good, summons us." It was thus imperative that each citizen renounce his or her "bad habits" and "erstwhile mistakes," first and foremost of which was "egoism," though "laziness, calumny, carelessness, and disorder" had played their part as well. "Everyone," Barnsby added, "must be in solidarity"—*solidaire*—"with his fellow man. No one has the right to fall short of their duty. THE FAULT OF ONE IS THE FAULT OF ALL." In conclusion, Barnsby reminded the personnel of the three words that Pétain had decreed as the "country's new framework": work, family, and fatherland—the new regime's official motto. Departing from the Vichy playbook, he added that the marshal had "cemented" the three words with a fourth: "DISCIPLINE." The language that Foucault associated with Vichy—the condemnation of egoism and the valorization of solidarity and sacrifice—lay at the heart of Barnsby's vision of the role doctors were to play under the marshal's new order.[111]

As Barnsby's speech suggests, Foucault's father, simply because of his profession, felt the pull of the forces rallying behind Vichy more than other members of his family. Precisely what political views Paul Foucault held are difficult to determine. What scant evidence we have suggests he was a somewhat conventional bourgeois liberal. Clearly, his commitment to the medical profession was one of the decisive traits of his identity. While many Poitiers doctors left some trail of their wartime activity—whether because they embraced Vichy, like Barnsby, or because they joined the Resistance, like some of his colleagues—Paul Foucault seems to have gone out of his way to avoid adopting any public political position during this difficult period. Foucault's brother, Denys, observes that "politics" was indeed a "major preoccupation" of family conversations. He recalls, however, no significant tensions. "My parents were on the right," he remembers, while quickly adding: "and yet . . ." (*quoique*).[112] But while Paul Foucault remained politically inconspicuous throughout the Occupation, his professional contacts with medical

Pétainism was most likely one of the primary ways in which the young Foucault acquainted himself with the new regime's ideology.

Given his commitment to his profession, it is not surprising that Paul Foucault was, before the war, an active member of his medical union, the Syndicat Médical de la Vienne (Medical Union of the Vienne). This organization was the local branch of the main French doctor's union, the Confédération Générale des Syndicats Médicaux (General Confederation of Medical Unions). This union was formed when two previous organizations merged in 1929 to defend the French medical profession as the country was moving toward a national health insurance system. In 1928, parliament had passed a "unified social insurance law that covered the risks of illness, disability, maternity, and old age."[113] A second law was passed in 1930. While the Confédération Générale worked to defend liberal medicine against advancing socialization, it also devoted its efforts to protecting the profession from what many regarded as the threat of foreign doctors, often from Eastern Europe, who arrived in the 1920s and 1930s. Since many of these doctors were Jewish, the union's protectionist measures often had an anti-Semitic character. One historian writes that in the 1930s, the union "tirelessly and continuously waged a fierce battle for the exclusion of foreigners and Jews."[114] In particular, union members complained about what they called a "medical plethora," that is, a surfeit of doctors who would lower the quality of—as well as the costs of practicing—medicine. This rhetoric was also, in many instances, residually anti-Semitic.[115]

Within two years of the union's creation, Paul Foucault had become regularly involved in the local chapter, the Syndicat Médical de la Vienne. For instance, he attended its general assembly in December 1931. Dr. Barnsby was also present, as was Dr. Morichau-Beauchant (who was discussed in the last chapter).[116] Paul Foucault regularly attended the organization's general assemblies in subsequent years (in December 1932, November 1936, November 1937, and May 1938).[117] In the late 1930s, he served first as deputy secretary, then secretary of the *syndicat*.[118] In 1937, he represented the Vienne at the interunion group for the Charentes-Poitou region.[119] Based on the minutes published in the union's professional journal, the Vienne union did not seem particularly concerned with the problem of foreign doctors, no doubt because few immigrants came to the region before 1938. The Syndicat Médical de la Vienne addressed issues such as health policy, medical ethics, and bread-and-butter issues like fee rates. At the 1931 meeting, for instance, Paul Foucault had presented a report with his colleague and neighbor

Dr. Maurice-Paul Veluet requesting an increase in the fees paid for reports by forensic pathologists.[120] The union's members were also concerned with protecting their status as a "liberal profession" in a decade in which there was growing momentum for national health insurance.

After France's defeat, however, medical unions were placed on a new footing, to ensure their compatibility with Pétain's national revolution. On October 7, 1940, the existing medical trade unions (including the Confédération Générale and its affiliates) were abolished and replaced with the Ordre des Médicins (Order of Doctors). In keeping with Vichy's corporatist principles, the Ordre des Médicins was intended to be a self-governing corporation that would include all French doctors and provide them with a conduit for interacting with the state. Such an idea was not, in itself, new: doctors had attempted but failed to organize their profession on a similar basis during the interwar years, while lawyers had established an *ordre* that dated back to the Second Empire. According to one historian, Vichy created the Ordre des Médicins to satisfy a long-standing demand of the medical profession, which the regime regarded as a sympathetic constituency.[121] Yet while the Ordre des Médicins did embrace xenophobic and conservative positions, its relationship with the regime was ultimately awkward. When Xavier Vallat, who ran the Commissariat Général pour les Questions Juives, Vichy's main Jewish affairs agency, proposed limiting the number of Jews in the medical profession to 2 percent of non-Jewish doctors, the Ordre des Médicins' governing council balked at the idea that the law would apply both to current doctors (rather than new ones) and to French Jews. Despite its objections, the August 11, 1941, law applying quotas to the medical (and other professions) went into effect. Thus while the Ordre des Médicins's leadership included avowed Pétanists and members who were close to L'Action française, their preferences were ultimately vetoed, Vichy's commitment to corporatism notwithstanding, as the regime veered increasingly toward biological racism.[122]

In Poitiers, the Syndicat médical de la Vienne became the Ordre des Médecins de la Vienne (Order of Doctors of the Vienne). Its first president was Pierre Barnsby, the same doctor who delivered the speech condemning egoism at Poitiers's Hôtel-Dieu in 1941. The *syndicat*'s regional journal—which covered the Vienne and four proximate departments—was reborn as the journal of the Ordre des médicins, under the title *Charentes et Poitou*. Since Paul Foucault was a member of the *ordre*, one imagines that this publication might have been found its way to the Foucault household. An early issue printed a speech by one Dr. Barraud, the Ordre des Médicins' president in nearby Charentes

Maritimes, suggests the flavor of its rhetoric. Echoing Marshal Pétain's own words, the doctor lamented the fact that the period preceding France's defeat was placed under "the double sign of the spirit of pleasure and the taste for lucre," two "seeds of death" that had "irreversibly infected French society." The "general decadence of French morality" that had prevailed over the previous quarter century had not only "murdered the nation's collective soul," but also "corroded the medical soul." The "wild and frantic egoism of those under forty did not hesitate to shamelessly trample on the venerated principles of the medical brotherhood." True, medical unions had done an admirable job protecting the profession, but their efforts had been limited to "particularistic needs." Man does not live by bread alone, the president recalled. Before the war, the "medical mystique was dying." [123] This trend was exemplified by prewar social legislation, which defined price scales for medical procedures that recognized only the "commercial value" of their work, making their charges indistinguishable from the "bill of a plumber or a car mechanic." [124] Thus it was imperative that the "Ordre des médecins think first of all about the soul!" Quoting Alphonse Daudet, he called on doctors to fulfill their mission to become the "last priest, the supreme belief"—to renounce, in other words, a purely materialistic understanding of their vocation. [125] The address concluded: "[Though they are] doctors of bodies, the practitioners of the Ordre des médecins can and must also be [doctors] of intellects and minds, which are intoxicated and led astray by bad shepherds." [126] Not only did this address partake in the critique of egoism and pecuniary interests that Foucault had been reminded of in 1983, but it also specifically referenced the idea, to which Foucault would refer on a number of occasions, that the doctor has "taken over from the priest"—only in this instance, the claim was not historical, but programmatic: doctors were summoned to assume, in Vichy's New Order, a spiritual role that supervened on their purely medical responsibilities. [127]

Far from being a straightforward scientific journal, *Charentes et Poitou* sought to rally the medical profession to the cause of Vichy's *révolution nationale*. Its pages are replete with examples of medical Pétainism: a concern with protecting society against is enemies, fighting various forms of medical and psychological "abnormality," and promoting "normalization" as a condition of national health. In this way, the medical Pétainism that expressed itself with such vigor in Paul Foucault's circles during this period uncannily prefigures some of his son's major concerns. Medicine, in this context, became one of the primary terrains on which society could be defended against threats to health, vigor, and moral rectitude. One article spoke of the importance of addressing

"problems of social defense" and "social peril[s]," [128] while another denounced
the "social gangrene" afflicting France. [129] Addressing the ravages of alcoholism,
the author of one article declared, in no uncertain terms: "The defense of this
country against alcoholics belongs to the immense task of 'social defense' for
which I cannot hide my admiration." [130] In 1976, Foucault, of course, devoted
an entire lecture series to the theme "Society Must Be Defended," examining
the notion—which in the wake of May 1968 had once again become commonplace—that "power has as its responsibility the defense of society." [131]

Among the threats to society that medical Pétainism feared were various kinds of "abnormality" and "abnormal" behavior. In *Charentes et Poitou*,
this issue was addressed in a tone of moral urgency by one Jacques Trivas,
a doctor who ran the psychiatric hospital in Niort, one department to the
west of the Vienne. In March 1941, Trivas published an article entitled "The
Problem of Abnormal Childhood," which amounted to a manifesto of sorts
of medical Pétainism. The premise of his essay was that abnormal childhood
constitutes a full-fledeged "social peril." [132] This problem took many forms,
which Trivas carefully classified: intellectual abnormalities, which could be
either uncurable or perfectible; abnormalities of character, which were also
either uncurable—as with perverts—or perfectible, through discipline; epi-
leptic or encephalitic abnormalities; sensory-motor deficiencies; and juvenile
delinquency. Because for years childhood had not "been protected from the
dangers lying in wait for it," the time was ripe for a "a new social policy"
allowing doctors finally to gain fully control of the problem of childhood. [133]

Trivas also published a two-part article on the ravages of alcoholism in
contemporary France. In addition to equating alcoholism with military defeat
and parliamentarism (since the wine lobby made sure that it had *députés*
looking out for its interests), Trivas tied it to an array of deviant behaviors.
The actions of alcoholics brought them to "psychiatric hospitals, hospitals for
the abnormal, [and] prisons, too." [134] He notes the impact of alcohol on crime,
both because some acts were committed in a state of inebriation and because
of the "number of abnormal people who commit crimes or misdemean-
ors and whose defects result from inherited alcoholism." [135] Trivas's report
received national attention, too: in 1941, the right-wing polemicist Léon Daudet praised it in an editorial in *L'action française*, asserting: "It remains obvious that the defense of the country against alcoholism is part of the vast work
undertaken by Marshal Pétain." [136] Vichy also encouraged a repressive policy
toward venereal diseases, which were viewed as a social threat but also as a
harbinger of moral dissolution. As *Charentes et Poitou* informed its readers

in an article from May 1941, the regime required afflicted individuals to tell their doctors who had contaminated them.[137] Medical Pétainism's obsession with abnormal behavior prefigures a pervasive theme in Foucault's work, one that he likely first grappled with as a justification for repressive social policies during Vichy. Not only did Foucault devote an entire lecture series to the problem of *les anormaux* ("abnormal people"), but the advent of "normalization" as a distinctly modern form of power became a leitmotif of his thought.

Medical Pétainism was also replete with the critique of "egoism" and the praise of robust social bonds that Foucault remembered as being so characteristic of Vichy's discourse. Trivas claimed that alcoholism was evidence of the "cellular anarchism of our social organism." His efforts to fight alcoholism were driven by a need for "social regeneration." This task was difficult because there were "too many egoisms, interests small and great" that had to be overcome.[138] Daudet maintained that individual liberty had no standing when efforts like the anti-alcohol campaign were being pursued to restore national health: "Individual liberty cannot be invoked to allow thousands of alcoholics to spread degeneration, crime, and misery." And alcoholism's ravages justified, in Daudet's view, the long-standing demand of "psychiatrists and criminologists" for "effective legislation" and a "medical-legal organization" of the problem.[139] There is no denying that Vichy's discourse was firmly anchored on the political right: Daudet invoked the old libel that the Paris Commune was fueled by absinthe, and Trivas argued that alcoholism had been exacerbated, in the interwar year, by laws giving workers fewer work hours (encouraging "laziness") and evolving gender roles (as it became socially acceptable for women to frequent cafés).[140] Yet as Foucault suggests in his comments from 1983, he was inclined to see rhetoric denouncing "egoism" and proclaiming "solidarity" as elements of a single discourse, admitting right-wing as well as left-wing variations. His belief that socialist speech relayed *Vichyssois* motifs—or at least, themes that socialism and conservatism shared—is a further reason for Foucault's ambivalence toward the political left.

Make Live and Make Die:
The Assassination of Doctor Guérin

A little before midnight on May 13, 1943, Paul Foucault was informed that his services were urgently needed. A colleague, a fellow doctor, had been attacked and was gravely wounded. The elder Foucault hurried to one of the clinics where he worked, the Clinique du Pont-Achard, located at 1, Rue Georges-Guynemer, less than a ten-minute drive from his home. There, he found Michel Guérin, a thirty-six-year-old doctor, in critical condition. He had at least a dozen wounds, some from blunt force, others from stabbing. His lung had been pierced by a stiletto that had entered below his right shoulder blade. Another weapon had penetrated his stomach. Before long, the police arrived. Doctor Foucault allowed them to question his patient. The latter told the police that he remembered his assailants crying "Kill him!" At 2:30 in the morning, Guérin died on the operating table. None of his wounds should have been life-threatening, but his profuse bleeding proved fatal.[141]

Guérin was not only a doctor, but an outspoken collaborator and notorious right-wing sympathizer. Born outside of Poitiers in 1907, he was, as a young man, drawn to the monarchical and ultra-Catholic ideas of Charles Maurras and joined his political movement L'Action française. Around 1938, Guérin completed his medical studies, defending a thesis at the University of Toulouse. He returned to Poitiers to practice medicine. He participated in the local medical society, where he crossed paths with Paul Foucault. Soon, however, he was called to the colors. After fighting in what he saw as a pointless war, he wound up in a German POW camp, embittered by a defeat that he blamed on a corrupt and decadent republic. While imprisoned, his spiritual mission was revealed to him: he would serve Marshal Pétain and his national revolution, which was founded, as he saw it, on "a new conception of life," requiring "abnegation, a spirit of sacrifice, and self-renunciation." "The national revolution," he asserted, "is, ultimately, nothing more than a Christian conception of existence." Upon release, he found his way back to Poitiers.

While continuing his medical practice, Guérin became one of the most distinctive voices at L'avenir de la Vienne, which, following the German takeover, became the leading collaborationist newspaper. Using the pseudonym "Pierre Chavigny"—though his true identity seems to have been widely known—he feverishly supported Pétain and expressed considerable sympathy for the Nazis. He frequently berated local officials for their lack of zeal for the national revolution. When Bourgain was named regional prefect, Guérin publicly welcomed him, lamenting the fact that the prefecture still displayed the motto "Liberty, Equality, Fraternity" and a bust of Marianne, the republican icon.[142] Guérin praised Hitler's willingness to meet Pierre Laval to discuss France's place in the "new Europe," touting the encounter as evidence that France could "dominate its defeat."[143] He led the local branch of the Parti Populaire Français (French Popular Party, or PPF), the fascist-inspired party led by Jacques Doriot. In April 1942, Guérin proudly welcomed Doriot to Poitiers. Fresh from fighting alongside the Germans in Russia as a member of the League of French Volunteers (Ligue des Volontaires Français), Doriot addressed a rally and was interviewed by Guérin for L'avenir de la Vienne.[144]

Guérin also partook in the anti-individualistic, prosolidarity rhetoric that Foucault associated with Vichy. For instance, in May 1943, Guérin observed that measures that the regime had recently implemented regulating potato growing would be met with the "howls of impenitent individualists" lamenting the loss of their prior freedom. He concluded: "Solidarity is no longer a vain word. If its application must change certain habits, no one can deny that the national interest can impose these measures, the excellence of which is evident."[145] In one of his final columns, he denounced Vichy as a "reign of mediocrities." The regime's personnel, he complained, was tone-deaf to the "mystique of the national revolution." They simply rallied to whichever political adventurer flattered the "egotistical sentiments" of "bureaucrats trained in the school of the Third Republic."[146]

Guérin's political outlook was intimately connected to his medical views: he embraced a particularly virulent form of medical Pétainism. Shortly before the war, Guérin published the thesis he defended at the University of Toulouse on contemporary doctrines concerning marriage and reproduction, entitled "Mariage et stérilite: Les problèmes médicaux et moraux de la continence périodique" (Marriage and sterility: the medical and moral problems of periodic continence). The thesis shamelessly laced an allegedly medical treatise with dogmatic Catholicism. Specifically, Guérin attacked the rhythm method of birth control, which he referred to it as the "Ogino-Knaus hypothesis" (after the two doctors, Kyusaku Ogino and Hermann Knaus, who independently discovered the contraceptive implications of calculating a woman's menstrual cycle). The rhythm method, Guérin contended, was "contrary to marriage's primary ends." It was "perverse" to follow a "calendar based on human calculations" that would "knowingly disregard marriage's goal."[147] Far from being a form of birth control consistent with Catholicism, the rhythm method exemplified the soulless materialism of contemporary society and negated authentic sexuality. Though, for animals, copulation is merely the "satisfaction of a physiological need," sex, for human beings, can be "the most poetic of actions, under the condition that it is the normal and logical culmination of pure love between two beings who have devoted themselves to one another," a story that ends happily with "fertilization." The "most beautiful pages of humanity's history," Guérin writes, "were written by fathers and mothers."[148] True medicine should never lend support to those who would deny the "laws of nature" or render it unworthy of "man, this being whom the Creator sought to make in his image."[149]

Yet Guérin's traditionalism paradoxically committed him to the very modern policy of natalism, the notion that governments should actively encourage citizens to have more children. For France, Guérin maintained, fertility is "a question of life and death."[150] The country faced a stark alternative: "Either the French family will once again become fertile, or the name of France will disappear from the world's map. And the fertility that French women did not want to accept of their husbands, will, tomorrow, be joyfully received by their daughters from conquering barbarian hordes."[151] While Guérin believed the state had a role to play in promoting births, special responsibility befell the medical profession. Doctors could contribute to "modifying the popular mentality" on this matter, not least through their own personal example. And they should address this matter with the requisite "seriousness": "easy jokes" and "immoral advice" should be "banished from their conversations" about childbirth.[152]

A little before 11 P.M. on May 13, 1943, a young man knocked at the door of the house in Poitiers where Guérin lived with his parents. Claiming that his aunt, whom the doctor knew and who lived nearby, had taken ill, he begged Guérin to accompany him. When they arrived at the address, located on a steep street leading to the Clain River, three other men emerged from the darkness. They fell on the doctor, assaulting him with hammers, nightsticks, and knives. Reaching for the pistol that he carried with him, Guérin managed to fire several times. But by the time the assailants had dispersed, he was gravely wounded.

A few hours later, he died in Paul Foucault's clinic.[153] The perpetrators were arrested soon afterward. One of them, a twenty-one-year-old named Jacques Delaunay, was in his third year at the Poitiers medical school, where he likely crossed paths with Paul Foucault. Attendees at Guérin's funeral in Poitiers included not only representatives of the collaborationist local government and the PPF, but also the ubiquitous Dr. Pierre Barnsby, who, in his capacity as president of the Conseil de l'Ordre des Médecins, delivered a "brief and moving address."[154]

Through their connection to Guérin, the Foucault family was dragged into one of the more dramatic episodes occurring in Poitiers under German occupation. Guérin exemplified the discourse that Foucault associated with the Vichy regime, with its denunciation of "egoism," understood as a synonym for prewar capitalism, materialism, and bourgeois republicanism, and its call for "solidarity" as a means to regenerate the nation. If he was indeed a friend of Paul Foucault's, Guérin may have been one of the individuals from whom Foucault heard this rhetoric; it was, in any case, available to most Poitiers residents through Guérin's regular columns in *L'avenir de la Vienne*. Guérin was also a fierce advocate of medical Pétainism and a member in good standing of Poitiers's medical community. Both he and Paul Foucault attended, for instance, meetings of the Vienne medical society.[155] As a member of Doriot's PPF, Guérin may have been the closest the Foucault family got to a bona fide French fascist.

Guérin epitomized, moreover, the contradictions that Foucault would later see as emblematic of fascism. Drawing on an ultratraditionalist conception of marriage to advocate natalism, Guérin's thinking lay at the crossroads of what Foucault called the deployment of alliance, based on marital relations and lineage, and the deployment of sexuality, premised on fertility. Guérin's story constitutes, finally, a kind of parable illustrating a further trait that Foucault attributed to Nazism: that fascists could not affirm life without tempting death. Guérin had endorsed a frankly biopolitical program for regenerating the French nation. Yet in his relentless denunciation of Vichy's traitors and even its lethargic supporters, he seems to have chosen the fate that befell him, promoting a society in which, as Foucault later put it, "everyone has the right of life and death over their neighbor," even as he fell victim to it.[156] This latter-day prophet of the biblical injunction to "be fruitful and multiply"[157] drew his last breath lying—his body drained of much of its blood—on Paul Foucault's operating table. Foucault once wrote that "the preoccupation with blood and law has haunted, for nearly two centuries, the management of sexuality."[158] Guérin's passion was the objective correlative of this idea, an experiential matrix in which it was formed.

Grotesque Power: Fascism (1)

The great modern philosopher of power never wrote a study of Nazism, despite its unique place in modern history. Yet in his analysis of power's various iterations, Foucault frequently referred to fascism, using it as a foil for pinpointing the distinctive ways in which power functions in modern societies. The high-water mark of his reflections on Nazism occurred between 1975 and 1977, when several decisive contexts converged: as he fine-tuned his genealogical method, Foucault began to devote himself explicitly to understanding power as such; in the wake of May 1968, the term "fascism" had, on the far left, become a commonplace for referring to modern society's most repressive tendencies; and the 1970s were also a period when the Nazi experience and the question of French wartime collaboration reentered the collective consciousness. During these years, Foucault not only reflected on the philosophical significance of Nazism and fascism but betrayed an intuitive understanding of and familiarity with those movements, rooted in his own experience. For a thinker whose thought is often seen as frustratingly abstract, Foucault's references to fascism have an immediate and emotional quality.

One of his first passing reflections on fascism occurs in an interview from the fall of 1975 when Foucault was lecturing in São Paulo, Brazil, where he arrived in early October. The previous month, he had traveled to Madrid with six other activists (including the magazine editor Jean Daniel, the writer Régis Debray, the Greek filmmaker Costa-Gavras, and Yves Montand, the singer and actor) to protest the imminent execution of eleven opponents to Franco's regime. When the group attempted to read a statement at their hotel in Madrid on September 22, policemen in civilian clothes brandishing machine guns pushed Foucault and his collaborators into a van, drove them to the airport, and expelled them from the country. Fascism forms the background to the 1975 interview in two respects: Foucault had recently experienced firsthand the security forces of one of the last regimes in Europe to trace its origins to the fascist moment of the 1930s; and in Brazil, Foucault found himself in a country undergoing similar repression and whose military dictatorship, which came to power in a 1964 coup, was described by many as fascist.[159] A visceral sense of fascism's nature, Foucault reflected, had been lost, at least in Europe. Hence the importance of the incident in Spain: "What frightened us," Foucault explained, "was to feel the presence of fascism. We have childhood memories of France under German occupation, but since then, we have lost contact with this presence. But there, we felt it."[160]

The incident in Spain specifically triggered one set of childhood memories: the silence of crowds as they witnessed arrests. As the journalists were handcuffed by the police and Foucault's group was escorted to the police van, Foucault "found once again the spectacle that we already knew from the German occupation: the silence of the crowd that sees and says nothing. We felt their sympathy for us, from the other side of the guards' and police's barrier. People who recognized a familiar scene and who say to themselves: more imprisoned people. People who observe, once again, the same rituals they have been seeing for a very long time. It is pathetic: the presence of fascism inscribed in the body and behavior of the people who are subject to it."[161] This passage sheds light on the intimate character of Foucault's experience with fascism. Fascism, as he saw it, made evident the fact that power is rarely a purely external phenomenon, but is often internalized by those who are subject to it. To live under fascism means not simply to take orders from fascists, but to have a fascist body, to engage in fascist gestures and motions. Fascism was, moreover, remarkable for the silence it produced and depended on. Silence, as we have seen, was an idea with deep emotional resonance for Foucault. It was a term he used to describe his father and the medical world, the silence of doctors underwriting their claims to knowledge. Significantly, Paul Foucault seems to have refrained (unlike some of his medical colleagues) from making any public political pronouncements during the Occupation: perhaps the elder Foucault's silence as a doctor became associated, in the mind of his son, with his silence in the face of fascism. At the same time, Foucault also believed that speaking out was crucial to challenging power: only when the mad and prisoners broke the deafening silence surrounding their confinement could their status be challenged. The silence of crowds pointed, in short, to one way to contest fascism. The experience in Spain (and, perhaps, Brazil) crystallized, from the vantage point of his fully developed theoretical positions, Foucault's lived experience of fascism as an adolescent in Poitiers.

In a lecture delivered on January 8, 1975, Foucault invoked fascism and Nazism to illustrate a particular way in which power operates: by brazenly displaying its "grotesque" or "ubuesque" qualities (the latter term being a reference to Alfred Jarry's 1896 play Ubu roi and its absurdist depiction of a dictatorial king). Certain forms of power, Foucault posited, derive their effects from their very preposterousness—from the fact that they are "manifestly, explicitly, voluntarily disqualified by the odious, the repugnant, and the ridiculous."[162] Power in its most ludicrous manifestations does not discredit itself but demonstrates its "unavoidability [and] inevitability," the way its "violent rationality" can continue without interruption even "in the hands of someone who has been effectively disqualified."[163]

While the precise experiences that generated these insights cannot be known, it is not difficult to imagine how the arrival of German troops in Poitiers might have inspired an uncanny terror of the ridiculous. In the early days of the Occupation, German marching bands paraded in Place des Armes, playing fifes, brass instruments, and drums. Wearing their Nazi insignia, German officers sat on the terraces of the cafés in the town center or dined in groups at the better restaurants. In the evenings, they caroused in nightclubs and bordellos reserved exclusively for Germans. They behaved, in short, like vulgar tourists, even as they impressed the reality of military occupation on the town's residents. A different form of grotesque was on display at local movie theaters, which played the grossly anti-Semitic *Jud Süß* (Süss the Jew) and the virulently anti-British *Ohm Krüger* (Uncle Krüger).

Perhaps the most likely model for Foucault's reflections on the grotesque was the notorious Milice Française. Created by Vichy in 1943, the Milice was a political police force charged with ensuring order, suppressing the black market, and cracking down on burgeoning Resistance forces.[164] The Milice was not established in Poitiers until the spring of 1944, after it had been authorized to operate in the occupied zone. Its headquarters were located on the Place d'Armes, just across from the town hall; its primary dormitory was situated on the Rue Jean Jaurès, two blocks from where Foucault attended school. At the Caserne des Dunes, the military barracks overlooking the city from the east, the Milice also opened a school for training the Franc-Garde, the organization's paramilitary wing. At the formal inauguration of the Milice's headquarters in May 1944—less than a month before D-Day—the local leader, Louis Aussenac, delivered an address that spelled out the group's blatantly fascist beliefs, using the same rhetoric that Foucault later compared to the Left's: "The Milice, born out of a desire for struggle, was raised in struggle: a struggle against the old regime, a struggle against bourgeois and liberal society, against the deep and distant causes of our fatherland's decadence." It was fighting for the "new France of tomorrow," which would be a "new land of liberty"—not the liberty that allows "the individual to act as they wish in all domains, the liberty of the jungle," but "liberties that would be the reward for communities that have demonstrated their vitality and, within these communities, for individuals who have demonstrated their sense of valor and duty." Meanwhile, the Milice waged war against "Gaullist dissidence, against Bolshevism, against Jewish imperialism, [and against] Anglo-Saxon freemasonry."[165]

Yet beneath the Milice's conservative, law-and-order rhetoric lurked a proclivity for chaos, deviance, and sadism that illustrated Foucault's reflections on power's "grotesqueness" all too well. Like other right-wing paramilitary groups, the Milice was immediately recognizable by its unusual uniforms: boots, dark trousers and waist jackets, khaki shirts, and a distinctive left-sloping beret. They also wore a lapel pin shaped like the Greek letter gamma, which represented the zodiacal sign of Aries, a symbol of energy and renewal. Yet while they cultivated an image of suave defenders of public order, the Milice's recruits consisted to a considerable degree of militant fascists and young men hoping to avoid obligatory labor service in Germany. Many were drawn to enlist because the organization promised free clothes, lodging, and a regular paycheck. Some joined to avoid prison.

Given the profile of their recruits, it is perhaps unsurprising that the Milice soon became associated with extreme behavior and gratuitous violence. The antics of the *miliciens* in Poitiers would almost have been comical were it not for their frank brutality. Even collaborators despised the Milice. Prefect Bourgain described Aussenac, the Milice's chief in Poitiers, as a "dangerous madman and a megalomaniac."[166] Aussenac and his men provided ample justification for such characterizations. For instance, in 1944, on Bastille Day— which Vichy regarded as a day of shame—a group of *miliciens*, some holding handguns, raided the prefecture to track down busts of Marianne, a symbol of the republican tradition they abhorred. When they discovered two reproductions of the statue of Minerva that had been founded in Poitiers decades earlier, they tried to whisk them off, confusing the Gallo-Roman goddess with the republican icon. Bourgain had to intercede to remove the *miliciens* from the premises, angrily deriding their leader as a *petit voyou*—a little punk.[167] Late one spring evening in 1944, Aussenac and his band were seen punching, kicking, and pistol-whipping a man at the Place d'Armes.[168] For many, the Milice was little more than state-sponsored delinquency. One police official remarked: "Aussenac literally invaded the city of Poitiers with his numerous and well-armed troops, against which police officers could oppose almost no resistance. . . . The Milice has engaged in genuine harassment toward the police, going so far as to arrest and detain officers of the peace under the pretext that they had not saluted officers of the Milice."[169]

The most horrific incident involving the Milice in Poitiers occurred in August 1944, barely two weeks before the town was liberated. As Occupation forces and Vichy personnel withdrew in the face of the Allied advance, a Milice unit from Bordeaux had retreated to Poitiers. When a young man in a café at the Place d'Armes dared to predict an imminent Allied victory a little too loudly, two of the Bordeaux *miliciens*, who happened to be sitting nearby, arrested him and took him to headquarters. The man refused to name the "terrorists" he knew; the *miliciens* proceeded to break his arm, burn his leg to the bone, and beat his face to a pulp. In agony, the prisoner muttered a few names. As a result, around eight other Poitevins were arrested the following day. That afternoon, the prisoners were brought to the Chateau de Porteau, an aristocratic residence perched on a hill northwest of Poitiers, where the Bordeaux unit was stationed. The *miliciens* brought the prisoners into the chateau's main hall, took their money and valuables, and beat them. When they protested, asking to speak to the leader, a *milicien* replied: "We have no leader; we are the only masters here." The *miliciens*, along with several German soldiers, raided the chateau's wine cellars, and spent the night drinking, eating, singing—and torturing their victims with orgiastic abandon. A German witness described the night as "one of the most awful of my life." One prisoner was undressed, and, as he stood naked, was ordered to identify his "accomplices" or be shot. They beat him and burned him with hot tongs, then crushed his skull with a piece of wood, gouged out his eyes, and threw his body down a well. Several other prisoners were dealt a similar fate. A female prisoner was allegedly gang raped. The other prisoners were released. The next day, the Bordeaux *miliciens* and their Poitiers counterparts retreated to the east.[170]

In Foucault's remarks on fascism, it is possible to detect both outrage and scorn—outrage at its violence, and scorn at the ludicrous, uncouth way in which it wields power. His concept of the "grotesqueness" of power captures both these sentiments. In his 1975 lecture, Foucault cited Mussolini as the embodiment of a form of power emanating from someone "theatrically disguised . . . as a clown, as a fool."[171] And who, Foucault asked, better exemplified the idea of the "repugnant sovereign" than "the little man with trembling hands who, from the depths of his bunker, with forty million dead under his belt, now asked for but two things: that everything that still remained above him be destroyed and that he be brought chocolate cakes until he had stuffed himself to death"?[172] It is striking that in each of these cases, grotesqueness implies adults behaving in childish ways—as if Nazism impressed the young Foucault in the way it disrupted acceptable adult behavior.

But Foucault's scorn was most evident when he described the Nazis as "petty bourgeois." In doing so, he was not being sociological, but simply insulting: as we have seen, "petty bourgeois" was a term he always used with obvious contempt (not least at what he saw as his own family origins, even if they were not petty bourgeois). This is particularly evident in an interview from 1975 (roughly contemporaneous with his "grotesqueness of power" comments) when Foucault was asked about a wave of recent films that eroticized Nazism, connecting it in particular to sadomasochism. This connection, Foucault insisted, was based on a "total historical mistake." "Nazism," he asserted, "was not invented by the great erotic madmen of the twentieth century, but by the most sinister, dull, and disgusting petty bourgeois imaginable." Foucault continues in a vein that blends antifascism with unapologetic *mépris social* (class contempt). Himmler, he notes, was "vaguely an agronomist"; to make matters worse, he married a nurse. Echoing Martin Heidegger's comparison of the death camps to the mechanized food industry, Foucault contends that the camps were the product of the "joint imagination of a hospital nurse and a poultry breeder." He goes on to say that the Nazis were "cleaning ladies in the bad sense of the word," in their embodiment of the "revolting petty bourgeois dream of racial cleanliness, which underpinned the Nazi dream."[173] If anything, it is Nazis' petty-bourgeois obliteration of eroticism that makes them so frightening.

Foucault's view of Nazism and fascism was thus premised on a patronizing scorn for their "grotesqueness" and "petty bourgeois" drudgery, not unlike the contempt with which many, in Poitiers, viewed the Milice. Yet he also came to realize that in asserting their very hideousness—as the Milice constantly did—fascist movements were no less terrifying, providing a sobering lesson on power's inescapability.

Exposure to Death: Fascism (2)

What struck Foucault most about the Nazis, at least once he was able to formulate his intuitions in explicit terms, was how they justified their authority on a willingness to expose *themselves*—and not just others—to death. A lucid recognition of one's mortality, as well as a disposition to precipitate death, became, for the Nazis, a font of strength and power. Discussing Nazism in his 1976 lectures, Foucault observes: "The destruction of other races is one facet of the project, the other facet being to expose one's own race to the absolute and universal danger of death. The risk of dying, exposure to total destruction, is one of the principles inscribed in the fundamental duties of Nazi obedience. . . . One must arrive at a point at which the entire population is exposed to death."[174] The Nazi state manages to be at once "absolutely racist," "absolutely murderous," and "absolutely suicidal." The superimposition of these attributes on another results "in both the 'final solution' (through which they sought to eliminate, by way of the Jews, all the other races of which the Jews were the symbol and the manifestation) of 1942–1943, and . . . telegram 71, through which, in April 1945, Hitler gave the order to destroy the conditions of life of the German people itself."[175] In the introductory volume to *History of Sexuality*, Foucault theorized this insight by situating Nazism in the transition from a "society of blood" to a "society of sex." In the former, "power speaks *through* blood": the "honor of war and fear of famines, the triumph of death, the sovereign with his sword, executioners and torture"; in the latter, "power speaks *of* and *to* sexuality": "health, offspring, race, the future of the species, the vitality of the social body."[176] While these power regimes are distinct, Foucault maintains, the transition from the one to the other involved frequent overlapping: "in various ways, the preoccupation with blood and the law has, for nearly two centuries, haunted the management of sexuality." The most striking examples of power forms blending these two models are biological racism and Nazism. In these instances, "theme of blood was called on to reinvigorate and to support . . . the type of political power that is exercised through the deployment of sexuality." Nazism is the "most naive and cunning—the one because of the other—combination of fantasies of blood with the paroxysms of disciplinary power." Foucault explained: "A eugenic ordering of society, with what it entailed in terms of the extension and intensification of micropowers, under cover of unlimited expansion of the state, is accompanied by an oneiric exaltation of superior blood: this implies both a systematic genocide of others and the risk of exposing oneself to a total sacrifice."[177] Nazism's appeal to the archaic mystique of blood provides a rationale to a distinctly modern ordering of society, on disciplinary and biological principles.

Yet a paradoxical caveat to the claims that Nazism made in the name of superior blood was, in Foucault's view, that they could be redeemed only by exposing the population endowed with this blood to annihilation. The idea that a willingness to die can justify claims to power and to knowledge and truth runs through much of Foucault's work. As a philosophical proposition, its origins undoubtedly lie in Foucault's reading, during his student years, of Heidegger's *Being and Time*. According to the German philosopher, authentic existence (*Dasein*) involves a resolute disposition in the face of death, understood not just as a point at which life ends, but as the way in which finitude molds existence as such. Heidegger writes: "Primordial and authentic coming-toward-oneself is the meaning of existing in one's ownmost nullity."[178] Only when humans grasp with utter lucidity the way finitude saturates their entire being can they achieve authenticity and coincide with being's purest possibility. In his earliest work, Foucault sought to show that Heidegger's insight was not pathbreaking, but already embedded in modern epistemology's most basic assumptions. As Kant's work demonstrates, the vast claims made by modern forms of knowledge lie in their refutation of the view that human beings can assume the standpoint of God precisely because they acknowledge and embrace their finite nature. The disingenuous humility inhering in arguments tying knowledge (in its empirical and transcendental forms) to human finitude is the essence, for Foucault, of the humanist swindle.

Yet this connection between mortality, knowledge, and truth could also assume, for Foucault, a more positive form. He liked to argue that propositional statements—the adequacy of words to facts—were far from being the only form of truth to have existed historically. At times, the ability to speak or reveal the truth is linked to the ability to make existential commitments that put life itself into play. This is the case, he explained in 1971, in ordeals, that is, in "physical tests" in which one "exposes oneself or exposes someone to indefinite danger."[179] In his studies of the relationship between law and truth in the early 1970s, Foucault contrasted the model of the medieval custom of the ordeal (*épreuve*), in which the truth of an allegation was determined by a battle to the death between two opponents, to the early modern idea of inquiry (*enquête*), in which a third-party judge proclaimed a seemingly disinterested verdict.[180] In the way that it asserted power—and the health of the German population—by exposing its own people to death, Nazism not only brought back the "regime of blood" but also revived the ordeal—a form of power and knowledge that was liberated from the modern will to truth. Beneath these fruits of Foucault's mature thought lurks a visceral fascination with a disposition to risk death and the truth effects that it entails.

Foucault shows, in his writings, an attitude toward Nazism and fascism that is at once derisive and ambivalent. In 1977, Foucault wrote a preface to the English translation of *Anti-Oedipus*, the rambling philosophical-political manifesto written by his friend the philosopher Gilles Deleuze and the anti-psychiatrist Félix Guattari. The book's "major enemy," its "strategic adversary," Foucault explained, was "fascism." In his explanation of what he meant by "fascism," the historical and personal overlap. Deleuze and Guattari's target, he maintained, is "not only historical fascism, the fascism of Hitler and Mussolini—which was able to mobilize and use the desire of the masses so effectively—but also the fascism in us all, in our heads and in our everyday behavior, the fascism that causes us to love power, to desire the very thing that dominates and exploits us."[181] Foucault's use of the first-person plural pronoun is revealing: in this way, he acknowledges, even as he presents his statement as an insight about human nature, that fascism implies an erotics of power—to which he was not immune. To reckon with fascism is to come to terms with the entwinement of power and desire, while recognizing that this entwinement is dangerous. An acknowledgment of fascist eroticism is evident in Foucault's claim that Nazism had revived the ancient practices of the "society of blood" from within the highly medicalized and biopoliticized "society of sex." To the masturbating child or the boy who longs for his classmate, fantasies of violent mastery might well "reinvigorate" (to use Foucault's term in *History of Sexuality*) these ambivalent desires.

Even so, the lesson of *Anti-Oedipus* was that fascism remained the enemy. Fascism focuses our attention on the concatenation of power and desire; yet it is equally important to recognize that, with fascism, power completely colonizes desire. Fascism may harbor an erotics of power, but this is the only erotics it allows. Foucault says as much in his analysis of the Marquis de Sade, whom he treats as a functional equivalent of Nazism, insofar as both make a half turn back to "the society of blood" from within the "society of sex." Foucault writes: "Sex, in Sade's work, has no norm, no intrinsic rule that could be formulated on the basis of its own nature; but it is subject to the unlimited law of a power that itself knows only its own." Sade champions the "unlimited right of an all-powerful monstrosity"; with him, "blood has reabsorbed sex."[182] For similar reasons, Foucault concludes, the Nazi regime, for all its bloodlust, remained curiously prudish: "Hitlerian sex policy . . . remained a derisory practice."[183]

While Foucault's insights about fascism and Nazism are the product of a thinker at the height of his intellectual powers, they were nonetheless rooted in earlier and more inchoate experiences. Fascism taught Foucault that something in "our heads and in our everyday behavior . . . causes us to love power." Yet the problem with desiring power is that it can be so all consuming as to leave little room for desire itself. There was little in Nazism's erotics of power that was genuinely erotic. Fascism is evidence of one of the most sobering lessons about power, the fact that people "desire the very thing that dominates and exploits" them. Desired servitude is, arguably, the ultimate political problem. But Nazism also instructs as to why we must learn to wean ourselves from our love of power. While sexual relations may also be power relations, the former must not be annihilated by the latter. An intuitive understanding of power's erotics, as well as a recognition of power's ability to obliterate and impoverish sexuality, constitute the experiential backdrop to Foucault's insights into fascism—and perhaps, into power as such.

"Whether We Would Die or Not": Poitiers Bombarded

During Foucault's adolescence, of course, Nazism's danse macabre was hardly an abstract proposition. By 1944, the annihilation to which Hitler's regime exposed Germany and the occupied countries had become a terrifying reality for many Europeans, including Foucault and his family. The Allied invasion on June 6, 1944, sparked hope, but it also marked a return to life-threatening combat. The Vienne witnessed a stream of German troops rushing through it to reach the front up north. "The uninterrupted flow of troops crossing [Poitiers] in disparate vehicles," one historian writes, "suggested an army in rout."[184] Resistance forces, under the leadership of the Forces Françaises de l'Intérieur (French Forces of the Interior, or FFI), launched a relentless sabotage campaign to slow down Germany's ability to reinforce its positions against the Allies. In Poitiers's environs, the battle raged between *résistant* and occupier: "Murder, rape, summary executions, [and] burned homes marked the path of these new 'infernal columns.'"[185] Prefect Bourgain negotiated with German authorities to discourage them from engaging in mass destruction as their imminent retreat became inevitable.[186]

Though the Germans did not destroy everything in their wake, their mere presence exposed Poitiers to the threat of aerial bombing. The Foucault household was particularly sensitive to this danger because of their proximity to the train station, which had already been bombed in June 1940. After D-Day, the family prepared for the worse. Foucault's brother recalled: "We knew that the neighborhood of the train station would be bombed. Thus everyone who lived around it was asked to go elsewhere. So my parents lived temporarily on the Place de la Liberté"—at the time, Place d'Armes—"while we children were already on holiday in Vendeuvre," the family's home outside the city.[187]

The Allied invasion thus set the stage for the most devastating bombing in Poitiers's history—which also posed an existential threat to the Foucault family. Poitiers attracted the attention of Allied forces because of its strategic location along the Paris-Bordeaux-Bayonne railroad line. On June 12, British intelligence was informed that a large number of German troops would be spending the night aboard trains in the Poitiers station. That evening some 116 Royal Air Force planes took off from England, headed toward France.

The planes reached the skies over Poitiers at 1:41 A.M. Air-raid sirens screeched; the sky, already lit by a full moon, was illuminated by the flares of the RAF's Mosquito Pathfinders. Their target was the area of the Boivre valley, west of central Poitiers, where the train station is located—a rectangular area measuring about a mile and half north-south and several hundred meters east-west. For nearly half an hour, 112 Lancaster bombers took their bomb runs in turn, unleashing ordinance onto the station and surrounding areas.[188] During the attack, fifteen hundred bombs—475 tons of iron and steel—fell on Poitiers.[189] Back in England, the RAF bomber command reported that the raid on Poitiers was the most successful of the night.[190]

On the ground, the devastation was total. One witness who lived in neighboring Civray recalled, upon learning that Poitiers had been bombed, cycling into town, where his wife was in the hospital: "The sky . . . was dusty. From time to time, deafening explosions here and there. On the rails, disemboweled train cars that civilians were starting to explore. One crossed people who, without a word, immobile, contemplated this desolation, completely dumbstruck." From the valley where the station is located, he took the debris-strewn stairs. "At the bottom of the Rue Arthur Ranc"—one block from the Foucault home—"there was a movie theater reserved for the [German] troops, the Soldaten Kino, [called] the Majestic. Perhaps it served as a dormitory, [as] wounded and dead people were being brought out of it."[191] The next day, L'avenir de la Vienne, reporting on the "night of terror" inflicted by so-called Allied aircraft, described the "slow and painful searches" for survivors: "to the spectacle of desolation was added the horror of the first victims, struck down without having attempted the slightest gesture of defense." Noting that the area immediately around the train station had been "pulverized," the article explained that parts of the city center had been hit by smaller, incendiary bombs. It named specific streets that had been struck, specifically Rue Arthur Ranc and adjacent streets such as Boulevard de Verdun and Rue de la Marne (Figure 10).[192]

Jacques Melin, a resident of Iteuil, ten kilometers to Poitiers's south, remembered being awakened by the noise of the planes and the intense light glowing through his open window. With his parents, he and other residents of the town went to a high spot from which they could watch the city's bombing. The next day, he came to town and discovered an "apocalyptic spectacle": "The entire valley, with the station, had been razed: train cars, locomotives, and rails were raised to the sky, buildings were crushed. . . . An acrid odor of dust and powder seized people by the throat."[193] Bernard Guionnet, a boy of fifteen at the time, visited the area several days after the bombing. Observing the station district from town, he later recalled: "The view was absolutely apocalyptic: the contours of the Boulevard du Grand-Cerf were no longer identifiable. Rubble was piled up everywhere, semicalcified skeletons of beams stood with nothing left to hold up, carcasses of cars covering, here and there, the entire scene. . . . The smell of burnt matter was mixed in with that of scorched cloth, carbonized wood, cooked paint and, at times, a whiff of decomposed flesh. Here and there one still found a few wisps of smoke that rose straight up into the summer sky." Guionnet further remembered: "And there reigned a haunting silence, interrupted only, from time to time, by the distant bark of a dog, without the din of

Figure 10. Poitiers after the June 13, 1944, bombing. The camera is facing east, toward the city center. In the foreground is what remains of the train station. In the upper right-hand corner lies Rue Arthur Ranc, where the Foucault home was located. The dark tower along the horizon to the right is the central post office, located one block east of the Foucaults'. P.2.4, Médiathèque François-Mitterrand, Grand Poitiers Communauté urbaine.

a city to cover them up. The effect was to give the impression that a world had ended, the night of June 13."[194] The official casualty count was 239 dead and 363 wounded. Some two thousand buildings had been damaged, of which two hundred were completely destroyed and 456 had to be torn down.[195]

Reflecting on this period of his life, Foucault later recalled: "We did not know whether we would die or not in the bombing."[196] Though the June 1940 air raid had also terrified the city, it was to the unprecedented destruction inflicted on June 13, 1944, that Foucault was presumably referring. On that night, Foucault, then seventeen, tasted death like never before. He and his siblings were twenty kilometers north of Poitiers in the family's country home in Vendeuvre. Perhaps, like Jacques Melin, they were awakened by the thundering explosions and the illuminated night sky. They too may have found a spot from which to observe the spectacle of the city's destruction from afar. We do not know if their parents were with them; if not, the children probably knew their parents were not at the Rue Arthur Ranc house, but at the slightly safer residence they had taken on the Place d'Armes. Even so, Foucault would have had no way of knowing, in the middle of the bombardment, if the city center had been spared. Telephone communications and electricity were cut after the bombing, making prompt communication difficult. Foucault may well have spent hours wondering if his parents were still alive. Even if he knew his parents were safe, he must have imagined all the people he knew who might have perished in the bombing. And Vendeuvre was hardly far enough from Poitiers to dispel the fear that Foucault's own life could be at risk.

The Foucault home escaped destruction by pure chance. The Cinéma Majestic on Rue Jacques de Grailly, which received a direct hit, was less than a hundred meters away. A slight modification of the bomb's trajectory could have devastated the townhouse at 10, Rue Arthur Ranc. This is borne out in a certified report by a bailiff who, at Paul Foucault's request, visited the property on June 21, a week after the bombing. The report noted that Paul Foucault had commissioned the bailiff to make note of the damage resulting from "the aerial bombardment of June 12 and 13," so that the family could make "urgent and necessary repairs" needed to prevent further damage. Most windows on the building's three floors had been blown out. The ceiling in Paul Foucault's examination room (where he received some patients) had collapsed. In the linen and maids' rooms, located on the top floor, the building's roof had been pierced in multiple places. "As for the greenhouse and the garage," the report added, "they were crushed by a bomb (one can see an automobile amid the debris). . . . The garden itself was devastated."[197] The garage, located just up the street, was totally destroyed, indicating that another bomb only barely missed the main house (Figure 11).[198]

As his subsequent remarks suggest, the June 13, 1944 bombings were the first of several experiences in Foucault's life in which he faced the imminent prospect of death. This incident foreshadowed his suicide attempts in Paris in the late 1940s and his collision with an automobile in 1978. The damage inflicted on his family home and the fact that it avoided destruction only thanks to a miniscule variation in a plane's flight plan and bomb run seem to have reinforced Foucault's view that his home provided no protection against a menacing outer world. Like the townhouse's roof following the bombings, the Foucault household appeared to be penetrated by hostile, life-threatening forces. Furthermore, the devastation inflicted on Poitiers—not by the grotesque Nazis, but by the British "liberators"—may well have given the lie to the repression of violent and aggressive impulses that was central to bourgeois child rearing and education. The psychoanalysts Anna Freud and Dorothy

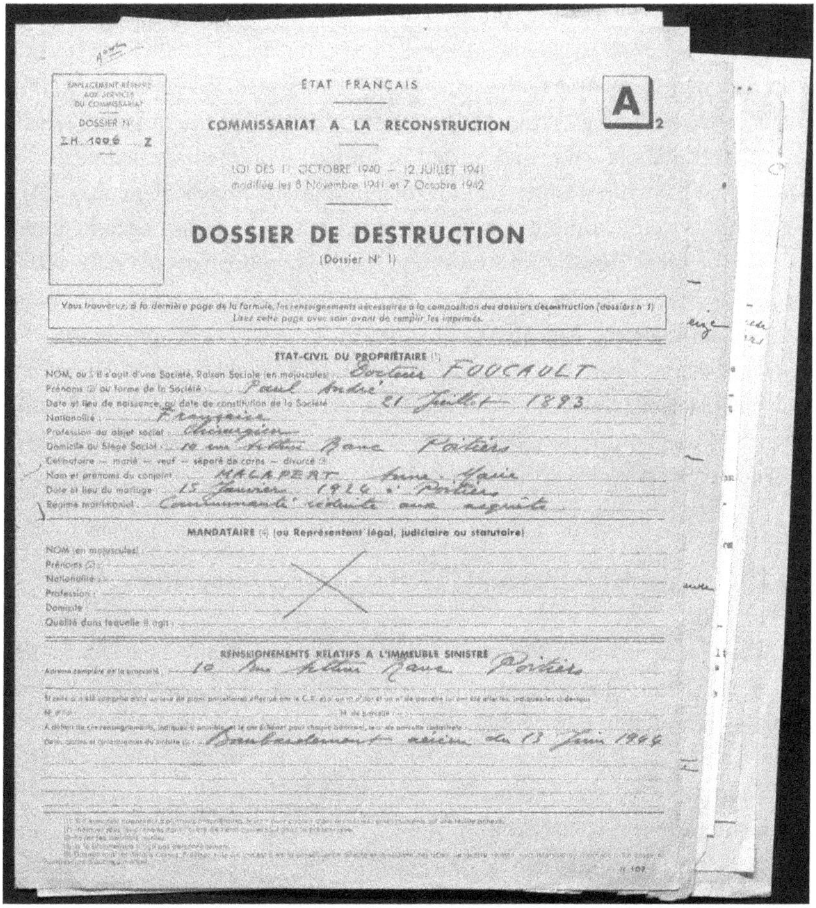
ÉTAT FRANÇAIS

COMMISSARIAT A LA RECONSTRUCTION

LOI DES 11 OCTOBRE 1940 — 12 JUILLET 1941
modifiée les 8 Novembre 1941 et 7 Octobre 1942

DOSSIER DE DESTRUCTION
(Dossier N° 1)

A 2

EMPLACEMENT RÉSERVÉ AUX SERVICES DU COMMISSARIAT
DOSSIER N°
ZH 1006 Z

Vous trouverez, à la dernière page de la formule, les renseignements nécessaires à la composition des dossiers de construction (dossiers n° 1)
Lisez cette page avec soin avant de remplir les imprimés.

ÉTAT-CIVIL DU PROPRIÉTAIRE (1)

NOM, ou s'il s'agit d'une Société, Raison Sociale (en majuscules): Docteur FOUCAULT
Prénoms (2) ou forme de la Société: Paul André
Date et lieu de naissance, ou date de constitution de la Société: 21 Juillet 1893
Nationalité: Française
Profession ou objet social: Chirurgien
Domicile ou Siège Social: 10 rue Arthur Ranc Poitiers
Célibataire — marié — veuf — séparé de corps — divorcé (3)
Nom et prénoms du conjoint: MALAPERT Anne-Marie
Date et lieu du mariage: 15 Janvier 1924 à Poitiers
Régime matrimonial: Communauté réduite aux acquêts

MANDATAIRE (4) (ou Représentant légal, judiciaire ou statutaire)

NOM (en majuscules):
Prénoms (2):
Nationalité:
Profession:
Domicile:
Qualité dans laquelle il agit:

RENSEIGNEMENTS RELATIFS A L'IMMEUBLE SINISTRÉ

Adresse complète de la propriété: 10 Rue Arthur Ranc Poitiers

Date, causes et circonstances du sinistre: Bombardement aérien du 13 Juin 1944

Figure 11. "Destruction Dossier," filed by Foucault's parents as part of their application to the Reconstruction Commissariat for funds to help repair their home. The reason given for the destruction: "aerial bombardment of June 13, 1944." Archives Départementales des Deux-Sèvres et de la Vienne.

Burlingham reflected on the different forms of "air-raid anxiety" experienced by children they encountered during the Blitz at Hampstead Nurseries in London. While children can often cope with the "real anxiety" provoked by air raids, a more difficult problem is the way bombings can rekindle the violent instincts they have just learned to control. A child, Freud and Burlingham write, "learns to criticize and overcome in himself certain instinctive wishes, or rather he learns to refuse them conscious expression. He learns that it is bad to kill, to hurt, and to destroy, and would like to believe that he has no further wish to do any of these things. But he can only keep up this attitude when the people in the outer world do likewise. When he sees killing and destruction going on outside it arouses his fear that the impulses which he has only a short while ago buried in himself will be awakened again."[199] Foucault's fascination with violence, death, and sadomasochism may trace their origins to the bombings and the feelings with which they became intertwined: the sense that the world was a perpetual conflict between destructive forces and that a heightened experience of one's own mortality was the purest form of authenticity. It is significant that in the lectures on psychology he delivered at the École Normale Supérieure in his twenties, some nine years after the bombings, Foucault specifically referenced Freud and Burlingham's work.[200] While Foucault's interest in death most likely preceded the bombing, the war years crystallized this obsession.

Popular Justice and Failed Revolution: Liberation

As Allied forces advanced through France toward Germany after D-Day, the region surrounding Poitiers degenerated into a war of all against all. As they redeployed to fight enemy forces and soon prepared to retreat, the Germans clashed with the Resistance forces that congregated in the Poitou's forests. The Germans' goal was to send reinforcements to the northern frontline and to safeguard major transportation routes, while the Resistance, in coordination with the Allies and de Gaulle's Free French forces, engaged in sabotage and military actions to slow down German troop movements. On June 27, German troops searching the Saint-Sauvant Forest south of Poitiers ran into a group of *résistants*, resulting in thirty-three French and twenty-seven German deaths. Not far away, in the town of Le Vigeant, on August 4, Germans punished local inhabitants they believed were providing supplies to the *maquis* (i.e., decentralized rural Resistance groups) by executing twenty-two of them, including two teenagers. In this context of generalized violence, the distinction between military actions, revenge, and crime became meaningless. On July 22, in the village of Bourg-Archambault, located southeast of Poitiers, a unit of Franc-Tireurs et Partisans (FTP), the Communist resistant organization, shot twenty-four men and women, burying them near a stream. A subsequent inquiry determined that the FTP unit in question was led by two Jews of Polish origin, and that they had stolen jewelry and 140,000 francs from their victims. The inquiry concluded that the killings had no motive but personal enrichment and revenge, calling the incident "an execution of bourgeois whose possible pro-German activity was not even investigated by their executors."[201] Writing to Prefect Bourgain around this time, one official commented: "The population is terrorized."[202]

The Gestapo and the Milice evacuated Poitiers on August 23. Six days later, they were followed by the Feldkommandantur. By September 4, there were no Germans remaining in the town. Poitiers was not, like many towns, liberated by regular armed forces. Rather, the vacuum left by the German retreat was replaced by the "army of the shadows"— *maquisards* who were now formally under the command of Charles de Gaulle and his newly proclaimed Provisional Government of the Republic. Thus Poitiers, as one historian describes it, found itself in the hands not of "disciplined soldiers, but men who had often proclaimed themselves colonels, captains, or lieutenants and who, in some cases, knew but one authority, one police, one justice: that of the submachine gun they held in their hands."[203]

To lay the legal basis for a new republican regime, de Gaulle had placed each liberated department under the authority of a commissioner of the republic, working in conjunction with a Department Liberation Committee. In the Vienne, the commissioner was an energetic thirty-six-year-old lawyer named Jean Schuhler. Regime change in Poitiers could not have been more dramatic. On September 5, Schuhler and a band of *maquisards* marched to the prefecture, where Prefect Bourgain greeted them with sparkling wine. Unfazed, Schuhler immediately placed Bourgain under arrest.[204] In the building that the Gestapo had just vacated on the Rue des Écossais, around the corner from the Foucault home, the FFI set up headquarters, from whence it began purging Poitiers of collaborators.

This purge—or *épuration*—was no neat, law-abiding affair. In the weeks following the Germans' abrupt retreat, it took the form of unabashed and frequently cruel acts of revenge that were only thinly disguised under a veneer of legality. After four years of foreign oppression aided by collaborators, many felt little disposed to exercise forbearance in dealing with those who had benefited from German rule. As Commissioner of the Republic Schuhler put it: "The Liberation was interpreted as the abolition of constraints." "Everywhere," he added, "men and women were detained in improvised prisons, threatened with summary judgments."[205] Like elsewhere in France, the *maquisards* and their supporters shaved the head of women accused of "horizontal collaboration" with the Germans and paraded them through the streets, to the jeers of local population. The mother and father of Dr. Guérin were among those marched through the streets, forced to wear signs marking them as *collabos* (collaborators).[206] In some instances, summary executions occurred with little pretense of legality. In late September, a group of around twenty Hindu and Sikh prisoners belonging to the Waffen SS's Free India Legion were being transported by the FFI through Poitiers when their truck was stopped in the city's main square, the Place d'Armes (where Foucault's parents had taken up residence during the June bombings). Before a crowd of spectators, several were shot in broad daylight.[207]

In other cases, however, *maquisards* established their own courts. Often, they wrapped themselves in the mantle of "popular justice," a major theme in *épuration* discourse, particularly in the Communist press. Maurice Rolland, a resistant who had been promoted to an inspector general of services, captured the atmosphere in Poitiers during these weeks: "This peaceful region, where temperaments are more inclined to calmness than to energy, was, at the moment of the Liberation, taken over by numerous Resistance organizations, who showed little discipline and were eager for revenge and rewards."[208] This spirit was captured by an article in *Libre Poitou*, a clandestine newspaper that went public after the Liberation, which listed the collaborators—particularly *miliciens*—who had been tried and summarily executed by FFI military tribunals before concluding: "Of course, there are still lots of bastards to be eliminated. But they will not escape from ineluctable justice."[209] In Poitiers, a *maquis* commander who was known as *"La Chouette"* (the owl) headed up a people's court comprising fellow combatants that issued several death sentences, as their deliberations were, according to one witness, "assiduously followed by a horde of shrews who expressed their opinion by crying out for death."[210] In some cases, this conception of popular justice was explicitly connected to the French revolutionary tradition: an article in the communist newspaper *Le patriote poitevin* reviewed the "lessons of the terror," encouraging the patriots of 1945 to consider the efforts of their counterparts in 1793. It concluded: "let us be sure to draw inspiration from the healthy vigor with which the men of '93 [that is, 1793] struck the enemies of the People within, in order to fight, with greater security, against enemies without, let us be worthy of these men who, in addition to a great example, bequeath to us one of the great pages in the history of France."[211]

In a context in which the line separating justice from vengeance had been practically effaced, Schuhler, as the representative of an incipient state authority, sought to channel popular outrage toward more conventional legal processes. In September, a military tribunal was created, which, after new instructions were issued by the provisional government, by a court of justice consisting of a presiding judge and a jury comprising four members of the Resistance or victims of the Occupation. The *Patriote poitevin* did not object, providing the program of revenge could continue without impediment: the newspaper maintained that "the defense, like the prosecution, [should] participate in the punishment of the traitors. Military tribunal, court of justice— it doesn't matter. One must judge, condemn, execute!"[212] Yet as it returned to principles of evidence and fairness, the court made acquittals, much to the audience's displeasure. The courtroom became a showdown between supporters of the vigilante spirit of the *maquis* and Schuhler's efforts to restore authority—though Schuhler recognized that, to do so, he needed to make sure that the court issued guilty verdicts at a steady clip.

Efforts to reimpose "republican legality" so rankled Resistance forces that they even attempted an insurrection. In the fall, the Army Ministry dismissed the *maquisard* in charge of Poitiers's military command, after Schuhler had complained of his unwillingness to discipline his men, most of whom had recently belonged to FFI units. Consequently, on the evening of December 2, 1944, a band of some thousand former *résistants* marched on the prefecture to the beat of military music, shouting slogans denouncing the commissioner of the republic. To forestall any intervention, they had already seized control of police and gendarmerie headquarters. The protestors filled the square in front of the prefecture—only two blocks from the Foucault home—before forcing open its gates and invading the building. Several officials tried unsuccessfully to block the crowd as it forced itself into Schuhler's personal suite.

Daniel Villey, a liberal economist who taught at the University of Poitiers, described the event in the local newspaper: "They cried out, they sang the *Marseillaise* and the *Internationale*, . . . mistreated the carpets in the Commissioner's private apartment, took his silver and other personal objects, kidnapped the hat and gloves of a political officer." Schuhler eventually met with them. Soon afterward, the mob dispersed. Reflecting on the incident, the subprefect at the time concluded: "It is certain that people are easily embittered, but most of them do not like disorder and, to the contrary, seek peacefulness."[213] Villey was appalled at the insouciance with which the *maquisards* resorted to force to achieve their political goals. "What distinguishes an army from a militia [i.e., *milice*]," he opined, "is that a militia pursues special political goals, while an army is a docile instrument in the service of the state. *La milice*, here, is of odious and recent memory. France needs a disciplined army.

The public use of force must be in the hands of the state and its authentic representatives."[214] By early 1945, the authority of the state and the rule of law were returning to Poitiers.[215]

Not only was the question of the relationship between revenge and law one that Foucault would later place at the heart of his reflections on punishment, but he would specifically explore the nature of "popular justice" that had figured prominently in Resistance ideology during the Liberation. Though he referred to it on several occasions in the early 1970s, his most extensive discussion of the concept occurred in a 1972 debate with two radical student Maoists, at a time when the idea of popular justice and popular tribunals had been embraced by the post-1968 radical left as a means for mobilizing workers against the alleged crimes of their capitalist employers. The main idea that Foucault defended in the exchange was that genuine popular justice never takes the form of a tribunal, but always involves direct action by the people against its enemies. He cited the example of the September massacres of 1792, when, responding to the attack on France's borders by conservative forces, Parisian crowds murdered over a thousand prison inmates suspected of treason. Popular justice, in this context, was "an act of war against internal enemies" an "act of vengeance against the oppressive classes," and "retaliation of the masses against . . . their enemies."[216] "Acts of justice that are truly popular," he explained, "tend to elude courts."[217] Rather than bringing in a third party—a judge who represents a neutral standpoint—popular justice consists of a faceoff between the "masses and their enemies." Furthermore, when the masses decide to "punish [their] enemy," they "do not refer to an abstract, universal idea of justice; they refer only to their own experience, the damages to which they were subject, the way they were wronged, the way they were oppressed." Nor does their decision invoke a formal authority, a state apparatus—they execute their decision, "purely and simply."[218] Though his main historical reference point is the Terror, Foucault's account of popular justice harmonizes perfectly with the actions of Resistance movements in Poitiers after the Liberation: in the rhetoric emphasizing popular justice and the punishment of enemies of the people, their disdain for legal formalities, their confidence in their own authority, and their fervent embrace of the purifying virtues of revenge.

The connection between the Terror and the Liberation was so glaring that the parallel could not be avoided—though it was the young radical Benny Lévy who first mentioned it, not Foucault. Lévy cited as "a real but ambiguous" "act of popular justice" the head shavings of the "horizontal collaborators" in 1944. Because "commerce in the most carnal sense of the word with the *Boches* [a derogatory name for Germans] . . . really did physically and morally harm the people," shaving the women's heads could indeed be deemed popular justice. Yet it remained a dubious choice, Lévy argued, because these women were publicly shamed even as more blatant collaborators were let off the hook.[219] Foucault did not respond immediately to Lévy's remark but returned to it several moments later to illustrate his claim that popular justice was incompatible with the court system: "To come back to the example that you gave," he said, "if the people rushed to the women to shave their heads, it is because the collaborators, who should have been [their] natural enemies and on whom popular justice should have been exercised, were stolen from the masses, were stolen away as it was said: 'Oh, those ones are too guilty, we're going to bring them before the court.' . . . They were put in prison, and they were brought to court, which, of course, acquitted them. In this instance, the court served as an alibi in relation to acts of popular justice."[220]

Though Foucault's comments about popular justice and collaboration had no autobiographical intent, they were nonetheless consistent with what happened in Poitiers in the late summer of 1944. After an eruption of acts of revenge and popular violence in August and September, officials of the new provisional government managed to replace vigilante justice with courts that punished some collaborators. In September 1945, Louis Bourgain, the former regional prefect, was condemned to "national indignity," eight years in prison, and the confiscation of his property. By 1948, the Poitiers court had completed its work, having condemned sixty-one individuals to death, 243 to hard labor, 646 to jail time, and 270 to loss of civic rights (*dégradation nationale*). Yet as with similar tribunals throughout France, this long list of sentences was not quite as punitive as it seemed. Only eighteen of the death sentences resulted in executions. Bourgain was pardoned in 1951, before he had completed his time. Even an abhorred figure like Louis Aussenac, the head of Poitiers's Milice, had his death sentence commuted to twenty years of hard labor.[221] Foucault was not wrong in saying that justice fell hardest on those who faced the people's cries for vengeance directly, rather than those who were channeled through the court system.

Resisting the Medical Revolution

In a world that was now defined by the position one had (or claimed to have) taken during the war—collaboration, resistance, and the vast gray area in between—it is striking how scrupulously Foucault's father seems to have avoided taking political sides. Paul Foucault was connected, as we have seen, to the *fascisant* collaborator Michel Guérin, who was still sufficiently reviled after the Liberation that his parents received prison sentences. He participated in the Vichy-controlled Ordre des Médecins. Yet he also had connections to the new, post-Occupation order. Several of Foucault's colleagues at the university and specifically in the medical school had joined the Resistance, some of whom now assumed political positions. René Savatier, a born Poitevin and a prominent legal scholar at the university's law school, was active in the Resistance before his arrest in 1942.[222] At the Liberation, he became the president of the Department Liberation Committee. He was joined by Daniel Villey, a young economist who also taught in the law school and who was active in the Resistance, particularly the underground press. He would later become a member of the Mont Pelerin Society and an outspoken champion of economic liberalism. At the medical school, Jacques Quivy—the colleague whom, as we saw in the first chapter, Paul Foucault once mocked before his students—had joined the Renard Network, an important local Resistance organization, for which he was arrested and spent time in prison.[223] One of the most interesting members of Poitiers's post-Liberation elite was Pierre Barnsby, Paul Foucault's longtime colleague at the medical school and the Hôtel-Dieu who, despite openly collaborating with Occupation authorities as a doctor, managed to acquire sufficient Resistance bona fides to be appointed to the Department Resistance Council. Foucault's father had, in short, managed to have a foot in both camps, with connections both to Vichy and Resistance figures, while closely associating himself with neither.

The reestablishment of the judicial authority of the state, which rechanneled and even disrupted the attempt by Resistance movements to purge France of collaborators through popular justice, represented one attempt to thwart the revolutionary élan of the Liberation. Another attempt occurred in the field of medicine, as certain members of the Resistance tried, with mixed results, to transform the French health-care system. This involved, in the first place, breaking with the medical regime instituted by Vichy. In Poitiers, this rupture was evident in the resurrection of medical trade unionism and a critique of medical Pétainism. In October 1946, nearly two years after Poitiers was liberated, the local medical community relaunched its journal, the *Revue médicale du Centre-Ouest*, announcing that it would now be the mouthpiece for the Vienne branch of the Syndicat des médecins.[224] The following issue included a blistering attack against Vichy and medical collaborators penned by a longtime colleague of Paul Foucault's, René Le Blaye. At least one witness claims that during the war, Doctor Le Blaye had prevented the Germans from arresting an elderly Jewish patient.[225] Le Blaye began by praising the prewar work of the doctors' trade union, which had "to the best of [its] ability served the interest of our profession." But he also recalled his surprise at the new tone adopted by the unions' regional journal in December 1940, once the union had been dissolved and replaced by the Vichy-backed Ordre des médecins. He specifically denounced—without mentioning him by name— the pro-Vichy speech delivered during the war by Dr. Barraud, who had pre-sided over the Ordre des Médecins' local branch. Barraud had welcomed the new regime as a cure to the Third Republic's spirit of "wild and frantic egoism" and the progressive thinking of the eighteenth and nineteenth cen-turies. Le Blaye conceded that Barraud had simply adopted contemporary propaganda, the "aberrations of troubled times." "*O tempora*," he quipped, "o Maurras!" He welcomed the rebirth of the union and its journal and the end of the long silence to which they had been subjected.[226] When Barraud responded by accusing Le Blaye of "aggression," the latter responded that he was simply denouncing Barraud's own "aggression . . . against medical trade unionism" at a time when "the new order was throwing [its supporters] overboard."[227]

Yet while many doctors welcomed the Liberation, they did not necessarily support the agenda embraced by the Resistance and their advocates in the new provisional government. Specifically, the program of the National Coun-cil of the Resistance had called for the establishment of a full-fledged system of social security, broadly similar to the Beveridge Plan, which paved the way for the creation of Britain's National Health Service in 1948. Even patriotic doctors who supported the Resistance opposed what they regarded as the socialist and communist-inspired idea of socialized medicine. In Poitiers, as throughout France, the question of how to respond to the new governments' decrees establishing social security was, in the immediate postwar years, one of the medical community's major preoccupations. The newly reconstituted doctors' unions feared that the 1945 decrees establishing the social security system would violate the Charter of Liberal Medicine, which the unions had drawn up as a condition for accepting the health insurance legislation adopted in 1930. In particular, they worried that that the postwar system would reject the principle of *entente directe*, which held that fees should be determined exclusively by an agreement between doctors and patients.[228]

In 1946, Poitiers's Ordre des Médecins addressed the issue of whether to accept the lower prices mandated by officials in Paris or the somewhat higher prices allowed for by an agreement the union had signed with local authorities. Pierre Laroque, the man de Gaulle had tapped to serve as the director general of Social Security, assured the doctors in a meeting in Limoges that he did not want to aggravate the "statefication [*étatisation*] of medicine."[229] Jacques Quivy, the main intermediary between the Vienne doctors' union and the Social Security administration, had impeccable Resistance credentials yet worried that the reform was threatening the profession's independence. He complained that the "doctrinaires of Social Security" saw the medical profession as a "vampire that takes fees that are far too high" and were committed to the kind of "salaried or bureaucratized medicine" found in "totalitarian states."[230] The goal, as he feared, was to establish a system of "medicine without doctors" (*médecine sans médecins*),[231] in which medicine would be distributed by social workers without medical consultations. What the reformers ignored, he believed, was that the principle of *entente directe*—the agreement between the doctor and patient on an acceptable price for medical services—and the market principles on which it was based could not be legislated out of existence. Doctors willing to charge less and clients prepared to pay more would always find customers and providers. "Little by little," he explained, "the law will be obliged to adopt itself to habits, rather than brutally modifying them."[232]

This discussion was the context for one of Paul Foucault's rare public statements on a political issue. At a meeting of Poitiers's doctors' union held on December 8, 1946, Quivy recommended that the union sign a department-level contract with the Social Security administration that would set prices at a level above the national rate. During this debate, the minutes note, Paul Foucault stated his belief that "it is difficult to apply the *tiers payant* in France."[233] The *tiers payant* or "third-party payer" refers to a system of social insurance in which doctors collect no payment for their services but are reimbursed directly by the state. The state had attempted to introduce this principle after the First World War, in legislation providing medical service for veterans, then in the series of laws that established a system of national health insurance between 1927 and 1930. French doctors' unions vehemently opposed the *tiers payant* principle as a violation of the principles of "liberal medicine" and as an assault on their professional integrity. This position reflected the "liberal and individualistic conception of medical practice" that, for reasons of professional ethics as well of economic self-interest, increasingly prevailed in the profession.[234] Paul Foucault's comment was nothing more and nothing less than a clear endorsement of the vision of liberal medicine and its concomitant distrust of state intervention, a set of beliefs that were constitutive of doctors' professional identity in the first half of the twentieth century. While it was hardly a manifesto, his remark nonetheless defines a coherent, if unremarkable position: as a doctor—his core public identity—Paul Foucault believed that doctors should be free to practice their art while being subject to no other regulations than those set by other members of the profession. He opposed the socialist and statist tendencies of the Liberation government, and, despite any ideological sympathies he may have had for medical Pétanism, he was probably skeptical of Vichy's consistent interference in medical practice. His instincts were those of a conservative liberal, suspicious of government meddling and the emerging welfare state.

In his own highly idiosyncratic way, Foucault shared some of his father's ambivalence towards the Social Security system. The notion of a "right to health" guaranteed by the state was, Foucault contended, meaningless. As an empirical condition, health does not admit "rights," and the boundary between health and sickness is historically and culturally relative (though Foucault recognized that one could demand a right to live and work in conditions that did not significantly harm one's health). The relevant questions were now: "Must a society seek to satisfy the health needs of individuals by collective means? And can [individuals] legitimately demand the satisfaction of these needs?"[235] The solutions to this question, Foucault implied, could only be practical and empirical: they were dependent on the "means of health" available to a given society and could be explored through transforming society into a field of experimentation in which new approaches to health could be tried out. This included, he noted, "an effort at decentralization," in order, for instance, "to bring consumers closer to the decision-making centers under whom they fall and to involve them in decision-making processes."[236] Such solutions needed exploration because the statist and collectivist solutions that had dominated in the immediate postwar years had been undermined by a new social concern with individual autonomy: when basic issues of survival prevailed, people tended not to be concerned by their dependence on the state; but as they became accustomed to better standards of living, dependence became increasingly problematic. Though his concern was with understanding social phenomena like the "right to health" and not the mechanics of social insurance, Foucault's views did overlap with those held by his father in the 1940s: both expressed instinctive unease about statist solutions and preferred to see medicine as a fundamentally relational field, consisting of a tapestry of exchanges between "consumers" and "providers" of health. Whatever Foucault's misgivings about his father's medical practice, he begrudged the older man neither his skepticism about Social Security nor (to a degree, anyway) the conception of the medical profession on which this skepticism was based.

In a 1975 interview, Foucault reflected on why, in recent years, people had begun to imagine that "certain erotic fantasies" could be accessed only through Nazism: "Why these boots, these hats, these eagles, for which there is such a craze?" He wondered if the reason did not lie in the poverty of contemporary sexual imagination: "Is the only vocabulary we possess for retranscribing the great pleasure of the exploding body the sad fable of a recent political apocalypse? [Can we not] think the intensity of the present except as the end of the world in a concentration camp?"[237] Perhaps this insight holds the key to Foucault's bad trip in the New York bathhouse. At first glance, it might seem that Foucault's nightmare—the return of fascism through Reagan—bore an uncanny resemblance to his own sexual desires—the eroticization of confinement, domination, and discipline in places like Man's Country. Yet Foucault suggests otherwise: fascism was not, for him, a trauma he grappled with by sexualizing it, but a direct threat to his desires, one that had to be directly and deliberately resisted. Fascism meant the impoverishment, not the enhancement of bodies and pleasures and a fixation on discipline that foreclosed any recognition of the innumerable relationships and intensities to which bodies are susceptible.

Overcoming fascism was thus a crucial element of Foucault's thought and the experiential matrix from which it emerged. It was one of several ways in which the Second World War contributed to the formation of his personality and intellectual outlook. Wartime Poitiers exposed Foucault to numerous lessons in the volatility and reversibility of power relations. Vichy's policies and the threat of military violence seem to have undermined, in his eyes, the bourgeois idea of the family as an institution intended to shield children from the dangers of the outside world. Most importantly, Foucault was permanently marked by the way in which the war made death an ever-present risk. He came to see death as the vantage point from which human endeavors had to be understood. And exposure to death became the template of the "intensities" he pursued, albeit in other ways, in his intellectual work and relationships. If Foucault spoke so little about his wartime experiences, it was perhaps because they secretly propelled his thinking—a hidden spring of his inner world, effective only insofar as it operated in silence.

CHAPTER 4

Philosophy

The war years, in addition to being experiential matrices in their own right, were also a formative moment in Foucault's education. In 1940, his parents withdrew him from Poitiers's Lycée Henri IV and placed him in the Catholic Collège Saint-Stanislas. During these years, Foucault's dedication to studying reached a fever pitch. In the process, he discovered philosophy, the discipline to which, in his own idiosyncratic way, he would devote his career.

Reflecting on his high school years later in life, Foucault described his schooling as a haven protecting him from the surrounding historical maelstrom: "When I was sixteen or seventeen I knew only one thing: school life was an environment protected from exterior menaces, from politics. And I have always been fascinated by living protected in a scholarly environment, in an intellectual milieu. Knowledge is for me that which must function as a protection of individual existence and as a comprehension of the exterior world. I think that's it. Knowledge as a means of surviving by understanding."[1] In this way, Foucault describes education as an almost ascetic pursuit, a voluntary seclusion from the storm and stress of the world through which one hones one's inner resources. At the very moment when Christian asceticism had begun to elicit his interest, it is as if Foucault were self-consciously identifying with the priests and monks who taught him.

Years earlier, in 1975, Foucault described this phase of his life to a radio interviewer in starkly different terms. Characteristically of what he dubbed the "provincial petty bourgeoisie," he explained that he had been "raised, brought up on knowledge [*savoir*]." "Even before primary school," he had been plunged into a "milieu in which the rule of existence, the rule for advancement, was knowledge—knowing a bit more than others, being a little better at school, . . . even sucking one's bottle better than others, walking for the first time before others." "Exams, competition, doing a little more than others, being number one . . . someone like me has always been part of that. So I did not really enter knowledge; I have always been in knowledge; I was immersed in it." The interviewer responded: "How lucky you are." Foucault sighed, then asked: "Is it luck?"[2] Knowledge, in this interview, appears not as a protective shield but as a terrifying imposition, compelling helpless children to play by the adult world's cruel rules. This picture of knowledge as a ruthless, meaningless game whose value its participants nonetheless celebrate recalls one of Foucault's favorite texts by Nietzsche, "On Truth and Lie in an Extra-Moral Sense." In that essay, after describing the invention of knowledge as the "most mendacious minute of 'world history,'" the philosopher writes: "that haughtiness which goes with knowledge . . ., which shrouds the eyes and senses of man in a blinding fog, [and] therefore deceives him about the value of existence by carrying in itself the most flattering evaluation of knowledge itself."[3] Commenting on this essay, Foucault lauded Nietzsche's conception of knowledge as "nastiness," as characterized by a "murderous tenacity" and a "will" manifesting itself as "violence."[4]

Of course, from the standpoint of Foucault's philosophical position, the two statements are hardly at odds. As Nietzsche contended, knowledge is a way that physically feeble beings can exhibit strength—a "means by which the weaker, less robust individuals preserve themselves, since they are denied the chance of waging the struggle for existence with horns or the fangs of beasts of prey."[5] This knowledge can be both a survival strategy and an act of violence. As a high school student, Foucault displayed both tendencies. His classmates and teachers noted his contrarian and defiant disposition. He quarreled with his father over the latter's expectation that he become a doctor. But Foucault also partook in his family's commitment to advancement through education. "We were born to learn, on my mother's side as much as my father's," Denys Foucault reminisced, adding: "my brother was a brilliant student."[6] And Foucault's claim that studying provided sanctuary from the outside world was not just idle sentiment: in a school that was pressured to embrace Vichy's ideology and where teachers were arrested and in some cases murdered for their political activities, immersing oneself in learning was an eminently plausible form of self-protection.

It was in these years that Foucault was first exposed to philosophy. Perhaps he saw philosophy, too, as a form of knowledge focused on "competition" and "being number one." After all, Nietzsche portrays the philosopher as "the proudest human being," who believes that he can see "the eyes of the universe telescopically focused from all sides on his actions and thoughts."[7] A relative

Figure 12. Foucault at the
Collège Saint-Stanislas,
1940–41. Foucault is on
the left, in shorts. Archives
historiques du diocèse de
Poitiers.

on his mother's side of the family was a prominent Third Republic philosopher. At the Collège Saint-Stanislas (Figure 12), Foucault was in regular contact with an erudite clergyman who would have been his philosophy teacher had he not been imprisoned and deported because of his involvement in the Resistance. An unintended consequence of this event was that it resulted in the young Foucault's introduction to two other philosophers: a monk from a nearby abbey and a university student hired to be Foucault's tutor.

The intellectual impact of his Poitiers upbringing on Foucault's outlook is even harder to pin down than its experiential and emotional impact. Pierre Rivière, a classmate of Foucault's at Saint-Stanislas who went onto become a senior civil servant, reflected: "The question I ask myself . . . is what remained of the Poitevin period in Foucault's education. And I am incapable of answering."[8] By reconstructing the educational world in which Foucault was schooled and focusing in particular on the ideas as well as the example of his teachers and other philosophers to which he was exposed, this chapter will attempt to answer Rivière's question.

In the first place, Foucault's education in Poitiers shaped his initial assumptions about the nature of philosophy. It fashioned, as it were, his philosophical common sense. Specifically, his teachers sanctioned a distinct account of philosophy's historical development, emphasizing—whether from a positive or negative standpoint—the overcoming of theological and metaphysical absolutes by positivism and a subject-centered account of rationality. This philosophical common sense also took for granted that psychology, notably in its most scientific iterations, was central to contemporary philosophical thought (as were, to a lesser extent, other social sciences, such as sociology and pedagogy).

Second, Foucault's early encounters with philosophy gave him firsthand experience with the conflict between secular and Christian thought. The high school Foucault attended was run by a religious order, and many of his teachers, including those who taught philosophy, were priests or monks. While they used standard philosophy textbooks and prepared students for the state-administered *baccalauréat*, these teachers nonetheless presented the conventional narrative of philosophy's history with a notably different emphasis. They examined with genuine erudition the doctrines of modern thinkers like Descartes and Kant, but without celebrating their advent as unequivocal progress. Specifically, these teachers questioned the disenchanted rationalism of the scientific worldview and the central place in modern thought of the individual and *cogito*. At the same time, outside of school (and later in *khâgne*), Foucault was also exposed to the secular philosophy of his day, which was the mainstay of the state educational system of the late Third Republic. Foucault was never, by any stretch of the imagination, a Catholic thinker. Yet his exposure to Catholic thought helped call attention to the shortcomings of mainstream secular philosophy and made alternatives conceivable.

Third, largely through his exposure to the Catholic-secular conflict, Foucault's Poitiers education made him aware of a major motif in this dispute that would become particularly important to his early thinking: the place of "man," humanism, and philosophical anthropology in modern thought. The teleological philosophical narrative endorsed by contemporary secular philosophy usually took for granted that the onset of a philosophical perspective focused on human beings, the inherent dignity of human life, and the limited nature of human knowledge was positive and necessary. Catholic philosophy, however, explicitly challenged the tenets of this thinking, by warning of the moral and intellectual dangers of abandoning theocentrism for anthropocentrism and misinterpreting the implications of modern thought's insights into the finite, contingent, and empirical character of human existence. By no means did these Catholic thinkers subscribe to what Foucault would later call the "death of man" or what became known in France as philosophical antihumanism. But their critique of secular thought's humanistic orientation heightened the visibility of this trend (as would Heidegger, that lapsed Catholic who proved so influential on the young Foucault) and challenged its self-evidence.

Finally, it was during these years that Foucault first learned of—and perhaps read—philosophers who would prove instrumental to the formulation of his own early thought. Of these, the most important was Immanuel Kant. It is, of course, a commonplace that a deeply Kantian strand runs through French academic philosophy of this period. Yet Kant was also a major point of intersection between secular and Catholic thought and exemplified philosophy's anthropocentric turn (a claim that the young Foucault would examine at length). The point is not that Foucault, during his Poitiers years, was decisively influenced by Kant, any more than he was by other philosophical ideas imparted to him by his teachers. It is, rather, that the philosophical common sense that he absorbed in Poitiers provided the background against which the philosophy he later discovered in Paris would appear innovative, while also instilling in him the conventional understanding of philosophy that his Parisian teachers would help him rethink. This chapter thus explores a layer of Foucault's thought in which experience and self-conscious thinking are intertwined, and that provided the immediate backdrop to his first original thought.

Teaching Humanity: Paulin Malapert

The first philosopher Foucault knew was probably his great-uncle Paulin Malapert. Malapert exemplified the bourgeois success achieved by Foucault's mother's family. Of Édouard Prosper Malapert's three sons, one became a doctor (Foucault's grandfather), another a military officer (Colonel Malapert, discussed in the previous chapter), and the third, Paulin, a philosopher and distinguished teacher. Born in 1862, Marie Édouard Jules Paulin Malapert studied at Poitiers's lycée (which his great-nephew Michel would also attend), where his philosophy teacher was Lucien Lévy-Bruhl, later known for his anthropological studies of the primitive mind. Malapert studied in Paris, where he passed the philosophy *agrégation*. After a string of postings at provincial schools, he returned to Paris, where, in 1898, he was appointed to Lycée Louis-le-Grand, one of France's most prestigious secondary schools. Over a career spanning twenty-seven years, he acquired a reputation as a remarkable teacher. In an obituary, a colleague recalled the impression Malapert had made on the "young people of the philosophy class"—that is, the final year of a lycée education—who "received from him such solid lessons in criticism and morality that they would remain alive in their memory."[9] Though he never obtained a university position, Malapert was recognized as a prominent academic philosopher. The great Henri Bergson, for instance, referred to Malapert as a preeminent "moralist."[10]

Because of his work on psychology, Malapert's interests dovetailed considerably with the scientific preoccupations so important to other members of his family. While his Latin thesis was a fairly traditional analysis of Spinoza's political thought,[11] much of his later work also focused on psychology and its philosophical implications. Like his great-nephew, Malapert was interested in the competing claims of traditional philosophical psychology and the emerging field of experimental psychology. In the first volume of a philosophy textbook he authored, Malapert explained that psychology, understood etymologically as "the study of the soul," seeks to grasp the "mysterious principle" that lies at the root of all mental phenomena. "Rational psychology" thus conceived constitutes a "chapter of metaphysics." But psychology can also be understood as "a science that presents itself as the positive study of the phenomena of internal life and their laws." This kind of experimental psychology eschews metaphysical speculation, embracing the project of a "psychology without the soul."[12] Similarly, in one of his first published essays, Foucault also reflected on psychology's alternative claims to epistemological legitimacy: "One of the historical *a prioris* of psychology, in its current form, is this possibility of being, in an exclusionary mode, either scientific or not."[13] Malapert examined many of the same natural psychologists that Foucault would reference in his writings from the 1950s: John Stuart Mill, Alexander Bain, Wilhelm Wundt, and Théodule Ribot. Malapert especially emphasized the role played by early psychiatrists—including those that would be central to Foucault's early thought—in psychology's development. "French *aliénistes*" like "Esquirol [and] Pinel," Malapert noted, had, through "their study of mental anomalies [and] pathological cases," and through their "'clinical' method" "provided precious models of what a psychological study of the mind might be."[14]

While Malapert recognized the importance of experimental psychology and clearly accepted its findings, he also believed that its conclusions confirmed psychology's autonomy from physiology. Anticipating arguments that would soon become mainstays of phenomenology, he defined psychology as the study of states of consciousness. Psychology, he maintained, must

renounce metaphysics and devote itself to positive facts, but the facts it considers must be "facts of consciousness."[15] Facts of this kind necessarily have
a subjective dimension: "Consciousness, in the psychological sense, is *immediate knowledge of an inner phenomenon that is characterized by this knowledge itself.*" From this premise, it followed that all facts of consciousness are
predicated on the existence of a "subject, an *I.*"[16] Psychology's "starting point,"
he contended, must be "inner observation."[17] In 1957, Foucault commented
that fifty years earlier, psychology had been "the good positivist and naturalist
conscience of philosophy curricula."[18] Because Malapert defended traditional
philosophy in an idiom that resonated with experimental psychology, Foucault's assertion applies to him almost perfectly.

Malapert's broader commitment to psychology as a form of knowledge
informed his interest in human character. He defended his major thesis,
entitled "Les éléments du caractère et leurs lois de combinaison" (The elements of character and their laws of combination), in 1897. It was deemed a
major contribution to the philosophical and psychological subfield of ethology—that is, the study of human character. His thesis jury consisted of several contemporary luminaries, including the neo-Kantian philosopher Émile
Boutroux, the educational theorist and politician Ferdinand Buisson, the
psychologist Pierre Janet, and the literary critic Émile Faguet.[19] In his thesis,
Malapert explained that whereas psychology studies the laws of the human
mind, ethology examines how, on the basis of these laws, character is formed.
Consistent with modern psychology's scientific orientation, ethology places
the study of character on rigorous empirical footing. As Malapert explained
at his thesis defense, by studying man not "from the standpoint of unity,"
but from "the standpoint of the multiplicity of psychological functions," the
ethologist circumvents "the terrain of metaphysics" and remains grounded in
the "the realm of facts."[20] In addition to its scientific significance, the study of
character also had, Malapert believed, important moral consequences. Insofar as ethology revealed the fundamental diversity of human character, the
highest ethical goal was for each individual to achieve "the ideal of [their]
own nature" and to strive for the "perfection of personality"—a goal that
Malapert asserted as a challenge to his contemporary Émile Durkheim, who
feared that individualism could result in social dissolution.[21]

The concept of personality, which lay at the core of Malapert's characterology, was also central to Foucault's early writings, particularly his first—and
later disowned—book, *Maladie mentale et personnalité* (Mental illness and
personality). In it, the young Foucault presented and seemed to subscribe

to the psychiatric viewpoint that the notion of personality was the optimal framework for understanding mental illness: madness is, fundamentally, something that happens to personality. "Personality," he observed, is "the element in which illness develops, and the criterion that makes it possible to judge it." "The science of mental pathology," he further remarked, "can only be the science of a sick personality."[22] While Foucault's ideas on personality in the 1950s were sifted through his contemporary readings—particularly psychoanalysis and existential psychology—the commonsense appeal of this category, which is patently absent from his later work, could well have been fixed by his exposure to the ideas of Malapert, as well as the broader intellectual environment to which his great-uncle belonged.

In his studies of human character, Malapert referred repeatedly to a book that would play a decisive role in his great-nephew's intellectual development: Kant's *Anthropology from a Pragmatic Point of View*. The book, comprising lectures delivered over many years at the University of Königsberg, is among Kant's more peculiar writings. It presents itself as a study of human beings (i.e., an *anthropos logos*) from the standpoint of their actions as free creatures (hence the "pragmatic" point of view) through an examination of their faculties (the subject of part 1, the "anthropological didactic") as well their character (the focus of part 2, the "anthropological characteristic"). Along the way, Kant addresses such seemingly disparate topics as desire, madness, physiognomy, and sexual traits. Malapert's interest in the book lay primarily in its prefiguration of characterology. Using Joseph Tissot's 1863 translation (which Foucault's translation would later supersede), Malapert reflected on Kant's attempt to distinguish "character" from mere character traits.[23] He also referenced Kant's ideas about our capacity to change our personalities, his fourfold division of the question of character into personal, sexual, national (or folk), and species characteristics, and his ideas about temperament.[24]

Malapert's nephew would also regard Kant's *Anthropology* as enormously important. In his Kant thesis, however, Foucault was less interested in addressing the book's discrete arguments than in reflecting on the project's broader intellectual significance and its relation to Kant's "Copernican Revolution" in philosophy. What interested Foucault was the way in which, in modern philosophy, "man" became not only the subject of a distinct set of philosophical questions, but the philosophical problem par excellence, through which all other philosophical and epistemological questions must be accessed. Foucault was also intrigued by the way in which a philosopher so concerned with knowledge's transcendental conditions (the crucial question of a priori knowledge, which preoccupied him so deeply) immersed himself, in *Anthropology*, with messy empirical topics such as taste and temperament. Though hardly his main concern, Malapert was clearly aware of these problems. For instance, while noting that in the first two critiques Kant alluded to the problem of character only in the most abstruse metaphysical sense, Malapert observed that *Anthropology* was an "exception" to this tendency in the attention it gave to character's empirical nature and the "psycho-physiological theory" of temperament.[25] The connection between transcendental philosophy and the empirical science of human beings—the problem of "empirico-transcendental doublets"—that was so central to the young Foucault's thought was, at the very least, intuited by Malapert. Despite the many differences between them, Malapert's interest in Kant's *Anthropology* connected his thought to his great-nephew's.

Malapert did not, however, confine himself simply to the theoretical questions raised by philosophy's ever more pronounced psychological orientation. He also invoked his authority as a philosopher to weigh in on social issues, notably pedagogy. In 1906, Malapert was, at least nominally, a candidate for the chair in the science of education at the Sorbonne being vacated by Ferdinand Buisson (a member of his thesis jury). The opposition was formidable: the clear favorite was Émile Durkheim, with Célestin Bouglé as the "phantom candidate" (the designated loser, as it were). The election report, written by Émile Boutroux and Gabriel Séailles, lavished praise on Durkheim and expressed admiration for Bouglé. Their comments on the third candidate were, however, rather cutting: "M. Malapert lacks neither refinement nor penetration" but seems of "lesser stature."[26] Durkheim's success as a philosopher, social scientist, pedagogical theorist, and public moralist cast a long shadow over Malapert's career.

Though lacking Durkheim's intellectual originality, Malapert also wrote pedagogical essays offering moral counsel to contemporary students that rested on broadly "humanistic" principles. At a time when a utilitarian approach to education was becoming widespread, Malapert emphasized the value of "teaching humanity."[27] While assenting to the contemporary doctrine of "solidarism," he nonetheless emphasized freedom and the will as the foundation of human dignity. He warned young people against the temptation of deterministic and materialistic philosophies, which reduce "man to an automaton." It is through man, he claimed, that "nature becomes self-conscious and illuminates itself by the light of reason."[28] Life's purpose, he concluded, is to exercise the will that is constitutive of human nature. Malapert's public philosophy was thus entrenched in his admittedly mainstream conception of humanism.

Another contemporary issue on which Malapert was particularly outspoken was sexual morality, particularly the place of sexual ethics in school curricula. In 1907, as president of the Parisian committee of the Ligue Française de Moralité Publique (French League for Public Morality), he delivered a lecture titled "Schools and the Teaching of Sexual Morality."[29] In 1909, as part of a series of talks organized by the Ligue Française pour l'Hygiène Scolaire (French League for School Hygiene) at the École des Hautes Études Sociales, he spoke on the topic of "sexual morality in schools."[30] A year later, he chaired a plenary session on sexual education at the Third International Conference on School Hygiene.[31] Finally, in 1911, he participated in a meeting of the Société Française de Philosophie devoted to "sexual education," in which Durkheim was one of his interlocutors.[32]

In his many pronouncements on sexual education, Malapert leveraged his status as a teacher and purveyor of knowledge to argue that sexual conduct should, in a modern society, be the object of an explicit pedagogy. Triangulating philosophy, pedagogy, and medicine, he made a case for teachers as agents of public morality and sexual health. Perhaps even more interesting than Malapert's views on sexual ethics as such were his ideas about how they should be taught. He emphasized that rather than simply relying on "attentive, scrupulous, well-considered, [and] prudent surveillance," it was imperative to have frank and open conversation about sex with adolescents. After all, he remarked, it is "not so difficult . . . to talk about sexual morality, without vulgarity but also without obscure obliqueness."[33] But who was best positioned to speak to teenagers about such matters? Parents were the obvious candidates. Mothers, he believed, had an especially important role to play. Chairing a panel at the International Conference on School Hygiene, Malapert said that it was "women and especially mothers that the teacher wants as auxiliaries."[34] "Better than anyone," he explained on another occasion, "mothers are in a position to judge when it is appropriate to provide the child with clarifications . . . [and] from what mouth would the child receive these words with such a degree of respectful and poignant gravity?" Yet Malapert feared that few parents "*dared* fulfill this duty." The education parents needed if they were to discuss these matters was almost as great as the sex education needed by their children.[35] Traditionally, of course, there existed an important alternative to sexual enlightenment by families: the priest. Malapert refused to be drawn into the question of whether the church should have "a monopoly over sexual education,"[36] insisting only that teachers had a special obligation to provide boys with insight into sexual matters—despite the titters and guffaws that the very prospect of mentioning "women" in a class of sixteen-year-olds might elicit.

As for the content of his proposed sexual education, Malapert maintained that premarital abstinence and sexual monogamy were justified within the limits of reason alone. His position was, in the first place, prudential: poor sexual morals were a major cause for the "disorganization of families"[37]—a phrase that evokes the title of Foucault's *Le désordre des familles* (The disorder of families), which examined how old regime families used *lettres de cachet* to rein in unruly and immoral behavior. Malapert was especially critical of the proverb *"il faut que la jeunesse passe"*—roughly, "boys will be boys." He reminded his audience of all the daughters and wives whose reputations were irreparably damaged in the name of allowing young men to sow their wild oats, while also condemning the modern slavery imposed on many women by prostitution. He warned of the ravages of syphilis, that "modern plague," which afflicted, he claimed, one in seven men and no less than one in four students. Lust and permissiveness also resulted in "physical degeneration," "chronic weakness," and "moral debasement," leading to a diminished intellectual ability and a predisposition to psychiatric problems.[38] But over and above sexual license's dangerous effects, Malapert insisted on its inherent depravity. "To dole out love in a mad and sordid way is to debase it," he intoned, "and one does not debase it without debasing oneself."[39] He presented the implications for practical reason in explicitly Kantian terms: "As you can clearly see, it is not simply prudence that recommends chastity to you; it is morality that orders it."[40] He concluded by admonishing his imaginary audience of *lycéens* to embrace an "elevated conception" of love and women and refrain from conduct that might result in their debasement. He advised his charges to get married at a young age to a wholesome girl.[41]

Foucault's great-uncle could be seen as almost the ideal type of a Third Republic philosopher—passionate about secondary education, steeped in a vague personalism, inclined to positivism, politically republican, and broadly humanistic. It is precisely this generic quality of his thought that may have informed—however indirectly and diffusely—Foucault's thought, particularly Malapert's investment in the period's prevailing shibboleths (which, in many ways, form the immediate historical backdrop to Foucault's philosophy). Malapert exemplified the belief that many of philosophy's problems could be resolved through empirical psychology and the social sciences. His

emphasis on Kant highlighted the strategic place that the German philosopher occupied in philosophy's orientation toward a kind of anthropologism.
At the same time, the humanist and positivistic orientation of Malapert's
thought underwrote a program of practical intervention in the lives of young
people, aimed at fostering their education, moral hygiene, and sexual health.
Even if he did not attach undue importance to the terms "human" or "human
nature," Malapert's thought was premised on the view that understanding
human beings lay at the heart of the philosophical enterprise.

Ego Contra: Foucault as Student

One Sunday in October 1947, during a high mass in honor of the Feast of
Christ the King at the chapel of the Collège Saint-Stanislas, a former student
was distracted when he recognized a familiar face. "At the back of our chapel
I had just noticed a sympathetic head, an imposing, even impressive one,
an alum's head, a well-known alum." Unable to put a name to this face, he
approached him. As they spoke, he noted that his old classmate had changed
little since their school days: "Does one not find in him the same facial traits?
Does the conversation not retrace the contours of the same mind, eager to
play the rebel, the *ego contra*, who stung our dear M. Bardinette so deeply,
particularly during religious discussions?" At last, he revealed the mysterious
alum's identity: "Those who go back to these days, I am sure you have already
put a name to this admittedly imperfect description: Paul [i.e., Michel] Foucault." Recounting the story for an alumni newsletter, he explained how Foucault had spent the three years since they last met: "He is living, he says, his
dream life: this year, he is beginning his second year at Normale Supérieure
Letters." In addition to attending "lectures at the Sorbonne," he was living a life
of "great freedom," absorbed in "the most interesting of studies" and devoid of
"rules that impose on us a rigid and detailed schedule" (the narrator added:
"what an advertisement for young people! But it is not for everyone").[42]

   This anecdote highlights a feature of Foucault's behavior that recurs in
accounts of his school days: his reputation as a "rebel," as an *ego contra*, as a
young man who—to state a patently obvious point, from the standpoint of
his later thought—bristled at discipline. This is evident in what is perhaps
Foucault's earliest available writing, an undated school assignment found
in the archives of Poitiers's Lycée Henri IV that seems to have been written
when he was twelve or thirteen years old. Foucault's essay is simply a reading

report—*un compte-rendu de lecture*—of a story from Alexandre Dumas's memoirs, in which the author describes one of the "great terrors" of his life.[43] Dumas wrote:

> I was playing at marbles at the door of a grocer called Lebègue, who was scraping and spreading out chocolate on a marble slab with a long, flexible knife that I believe they call a spatula. I began a dispute with my companion, and we fell to pummeling one another. Please take note that when it was a question of fists, I was never a coward. He was stronger than I, he pushed me roughly back and I fell over backwards into a tub of honey.
>
> I at once saw the consequences of my accident, I uttered a cry which made the grocer look up, and he soon saw what had happened, namely, that, as I have said, I was seated in a tub of honey. I sprang up as though springs were attached to my legs, in spite of the resistance of the substance to which I was glued: and I fled incontinently.
>
> My prudent and rapid flight was due to a view of the grocer dashing out knife in hand at the same time.
>
> I naturally ran in the direction of my home, but it was in the center of the Rue de Lormet, and a good way off the scene of the accident. I ran with all my might, but the grocer's legs were double the length of mine; I was driven by terror, but he was moved by greed. I turned to look behind me as I ran, and saw that awful tradesman, with fiery eyes and open lips and frowning brow, knife in hand, gaining upon me every minute. At last, weltering with heat, panting, speechless, and on the point of a collapse, I flung myself on the pavement ten paces from our door, convinced that it was all over with me, and that Lebègue was pursuing me for no other purpose than to cut my throat.
>
> Nothing of the kind happened. After a struggle, in which I resisted him tooth and nail, he laid me face down on his knees, and scraped the seat of my trousers with his spatula, set me on my feet, and returned perfectly content to his shop.[44]

Foucault's essay, which takes two and a half pages of a *copie double* (two connected leaves of paper, which are commonly used in French schools), is entitled "In the Honey." It is nothing more than a routine assignment,

completed in class or as homework, that for some arbitrary reason was preserved in his school file. In his retelling of Dumas's story, Foucault notes that
the incident occurred while Alexandre is "still a child." He emphasizes the
marble game and the fight with his friend, noting the latter's greater strength.
Foucault makes the connection between the unexpected outcome of the
boys' brawl and the intrusion of a threatening adult into the children's play
even tighter than in the original version. No sooner had the young Dumas
fallen into the tub of honey, Foucault wrote, than the grocer appeared "with a
knife in hand as if to kill the victim." Dumas does not make his fear that the
grown-up might "cut [his] throat" clear until the story's conclusion, nor does
he refer to himself as a "victim." Foucault also dwells on the twist that occurs
at the tale's end, when the grocer "caught up with Alexandre, laid him on
him, scraped the seat of his trousers [*son fond de culotte*], and left." Presumably in response to a teacher's instructions, Foucault, in the next paragraph,
describes "the details that struck him": "when the little boy fell into the honey,
when Alexandre thought that the grocer was going to kill him, and when the
grocer did not get upset."[45]

Reflecting on the significance of a randomly preserved school assignment
might seem fruitless—no different from trying to assign meaning to Nietzsche's
notorious fragment, "I have forgotten my umbrella," given that, as one of Foucault's more famous students would later write, "we never will know *for sure*
what Nietzsche wanted to say or do when he noted these words, nor even that
he actually *wanted* anything."[46] At minimum, the story, in Foucault's recounting, describes a world in which children and their games are subject to terrifying and inscrutable retribution from adults. After engaging his friend in
a brawl, which is presumably forbidden behavior, and failing, moreover, to
assert himself, the young boy involuntarily sullies himself when he falls into
the tub of honey. This action triggers a sudden and frightening reaction on the
part of the story's only adult, who is portrayed as physically overpowering. The
adult's action is perceived, moreover, as an existential threat, as if falling into
the honey—and tarnishing his trousers with a viscous substance—made him
deserving of the highest punishment. In Foucault's retelling, this fear of death—
of being killed by a grown man—is central to the narrative.

In Foucault's account, the story ends on an ambivalent note. On the one
hand, Foucault is surprised by the fact that, contrary to what his actions had
suggested, the grocer was not angry. On the other hand, the story's conclusion
is unsettling, even perverse. By bending him over his knee, the grocer seems
to prepare the boy for a spanking. Instead, he uses a spatula—which Foucault

refers to as a knife—to scrape the honey off the "seat of his pants." Despite its punchline's humor—the grocer intended no harm, he just wanted his honey back—there is something disturbing about the way the adult authoritatively takes hold of the boy's body, runs his tool over his backside, and lays claim—and implicitly valorizes—something that the boy had, moments ago, assumed to be transgressive. The French phrase—*"fond de culotte"*—lends itself, moreover, to a double entendre: while referring to the boy's pants, the word "culotte" can also refer to underwear. Thus while we know nothing about what Foucault thought when he completed his assignment, it does seem to revolve around a number of motifs: disobedient behavior (specifically fighting), a threatening male adult, fear of punishment and even death, shame, and implicit sexualization or objectification.

Several years later, during the war, Foucault had been identified as a problem by his new philosophy teacher at Saint-Stanislas. Marcel Pierrot, a Benedictine monk at the abbey in nearby Ligugé, had replaced Father Bardinette—the teacher who, according to the alumni newsletter, had been the target of Foucault's rebellious behavior. When in old age he wrote his autobiography, Pierrot included the following story from January 1943:

> I have among my philosophy students Michel Foucault, the son of a surgeon in Poitiers and who has since made a name for himself in contemporary philosophy.
>
> He is seventeen years old. He is exceptionally intelligent. [Father Joseph] Braud [the headmaster] fears him and rightly considers him to be the class ringleader.
>
> "If you can win him over [*faire sa conquête*], you will have peace," he tells me.
>
> After a few days, Michel Foucault comes to see me. Very laid back and confident in himself, he began to disparage the school and its administrative staff, the teaching offered, etc.
>
> I let him speak, listening attentively to him. I answered simply:
>
> "Thank you, Michel, but I thought if you came to see me, it would be to tell me something other than school gossip. A boy like you must have something else to say. Would you like us to talk about philosophy?[47]

The struggle between the boy and the adult that Foucault described in in his *compte-rendu* now took the form of a conflict between a student and his teachers—one in which the student at least temporarily had the upper hand. Fear has changed sides: the youth inspires trepidation, not the adult. Rather than running away, the young man approaches his teacher with assurance, unafraid to berate the latter's peers. Even so, the adult, once again, prevails, and manages to *faire sa conquête*—not by making a perverse claim on his body, but by admonishing him to philosophize.

After earning his *baccalauréat* at Saint-Stanislas, Foucault returned to Poitiers's Lycée Henri IV to do his *khâgne*—the rigorous humanistic training taken in view of passing the entrance exam to the École Normale Supérieure. The question of discipline continued to hound him. In his school file, one finds a brief statement in Foucault's hand, dated January 17, 1945, when Foucault was eighteen: "I swear on my honor that I will not participate in bullying inside and outside the school on the part of old students against the young and which result in physical abuse, blackmail, [and] the extortion of money."[48] Despite its cryptic nature, the statement seems to allude to the long-standing practice of *bizutage* or "hazing," a notorious rite of passage for new entrants into preparatory courses for the *grandes écoles*. These rituals typically involve older students assuming the roles of *bourreaux*—"executioners" or "torturers"—subjecting newcomers to ordeals of physical pain, vilification and, in some instances, sexual abuse. According to one study, *bizutage* is intended to produce "regenerative depersonalization," creating solidarity among a cohort through "radical physical humiliation."[49] Foucault's signed statement does not, of course, mean that he participated in such rituals; the document may have been a preemptive effort by school officials to prevent the notorious practice from occurring. But the document does suggest that *bizutage* was part of the culture and common sense of "*prépa*" students in the Poitiers of Foucault's generation (Figure 13).

Even as Foucault honed his identity in the field of philosophy, he simultaneously fashioned himself as *ego contra*. The sources discussed above portray Foucault as engaged in an adolescent revolt against an adult world of dubious merit. They suggest, too, that at a young age, Foucault sensed that institutions devoted to the pursuit of knowledge could become arenas for power struggles—hence his willingness to tussle with a priest over "religious questions," his assumption of the role of class "ringleader," and his criticism of his school's administration and pedagogy. Schools were a context in which Foucault came to realize he could succeed, even as he viewed them as oppressive institutions—precisely insofar as they were dedicated to learning—against which he instinctively rebelled.

Figure 13. Foucault at the Collège Saint-Stanislas, 1941–42. Foucault is in the
middle, with glasses. Archives historiques du diocèse de Poitiers.

Supernatural: Georges Duret

The 1941–42 class photograph for the Collège Saint-Stanislas is in many ways
typical. It shows nearly fifty teenagers—some in ties, some with open col-
lars—standing and sitting in the school courtyard. At the center sit two men,
both priests. The elder is short and frail. His gaze, through his wire-framed
glasses, is impassive yet alert, his face gaunt, with slight hollowing beneath his
cheekbones. His pale skin and striking white hair contrast with his clothes'
austere darkness. Surrounded by adolescents whose fidgeting and slumping
have been frozen in time, the priest seems at home in his stillness. A little
to the priests' left and one row behind him, stands, at the margins of the
group, a young man of fifteen or sixteen. He is dapper, proud, and, like the
priest, vaguely distant. As he holds his hands behind his back, he sports a
light-colored jacket, his tie nonchalantly dangling on top of his sweater. His
hair is brushed into a wavy pompadour, his gaze, through his thick-rimmed
glasses, veers off to the side, away from his classmates as well as the camera.

Perhaps ten or twelve feet separate the priest and the student. Each looks in the opposite direction.

The student is Michel Foucault. The priest is perhaps one of the most intriguing and—at least in some circles—renowned of Foucault's teachers: Georges Duret. If everything had gone according to plan, Duret would have been Foucault's philosophy teacher (in his final year, when French students take the state-mandated, education-crowning course in *philosophie*). But history got in the way: in September 1942, on the first day of the new academic year, Duret was arrested on the school's premises by the German police because of his participation in a local Resistance cell. By this point, Duret had already established an impressive local reputation—not only as an exceptional teacher, but also as a philosopher and pedagogical theorist (who had published in local and national venues), a poet, and a priest whose ascetic disposition and pastoral devotion left a lasting impression on his contemporaries. In 1943, this man who so exemplified Christian virtues became, quite literally, a martyr. Those who knew him called him a saint. As the 1941–42 school picture makes clear, Foucault unquestionably knew Duret. He may have had him at one point as a teacher. Duret, in any case, was a local celebrity. A classmate asserted that Foucault was certainly marked by the philosopher-priest.[50] But as with much in his childhood, Foucault never uttered a recorded word about his best-known teacher. Yet given that, like Malapert, Duret was among the first philosophers Foucault knew, it is worth examining Duret's philosophical persona and considering the experiential matrix he constituted for the young man (Figure 14).

Born to a farming family in the Vendée in 1887, Duret always identified with his provincial background and peasant roots. Despite a conservative upbringing in a region whose name is synonymous with reactionary Catholicism, Duret exhibited great intellectual curiosity from early on, and his deep faith was nourished by an openness to contemporary currents seeking to transform the church. As a student, he was attracted to Le Sillon (The Furrow), an organization founded in 1894 in the wake of Leo XIII's bull *Rerum Novarum*. Inspired by incipient Christian-democratic principles, Le Sillon undertook to engage with modern social issues, notably the labor movement. As a seminary student, Duret publicly disagreed with a teacher who had criticized the movement in class. Thanks to this disobedience, Duret was discreetly transferred to the seminary at Poitiers, where he would live for the rest of his life. He was ordained in 1912, the same year he began teaching at the Collège Saint-Stanislas.[51]

Figure 14. Foucault and Georges Duret at the Collège Saint-Stanislas, c. 1942. Duret is in the second row on the far left, Foucault on the third row on the far right. Archives historiques du diocèse de Poitiers.

While Duret never became a prominent philosopher or scholar—not least because, by all accounts, he was too spiritually invested in his roles as teacher and priest—he consistently marked those who knew him with his great learning and formidable intellect. He also became the nexus of a regional intellectual scene, centered in Poitiers, which participated in the ferment then transforming Catholic thought. At the seminary in Poitiers, Duret formed several close intellectual friendships, notably with the Abbot René Aigrain, a learned monk whose legendary library the young Foucault would consult.[52] Duret completed a first thesis in Poitiers on the plays of Pierre Corneille, before starting a philosophy doctorate that he would never finish. Despite his teaching responsibilities, he published with some regularity. He contributed essays on a regular basis to the journal *L'enseignement chrétien* and wrote a contribution on medieval literature to a popular encyclopedia of Catholicism edited by his friend Aigrain.[53] For years he was the head priest for Poitiers's university parish, cementing his ties to the local academic community.

A key to understanding Duret's faith was his passion for Charles Péguy, the French writer and journalist. Turning against the rationalist and anticlerical inclinations of his youth, Péguy had embraced a mystical faith in the years prior to the First World War, before being killed at the Marne in 1914. Péguy's writing and example resonated with Duret at many levels. Like Péguy, Duret was a poet. As a Vendée peasant, Duret identified with Péguy's plebian origins. Though Duret did not serve in the Great War—much to his regret—he enthusiastically embraced Péguy's mystical nationalism, centered on Joan of Arc. Finally, at an intellectual level, Duret was drawn to Péguy's conception of a natural, immanent world infused with divinity. Aimé Forest, who knew Duret while teaching in Poitiers in the 1920s and 1930s before Forest went on to become a prominent Thomist philosopher, said of his friend: "Péguy represented for Duret the genuine spirit of Christian philosophy, the sense of the accord between distinct values, the understanding of a genuine union of soul and body 'like two hands joined in prayer.'"[54] In his poem *Ève*, Péguy had written: "*le surnaturel est lui-même charnel*"—"the supernatural is itself corporeal."[55] Duret, in particular, embraced the famous formula Péguy had coined to describe his generation's trajectory: "Everything begins in mysticism and ends in politics."[56] In his teaching notes for his class on moral philosophy, one finds a list of four quotes that Duret considered to be guides for "personal morality," one of which is by Péguy: "The essential is that, in each order, mysticism not be devoured by the politics to which it gave birth." Duret glosses this quote as follows: "mysticism" means "acting on the basis of an idea; disinterestedness," while "politics" means "acting on the basis of interest." Duret concludes: "One must have character, that is to say, to decide on the basis of principles, and not on the basis of interests, which change."[57] Péguy's influence also loomed over Duret's literary tastes, in particular his passion for Corneille. Duret argued that the teaching of Corneille was crucial to Christian pedagogy, because in his theater, the traits of ancient tragedy are infused with the "*surnaturel*," or supernatural[58] (particularly in the last of Corneille's great plays, the Christian-themed *Polyeucte*). This is why, he suggested, young people learn more about love and faith from Corneille than from his contemporary Racine, who, for all his Augustinianism, could never free his verse from the hothouse of human passion. In this way, Duret drew directly from Péguy's literary criticism, notably when the latter praised Corneille for expressing a "a natural and supranatural supernatural," that is "literally *super*natural." For Péguy, the "mystery of the incarnation"—the presence of the supernatural in the natural—was Corneille's signal achievement.[59] For Duret, it was the insight that Péguy had rekindled in modern culture.

Péguy's influence was evident in the most developed expression of Duret's intellectual outlook, a magazine of sorts that he edited and produced between 1918 and 1924. Its title, *Série préparatoire aux cahiers pour les professeurs catholiques de France* (Preparatory series to notebooks for Catholic teachers of France) was cryptic but clearly referenced Péguy's famous journal *Cahiers de la quinzaine* (Fortnightly notebooks). The most idiosyncratic feature of Duret's magazine was that he wrote it out entirely longhand, in his own meticulous script, before having it lithographed. On several occasions, Duret explained his *Cahiers* program. In a slogan that presented itself as a gloss of the phrase *homo sapiens*, Duret asserted: "we are lost because of rhetoric and scientism; we will be saved by doctrine." The purpose of the *Cahiers* was to introduce readers to theological and philosophical topics in a manner consistent with Duret's broader religious aims, according to which "the spiritual and the supernatural . . . are integrated into the temporal."[60] In his careful handwriting, Duret produced fifty-two issues of the *Cahiers*, which became an underground success with local students and intellectuals. The *Cahiers* addressed a range of questions, including theology (with issues such as "On Holiness," "On the Nature of Grace"), philosophy ("The Life of Blaise Pascal," "The Lesson of Socrates"), literature and aesthetics ("Chateaubriand as Traveler," "Corneille's Scruple"), and even Duret's own autobiography (in the thinly disguised account found in "The Spiritual Childhood of Pierre Peccator").[61] In 1924, however, the bishop of Poitiers forbade the magazine from continuing. With an "adieu" by Duret to its readers, the *Cahiers* came to an end.

In addition to advancing his theological vision, the *Cahiers* also promoted a scholarly concern of special importance to Duret: the rediscovery of the Church Fathers. One of Duret's students observed: "Now that any library, not only of a priest, but of any cultivated man, includes a shelf devoted to patristics, it is difficult for us to imagine the novelty, the audacity of this choice."[62] Though Duret himself was not an expert on the Fathers, his friend and colleague René Aigrain was a major authority. On several occasions, Duret invited Aigrain to make contributions on patristics. An issue from 1920 was devoted to a learned essay by Aigrain on Saint Polycarp of Smyrna who, according to tradition, knew the evangelist John and later became a martyr. Aigrain's essay examined his life and teachings through an analysis of extant sources, while pursuing tangents relating to Eursebius and Saint Ire- naeus's polemics against the Gnostics.[63] This essay was reprinted in Aigrain's programmatic book *Pour qu'on lise les pères* (roughly, the case for reading the [Church] Fathers).[64] Later that year, Duret devoted an issue to a piece by Aigrain on Origen, who was perhaps the Church Fathers' greatest theo- logian.[65] He also favored assigning Augustine and other Church Fathers in the high school philosophy course.[66] The Church Fathers, championed by his teacher Duret and studied by his mentor Aigrain, were the main material to which Foucault would turn when, in the final years of his life, he began to study early Christian attitudes toward sexuality and selfhood. Most likely he owed his first exposure to Origen and Augustine—and even Polycarp—to these two priests.[67] The late Foucault's interest in early Christianity was, in this sense, a return to the intellectual world of his childhood.

However peripherally, Duret thus seems, in various ways, to have par- ticipated in the intellectual renewal underway in twentieth-century French Catholic thought, which culminated in the so-called *nouvelle théologie*. Duret never endorsed modernism—the controversial movement that sought to rethink Christian theology in radically historical and quasi-anthropocentric terms—though one wonders if his *Cahiers* was banned by diocesan author- ities because its contents were seen as flirting with unorthodoxy. Yet Duret's emphasis on the supernatural as a dimension of nature, and even as its reali- zation, harmonizes with some of the arguments that new theologians such as Henri de Lubac would develop more fully. For instance, the philosopher Maurice Blondel, who pioneered the views defended by the *nouveaux théol- ogiens*, insisted that Catholic thinkers must take seriously the subjectivist stance of modern philosophy and see it not as an obstacle, but as an oppor- tunity for a new apologetics. Blondel, according to one scholar, embraced "not a 'doctrine of immanence,' which merely begins and ends with subjective reality, but rather a 'method of immanence,' seeking to prove that an imma- nent and phenomenological examination of human action and aspiration ultimately might lead to transcendence."[68] This project of demonstrating how the supernatural undergirds ordinary human action closely aligns with Duret's thinking in the *Cahiers* and other writings. Though he does not seem to mention de Lubac himself, Duret was familiar with other thinkers who helped to formulate the *nouvelle théologie*. In 1933, in a talk to local Catholic women, Duret cited the Jesuit archeologist and theologian Pierre Teilhard de Chardin, who at the time was virtually unknown.[69] He admired the work of the Jesuit theologian Pierre Rousselot, particularly his thesis *L'intellectualisme de Saint Thomas* (The intellectualism of Saint Thomas), which he cited in class and assigned to his students.[70] Drawing on his reading of Aquinas, Rousselot maintained that intelligence is the essence of goodness, in the way that it both engenders and merges with being. The highest form of intelligence, the endpoint to which it tends, is the beatific vision, which only angels, as incorporeal beings, can truly achieve. Intelligence in this sense is beyond the limits of human reason, making it accessible only through participation in divinity. In this way, Rousselot sought to propose a philosophical anthropology of humanity's epistemological limitations, while showing that they could be transcended only through the Christian God.[71]

Duret also crossed paths with Jean Daniélou, who went onto become a significant figure in the *nouvelle théologie*. As a Jesuit novice, Daniélou taught from 1934 to 1936 at the Collège Saint-Joseph, another Catholic school in Poitiers. During these years, he came to know Duret. In 1936, Poitiers hosted the *journées universitaires*, a spiritual retreat of sorts for Catholic university professors. Daniélou described the occasion for *Études* (Studies), the Jesuit journal he would later edit. In an essay brimming with spiritual enthusiasm, emphasizing Poitiers's stature as "the holy city of the Cross" and one of the "oldest centers of Christian Gaul,"[72] he recounts Duret's role during the events: "The canon Duret made himself the historian and theologian of this Poitevin devotion to the Cross, in a particularly moving ceremony that would be one of the *journées'* high points: the veneration, at Saint Hilaire [one of the city's churches], of the precious relic preserved since Saint Radegund at the Saint-Croix monastery."[73] Daniélou was referring to perhaps Poitiers's most celebrated saint, known in French as Radégonde, the sixth-century Thuringian princess-turned-ascetic who founded an abbey in honor of a fragment of the True Cross given to her by the Byzantine emperor. Foucault's mother—Anne-Marie Radégonde Malapert—was named after her. Daniélou's essay references several prominent members of the university parish that Duret served. Given his family's Catholicism and university affiliations, it seems almost certain that Foucault's father would have known of the event and perhaps even participated. Daniélou would go on to study with de Lubac, with whom he collaborated in promoting the study of patristics. Pope Paul VI later made Daniélou a cardinal.

Duret was not only a philosopher, but a teacher of philosophy. Without question, Foucault would have known of Duret's legendary reputation as a teacher. A former student described the impression the priest made on his charges: "While, in the sluggishness of a summer that was drawing to an end, a horde of children grew agitated and chatty . . . a slight priest, with gray hair, already wearing a cape and a coat, a scarf around his neck, paced quickly, while coughing, in the covered area of the playground. His head lowered, his hat resting lightly at his eyes or pushed frankly back, his hands slipped under the belt of his cassock, he walks this way, several times a day, without worrying about what is going on around him. For the entire town, the priest is 'M[onsieur] Duret' or, more familiarly, 'Father Duret': but for the *mocking schoolboy*, he is 'the rat.' A man who is not like everyone else, some people say, who lives in the clouds: in short, a philosopher."[74] Duret's classroom demeanor was also distinctive: "He holds himself upright on his chair, leans back rarely, avoids stretching his legs or crossing his feet: he is on guard against slackness. He makes no gestures, just a few movements of his right fist, his thumb raised, to emphasize ideas. He is simple and reacts against all whimsey. But there is nothing affected or stiff about his attitude: he is himself. His diction is carefully articulated, deliberately slow and without fits and starts, modulated only after one or two notes, given rhythm by the rolling of his r's. His language is clear, pared down, without metaphor or circumlocution, even without adjectives. . . . He seems interested in no one; and even less in himself. Ideas alone matter to him." The student concludes: "Ultimately, he says . . . . only one occupation is worthwhile for a man: that of searching for the truth. Any life from which this care is excluded is a failed life. . . . And through him, [his students] already feel in contact with the truth. In this ascetic face, nothing more appears, behind the little spectacles belonging to an earlier generation, but a gaze that is gray, a little sad, [and] extraordinarily deep and calm."[75]

Through his compelling personality, Duret seems to have breathed life into an otherwise conventional Catholic philosophy course. Though fate would deny Foucault the opportunity to study philosophy with Duret, he probably had him as a French teacher earlier in his schooling and may have taken Duret's extracurricular "general culture" course,[76] giving him other occasions to be exposed to his ideas and personality. Moreover, given the unexpected interruption of Duret's teaching in fall 1943, the year Foucault would have done his *philosophie*, one suspects that those who suddenly had to replace him largely stuck to his curriculum. Duret assigned *Cours de psychologie* (Course on psychology), a textbook published in 1917 by Father Émile Baudin,[77] as well as *Éléments de philosophie scientifique et de philosophie morale* (Eléments of a scientific philosophy and a moral philosophy), by the Jesuit Charles Lahr.[78] A character in one of François Mauriac's early novels describes the latter work's tenor: "Each theory, presented in a simplistic manner, is followed by a peremptory phrase in italics: *This theory is wrong for the following reasons....* The Father, full of confidence, then concludes: *Here is the true solution.*"[79] In addition to these textbooks, Duret also assigned Léon Brunschvicg's edition of Pascal's *Pensées* and Descartes's *Discourse on Method*.[80] His course covered what, at the time, were conventionally regarded as philosophy's four primary subfields: logic, psychology, morality, and metaphysics.

Though Duret's course was intended to ensure that students would pass the state-sponsored baccalaureate exam, its primary purpose, unsurprisingly, was to justify the revealed truths of the Christian religion and to solidify his pupils' Christian faith. In order to do so, of course, Duret had to present the story of philosophy, as well as all the discrete problems philosophy has addressed, as *"finding themselves and coming together in God."*[81] Duret's student Marcel Guilloteau specifically describes his teacher's course as based on the distinction and connection between the "order of nature" and "the supernatural order," which itself was inseparable from the "Christian order."[82] He seems to have agreed with the thinkers who would soon launch the *nouvelle théologie* that philosophy's development had reached an impasse in "immanentism," which made necessary a return to and redefinition of transcendence. Duret began his course by describing "this great adventure of the mind rising from the *Dialogues* and the *Metaphysics* from the two *Summae*, then descending to the *Meditations* and the *Critiques*."[83]

Central to this Christian conception of philosophy and its story was a particular understanding of the nature of human beings and their role in God's order. Following Aquinas, Duret explained how the natural order consists of a hierarchy of realms ranked according to the degree to which the entities constituting them are material or spiritual: the mineral, the vegetative, the animal, and the human. This proves the "admirable order of the world," the fact that it is a "cosmos": Aquinas's hylomorphic theory shows, Duret explained to his students, that this cosmos exists as "harmony."[84] While belonging to this integrated cosmos, man nonetheless occupies a unique place in it. "Whereas an animal acts without reflection, man proposes an end to his action and organizes the means to reach this goal."[85] "The existence of liberty," Duret explained (according to one student's notes), "thus poses the problem that is unique to man."[86] Duret proceeded to explain how different philosophers had grappled with this problem. Hedonists and utilitarians see moral considerations as driven purely by external considerations, such as pleasure. In different ways, the Stoics and Kant saw morality as an end in itself and as arising from an inner sense of obligation. For Duret, neither argument was convincing. Citing the theologian Jacques Chevalier, Duret asserted that morality is neither autonomous nor heteronomous, but theonomous—that is, founded on the need for God.[87] The "shortcomings of human consciousness allow us to reach the conclusion of the moral necessity of Revelation and a social authority of a spiritual nature to maintain the purity of the moral law and to educate consciences."[88]

Human beings, according to Duret, are contingent creatures inhabiting an immanent reality in which they can nonetheless discern the transcendent world to which they are deeply if obscurely connected. Humans are drawn to God because they spontaneously intuit their own insufficiency. Reflecting on Pascal's observation that human beings are "full of needs, passions that throw us outside," Duret concludes: "This is why no man can find happiness in himself; no man suffices to himself."[89] In the issue of *Cahiers* he devoted to the nature of grace in 1921, Duret had spelled out this claim, that human existence is defined by a kind of ontological vulnerability that means that we cannot but "accept" the world's offerings: "Nothing is ultimately as natural to man as believing and accepting, as asking. They too (Cartesians and Kantians), they asked and received their first nourishment and their first knowledge. All life is founded on acceptances; it is made up of them. A science can constitute itself only by first accepting a given. Mathematics is not a product of logic; physics starts with the testimony of the senses; history cannot be deduced from a philosophy of man. Action is not analytical. Love does not feed on itself; it is ecstatic. We are filled with things"—Duret returns to Pascal—"that throw us outside [*qui nous jettent en dehors*]."[90] This passage clarifies what Duret meant when he told his students that moral consciousness is "finite, contingent," and "not infallible" and that human intelligence is a "finite participation in God's infinite intelligence."[91] Duret's emphasis on immanence also explains his rejection of idealism: paraphrasing a remark by Péguy on the limitations of Kant's thought, Duret told his students: "Idealism's hands are pure, but it has no hands."[92] In other words, idealism sidestepped the key philosophical problem—the fact that human beings are destined to exist in a material dimension that they did not create. Human existence is immanent and contingent, but by this very condition opens us to participation in God's transcendence and necessity.

A further role that Duret embodied, for those who knew him, was that of an ascetic. Not only did those who knew him repeatedly describe him as such, but they frequently insisted on Duret's physical appearance, demeanor, and way of life, as if to emphasize how perfectly he embodied the ascetic ideal. Jean Toulat, who studied at Saint-Stanislas before becoming a priest and a resistant, recalls the simple classroom in which "fifteen adolescents, philosophy students, directed their gaze toward a frail black silhouette with the ascetic head of the Curé d'Ars"[93] (that is, Jean-Marie Vianney, a nineteenth-century saint who epitomized the virtues of the postrevolutionary parish priest).[94] Duret's living conditions made an impression on many. A student who knew him while attending seminary remembered that Duret lived in a room provided by the school at "the end of a tortuous and dark corridor," which, besides its many books, contained little more than an iron bed. For Duret, "clothing [and] comfort did not count: he spent his winters without fire." The same student described Duret as the "ascetic of the fire-less room, of Franciscan poverty."[95] Duret's voluntary subjection of himself to the cold struck many who knew him. One student speculated that it required a "heroic will" and wondered if this disposition to suffering suggested that Duret foresaw his fate.[96] Father André Beaufine, a colleague at Saint-Stanislas, recalled Duret's disregard for "preoccupations having to do with clothing," evident in his "hole-covered cape, his shabby hat, and his shoes with gaping soles." Beaufine also remembered Duret's apathy toward food: "For ten years, I took my meals across from him. Not once did I hear him speak of what he was eating or drinking. He took what he was offered, without discrimination. Sometimes he arrived late: everything was cold, the soup, the meat, the vegetables. He did not seem to notice and asked for nothing he lacked. I have never seen such complete, such constant indifference."[97] His ascetism extended well beyond material renunciation. Simone Landry, a nun who followed Duret's teaching and later corresponded with him, asserted: "Duret lived as an ascetic. Everyone knew it and could attest to it." In addition to his disregard for physical comfort, Duret also "spurned marks of admiration addressed solely to him." For Duret, asceticism was necessary for intellectual as well as spiritual pursuits (though the two could never truly be separated for him): rather than praise or recognition, "all that mattered to him was the truth of the message conveyed." Asceticism lay at the heart of Duret's "spiritual attitude, which consisted of resolute Christocentrism."[98]

Yet the role that Duret played that most awed his contemporaries, the one that threw every other facet of his personality into relief, was that of martyr. For the Collège Saint-Stanislas, September 30, 1942, was the *rentrée*, the first day of classes after the long summer break. On this day, Foucault began his final year of high school, when he planned to take Duret's renowned philosophy course. Yet the new academic year was interrupted by the arrival on the school's premises of two Gestapo agents, who requested to see Duret. His colleagues encouraged him to flee; instead, the priest met the Germans in the parlor.[99] Soon after, Duret was placed under arrest on suspicion of belonging to the Resistance. Saint-Stanislas's headmaster scrambled to find a substitute.

Duret's path to martyrdom began with his early and visceral rejection of German occupation. Though Duret seems, for a time, to have been drawn to Maurrasian nationalism, his Christian democratic inclinations made him ill disposed to fascism and the far right. After France's defeat, René Savatier, a prominent law professor at the University of Poitiers, hosted a meeting of local Catholics to discuss the proper attitude toward the new French government. Many were struggling with the question of whether Christian teachings emphasizing respect for established political authority should apply to Vichy. Duret's position was unambiguous. Even if Pétain's regime was legitimate—which, according to Duret, was far from certain—its policies were contrary to Christian duty, which mandated resistance. "Refusing to collaborate with Hitler's Germany, [which was] anti-Christian and [France's] enemy," Christians, Duret taught, must, "whatever the risks, refuse to obey the French government in every matter that could relate to this collaboration."[100] A student recalled that Duret sensed the "deceit of a regime inclined to bring Nazi paganism into France under the guise of a new order." The same student described how Duret, as a theologian, "analyzed with calm and implacable rigor the antinomies between *Mein Kampf* and the Gospel."[101] With Savatier, Duret wrote pamphlets against the Germans and collaboration. One fellow resistant recalled a pamphlet penned by Duret in which the priest, citing Aquinas, demonstrated that "resistance to oppression could sometimes constitute the most sacred of duties."[102] Duret also engaged in passive resistance when he, along with a number of colleagues and students, was conspicuously absent from a ceremony at Saint-Stanislas at which the Vichy anthem "*Maréchal, nous voilà*" was sung. The incident was reported to local authorities, though nothing came of it.[103]

Duret's active resistance began with his involvement in one of the earliest and most important local Resistance groups, the *réseau* Renard, or Renard Network. Louis Renard, a Poitiers attorney, founded the organization in 1941, making it one of the earlier Resistance movements. Believing that Britain would ultimately prevail, he wanted to plan an uprising in Germany's rear when an allied invasion finally came.[104] Politically, his group was broadly republican and left of center. The movement recruited among local professionals, notably university professors. Yet despite the anticlerical tendencies of some members, the Renard Network had a considerable following among Catholic priests and monks. In addition to embracing theological principles like the "duty to resist," many had strongly patriotic sentiments, and some were even veterans. The charges later brought against Duret specifically mentioned his efforts "to cultivate relationships with Catholic milieus, whose influence on the population, particularly in the countryside, he was familiar with."[105] Though Duret was the most prominent Catholic recruit, others included Father Aimé Lambert, who ran the famous library at the Benedictine monastery at Ligugé, and the canon Henri Chollet, who was the priest at Saint Porchaire—the parish of Renard, as well as the Foucault family. While little is known about Duret's specific role in the Renard Network, Henri Auroux, a friend who was later imprisoned with Duret, speculated that the priest was a valued adviser and a recruiter among Poitiers's clerics. Auroux also claims that, in June 1942, Duret participated in a clandestine meeting with British intelligence agents.[106]

The Renard Network unraveled in the summer of 1942. A package sent by a member was intercepted in late July, leading to a series of arrests. A first attempt by the Gestapo to detain Duret occurred in mid-September but was averted because of confusion about his name and his absence from Saint-Stanislas. Those close to Duret remember the way he almost welcomed arrest. Many recall him saying (though there is disagreement as to when): "Our cause lacks martyrs." His arrest on September 30 occurred when he had returned to his lodgings at the school despite warnings from his colleagues that he was being sought by the Germans.

In addition to being a model of Christian asceticism, Duret may well have been the first political prisoner that Foucault knew. His teacher was first jailed at Poitiers's Pierre Levée prison which, by 1942, had been taken over by the Sicherheitsdienst and was being used as the primary regional detention center for resistants. In early 1943, Duret was transferred to the notorious Fresnes Prison—one of the country's largest—located south of Paris. Less than a decade later, Foucault would participate in psychiatric experiments at the same prison while studying in Paris. From Fresnes, Duret was transferred to Germany, first to the concentration camp at Hinzert, and then to a prison in Wolfenbüttel. In each case, he was confined alongside other Resistance figures. Not until his final destination was he formally charged with belonging to "a secret organization directed against the security of occupation troops and espionage."[107]

Duret's conduct during his imprisonment convinced his acquaintances that he was a genuine Christian martyr. Sister Landry recalls that shortly after he was transferred to Fresnes, Duret sent back to her a copy of *The Imitation of Christ* she had given him, inscribed with one of his own poems.[108] Auroux remembers how, in Germany, Duret would, at night, secretly take confession from his fellow prisoners at their bedside or in the lavatory. When a guard at Wolfenbüttel asked why Duret had not followed Joan of Arc's example (that is, of fighting the English), he replied: "if she returned to Earth, it is you that . . . she would chase from French soil." Duret suffered like a martyr, too. In prison, he was repeatedly forced to undress, an affront to his "modesty and reservation." Despite his frail constitution, he was exposed to various forms of torture, including freezing cold showers. A witness described the scene: during the twenty minutes the ordeal endured, Duret "remained motionless, his hands crossed as in prayer, in a kind of ecstasy in which he seemed to experience a divine pleasure in suffering for the cause to which he had given his entire self."[109] After he was moved to Wolfenbüttel—in the cramped, suffocating heat of a transportation train—he was confined to a solitary cell and his health began to deteriorate. To Auroux, who saw him only during the daily walk, his declining health was evident: "his face was emaciated, his body skeletal, his legs struggled to keep him up, and one day he fell. Some of his fellow Poitevin resistants, such as Father Lambert, the Liguge librarian, were beheaded at Wolfenbüttel. Duret, for his part, died alone in his cell on May 30, 1943.[110]

Duret seems to have intuited his fate, embracing an opportunity to die for this faith. Many of his friends seized on lines from Duret's final volume of poetry, which in retrospect seemed prophetic: "A thousand prudent lies / Will never make up for the absence of martyrdom."[111] A fellow inmate observed: "Sixteen or seventeen centuries earlier, he would have been martyr and probably a saint."[112] A colleague from Saint-Stanislas stated: "Now that I know he died a martyr for his fidelity to the principles of his faith and his patriotism, to his God and his country, I honor him like a saint."[113] In the 1990s, a former student initiated the procedure for Duret's beatification.[114]

What impact, then, did this priest, philosopher, ascetic, and martyr have on the young Foucault? The biographers who consulted his family members directly stress the educational expectations that the Foucaults had invested in the philosophy course that Michel would take with Duret. One Foucault biographer observes that Duret was seen as an "eminent figure that university professors did not hesitate to consult. All students expected a great deal from the year they would spend with him."[115] Another describes Duret as "a man greatly respected by his colleagues."[116] Besides the connections resulting from Foucault being enrolled at Saint-Stanislas, Duret intersected with the family's social circles as well. In addition to being a prominent and long-standing citizen of Poitiers, Duret had, for example, close connections to the university. When Foucault's classmate and occasional rival Pierre Rivière was asked if he believed Duret had left an impression on Foucault, he replied: "Yes."[117]

But where do the specific traces of Duret's imprint lie? First, while Foucault never mentions Duret or his influence, a consideration of his teacher's conception of philosophy highlights important strands in Foucault's early thought. Like Duret, Foucault was interested in the relationship between a divinely ordered and teleological conception of the cosmos, on the one hand, and human nature and knowledge, on the other. Duret's Christian philosophy pinpointed, in short, the problem of anthropology, by showing how it became the basic paradigm of modern thought once philosophy sought to emancipate itself from divine tutelage. It is significant, too, that Duret was fully aware of the trends in modern thought that replaced "rational psychology" with "scientific psychology"—with what Duret called a "psychology without a soul."[118] At the same time, Duret was also remarkably innovative in the way that he described the human condition as defined by contingency, immanence, and finitude, in ways that challenged some of the basic assumptions of modern philosophy, notably the primacy of the subject and its interiority. Duret's claim that we "are filled with things that throw us outside" prefigures Edmund Husserl's concept of intentionality, not to mention what Foucault called "thought from outside."[119] The first time that Foucault encountered this distinctive anthropology, emphasizing the finitude and contingency of human existence, may have been through Duret or others who came under his influence at Saint-Stanislas. While Duret provided an alternative to anthropocentric thinking, it must nonetheless be emphasized that he ultimately embraced a form of "Christian humanism": though he recognized the poverty of man shorn of his sacred canopy, he had no doubt that human beings occupied a central place in God's plan. Foucault's later notion that "man" did not exist as an epistemological or philosophical problem before the eighteenth century would have been completely alien to Duret's thought.

Second, it is intriguing to consider the role that Duret played in shaping Foucault's ideas about Christianity—more precisely, the various points at which his thought intersected with Christianity. The Church Fathers constitute the subject matter of much of Foucault's late work—particularly the 1979–80 Collège de France lectures, *On the Government of the Living*, and the final volume of *History of Sexuality*, *Confessions of the Flesh*. Foucault most likely read or at least heard of these authors for the first time at Saint-Stanislas, perhaps under Duret's guidance. It is difficult not to detect traces of Duret's impact, at least as a kind of model, in Foucault's late reflections on asceticism and its relationship to truth. In his final lecture series—delivered in February and March 1984, as he was dying—Foucault explored the ancient art of truth telling or *parrhesia*, notably as practiced by the Cynic philosophers. In the final lecture, Foucault discussed how the Cynic project of reforming oneself and others through truth telling paved the way for a conception of truth as the harbinger of a thoroughgoing transformation of the world as such. This conception of *parrhesia* was especially evident in early Christianity and Christian asceticism, which promoted the idea of a "missionary of truth, coming amid men to give them the ascetic example of the true life, to call them back to themselves, to put them back onto the straight path."[120] Duret was indeed seen by his contemporaries as a "missionary of truth," and his asceticism was widely viewed as living testimony to the faith he practiced and imparted. In the same lectures, Foucault discusses the centrality to early Christianity of a form of asceticism widely associated with Duret: indifference to food. Abstention from nourishment, Foucault observes, was common to both the Cynics and early Christian ascetics, though the latter, he argued, did so in a more systematic way, taking the Cynical idea of reducing bodily dependence "to the limit": in Christianity, one sees "the reduction of all pleasure, in such a way that neither food nor drink would ever, in themselves, provoke any form of pleasure." Between its predecessors and Christian asceticism, there is thus both "continuity and a certain passing to the limit [*passage à la limite*]."[121] This quest to purge one's experience of all bodily comfort and pleasure is one that Duret's acquaintances strongly associated with him, to the point that even fellow priests were struck by his "complete [and] constant indifference" to physical gratification.[122] As his interest shifted toward ancient arts of living—and as the sexual revolution seemed to run out of steam—Foucault became struck by the similarity between extreme license and radical asceticism: both were practices by which "very cultivated people . . . [sought] to give their life much more intensity, much more beauty."[123] Similarly, in the final volume of *History of Sexuality*, Foucault argued that the most distinctive trait of early Christian practices of selfhood was not their repressive character, but the way that they inaugurated a new experience of the self, in particular through self-understanding and self-transformation.[124] In the last lecture of this final series, Foucault reflected on Christianity's complex reconfiguration of the ancient practice of truth telling. One tendency in Christianity viewed *parrhesia* as anarchic, disorderly speech that exposed itself to sinfulness and could be reined in only through obedience. But another trend, which Foucault found in Christian mysticism, conceived of *parrhesia* in far more theologically positive terms. For the latter, *parrhesia* means "confidence in God, confidence as the means by which man can tell the truth for which he is responsible if he is an apostle or a martyr."[125] Throughout his life, Duret embraced this ecstatic conception of God—a supernatural, transcendent God that he came to understand thanks to Péguy. And, as many witnesses attest, it seems to be this very experience of divinity that informed Duret's engagement in the Renard Network and his final passion: his refusal to flee arrest, his conviction that his cause "lacked"—and thus *needed*—"martyrs," his performance of his duties as a priest in German prisons, his ability to bear witness to his faith even before his jailors and torturers. While Duret and the priests who populated the world of his youth did not cause Foucault's late reassessment of Christianity's significance, it seems plausible that they—and Duret in particular—provided the experiential matrix for this subsequent position. Duret was, for Foucault, the template for the intensities and the relationship to truth that Christian asceticism made possible.

Against Descartes: Marcel Pierrot

Beyond its significance for Duret, his arrest in September 1942 posed an immediate personnel question: who would replace him as Saint-Stanislas's philosophy teacher? The first substitute was Father Bardinette, who usually taught literature to the *premières* (the penultimate year of lycée). A former student described him as "very honorable and . . . extremely nice" but acknowledged that the priest confined himself to "sleep-inducing" commentaries on the textbook and correcting his students' spelling mistakes.[126] It was Bardinette that Foucault, according to the alumni magazine referenced earlier, "stung so deeply . . . , particularly during religious discussions."[127] Yet Bardinette did not last for long. Some claim he simply got sick.[128] A different version of the story, however, says that Foucault's mother objected to the decision on pedagogical grounds. Denys Foucault, the philosopher's brother, recalls: "The superior [Father Braud, the school's director] wanted the course to be taken over by a literature professor. But my mother, who was a little wary of private schools, protested by saying: 'That's literature, not philosophy!' Furthermore, my brother couldn't stand that teacher."[129]

Bardinette was replaced by Marcel Pierrot—known as Dom Pierrot—a monk at the Saint Martin Abbey at Ligugé, just south of Poitiers. Several accounts emphasize the role played by the Foucault family in securing Pierrot's appointment. Didier Eribon claims that Foucault's father had served with several Ligugé monks in the eastern campaign during the First World War.[130] Denys Foucault contends that his mother was instrumental in bringing Pierrot to Saint-Stanislas.[131] At least for a short period, an "acceptable substitute for Duret" was found in Dom Pierrot of Ligugé.[132]

That Foucault met monks from Ligugé is not surprising, given the monastery's place in his family history. The Saint Martin Abbey of Ligugé was first founded in the fourth century, on a site offered by Saint Hilary, Poitiers's bishop, to Saint Martin of Tours, making it an ancient and revered site in early French Christianity. It was closed during the Revolution but revived in the mid-nineteenth century as a Benedictine monastery. Its striking architectural beauty, including a cloister with vaulted alleys surrounding a central courtyard, and its peaceful setting have made it appealing to writers and artists. Rabelais lived there briefly, and, more recently, it functioned as a retreat for modernist authors who wanted to explore their faith: Joris-Karl Huysmans and Paul Claudel both sojourned at Ligugé and wrote about their experiences.[133] A further attraction of the abbey was its magnificent library, one of the largest private collections in France. As we have seen, during the war, several of the Ligugé monks (including the librarian) were arrested for their involvement, alongside Duret, in the Renard Network and executed in Germany. The monastery also served as a safe house for Resistance members and those fleeing from the free zone. One of Foucault's biographers notes that, as a doctor, Paul Foucault was "consulted by the Benedictines at Ligugé."[134] As Pierrot recalled in his memoirs, Foucault would visit him there, riding his bicycle from Poitiers.

Marcel Pierrot's path to Ligugé and the monastic calling occurred by way of his discovery of philosophy. He was born in Laon in 1903 and raised in an emotionally asphyxiating bourgeois family, from which he escaped through

"reading, which revealed to him monastic life."[135] In Paris, at the Collège Stanislas (not to be confused with the similarly named Poitiers institution), he
was taught by the budding Catholic philosopher Jacques Maritain. Pierrot
failed the entrance exam to the École Polytechnique, to his father's considerable disappointment, after which he enrolled in the École des Hautes Études
Commerciales. Yet all the while, Pierrot felt called on to nurture his growing faith through spiritual reflection and the study of philosophy. He became
involved with the Solesmes community, a major center of Benedictine revival
in the previous century. When he turned twenty-one, Pierrot cut off contact
with his family and began his novitiate. At the same time, he started his formal studies in philosophy and theology. In addition to Maritain, he was also
attracted to the work of Étienne Gilson, the Catholic philosopher and medi-
evalist. Father Marie-Albert Janvier, who preached at Notre Dame in Paris,
advised Pierrot to read Aquinas directly, dispensing with commentaries and
summaries. Around this time, he also made it a custom to read the entire
Gospel, as well as *The Imitation of Christ* and Pascal's *Pensées*, each year. After
becoming a monk, he was encouraged to join the Benedictine community at
Ligugé, where he arrived in 1930. In 1939, he was asked to prepare lectures on
the history of philosophy to educate his community.[136]

A key moment in the articulation of Pierrot's own outlook occurred when,
after being mobilized during the Phony War, he began sharing his thoughts
about the causes of the war and France's national decline. Various acquaintances, including his officers, asked him to lecture on the topic. Once France
fell, he was invited to deliver his talk in Tours, Rennes, Reims, and other cities.[137] The broad theme of the lecture was the "crisis of Western civilization."
The deep roots of the Second World War, Pierrot argued (as we know from
a detailed account of the lecture he gave in Cholet, which was published by
a local journal), were to be found in the "secularization" of Europe that had
occurred since the unravelling of medieval Christian society. Pierrot's analysis
partook, somewhat generically, in the cultural pessimism of the age, though
he presented it in a distinctly religious key. The "fatal rupture" between Christ
and Europe that began in the Renaissance had led to the rise of secularized
habits of thought, the rejection of authority, and science's emergence as the
dominant intellectual idiom, resulting in confusion about the ultimate "purpose of life." But the most poisonous facet of secularization, Pierrot argued,
was "individualism," which he characterized as nothing less than the "deep
cause of the French disaster." In addition to lamenting egoism as a moral
attitude, with its political and economic consequences, Pierrot also held it

responsible for intellectual "anarchy," the belief that each person could decree their own law, the preference for rights over duties, and the confinement of human aspirations to the present world. As a philosopher, it is not surprising that Pierrot blamed the rise of individualism on "Cartesianism," and the "rationalist individualism" that it generated. The nefarious effects of the Cartesian turn were multiple. Reason was entirely reduced to its mathematical dimension, rendering rationality "inhuman," as "mathematical disciplines occur . . . beyond the human." Mathematics, moreover, focuses on "abstract" and "absolute" considerations, whereas life's deeper problems are "concrete, relative, and tied to particular cases." He also noted that mathematics emphasizes quantity over quality, making it problematic for approaching matters in which "inner value" prevails. Finally, Pierrot concluded, the Cartesian disposition orients the mind toward "the external side of things, their profitability, their utility." In this way, Pierrot attributed France's decline—as evidenced most dramatically by its 1940 defeat—to modernity's underlying trajectory, as construed from a conservative Catholic standpoint. Pulling France back up would require a new spiritual élan, akin to the commitment medieval workers displayed in building the cathedrals—though the cathedral to be rebuilt was France itself.[138]

While there is no clear record of what Pierrot taught during the short period in which he was Foucault's teacher at Saint-Stanislas, it seems likely that he would have had an occasion to share his personal views about philosophy and its role in the West's decline. According to his papers, it was on January 13, 1943, that the school's director asked Liguge's abbot to let Pierrot replace Father Bardinette. Pierrot described himself as a "very surprised" and "rather worried" by the offer, presumably because, in addition to having a shy temperament, he did not have the same breadth of philosophical knowledge as the widely respected Duret. Under pressure, he nonetheless acquiesced. That Monday, he walked to Poitiers, and by that afternoon he had "improvised his first class."[139] Neither Pierrot nor other commentators were particularly enthusiastic about his pedagogical abilities. One Foucault biographer characterized his teaching as "no more than adequate."[140] Pierrot remembers that he provided commentary on their philosophy textbook "for better or for worse." Even so, he was able to write that "classes are going well. The pupils are behaving and seem to be interested in the improvised teaching provided to them" (Figure 15).[141]

Yet whatever his shortcomings as a teacher, Pierrot appears, during his time at Saint-Stanislas, to have extended his pedagogical responsibilities

Figure 15. Dom Pierrot at
Ligugé, July 1943. © Abbaye
Saint-Martin de Ligugé.

beyond the classroom. The school's director asked him to present "the lectures on France that [he] had already given in Poitiers and other cities" for
the benefit of "the school's teachers and pupils in the upper classes."[142] Thus
it is possible that Foucault heard Pierrot's reflections on the role played by
individualism and Cartesianism in France's decline. Pierrot's views seem to
have been quite well known: Foucault's future philosophy tutor recalled, in an
interview from 2001, that Pierrot was "erudite," but also a "dogmatic Thomist,"
"hostile to everything that, since and including Descartes, thought of itself as
philosophy."[143] Furthermore, Pierrot also sought to interact with his charges
one on one—a task simplified by the fact that there were only twelve students
in his philosophy class. As a new teacher, he "received [his] students individ-
ually," allowing him to gauge who they were "intellectually and socially."[144] As
we saw earlier, he had an early interaction with Foucault—identified both as

a doctor's son and as the class leader—in which the young man tried to draw his teacher into a gossip about the school administration, only to have the Benedictine call him to order. Afterward, their relationship developed. Pierrot writes: "we became good friends. He even came to see me several times in the monastery over the next few years."[145] Of Foucault's character as a philosophy student, Pierrot said the following to Didier Eribon: "The young students in philosophy that I knew, I classify them into two categories: those for whom philosophy would always be an object of curiosity and who seek to orient themselves in the study of great systems, great works, etc. And those for whom it rather be a matter of personal anxiety [*inquiétude*], of vital anxiety. The former are marked by Descartes, the latter by Pascal. Foucault belonged to the former category. One sensed in him formidable intellectual curiosity."[146]

Pierrot's stint teaching at Saint-Stanislas ended after six weeks. Though Foucault may have continued to see him in Ligugé, the relationship does not seem to have been particularly close. There is no evidence that Foucault ever sent Pierrot any of his books.[147] Pierrot's characterization of Foucault as a "Descartes" rather than a "Pascal" type amounted, if not to a jab, at least to a suggestion that, in contrast to Pierrot's own experience (which he clearly understood as Pascalian), it was not a tormented soul that drove Foucault to philosophy. Given the concerns with tragedy, death, and even angst that haunted the early Foucault's work, one wonders how close the bond between the teacher and student could have been.

And yet, even so, some of the broad strokes of Pierrot's ideas are apparent in Foucault's thought. The notion that Descartes is the hinge on which philosophy turned and entered the modern era is one that Pierrot and Foucault shared, as is the view that the kind of philosophy Descartes inaugurates was simultaneously subject-centered and rationalistic. In *Madness and Civilization*, Foucault famously described Descartes's thought as part of the "great confinement," when the mad were first locked up. Descartes's contention, in *Meditations*, that madness—unlike dreams and illusion—provided no serious ground for methodic doubt, was premised on the claim that while "*man can still be mad, thought, as the exercise of the sovereignty of a subject who makes it their duty to perceive the truth, cannot be insane.*"[148] In *The Order of Things*, Foucault identified *mathesis*—the "science of calculable order"[149]—as an important component of the classical episteme's "general science of order" (which he associated, among others, with Descartes). Moreover, Pierrot later described modern philosophy as both "humanistic" and "anthropocentric." He lamented the tendency of modern thinkers to consider man as an absolute, which he viewed as a reversion to paganism, and to make a god of the "self." He regretted that modern thought has pitted "humanism without Christianity" against "Christianity without humanism"—he specifically described Pascal as an "antihumanist"—when Christianity properly experienced should integrate an understanding of man into a "theocentric" outlook.[150] These passages are particularly interesting, as they seem to have been written after the publication of *The Order of Things*, in which Foucault takes on a version of these issues, albeit from an extremely different philosophical standpoint. Might Pierrot have read his former student's work without referencing it? What can be said with certainty is this: whether or not Pierrot directly influenced the future philosopher, Foucault was, thanks to Pierrot, exposed to a generic critique of modernity, which his subsequent thought significantly enriched and complicated. In Foucault's hands, the old lament about Descartes's corrupting individualism becomes a more subtle examination of the hubristic epistemological claims that are authorized by Descartes's reorientation of thought in a subject-centered and anthropocentric direction.

The only other reference in Pierrot's papers to his former student is from June 1984. Of that date, the elderly Benedictine wrote: "I have learned of Michel Foucault's death. This news has shaken me more than I would have thought."[151] Pierrot died in 1991 and is buried on Liguaé's grounds.

"Kantianism with a French, Secularized Sauce": Louis Girard and Jean-Raoul Carré

A further consequence of Duret's arrest was the family's decision to hire a philosophy tutor for the young Foucault. Just as she had mobilized the family's personal connections to the Liguaé monastery to bring Pierrot to Saint Stanislas, Anne Foucault also drew on the family's social network to find an appropriate instructor for their son. The young student she chose, Louis Girard, recalls what happened: "Before [Pierrot's arrival], Madame Foucault had asked Dean [Jean-Raoul] Carré of the University of Poitiers's faculty of letters to recommend someone who was able to give private philosophy lessons to her son. This is how I found myself every Thursday at Michel Foucault's home, on Rue Arthur Ranc, in 1942 and 1943. I was twenty two-years old, so only a little older than him."[152] At the time, Girard was a second-year philosophy student at Poitiers.[153] His social background was very different from Foucault's. Born in 1921 to a working-class family, Girard was raised in the village of Mirebeau, outside of Poitiers, where his father worked as a carpenter. As we have seen, he recalled the contrast between the grandiose household in which the Foucaults lived and his "hovel." His parents were conservative Catholics who, presumably because of their skepticism toward the state education system, sent him to the Collège Saint-Stanislas, where he studied—notably with Duret—while also serving as a monitor.

While working as an elementary school teacher, Girard earned a *licence* in philosophy from University of Poitiers in 1942 and began preparing for the state competitive examination to teach high school. It was the fruits of his undergraduate philosophy education that he presented to Foucault at his weekly tutorials. To one Foucault biographer, he said: "The philosophy that I got at university was a sort of fairly vague Kantianism, arranged nineteenth-century style, in [Émile] Boutroux's style, and it was this Kantianism that I brought out to him."[154] In another instance, he explained that he modeled his lessons on the teachings of the professor who had recommended him to Foucault's mother, Jean-Raoul Carré, who was also the university's dean: "I brought out to him what Dean Carré taught us, that is, Kantianism with a French, secularized sauce," adding: "Generations of schoolteachers, the 'hussars of the Republic,' were trained in that kind of Kantianism."[155] He told a journalist that he had introduced Foucault to just a bit of Hegel, but a great deal of Kant.[156]

Girard emphasized that Kant was the focus of his lessons. At the time, Kantianism was seen in France as philosophy's essence, even its *lingua franca*. But Girard also stressed that he did little more than pass his own professor's ideas onto Foucault. The professor in question, Jean-Raoul Carré, was a respected figure in Poitiers's intellectual life. Contrary to Girard's rather uninspiring characterization, Carré was a distinctive figure. Born in 1887, he studied philosophy at the École Normale Supérieure, before serving as an officer (specifically, a battalion commander) in the First World War. To his contemporaries, Carré's military accomplishments were at least as impressive as his scholarly achievements. He was again mobilized in 1939, successfully leading his regiment back to safety after France's defeat.[157]

Despite Girard's emphasis on Carré's "Kantianism," the German philosopher does not figure all that prominently in Carré's thought, at least in his published work. Carré was more a historian of philosophy than a philosopher per se. His interest lay primarily in reconstructing the philosophical systems of thinkers belonging to what is now called the "radical Enlightenment." His thesis was a comprehensive study of Fontenelle; he also wrote two books on

Voltaire and one on Spinoza. Despite its historical character, Carré's concerns were focused on defending the philosophical anthropology of Enlightenment materialists, who saw man as a material being endowed with thought and who viewed the idea of God as reflecting the human mind's need for order and coherence, rather than any transcendental or supernatural principle (for instance, he described with considerable sympathy Voltaire's critique of Pascal's ideas about the supernatural). In 1939, for the sesquicentennial of the French Revolution, Carré delivered a lecture on the idea of "spiritual freedom." He argued that the principles laid out in the Declaration of the Rights of Man and the Citizen were conceived by their authors not "as the object of the selfish desires of men of just one country, but as the legitimate demands of men of all times and all countries, because they were for them nothing more than the definition of man himself, insofar as he is a man, and the articulation of the conditions necessary for the total development of his nature."[158] After the war—he was eventually arrested by the Gestapo for Resistance activities, imprisoned in Germany, and, though he survived, returned to France physically broken—Carré gave a talk in which he described himself as a "relativistic idealist." Developing the idea, he added: "My general position is a combination of Berkeley and Kant. I do not know what is meant by value in itself, nor by the absolute in itself. I know the absolute for man, [which] to me is the love of order."[159]

Thus to the extent that Carré was a Kantian at all, it seems to have referred to the fact that, building on Enlightenment thought, he conceived of philosophy as a largely anthropocentric activity aimed at understanding how human beings, as finite creatures, make sense of themselves and the world, in a manner that breaks free from theology's strictures. His philosophy was not so much "Kantianism with a French . . . sauce" as "enlightenment rationalism with a Kantian sauce." Though he was never exactly a top-tier thinker—even if his books were widely and often enthusiastically reviewed—he did have significant connections in the field. For one of his students, he wrote a letter of introduction to the great Hegelian philosopher Jean Hyppolite (who had attended high school in Poitiers); and he sent an autographed copy of one his essays to the existentialist thinker Jean Wahl. Both would become early mentors to Foucault.[160]

As for what Foucault got from his secondhand accounts of Carré's lectures, Girard remarks: "I cannot say that my teaching was very original."[161] Nor does he overplay Foucault's interest: his pupil "tried to understand" the philosophy lessons—no more, no less. Indeed, Foucault was very "demanding," and Girard claims that while he had more "gifted" students, he had never had one "as capable of quickly grasping the essential, and organizing their thought with such rigor."[162] He also learned that Foucault had an "extraordinary capacity for work."[163] Yet Girard also notes—as did other contemporaries—that Foucault at the time seemed more interested in history than philosophy. There is little reason to believe that Foucault found Girard's lessons particularly inspiring. In any case, they did not go on for long. In August 1943, Girard was recruited by Germany's forced labor program (the Service de Travail Obligatoire) to work in Nuremburg. There, he was arrested for engaging in political agitation and interned in several concentration camps, including Dachau. After being liberated by American troops, he returned to Poitiers in 1945, where he began a career as a high school philosophy teacher. Though Foucault by this point was headed to Paris, Girard recalls that when the family was staying in Vendeuvre, his former student would ride his bicycle to Mirebeau to visit him. Over the years, they saw each other occasionally.[164]

Reflecting on Foucault, Girard mused: "I think that he felt deep inside himself the constraints of the bourgeois norms that bound him and that he could not reject except by wiping the slate clean."[165] In a sense, the philosophy that Girard passed onto Foucault was the epitome of a certain kind of bourgeois philosophy: rationalistic, progressive, secular, and humanistic. It also stood in contrast to the philosophy he was taught at Saint-Stanislas, with its theocentric focus and more skeptical attitude toward modernity (even if this thought could also be associated with a subset of the bourgeoisie). As a term for describing a thinker like Carré, "Kantianism" was little more than a synonym for the prevailing orthodoxies and philosophical prejudices of the age. Perhaps Foucault took note of the very divergent interpretations to which thinkers like Kant and Descartes could lend themselves. And perhaps his interest in Girard lay in the fact that he managed to be a leftist activist while remaining in the church—and, more important, had never been bourgeois.

On the rare occasions when Foucault discussed his early years, he insisted on the "provincial" and "petty bourgeois" nature of his upbringing. No doubt these characterizations were meaningful for him. But one should not take Foucault entirely at his word, or—and more to the point—one must interpret such descriptions correctly. However harshly he came to judge its shortcomings, Foucault's Poitiers education had a cognitive dimension: it acquainted him with the philosophical common sense of the age, familiarized him with the tensions between secular and Catholic conceptions of philosophy, accustomed him to thinking of "humanism" (or "anthropocentrism") as a major theme in modern thought, and introduced him to key thinkers—notably Kant—who would later become decisive to his own thinking. Foucault often described his intellectual generation as engaged in a revolt against the subject-centered thought of existentialism and phenomenology. This is undeniably true. But these schools of thought also crystallized and upgraded the philosophical common sense instilled in him in Poitiers. If Foucault would later interrogate the epistemological primacy of the subject, of "man," of philosophical anthropology, and conventional accounts of Kant's significance, the reasons lie, in part, in his early encounter with these ideas during his Poitiers adolescence.

Conclusion

B y the time the war ended, Foucault's Poitiers years were drawing to a close. After earning his *baccalauréat* (the final diploma and exam for high school) in 1943, he entered the *classes préparatoires* at Henri IV, Poitiers's lycée, where he began rigorous preparation for the admissions exam to the École Normale Supérieure in Paris. When he took the exam in 1945, however, he failed. On the written portion of the test, which included papers on French literature, French-to-Latin and Latin-to-French translations, philosophy, history, and Greek-to-French translation, "Paul Foucault" (as he was listed in the gradebook) came in 103rd out of two hundred candidates.[1] Consequently, he was not among the fifty-seven who qualified to take the oral exams, of whom twenty-four were ultimately admitted.[2] Curiously, in light of both Foucault's high school education and his subsequent interests, the philosophy paper asked candidates to reflect on whether "man is simply a part of nature." The two professors who graded it—Georges Canguilhem, who would soon become extremely important for Foucault, and René Le Senne—regretted that candidates had tended to "substitute pathetic descriptions of the human condition for philosophical and even logical analysis of the relationship between nature and the human mind."[3]

To improve his chances on the next try, Foucault moved to Paris in the fall of 1945. He enrolled in the *classes préparatoires* at the Lycée Henri IV, an institution that, while it bore the same name as his Poitiers school, enjoyed a much greater reputation and possessed one of the best track records for securing admission to the École Normale Supérieure. A year later, Foucault sat for the entrance exam again: he came in seventh place on the written tests, qualifying him for the round of oral exams, in which he ranked fourth.[4] In the fall of 1946, as he turned twenty, Foucault became a *normalien* (as students and alumni of the École Normale Supérieure are known), with all that this entailed in terms of intellectual recognition and career prospects. Paris became his new home—even if, for the rest of his life, he would periodically return to Poitiers.

In Paris, with all the intellectual opportunities it afforded, Foucault was soon finding his own philosophical voice. By 1954, he had published two significant works: a short book, *Maladie mentale et personnalité* (Mental illness and personality), and a long introduction to a translated essay by the Swiss psychoanalyst Ludwig Binswanger.[5] He also wrote, in his difficult-to-decipher hand, a trove of essays and lecture notes that he never published.[6] In these works, Foucault began to explore his own ideas and intuitions in the idiom of academic philosophy. Thanks to the training he had received from philosophers like Jean Hyppolite, Jean Beaufret, Maurice Merleau-Ponty, and Georges Canguilhem and psychologists such as Daniel Lagache and Jean Delay, as well as his assiduous reading of G. W. F. Hegel, Martin Heidegger, Edmund Husserl, Sigmund Freud, and Friedrich Nietzsche, Foucault acquired an array of linguistic and conceptual tools that he employed to construct an increasingly original philosophical vision.

Foucault's concerns during this formative period appear, at first glance, to be largely immune from his early experiences—and indeed, from any personal experience whatsoever. The topics that attracted him included the nature of transcendentals in critical philosophy and German idealism, the relationship between psychology and phenomenology, the problem of the human sciences in post-Cartesian philosophy, and the concept of culture in contemporary psychology.[7] And yet, however dimly, the interests kindled during his Poitiers years managed to mark his writing during this period. In his reflections on psychology, Foucault displayed an ambivalent attitude toward medicine, at once lamenting the way that psychology modeled itself on medical positivism and denouncing psychology's failure to become as rigorous as medical science. Psychology, he noted, "has never been able to offer psychiatry what physiology offered medicine."[8] Foucault's interest in psychiatry and psychoanalytic practice, including figures like Binswanger and Roland Kuhn, led him to consider how mental illness arose from familial relationships, including cases in which homosexuality was a factor and that resulted in institutional confinement.[9] During these years, moreover, Foucault explored the philosophical significance of death, often by drawing on Heidegger's existential philosophy. This can be seen, for example, in Foucault's reflections on Ellen West, Binswanger's suicidal patient and the focus of Foucault's 1954 introduction.[10] Finally, the point at which many of these interests converged, in Foucault's view, was philosophical anthropology—that is, the branch of philosophy devoted to studying human nature. The point is not that Foucault, in these years, was thinking about his father's profession, his family and personal relationships, the war, and the conflict between secular and Christian philosophy he had encountered in high school. It is, rather, that the latter experiences were the matrices of a range of concerns—with medicine, relationships and their emotional import, death and finitude, and human nature—that shaped and even guided his outlook once it was recast as an intellectual project articulated in philosophical terms.

This is not to suggest a deterministic reading of Foucault, in which his childhood experiences rigidly prefigure his later work. Rather, in this book, I have attempted to identify a particular stratum of Foucault's thought that can be accessed and analyzed through the concept of experiential matrices. These experiences constituted the raw material of Foucault's subsequent reflections. As such, they did not determine Foucault's intellectual positions—that is, what he would think *about* this unprocessed material. The fact that Foucault was fascinated by medicine did not predetermine his conceptualization of the historical a priori; that he was exposed to discourses of social control and normalization under Vichy did not make it inevitable that he would conceive of power as microphysical and productive. Philosophy is not simply childhood experiences on intellectual stilts; it consists, rather, of linguistic and conceptual tools that can be used to make sense of these experiences and, in some cases, achieve a discursive purchase on them. Nor are the only philosophically salient experiences those that occur in childhood: Foucault's activism relating to prisons and his involvement in the West Coast's liberated gay culture of the 1970s and 1980s also altered, at a later point, his thinking's course. Yet the clues that Foucault provides to the earliest matrices of his thought (as evidenced in such remarks as "I am the son of a surgeon" and "The menace of war was . . . our framework of existence") cannot be ignored. While this early stratum may be relevant for many thinkers, it is particularly important to Foucault, given his emphasis on the centrality of experience to thought.

A second stratum of Foucault's thought is associated with the "young Foucault," narrowly construed. It begins with his earliest attempts, in the late 1940s and the 1950s, to formulate a consistent philosophical outlook. While one should not exaggerate the coherence of this phase, it would be equally mistaken to deny its distinctness or to dismiss it as no more than an inchoate first draft of his mature thought.[11] Like the young Hegel, the young Marx, and even the young Derrida, the young Foucault developed an innovative and compelling philosophical stance that, while interesting on its own terms, brings into relief his mature thought's originality and significance.

In a nutshell, the young Foucault proposed a historical reflection on philosophy and epistemology that highlighted the moment when thought became anthropologized—when "man," in short, became the measure of knowledge, both as its object (what must be known) and as its subject (the being that, by its nature, is destined to know). Breaking with centuries-long efforts to grasp the universe in theological terms, European thinkers in the eighteenth century concluded that human beings were the Archimedean point on which all forms of knowledge could rest. Rather than grounding the pursuit of knowledge on the assumption of an infinite creator, anthropologized knowledge, Foucault argued, made its claims on the basis of human finitude itself. For Foucault, the incoherence of this project lay in in its attempt to derive transcendental (that is, necessary and universal) truths from an empirical being—that is, human beings.[12] These insights informed *Madness and Civilization*, Foucault's first major work. Between the Middle Ages and the dawn of the modern period, he argued, madness ceased to evoke the theological problem of human fallenness as it became integrated, through modern medicine and psychiatry, into a purely immanent, purely human realm.[13] Though this was perhaps the most abstract and traditionally philosophical phase of Foucault's career, the impact of the youthful experiential matrices remains, as we have seen, discernable.[14]

The young Foucault's last major statement is 1966's *The Order of Things*. The critique of philosophical anthropology that had, in many ways, been the focus of the young Foucault's project still occupies a central place in this book, particularly in its analysis of the modern episteme's irresolvable contradictions and Foucault's notorious prediction that "man," as an epistemological concept, could soon disappear, "like, at the sea's limit, a face in the sand."[15] Yet at the same time, Foucault rendered explicit the "archaeological" method he elaborated in his work from the 1960s. This method rested on the premise that knowledge depends—as Kant had argued—on a priori conditions, but that these a priori conditions are—in contrast to Kant—historically variable. As Foucault's more astute commentators have noted, these two arguments (that is, the critique of philosophical anthropology and the archaeological method) were, for Foucault, closely connected: modern philosophy's problematic "anthropologization" of Kant's thought (that is, the reduction of Kant's claims concerning the transcendental conditions of knowledge to arguments about human nature) necessitated a return to Kant's core insight—that knowledge always rests on premises that precede experience itself.[16] In many ways, the archaeological method is something that Foucault happened on while elaborating his historical critique of philosophical anthropology. The methodology now regarded, no doubt correctly, as Foucault's main contribution to philosophy began as a by-product of the young Foucault's initial project—one that he had to abandon to bring his mature thought to fruition.

While the prior claim would seem to lie beyond the present book's scope, it is central to its claim that Foucault's thought consists of three successive strata. While this book maintains that experience is a major spur for philosophical reflection, it by no means seeks to reduce philosophy to the working out of purely personal concerns. His experiences alone are not what makes Foucault intellectually significant. Foucault, no doubt, was marked by his family's connection to the medical profession and his experience under German occupation. But not every doctor's son who lived under German Occupation is Foucault.[17] Experiential matrices are vectors of thought, plotting its course and fixing its interests. But they are only matrices. Without intellectual elaboration, they remain embryonic.

This approach offers us a better understanding of the mature Foucault—in my terms, the third and most influential stratum of his thought. This is the period, between the 1960s and his death in 1984, when Foucault wrote his most influential works and conceptualized, in turn, archaeology, genealogy, and technologies of the self. This stratum overlaps with the preceding one: works like *Madness and Civilization* and *The Order of Things* blend the philosophy of the young Foucault and his mature positions. In other words, this later stratum draws on experiential matrices from Foucault's earliest years. I do not claim that Foucault's childhood and youth can account for the methodologies on which his philosophical reputation rests. I argue, rather, that much of the material that ultimately became the object of his philosophical reflection first attracted his attention in his youth. Without a doubt, Foucault needed Canguilhem and Gaston Bachelard to arrive at his understanding of medical science, just as he needed avant-garde literature (of the Marquis de Sade and Georges Bataille, among others) to fine-tune his thoughts about relationships and intimacy, Heidegger to conceptualize finitude and death, and Nietzsche, Hyppolite, and the structuralists (as well as Heidegger) to identify humanism as a philosophical problem. But these concerns *became* problems—if not always philosophical ones—during his youth.

Viewing Foucault as a philosopher of experience provides an underlying intellectual rationale to something that Foucault's critics have long intuited:

that Foucault's thought, despite its radical and often unsettling character, can be self-referential and oddly parochial. This critique has been made, notably, from a feminist and postcolonial perspective. While many feminists have embraced Foucault's thought, others have regretted that Foucault failed to fully integrate gender into his understanding of modern power relations. Others have accused him, particularly in his *History of Sexuality*'s later volumes, of overidentifying with the ancient male philosophers he discusses.[18] Meanwhile, postcolonial theorists, while acknowledging the utility of Foucault's conceptions of discourse and power, lament his failure to take seriously the question of race and the complete omission from his oeuvre of a sustained analysis of imperialism.[19] The position defended in this book suggests that Foucault's failure to address these admittedly crucial issues is hardly surprising. To a significant degree, Foucault's interest, as a thinker, was in making sense of *his own experience* or, more precisely, questions *that had been raised by his experience*. He never served time in prison or in an asylum; yet confinement was, for him, a "personal obsession."[20] This does not mean that Foucault was narcissistic or narrow-minded; anyone with even a passing familiarity with his work realizes such a claim to be absurd. The point, rather, is that Foucault's philosophical outlook was directed both at making sense of experience and at exploring the kinds of experience that new theoretical perspectives and new conceptions of knowledge made possible. Understanding experience is what philosophers do—or, at least, an important part of what they do. This is a key element of what Foucault was getting at when, near the end of his life, he observed that all his books "revolved around the problem, which is always the same, . . . of the relations between subjects, truth, and the constitution of experience."[21]

While this book contends neither that Foucault's early years rigorously determined his later years, nor that the young Foucault somehow has priority over the mature Foucault, it seeks, nonetheless, to contribute to a renewal of Foucault studies. Despite the canonical stature that Foucault's work has now assumed, it is often encrusted in sediments of scholastic interpretations and hermetic verbiage that tells us more about his would-be glossators than about the philosopher's own ideas. Debates about structuralism, poststructuralism, and postmodernism were obviously central to the initial reception of his work, but viewing Foucault primarily through these lenses prevents a deeper and more judicious reading of his work—and specifically the idiosyncratic and personal elements of his thought that are, as this has book has shown, so central to his philosophical personality. Far from being a daunting

and pedantic theorist whose decoding requires great feats of intellectual discipline (as some of his champions see him) or a savvy con artist conjuring
up an illusion of depth from dazzling but ultimately artificial philosophical
fireworks (as some critics imply), Foucault was a vital thinker, consumed
with the need to understand himself and his life. Identifying the experiential
matrices of his thought is not, in itself, a sufficient basis for understanding his
philosophy. But it is necessary for grasping the kind of thinker he was.

A NOTE ON BIOGRAPHY

Though this book does not aspire to be a traditional biography, it is worth saying a few words about the three existing biographies of Michel Foucault. A humorous anecdote mentioned by Luc Ferry and Alain Renaut in *French Philosophy of the Sixties*—their polemical critique against the so-called antihumanism embraced by Foucault and other thinkers of his generation—captures the different perspectives embraced by Foucault's three major biographers. It concerns a Frenchman, an Englishman, and a German who independently undertake to study the camel. The Frenchman strolls down to the Jardin des Plantes, a Paris zoo. He finds a caged camel, which he feeds and plays with, before returning home to write "an article for his paper full of sharp and witty observations." The Englishman packs his bags and sets out for a long journey. He eventually returns "after a sojourn of two or three years with a fat volume, full of raw, disorganized, and inconclusive facts which, nevertheless, had real documentary value." As for the German, who is contemptuous of "the Frenchman's frivolity and the Englishman's lack of general ideas," he "lock[s] himself in his room," where, in utter solitude, he completes a tome entitled "The Idea of the Camel Derived from the Concept of the Ego."[1] The three intellectual personalities that this story identifies—and gently mocks—captures with uncanny accuracy the approaches pursued by Foucault's three biographers.

Didier Eribon's *Michel Foucault*, published in 1991, seven years after the philosopher's death, echoes the Frenchman's clever and insightful essay. At first blush, this claim seems unfair. Far from being superficial, Eribon's biography is an extensively researched work, drawing on archives, unpublished manuscripts, and scores of interviews. Yet Eribon resembles our Frenchmen in the way that he approaches Foucault as part of his world. Like the camel at the zoo, Eribon's Foucault belongs to the same milieu as the author. If Eribon's biography was the first to be published, it is, in part, because he belonged to Foucault's circle of friends. As Eribon notes, he knew Foucault between 1979 and 1984. On four occasions, he interviewed Foucault. But as a conscientious biographer, he is careful to extricate himself from his narrative. "In a few instances," he notes, "I am present or involved in the events that I recount. I have systematically avoided speaking in the first person."[2]

While offering the first meticulous account of Foucault's life, Eribon also sketches a valuable character portrait. So immersed is he in Foucault's world that one tacitly trusts his judgment when he assesses Foucault's personality and motivations. This is not simply because Eribon's conclusions are always judicious and evidence-based, but because of what he and Foucault had in common: in addition to being Paris-based intellectuals, Eribon and Foucault shared the same sexual orientation. Eribon walks a fine but, in his view, very important line between avoiding a reductive reading of Foucault as a "gay philosopher" and emphasizing the centrality of his sexual identity. Indeed, some of the resistance Eribon encountered to the very idea of writing a Foucault biography was tied to the "scandal involved, even today, in mentioning homosexuality." Eribon had to resist "the soft forms of repression and censorship" inherent in passing over any discussion of Foucault's sexual orientation, while also avoiding unseemly "exhibitionism," which risked "acknowledging the force of these powers and the voyeurism the entail."[3] For instance, Eribon describes, with considerable empathy and imagination, the young Foucault's erratic behavior and suicidal tendencies as a student in the 1940s, when he would return "from his frequent nocturnal expeditions in pickup sites and gay bars," "sick [and] annihilated by shame."[4] Insights such as these lead Eribon to conclude that Foucault's life and work were intimately related. In a later work, he goes so far as to argue that *Madness and Civilization* was a "theoretical act anchored in personal experience."[5] Ultimately, it is because Eribon belonged to Foucault's world that we accept his judgments. He is the Boswell of Foucault studies: the witness-participant turned biographer-historian.

The Foucault biographer who corresponds to the anecdote's Englishman—who spent years studying camels in their natural setting—is the British author David Macey. *The Lives of Michel Foucault*, published in 1993, is the longest and arguably the most exhaustive of the three biographies. Some regard it as Foucault's "authorized" biography, as Macey worked closely with Daniel Defert, Foucault's partner.[6] In his introduction, Macey writes: "Foucault lived many lives—as an academic, as a political activist, as a child, and as a lover of men. He lived a very public life, and also a very private one."[7] This conceit, while undoubtedly correct, is a thin conceptual justification for the relentlessly empirical approach that Macey pursues. Because of his proximity to his subject, Eribon permits himself to make character judgments; because of his extensive research, Macey recounts every character assessment shared by his interlocutors. It is no surprise that the resulting account is contradictory: Foucault is secretive, yet narcissistic; warm, yet distant; misogynistic in the company of men, but not that of women; well traveled, yet "profoundly French, or rather Parisian." Alive, he proclaimed the "death of the author"; dead, his estate jealously controlled his authorial rights.[8] Rather than an intimate assessment of Foucault's intellectual personality, Macey provides us with multiple interpretations of it, confining his own role, like a good positivist, to discounting accounts that strain credulity and making reasonable inferences based on imperfect evidence.

Macey's approach can be highly useful. He provides, for instance, the most detailed account of Foucault's early life in Poitiers—though even he limits it to a chapter. While the corresponding chapter in Eribon's account is insightful, its view of Poitiers as the provincial town from which the gay subject must flee to realize his identity limits its scope. Macey takes the time to explain *why* Foucault might have found it suffocating—though also why he regularly returned to Poitiers throughout his life. In a passage that typifies Macey's even-handed approach, he considers multiple accounts of Foucault's relationship with his father: "Accounts of the bad relations between Foucault and his father have no doubt been inflated. In later life, Foucault reputedly often spoke to friends of having hated his father and of having quarreled bitterly with him. Surviving members of the family speak of a relationship which was at times difficult and which cooled over the career issue, but regard talk of bitter hatred as exaggerated."[9]

Macey provides the reader with a wealth of information about Foucault's life. His portrait of Foucault is more multifaceted and nuanced than Eribon's more intimate sketch. Yet despite his immense knowledge, Macey shies away from offering his own assessment—his sense of which, of the many pictures he presents, gets Foucault right. Like his English counterpart's tome on camels, Macey's "fat volume" combines "real documentary value" with "inconclusive facts."

Finally, the place of the scholar who deduced the camel's meaning from the "concept of the ego" alone is occupied, in Foucault-biographical terms, not by a German but by an American. James Miller's *The Passion of Michel Foucault*, published in 1993, is undoubtedly the most provocative interpretation of the philosopher's life. Once again, the analogy with the camel-contemplating philosopher is not entirely merited: far from simply locking himself in a room, Miller has tracked down scores of Foucault interlocutors and obscure texts, many of which were not referenced by the other biographies. But like his German counterpart, Miller is troubled by "the Frenchman's frivolity and the Englishman's lack of general ideas." His primary concern is the big philosophical picture. Consequently, he explains, his book is neither a biography nor a survey of Foucault's works, but rather an account of "one man's lifelong struggle to honor Nietzsche's gnomic injunction, 'to become what one is.'"[10] Drawing on Foucault's own writings, Miller calls his book a "philosophical life."[11] While he, too, is scrupulous about the facts, his main concern is to intuit the "Idea of Michel Foucault." Where Eribon's and Macey's accounts are synoptic, Miller seeks to interpret the meaning of Foucault's philosophical ministry, as his book's Christological title suggests.

Miller emphasizes Foucault's lifelong fascination with death and its implications for knowledge, truth, and identity. We must take seriously, Miller argues, "what at first glance must seem among the most startling and farfetched of Foucault's apparent convictions: that a man's manner of dying, as the capstone of his 'whole life,' may reveal, in a flash, as it were, the 'lyrical core' of his life—*the* key to a writer's 'personal poetic attitude.'"[12] Like Martin Heidegger, a philosopher who profoundly marked his thinking, Foucault "believed that only death, in its culminating conquest, could define the unmistakable singularity—the authenticity—of a human life."[13] Central to the value that Foucault placed on death was his idea of "limit-experience." Miller thus extracts from Foucault's oeuvre a term that he used in *Madness and Civilization* and an early essay on Georges Bataille, using it as a prism from which to view Foucault's philosophical quest. Foucault understood limit-experience as a "kind of atheist ecstasy, an unholy revelation of the human being in its unformed, Dionysian essence."[14] Yet in addition to being a way of living, limit-experience also had a conceptual meaning: for Foucault, the very idea of "limit" always had a Kantian resonance (in the vein of "within the *limits* of reason alone"). It entailed a conception of philosophy as the enterprise of probing the boundaries of the thinkable and knowable in a particular time and place, and the embrace of transgression as a form of "post-Kantian 'critique,'" insofar as it "makes possible a revelation of the limits of reason and of the human being."[15]

Miller maintains that the preoccupation with death and limit-experiences were the leitmotifs of Foucault's thought *and* his life. These obsessions—and not intellectual trends such as structuralism and postmodernism, with which Foucault is commonly associated—formed the threads from which Foucault wove his philosophical quest. Yet if *The Passion of Michel Foucault* is seen as controversial and even inflammatory in the eyes of Foucault enthusiasts, it is because Miller maintains that these conceits illuminate not only the philosopher's thought, but also his personal desires and life choices. Foucault's 1975 LSD trip in the Mojave Desert is one example of a limit-experience; so was his practice of sadomasochism.[16] Most disturbingly, Miller suggests that Foucault's AIDS-related death can be understood in similar terms. Defert, Foucault's longtime companion, tells Miller: "When [Foucault] went to San Francisco for the last time, he took it as a *limit-experience*."[17] Much of the criticism directed at Miller's book stems from his account of the book's genesis in his postscript: that his interest in writing about Foucault's life was piqued by a rumor that Foucault allegedly had sex with men in San Francisco bathhouses when he knew that he was HIV-positive. While concluding that this allegation is groundless, Miller suggests that Foucault's final agony, in which death, sex, and disease merged into a single experience, might be seen as his "deliberately chosen apotheosis."[18]

In all three accounts, Foucault's biographers circle around the question of the relationship between experience and thought. Eribon and Miller have the clearest positions on this question, whereas Macey explores the harmonies and dissonances between Foucault's life and work, never reducing one to the other. Eribon's and Miller's biographies show, moreover, two different approaches to connecting Foucault's life and thought: the former, through a character portrait, albeit one that recognizes how personality intersects with social structures (such as heteronormativity); the latter, by identifying a conceptual leitmotif, in which Foucault's oeuvre becomes thought experience and his life philosophy-in-action. Miller's biography also displays the pitfalls of a bold thesis: that it unwittingly essentializes "abnormal" behavior and thus delegitimizes the main thrust of its subject's thought, and that it fails to account for the complexity of its subject's character.[19]

The aim of the present study is to build on the core insight of Miller's biography while taking seriously the more tempered perspectives of Eribon and Macey. Miller makes a persuasive argument that *experience*—specifically "limit-experience"—was one of Foucault's major philosophical concerns. He also shows that Foucault used a similar vocabulary to articulate his thought and reflect on his life. Miller's many critics accuse him of reducing Foucault's life to the enactment of a philosophical problem and, by the same token, giving credence to homophobic stereotypes. *E pur si muove*: the themes Miller highlights in Foucault's work are still there. Even so, this study does suggest that Miller's approach necessitates two qualifications. First, as we have seen, Foucault has as much to say about *experience* in general as about *limit-experiences* in particular. The importance Foucault attached to experience was not confined to its boundaries and the possibility of transgression. Second and more empirically, Miller's narrative (unlike Eribon's and Macey's) begins when Foucault is already a young adult. Surely experience—including philosophically salient experience—begins earlier. For this reason, it is necessary, if one wants to grasp the relationship between experience and thought, to consider the philosopher-as-youth.

NOTES

Introduction

1. This account draws on David Macey, *The Lives of Michel Foucault* (New York: Pantheon Books, 1993), 471–72. For the news segment, see "Levée du corps de Michel Foucault," INA, https://www.dailymotion.com/video/xfdxfb.

2. Announcement in "Le carnet de *Centre Presse*," *Centre Presse*, June 28, 1984, 2.

3. "Dernier hommage à Michel Foucault," *Centre Presse*, July 1, 1984, 5. My account also draws on Macey, *Lives of Michel Foucault*, 472–73.

4. Hervé Guibert, *À l'ami qui ne m'a pas sauvé la vie* (Paris: Gallimard, 1990), 113–14. This book is generally interpreted as an autobiographical roman à clef. For this reason, I have substituted, in the quote, Foucault's name for that of "Muzil," the name Guibert assigns to his Foucault-inspired character.

5. Michel Foucault, "The Minimalist Self," interview with Stephen Riggins, in *Politics, Philosophy, Culture: Interviews and Other Writings, 1977–1984* (New York: Routledge, Chapman and Hall, 1988), 3–16, at 4.

6. See Jerrold Seigel, *Marx's Fate: The Shape of a Life* (University Park: Pennsylvania State University Press, 1993 [1978]); and Peter Gay, *Freud: A Life for Our Time* (New York: W. W. Norton, 1988). "A Greed for Knowledge"—which draws on a quote from Freud—is the title of Gay's first chapter.

7. Foucault, "La constitution du transcendantal dans la Phénoménologie de l'Esprit de Hegel" (1949); Fonds Michel Foucault, NAF 28803, Manuscripts Department, Bibliothèque Nationale de France, Paris, France.

8. An example of this interpretation can be found in an early study of Foucault's work by Hubert L. Dreyfus and Paul Rabinow. Analyzing *Madness and Civilization*, Foucault's first major book, Dreyfus and Rabinow rightly observe that Foucault was concerned with retrieving an "experience" of madness that had been silenced and suppressed by centuries of medical discourse and institutional practices. Foucault intuited a "fundamental experience of unreason which beckons us beyond the bounds of society"—an authentic voice drowned out by the monotonous drone of scientific chatter. But by the time he was writing his *History of Sexuality*, Dreyfus and Rabinow maintain, Foucault interpreted the "search for a secret, inaccessible sexuality behind experiences" as a "mythic construction of modern thought." Rather than search for a "deep meaning behind appearances"—of the kind that might originate in something like

experience—he began "to interpret those appearances as an organized set of historical practices," which, among other things, gave rise to the human sciences. Only by overcoming his "search for deep truth behind experience" did Foucault arrive at his mature and most distinctive thought. See Dreyfus and Rabinow, *Michel Foucault: Beyond Structuralism and Hermeneutics* (Chicago: University of Chicago Press, 1983), 11-12.

9. Immanuel Kant, *Critique of Pure Reason*, trans. Norman Kemp Smith (New York: St. Martin's Press, 1965), 45.

10. Foucault, "Introduction," in Ludwig Binswanger, *Le rêve et l'existence*, trans. Jacqueline Verdeaux (Paris: Desclée de Brouwer, 1954), 9-128, at 16, 42, and 49. This text is also found in *Dits et écrits*, ed. Daniel Defert, François Ewald, and Jacques Lagrange, vol. 1, *1954-1969* (Paris: Gallimard, 1994), 65-119, at 68, 80, and 83.

11. Foucault, *Maladie mentale et personnalité* (Paris: Presses universitaires de France, 1954), 53.

12. Foucault, "La recherche scientifique et la psychologie," in *Des chercheurs français s'interrogent: Orientation et organisation du travail scientifique en France*, ed. Jean-Édouard Morère (Paris: Press Universitaires de France and Éditions Privat, 1957), 171-201, at 196. This text is also found in *Dits et écrits*, ed. Defert, Ewald, and Lagrange, vol. 1, *1954-1969*, 137-58, at 154.

13. Foucault, *Folie et déraison: Histoire de la folie à l'âge classique* (Paris: Plon, 1961), ix, vii.

14. Foucault, "Dire et voir chez Raymond Roussel," *Dits et écrits*, ed. Defert, Ewald, and Lagrange, vol. 1, *1954-1969*, 205-15, at 215; Foucault, "Préface à la transgression," in *Dits et écrits*, ed. Defert, Ewald, and Lagrange, vol. 1, *1954-1969*, 233-50, at 235 and 241; Foucault, "La prose d'Actéon," in *Dits et écrits*, ed. Defert, Ewald, and Lagrange, vol. 1, *1954-1969*, 326-37, at 326; Foucault, "Distance, aspect, orgine," in *Dits et écrits*, ed. Defert, Ewald, and Lagrange, vol. 1, *1954-1969*, 272-85, at 280; Foucault et al., "Débat sur le roman," in *Dits et écrits*, ed. Defert, Ewald, and Lagrange, vol. 1, *1954-1969*, 338-90, at 339.

15. Foucault, *Naissance de la clinique* (Paris: Presses universitaires de France, 2009 [1963]), 202.

16. Ibid., xv.

17. Foucault, *Histoire de la sexualité*, vol. 2, *L'usage des plaisirs* (Paris: Gallimard, 1984), 10. Though Foucault appears to be referring to *History*'s first volume, Foucault never, in this work, puts the term "experience" to work to analyze sexuality.

18. Ibid., 13.

19. Foucault, "Preface to *History of Sexuality*, Volume II," trans. William Smock, in *The Foucault Reader*, ed. Paul Rabinow (New York: Pantheon Book, 1984), 333-39, at 334, 335.

20. "Michel Foucault: 'L'expérience morale et sociale des Polonais ne peut plus être effacé" (interview with G. Anquetil, 1982), in *Dits et écrits*, ed. Defert, Ewald, and Lagrange, vol. 4, *1980-1988* (Paris: Gallimard, 1994), 343-50, at 345.

21. Foucault [Maurice Florence], "Foucault" (1984), in *Dits et écrits*, ed. Defert, Ewald, and Lagrange, vol. 4, *1980-1988*, 631-36, at 634.

22. Foucault, "Une esthétique de l'existence" (interview with Alessandro Fontana, 1984) in in *Dits et écrits*, ed. Defert, Ewald, and Lagrange, vol. 4, *1980–1988*, 730–35, at 731.

23. Foucault, "Est-il donc important de penser?" (interview with Didier Eribon, 1981), in *Dits et écrits*, ed. Defert, Ewald, and Lagrange, vol. 4, *1980–1988*, 178-82, at 181. Eribon refers to this quote while reflecting on its content in *Réflexions sur la question gay* (Paris: Champs-Flammarion, 2012 [1999]), 382.

24. Key interventions in this debate include Wilhelm Dilthey, *Die Jugendgeschichte Hegels und andere Abhandlungen zur Geschichte des deutschen Idealismus* (Stuttgart: B. G. Teubner Verlagsgesellschaft and Vandenhoeck and Ruprecht, 1963); and Georg Lukács, *The Young Hegel: Studies in the Relations Between Dialectics and Economics*, trans. Rodney Livingstone (Cambridge, Mass.: MIT Press, 1976 [1966]).

25. Key statements in this debate include Erich Fromm, *Marx's Concept of Man* (New York: Ungar, 1966); Louis Althusser, *Pour Marx* (Paris: La Découverte, 1986 [1965]).

26. Edward Baring, *The Young Derrida and French Philosophy, 1945–1968* (Cambridge: Cambridge University Press, 2011).

27. José Luis Moreno Pestaña, *En devenant Foucault: Sociogenèse d'un grand philosophe*, trans. Philippe Hunt (Broissieux: Éditions du Croquant, 2006).

28. Stuart Elden, *The Early Foucault* (Cambridge, Mass.: Polity, 2021), 3.

29. Foucault, *Le beau danger: Entretien avec Claude Bonnefoy* (Paris: Éditions de l'École des Hautes Études en Sciences Sociales, 2011), 32.

30. Jacques Derrida, "Circonfession," in Geoffrey Bennington and Derrida, *Jacques Derrida* (Paris: Seuil, 1991), 7-292; Pierre Bourdieu, *Esquisse pour une auto-analyse* (Paris: Raisons d'agir, 2004).

31. Jerrold Seigel, "Autonomy and Personality in Durkheim: An Essay on Content and Method," *Journal of the History of Ideas* 48, no. 3 (1987): 483–507, at 505.

32. Seigel, *Marx's Fate*.

33. Seigel, "Autonomy and Personality in Durkheim: An Essay on Content and Method," 505.

34. Foucault, "Est-il donc important de penser?," 181–82.

Chapter 1

1. Michel Foucault, *Le beau danger: Entretien avec Claude Bonnefoy* (Paris: Éditions de l'École des Hautes Études en Sciences Sociales, 2011), 33.

2. Ibid., 31.

3. Ibid., 32.

4. Ibid., 32–33.

5. Ibid., 33.

6. Foucault, "Le 'non' du père" (1962), *Dits et écrits*, vol. 1, *1954–1969*, ed. Daniel Defert, François Ewald, and Jacques Lagrange (Paris: Gallimard, 1994), 189–203, at 199.

7. Foucault, "Préface" (1961) (original introduction to *Folie et déraison*), in Defert, Ewald, and Lagrange, *Dits et écrits*, vol. 1, *1954–1969*, 159–67, at 160.

8. Ibid., 166.

9. Ibid., 162.

10. Ibid., 166.

11. Foucault, *Le beau danger*, 35.

12. Ibid., 33.

13. Foucault, "Conversation with Michel Foucault," interview with Millicent Dillon, *Threepenny Review* 1 (Winter–Spring 1980): 4–5, at 4. A slightly different version of this interview was published as "Foucault Examines Reason in Service of State Power" in *Campus Report*, October 24, 1979, 5–6. The quote comes from the lead-in to the interview, which is not included in the French version: "Foucault étudie la raison d'État," in *Dits et écrits*, vol. 4, *1980–1988*, ed. Daniel Defert, François Ewald, and Jacques Lagrange (Paris: Gallimard, 1994), 37–41.

14. Foucault, *Le beau danger*, 34, 35.

15. Ibid., 35.

16. Ibid.

17. Ibid.

18. Ibid., 35–36.

19. Ibid., 36.

20. Ibid.

21. Ibid., 37.

22. Ibid., 40.

23. Ibid., 41.

24. See Didier Eribon, *Michel Foucault (1926–84)* (Paris: Flammarion, 1991), 27–28; and David Macey, *The Lives of Michel Foucault* (New York: Pantheon Books, 1993), 11. Both place this incident around the time Foucault completed his *baccalauréat* in 1943.

25. Pierre Rambaud, "Nécrologie: P. P. Malapert," *Le Poitou médical*, May 1, 1887, 116–20. See, too, Paul Mantrant's account of a presentation on Prosper Malapert by M. A. Guillon, "Séance du 21 février 1980," *Bulletin de la Société des antiquaires de l'Ouest et des musées de Poitiers* 15, no. 1 (1980): 325–29, at 328–29.

26. Édouard-Prosper Malapert, *Synthèses de pharmacie et de chimie, présentées et soutenues à l'Ecole de pharmacie, le samedi 14 janvier 1854* (Paris: E. Thunot et Cie., 1854).

27. Untitled death notice, *Le libéral de la Vendée*, August 25, 1876, [3].

28. See the entry "Malapert (Prosper)" in Le Doyen Boissonnade, ed., *Histoire de l'Université de Poitiers: Passé et présent (1432–1932)* (Poitiers: Nicolas, Renault et Cie., 1932), 516. While this entry identifies its subject as "Prosper Malapert," it is clearly referring to Henri Paulin Malapert.

29. Jacques-Symphorien Foucault, "Propositions sur quelques points de médecine et de chirurgie," Medical thesis, Faculté de Médecine de Paris, Paris, 1835.

30. *Préfecture de la Seine: Recueil des actes administratifs*, no. 6 (Paris, 1844): 129.

31. M. le docteur Foucault de Nanterre [Jacques-Symphorien Foucault], "Mémoire sur les irrigations prolongées ou continues dans toutes les affections des organes

accessibles aux liquides," *L'union médicale* 8, no. 110 (September 14, 1854): 450–51, at 451.

32. "Lecture. Symphyséotomie," report read by "M. Foucault of Nanterre," on behalf of himself and "M. Dairaux" of Reuil to the Académie Impériale de Médécine, session of September 18, 1860, *Gazette des hôpitaux civils et militaires*, September 20, 1860, 443.

33. "Le Dr. P. Foucault" (Paul Victor Foucault), *Mémoire sur une épidémie de rougeole* (Fontainebleau: Ernest Bourges, 1872).

34. Foucault described assisting the French wounded near Mont-Mesly in Créteil during the Battle of Champigny in November 1870. See "Le régime alimentaire des grands blessés," in *Société française de secours aux blessés militaires. Conférences par le Dr. Foucault de Fontainebleau* (Fontainebleau: Maurice Bourges, 1901), 17–30, at 22–23.

35. Paul Denis du Péage, *Recueil de généalogies lilloises*, vol. 3 (Lille: Lefebvre-Ducrocq,1908), 956–57.

36. Entry on "Cuvillon (Jean-Baptiste-Philémon de)," in François-Joseph Fétis, *Biographie universelle des musiciens et bibliographie générale de la musique*, vol. 2 (Paris: Firmin Didot, 1867), 406–7; *Annuaire de la noblesse de France et des maisons souveraines de l'Europe* (Paris: Bureau de la publication, 1858), 201.

37. Alexis de Tocqueville, *Democracy in America*, trans. Harvey C. Mansfield and Delba Winthrop (Chicago: University of Chicago Press, 2002), 483.

38. Rambaud, "P. P. Malapert," 116, 120.

39. Henri Delaunay, *Historique de l'École préparatoire de médecine et de pharmacie de Poitiers: 1806-1900* (Poitiers: Fayoux, 1900), 10.

40. "Malapert (Prosper)," 516.

41. Untitled death notice, *Le libéral de la Vendée*, [3].

42. See Macey, *Lives of Michel Foucault*, 483n1.

43. André Guillon, "Un pharmacien poitevin, élève d'Orfila," *Revue d'histoire de la pharmacie*, 64, no. 231 (1976): 260–68, at 268.

44. Paul Foucault [Paul Victor Foucault], *Essai sur les tumeurs des nerfs mixtes: Thèse pour le doctorat en médecine; Faculté de médecine de Paris* (Paris: Parent, 1872), n.p.

45. Paul Foucault [Paul André Foucault], *Occlusions intestinales et coudures iléales: Thèse pour le doctorat en médecine* (Paris: Librairie Louis Arnette, 1923), n.p.

46. Jerrold Seigel, *Modernity and Bourgeois Life: Society, Politics, and Culture in England, France, and Germany Since 1750* (Cambridge: Cambridge University Press, 2012), 312.

47. Ibid.

48. Foucault, *Le beau danger*, 32. Foucault first referred to this idea in *Naissance de la clinique* (Paris: Presses Universitaires de France, 1963), attributing it to the doctor and medical historian José Miguel Guardia: "health replaces salvation, as Guardia said" (201). He referred to it, too, in his 1964 talk "Nietzsche, Freud, Marx," in *Dits et écrits*, vol. 1, *1954-1969*, 564–79, at 579 (with "Guardia" presumably misspelled as "Garcia"). Finally, Foucault alludes to this idea in a 1968 article for *Esprit*, referring to explanations of the rise of clinical discourse in terms of changing consciousness, notably a new

worldview in which "the concern for health replaces the preoccupation with salvation." Foucault, "Réponse à une question" (1968), *Dits et écrits*, vol. 1, *1954-1969*, 673-95, at 689. Philippe Theophanidis has usefully traced all these allusions in Foucault's work to this quote ("'La santé remplace le salut' in the Work of Michel Foucault," *Aphelis*, https://aphelis.net/sante-salut-michel-foucault/, accessed February 23, 2018). Theophanidis suggests that Foucault may have learned of the Guardia quote from Georges Canguilhem's book, *Le normal et le pathologique* (Paris: Presses Universitaires de France, 1993 [1966]), a reworking of his 1943 thesis (which may have been the text Foucault knew). On p. 61, Canguilhem quotes "a history of medicine" that refers to the fact that the Paracelsian chemist Jan Baptist van Helmont "confused health with salvation and sickness with sin." Confusingly, the source of this quote is not made clear in the 1966 edition (though it is in the English translation). It comes from Jean-Michel Guardia, *Histoire de la médecine, d'Hippocrate à Broussais et ses successeurs* (Paris: Octave Doin, 1884), 311. In short, the version of the quote that Foucault liked to reference was a considerably mangled version of the original. Yet there are, of course, plenty of reasons to believe that Foucault's own family upbringing would have familiarized him with a more general version of the same idea, as the reference to the quote while discussing his own background in *Le beau danger* suggests.

49. Maximilien Isidore Simon, quoted in Hervé Guillemain, "Devenir médecin au XIXe siècle: Vocation et sacerdoce au sein d'une profession laïque," *Annales de Bretagne et des Pays de l'Ouest* 116, no. 3 (2009): 109-23, at 113.

50. [Paul Victor Foucault], *Mémoire sur une épidémie de rougeole*, 1.

51. Foucault, "Qu'est-ce qu'un auteur?" (1969), in *Dits et écrits*, vol. 1, *1954-1969*, 789-821, at 800.

52. See, for example, *Journal officiel de la République française*, March 15, 1917, 2071.

53. Jacques Léonard, *La vie quotidienne du médecin de province au XIXe siècle* (Paris: Hachette, 1977), 30. Léonard's numbers refer to the nineteenth century, so they presumably had increased somewhat by the early 1920s.

54. On Arrou, see Joseph Uzanne and Angelo Mariani, "Le docteur Joseph Arrou," in *Figures contemporaines, tirées de l'album Mariani*, vol. 9 (Paris: Libraire Henri Floury, 1904), n.p.

55. Paul Foucault, *Occlusions intestinales et coudures iléales*. On Lejars, see Uzanne and Mariani, "Le docteur Lejars," in *Figures contemporaines, tirées de l'album Mariani*, vol. 8 (Paris: Libraire Henri Floury, 1903), n.p.

56. Placide Mauclaire referred to work that had been presented by Paul Victor Foucault when still an intern at the Academie Impériale de Médecine and commented on by Dr. Georges Hayem. See "Extrait du rapport de M. Hayem sur la candidature de M. Foucault," *Bulletins de la Société anatomique de Paris*, November 1869, 509-12. Placide refers to the same work by Foucault in his *Chirurgie générale des muscles, des tendons, des bourses séreuses et de la peau* (Paris: Octave Doin, 1901), 48. In a treatiste that he wrote with L. Picqué, Mauclaire mentioned the "device of Foucault of Nanterre"—i.e., Jacques-Symphorien Foucault—for reducing joint dislocations, *Thérapeutique chirurgicale des*

maladies des articulations: Muscles, tendons, synoviales tendineuses (Paris: Octave Dion, 1895), 1:83.

57. *Guide Rosenwald. Annuaire médical et pharmaceutique: 1925* (Paris: Rosenwald, 1925), 1526.

58. The name of these clinics is found in Paul-René Martin, *Fruchaud d'Angers (1894-1960)* (Angers: Éditions du Martinet, 2008), 103. The location of these clinics can be found in *Annuaire 1950 de Poitiers et du département de la Vienne* (Poitiers: Texier, 1952), 374. Not including the Hôtel-Dieu, this town directory lists six clinics in Poitiers at this time.

59. See Eribon, *Michel Foucault*, 21; and Macey, *Lives of Michel Foucault*, 2-3.

60. See *Annuaire de l'Université de Poitiers 1924-1925* (Poitiers: Lévrier-Labouygue, 1924), 159-61; *Annuaire de l'Université de Poitiers 1925-1926* (Poitiers: Lévrier-Labouygue, 1925), 163-65.

61. Gérard Simmat, *L'Hôtel-Dieu de Poitiers: L'Hôtel Pinet; Deux siècles de médecine* (Poitiers: Centre Hospitalier Universitaire de Poitiers, 2015).

62. "Témoignage de Maître Jacques Grandon (janvier 2015)," in Simmat, *L'Hôtel-Dieu de Poitiers*, 42. On Jacques Quivy, see "Décès de Jacques Quivy (1904-65), de Poitiers, associé national. Allocution de M. le Président," *Mémoires: Académie de chirurgie* 24, no. 91 (1965): 802-3.

63. Macey, *Lives of Michel Foucault*, 16. After Foucault's death, the Masson painting became the property of Foucault's brother, Denys—the surgeon.

64. Hervé Guibert, "Les secrets d'un homme," *Mauve le vierge* (Paris: Gallimard, 1988), 105-6. James Miller, to whose book I owe this reference, offers a powerful interpretation of this passage in *The Passion of Michel Foucault* (New York: Simon and Schuster, 1993), 364-67.

65. Drs. [Fernand] Landry and [Paul] Foucault, "Perforation vésicale par corps étranger," *Revue médicale du Centre-Ouest* 5 (1939): 118-25.

66. Drs. [Paul] Foucault, Boucheronde, and Boursegain, "Corps étrangers du vagin," *Revue médicale du Centre-Ouest* 3 (1947): 108.

67. Dr. [Paul] Foucault, "Torsion totale de l'appareil utéro-annexiel par tumeur ovarienne," *Revue médicale du Centre-Ouest* 5 (1938): 131-32, at 131.

68. Drs. Gabette, [Pierre] Ducellier, and [Paul] Foucault, "Un cas de malformation vaginale," *Revue médicale du Centre-Ouest* 7 (1937): 208-12, at 211, 212.

69. [Jacques Bénigne] Bossuet, "Sermon sur la mort" (1662), in *Oraisons funèbres et sermons I* (Paris: Librairie Larousse, 1942), 11-23, at 11.

70. Foucault, *Leçons sur la volonté de savoir: Cours au Collège de France; 1970-1971* (Paris: Gallimard/Seuil, 2011), 6.

71. Foucault, "Nietzsche, Genealogy, History" (1971), in *The Foucault Reader*, ed. Paul Rabinow (New York: Pantheon, 1984), 76-100, at 88. This essay was originally published as "Nietzsche, la généalogie, l'histoire" in *Hommage à Jean Hyppolite* (Paris: Presses universitaires de France, 1971), 145-72. It can also be fond in *Dits et écrits*, vol. 2, *1970-1975*, ed. Daniel Defert, François Ewald, and Jacques Lagrange (Paris: Gallimard, 1994), 136-56.

72. Paul Foucault, *Titres et travaux scientifiques* (Poitiers: Imprimerie du Poitou, 1926).

73. James C. Whorton, *Inner Hygiene: Constipation and the Pursuit of Health in Modern Society* (New York: Oxford University Press, 2000), 58.

74. Arbuthnot Lane, quoted in ibid., 56.

75. Lane, quoted in ibid., 62.

76. Alison C. Bested, Alan C. Logan, and Eva M. Selhub, "Intestinal Microbiota, Probiotics and Mental Health: From Metchnikoff to Modern Advances: Part I—Autointoxication Revisited," *Gut Pathogens* 5, no. 5 (2013): 1–16, at 4.

77. Statistic and quote (from Sir Arthur Hurst) in J. Lacey Smith, "Sir Arbuthnot Lane, Chronic Intestinal Stasis, and Autointoxication," *Annals of Internal Medicine* 96, no. 3 (1982): 365–69, at 367.

78. Andrew Scull, *Madhouse: A Tragic Tale of Megalomania and Modern Medicine* (New Haven, Conn.: Yale University Press, 2007), 259.

79. W. Arbuthnot Lane, "The First and Last Kink in Chronic Intestinal Stasis," *Lancet*, December 2, 1911, 1540–41, at 1540.

80. Paul Foucault, *Occlusions intestinales et coudures iléales*, 9.

81. Ibid., 82.

82. Paul Foucault, "Volvulus du caecum," *Archives médico-chirurgicales de province*, March 1924. See Paul Foucault, *Titres et travaux*, 26–43, at 32.

83. Smith, "Sir Arbuthnot Lane," 369.

84. Macey, *Lives of Michel Foucault*, 16. Macey also notes that Piel had, as a student, studied the philosophy textbook written by Foucault's maternal uncle, Paulin Malapert, who will be discussed in the next chapter.

85. Jean Piel, *La rencontre et la différence* (Paris: Fayard, 1982), 269.

86. Given that the accident occurred in Versailles, at some distance from Poitiers, it seems likely that Paul Foucault may not have been the initial surgeon.

87. Piel, *La rencontre et la différence*, 269–70.

88. Macey, *Lives of Michel Foucault*, 16. It was also around this time that Paul Foucault treated André Masson (a brother-in-law of Piel's, by way of the Maklès sisters, through whom both were also related to Georges Bataille), in the incident discussed earlier.

89. Foucault, "Entretien enregistré le 3 avril 1978: Michel Foucault, Colin Gordon, Paul Patton," in "Papers from the UC Berkeley French Studies Program, Pertaining to Michel Foucault's Visits at Berkeley and Stanford University, 1975–1984," BANC MSS 90/136z, 22, Bancroft Library, University of California at Berkeley. Note that this paragraph draws on a point I made in "Foucault and Technology," *History and Technology* 29, no. 1 (2013): 54–104, at 94–95.

90. Michel Foucault, "La politique de la santé au XVIIIe siècle," in *Les machines à guérir: Aux origines de l'hôpital moderne*, ed. Foucault, Blandine Barret Kriegel, Anne Thalamy, François Beguin, and Bruno Fortier (Brussels: Pierre Mardaga, 1979), 7–18, at 7. An earlier edition of this book and Foucault's essay appeared in 1976.

91. Simmat, *L'Hôtel-Dieu de Poitiers*, 25.

92. Foucault, "La politique de la santé au XVIIIe siècle," 7.

93. Rambaud, "P. P. Malapert," 116.

94. Foucault, "La politique de la santé au XVIIIe siècle," 7.

95. Ibid.

96. Foucault, "Réponse à une question," *Dits et écrits*, vol. 1, *1954–1969*, 673–95, at 688–89. Foucault makes this point when he is refuting a model of thinking about the political character of discourse that would associate evolving medical ideas with the changing outlook of the dominant class, that is, the nineteenth-century bourgeoise. Consequently, Foucault uses language here that is self-consciously simplistic. But this choice implies that many of his interlocutors may have thought about this period in similarly simplistic terms. This essay originally appeared in *Esprit* 371 (1968): 850–74.

97. Foucault, "La politique de la santé au XVIIIe siècle," 14.

98. M. Doucet in 1892, quoted in Simmat, *L'Hôtel-Dieu de Poitiers*, 34.

99. Foucault, "La politique de la santé au XVIIIe siècle," 16.

100. Simmat, *L'Hôtel-Dieu de Poitiers*, 34, 36.

101. Foucault, "La politique de la santé au XVIIIe siècle," 16.

102. Ibid.

103. Ibid.

104. Simmat, *L'Hôtel-Dieu de Poitiers*, 34, 43.

105. Ibid., 41.

106. Foucault, "La politique de la santé au XVIIIe siècle," 15.

107. Simmat, *L'Hôtel-Dieu de Poitiers*, 34, 41.

108. Ibid., 37.

109. Foucault, *Histoire de la folie à l'âge classique*, 60, 61.

110. Quoted in Pierre Rambaud, "L'assistance publique à Poitiers jusqu'à l'an V," in *Mémoires de la Société des antiquaires de l'Ouest* 3rd series, vol. 5 (1911): 1–663, at 421.

111. Emmanuel Thévenet, "La pauvreté en Poitou sous l'Ancien Régime vue à travers le prisme de l'hôpital général de Poitiers," *Annales de Bretagne et des Pays de l'Ouest* 113, no. 4 (2006): 159–82, at 160.

112. Charles de Chergé, *Le guide du voyageur à Poitiers* (Poitiers: Henri Oudin, 1851), 120.

113. Simmat, *L'Hôtel-Dieu de Poitiers*, 40n; and Dr. [Maurice-Paul] Veluet, "L'École de médecine et de pharmacie de Poitiers," *Revue médicale du Centre-Ouest* 5, no. 8 (1933): 217–57, at 229–30.

114. Foucault, "La politique de la santé au XVIIIe siècle," 16.

115. Veluet, "L'École de médecine et de pharmacie de Poitiers," 223–24.

116. Ibid., 248.

117. Ibid., 224.

118. Foucault, "La politique de la santé au XVIIIe siècle," 17.

119. Foucault, *Histoire de la sexualité*, vol. 1, *La Volonté de savoir* (Paris: Gallimard, 1976), 25, 42.

120. Ibid., 56.

121. Ibid., 64.

122. Ibid., 62.

123. Uzanne and Mariani, "Le docteur Joseph Arrou," n.p. Arrou was indirectly connected to Charcot through the latter's student Alfred Pitres (1848–1928), with whom Arrou studied.

124. Foucault, *La volonté de savoir*, 60, 61.

125. Joseph Arrou, *Chirurgie de l'appareil génital de l'homme* (Paris: Octave Dion, 1901), 278.

126. Ibid., 285, 286.

127. Ibid., 324.

128. Paul Foucault, "Les torsions du testicule et du cordon spermatique," *Archives médico-chirurgicales de province*, September 1924, 346–52, at 348.

129. Louis Ombrédanne, "L'orchite aigüe primitive des enfants," *La presse médicale* 59 (July 19, 1913): 595–98, at 596. Ombrédanne is referring to Gosselin, Curling, and Brodie's research at the Cliniques de la Charité. Ombrédanne concludes, somewhat non-committally: "The determining action of masturbation on testicular accidents no longer seems particularly in favor at present" (596).

130. Foucault, *La volonté de savoir*, 138.

131. Paul Foucault, "Les torsions du testicule et du cordon spermatique," 350–51.

132. Ibid., 352.

133. Foucault, *La volonté de savoir*, 204.

134. R[aymond-Noël] Darget and P[aul] Foucault, "De la conduite à tenir en présence de l'impuissance sexuelle chez l'homme," *L'actualité médico-chirurgicale*, November 1938, 270–83, at 270.

135. Ibid., 271; Foucault, *La volonté de savoir*, 32.

136. Darget and Foucault, "De la conduite à tenir en présence de l'impuissance sexuelle," 271.

137. Foucault, *La volonté de savoir*, 72.

138. Darget and Foucault, "De la conduite à tenir en présence de l'impuissance sexuelle," 275.

139. Ibid., 278.

140. Ibid., 276.

141. Paul Foucault, "Les torsions du testicule et du cordon spermatique," 352.

142. Darget and Foucault, "De la conduite à tenir en présence de l'impuissance sexuelle," 283.

143. Thomas Schlich, *The Origins of Organ Transplantation: Surgery and Laboratory Science, 1880–1930* (Rochester, N.Y.: University of Rochester Press, 2010), 99.

144. Ibid., 103.

145. Ibid., 106.

146. Dan Piepenbring, "Monkey Glands for Everyone," *Paris Review*, June 17, 2015, https://www.theparisreview.org/blog/2015/06/17/monkey-glands-for-everyone/. The

e. e. cummings poem, entitled "why are these pipples taking their hets off," appeared in *is 5*. See, too, Jean Réal, *Voronoff* (Paris: Stock, 2001).

147. Darget and Foucault, "De la conduite à tenir en présence de l'impuissance sexuelle," 281.

148. Ibid.

149. Dr. Louis Dartigues, *Le renouvellement de l'organisme: Endocrinothérapie chirugicale* (Paris: Gaston Dion, 1928), 229.

150. Ibid.

151. Ibid., 230.

152. Ibid., 231.

153. Ibid.

154. Ibid., 234.

155. Ibid., 239.

156. Darget and Foucault, "De la conduite à tenir en présence de l'impuissance sexuelle," 279.

157. Ibid., 271.

158. Schlich, *Origins of Organ Transplantation*, 112.

159. Quoted in ibid., 115. The quote is drawn from Eugen Steinach and Robert Lichtenberg, "Unstimmung der Homosexualität durch Austausch der Pubertätsdrüsen," *Münchener medizinische Wochenschrift* 65 (1918): 145–48, at 147.

160. Schlich, *Origins of Organ Transplantation*, 115.

161. Foucault, *La volonté de savoir*, 51.

162. Ibid., 55, 53.

163. Ibid., 53–54, emphasis added.

164. Ibid., 59.

165. Foucault, "Résumé du cours," in *Théorie et institutions pénales: Cours au Collège de France, 1971–1972* (Paris: Gallimard/Seuil, 2015), 231–34, at 234.

166. Foucault, "Résumé du cours," in *La société punitive: Cours au Collège de France, 1972–1973* (Paris : Gallimard/Seuil, 2013), 255–69, at 269.

167. Foucault, "Le pouvoir psychiatrique [résumé du cours]," in *Dits et écrits*, vol. 2, *1970–1975*, 675–86, at 686.

168. Foucault, *Les anormaux: Cours au Collège de France, 1974–1975* (Paris: Gallimard/Seuil, 1999), 29.

169. Foucault, "Entretien sur la prison: Le livre et sa méthode" (interview with J.-J. Brochier) in *Dits et écrits*, vol. 2, *1970–1975, 740–53, at 746*. This interview was originally published in *Le magazine littéraire* 101 (1975): 27–33. The previous year, Foucault was involved in a panel on forensic psychiatry, which was published as "Table ronde sur l'expertise psychiatrique," in *Actes: Cahiers d'action juridique* 5–6 (1974–1975): 45–52. It can also be found in *Dits et écrits*, vol. 2, *1970–1975*, 664–75.

170. Rambaud, "P. P. Malapert," 118.

171. José Ramón Bertomeu-Sánchez, "Classrooms, Salons, Academies, and Courts: Mateu Orfila (1787–1853) and Nineteenth-Century French Toxicology," *Ambix* 61,

no. 2 (2014): 162–86, at 163. On Orfila, see, too, José Ramón Bertomeu-Sanchez and Agustí Nieto-Galan, eds., *Chemistry, Medicine, and Crime: Mateu J. B. Orfila (1787–1853) and His Times* (Sagamore Beach, Mass.: Science History, 2006); and Amédée Fayol, *La vie et l'oeuvre d'Orfila* (Paris: A. Michel, 1930).

172. Bertomeu-Sánchez, "Classrooms, Salons, Academies, and Courts," 163.

173. Esquirol, Orfila, Marc, Pariset, Rostan, Mitivié, and Leuret, "Consultation délibérée à Paris, sur l'état mental de Pierre Rivière," in Foucault, ed., *Moi, Pierre Rivière, ayant égorgé ma mère, ma sœur, et mon frère . . . Un cas de parricide au XIXe siècle* (Paris: Gallimard/Juliard, 1973), 205–7.

174. Robert Castel, "Les médecins et les juges," in ibid., 315–31, at 327.

175. Foucault, "Résumé du cours," in *Théorie et institutions pénales*, 234.

176. Guillon, "Un pharmacien poitevin," 264.

177. Ibid., 264–66.

178. Ibid., 265. This quote is also cited in the opening paragraph of Rambaud's obituary, "P. P. Malapert," 116.

179. Rambaud, "P. P. Malapert," 118.

180. Guillon, "Un pharmacien poitevin," 166.

181. Archives de Paris, 8eme arrondissement, Mariages, 1879, 486.

182. "Nécrologie," in *Journal de chirurgie et de médicine pratiques* 87 (1916): 48.

183. See Jeffrey Moussaieff Masson, *The Assault on Truth: Freud's Suppression of the Seduction Theory* (New York: Farrar, Strauss and Giroux, 1984), chapter 2, "Freud at the Paris Morgue," 14–54.

184. Ambroise Tardieu, *Étude médico-légale sur les attentats aux mœurs*, 3rd ed. (Paris: Baillière, 1859). These quotes (and translations) are taken from Scott Long, "When Doctors Torture: The Anus and the State in Egypt and Beyond," *Health and Human Rights* 7, no. 2 (2004), 114–40, at 117–19. On the influence of Tardieu's "signs" for recognizing pederasty and related ideas, see Victoria Thompson, "Creating Boundaries: Homosexuality and the Changing Social Order in France, 1830–1870," 102–27; William A. Peniston, "Love and Death in Gay Paris: Homosexuality and Criminality in the 1870s," 128–45; and Vernon A. Rosario, "Pointy Penises, Fashion Crimes, and Hysterical Mollies: The Pederasts' Inversions," 146–76; all in Jeffrey Merrick and Bryant T. Ragan, eds., *Homosexuality in Modern France* (New York: Oxford University Press, 1996). See, too, Rosario, *The Erotic Imagination: French Histories of Perversity* (New York: Oxford University Press, 1997).

185. Foucault, *La volonté de savoir*, 34n2.

186. Laugier, "Du rôle de l'expertise médico-légale dans certains cas d'outrage public à la pudeur," *Annales d'hygiène publique et de médecine légale* 50 (1878): 164–73, at 165, 166. For an intriguing account of the problems public urinals posed to nineteenth-century French society, see Andrew Israel Ross, "Dirty Desire: The Uses and Misuses of Public Urinals in Nineteenth-Century Paris," *Berkeley Journal of Sociology* 53 (2009): 62–88.

187. "Deuxième partie: Histoire d'Alexina B.," in Tardieu, *Question médico-légale de l'identité dans ses rapports avec les vices de conformation des organes sexuels,* 2nd

ed. (Paris: J.-B. Baillière, 1874), 61–174. An excerpt of Tardieu's report is included in Foucault, *Herculine Barbin, dite Alexina B.* (Paris: Gallimard, 2014 [1978]), 145–46, 61–174. It is worth noting that in that Tardieu concludes Barbin's memoirs with a bracketed conclusion, noting that the memoirs were completed shortly after her death. In Foucault's version, Tardieu's remarks are replaced with a bracketed conclusion by Foucault himself.

188. Foucault, "Introduction," in *Herculine Barbin, Being the Recently Discovered Memoirs of a Nineteenth-Century French Hermaphrodite*, trans. Richard McDougall (New York: Pantheon Books, 1980), xi.

189. Laugier, "Hermaphrodisme, anatomie et physiologie," *Nouveau dictionnaire de médecine et de chirurgie pratiques*, vol. 17 (Paris : J.-B. Baillière, 1873), 488–507, at 493.

190. Tardieu and Laugier, "Hermaphrodisme, médecine légale," in ibid., 507–12, at 508.

191. Ibid., 509.

192. Ibid., 511.

193. Another figure in Paul Foucault's circle who was particularly interested in hermaphroditism was André Lapointe (1869–1931). In his thesis, he also expresses gratitude to one Dr. Lapointe, who "offered me his advice and his encouragement." André Lapointe was an important surgeon with whom Foucault had also crossed paths at the Hôpital Saint-Antoine. While his scholarship was, like most of Paul Foucault's mentors, focused on surgery, Lapointe was particularly concerned with medical matters pertaining to sexuality and perversity. The author of a thesis on noncongenital shrinkage of the rectum (*Titres et travaux scientifiques du Docteur André Lapointe* [n.d.: n.p., n.p.], 9–16), he also published, with fellow surgeon Théodore Tuffier, a major study of hermaphrodites, "L'hermaphrodisme: Ses variétés et ses conséquences pour la pratique médicale (d'après un cas personnel)," in *Revue de gynécologie et de chirurgie abdominale* 16 (1911): 209–68.

194. Foucault, "Introduction," in *Herculine Barbin*, vii.

195. Foucault, *L'archéologie du savoir* (Paris: Gallimard, 1969), 28. The English translation, while successfully capturing the spirit of Foucault's words, leaves out the reference to *état civil*, presumably because there is no obvious English translation that has the same associations: "Do not ask who I am and do not ask me to remain the same: leave it to our bureaucrats and our police to see that our papers are in order." Foucault, *The Archaeology of Knowledge*, trans. A. M. Sheridan Smith (New York: Pantheon Books, 1972), 17.

196. Foucault, *L'archéologie du savoir*, 28.

197. Denys Foucault, *Les duplications abdominales du tube digestif (à propos de 23 observations)*, medical thesis, Paris Medical Faculty, Paris, 1963.

198. Paul Foucault, *Planches coloriées d'anatomie: Membre supérieur; Deuxième série* (Paris: Librairie des Sciences et des Arts, 1946).

199. Review of Paul Foucault, "Planches coloriées d'anatomie," *Gazette des hôpitaux civils et militaires*, August 15, 1946, 360.

200. Ibid.

201. Foucault, "Ceci n'est pas une pipe" (1968), in *Dits et écrits*, vol. 1, *1954–1969*, 635–50, at 637.

202. Ibid., 643.

203. Ibid., 644.

204. Ibid., 646.

205. Foucault, *Le beau danger*, 33, 34.

206. Ibid., 34.

207. Foucault, "Ceci n'est pas une pipe," 645.

208. Foucault, *Le beau danger*, 35.

209. Foucault, "Ceci n'est pas une pipe," 644.

210. "Le docteur Foucault n'est plus," *Centre Presse*, September 15, 1959, [2].

211. "Tout Poitiers assistait aux obsèques du Dr. Foucault qui ont été célébrées hier matin," *Centre Presse*, September 18, 1959, [2].

212. Daniel Defert suggests that Foucault's time in Poland ended with some difficulty, when Polish secret police sought to compromise him by and force him to leave by trapping him in a relationship with a younger interpreter. "Chronologie," in *Dits et écrits*, vol. 1, *1954–1969*, 13–64, at 23. Given that Foucault moved to Hamburg in early October 1959, it is possible his situation in Warsaw prevented him from returning to Poitiers.

213. "Mme. Paul Foucault," *Centre Presse*, November 13, 1987, [2].

214. Thierry Voeltzel, *Vingt ans et après* (interviews with Michel Foucault) (Paris: Verticales, 2014), 49.

Chapter 2

1. Michel Foucault, "The Minimalist Self," interview with Stephen Riggins, in *Politics, Philosophy, Culture: Interviews and Other Writings, 1977–1984* (New York: Routledge, Chapman and Hall, 1988), 3–16, at 4, 3. This interview, which was conducted in English, was first published as "Michel Foucault: An Interview" in *Ethos* 1, no. 2 (1983): 4–9. It appears in *Dits et écrits* as "Une interview de Michel Foucault par Stephen Riggins," trans. F. Durand-Bogaert, vol. 4, *1980–1988*, ed. Daniel Defert, François Ewald, and Jacques Lagrange (Paris: Gallimard, 1994), 525–38.

2. Denys Foucault, "Nés pour apprendre," interview with Jean-Luc Terradillos, *L'actualité Poitou-Charentes* 51, January–March 2001, 27–29, at 29.

3. Foucault, "Préface" (original introduction to *Folie et déraison*, 1961), in *Dits et écrits*, vol. 1, *1954–1969*, ed. Daniel Defert, François Ewald, and Jacques Lagrange (Paris: Gallimard, 1994), 159–67, at 166.

4. Thierry Voeltzel, "Letzlove: L'anagramme d'une rencontre" (2014), in Voeltzel, *Vingt ans et après* (interviews with Michel Foucault) (Paris: Verticales, 2014), 203–11, at 203. Originally published as Thierry Voeltzel, *Vingt ans et après*, ed. Mireille Davidovici, with a preface by Claude Mauriac (the series editor) (Paris: Grasset, 1978). As Voeltzel explains in the aforementioned essay, written on the occasion of the book's republication, Mauriac and Foucault (who were close friends at the time) deliberately left out any mention of Foucault's name in the original edition, despite the fact that the book

consisted entirely of conversations between Foucault and Voeltzel, lest Foucault become the focus of attention.

5. This account is drawn from Voeltzel, "Letzlove: L'anagramme d'une rencontre," 203–5.

6. Voeltzel [and Foucault], *Vingt ans et après*, 50, 54.

7. Foucault, "De l'amitié comme mode de vie," interview with René de Ceccaty, Jean Danet, and Jean le Bitoux, in *Dits et écrits*, vol. 4, *1980–1988*, 163–67, at 164. This interview originally appeared in *Gai pied* 25, April 1981, 38–39.

8. "À propos de la généalogie de l'éthique: Un aperçu du travail en cours," exchange with Hubert Dreyfus and Paul Rabinow, in *Dits et écrits*, vol. 4, *1980–1988*, 609–31, at 616. This interview originally appeared as "On the Genealogy of Ethics: An Overview of Work in Progress" in Hubert L. Dreyfus and Paul Rabinow, *Michel Foucault: Beyond Structuralism and Hermeneutics* (Chicago: University of Chicago Press, 1983), 229–52.

9. See Adeline Daumard, *Les bourgeois de Paris au XIXe siècle* (Paris: Flammarion, 1970 [1963]). See, too, Lenore O'Boyle, "The Middle Class in Western Europe, 1815–1848," *American Historical Review* 71, no. 3 (1966): 826–45; Alfred Cobban, "The 'Middle Class' in France, 1815–1848," *French Historical Studies* 5, no. 1 (1967): 41–52; Sarah Maza, *The Myth of the French Bourgeoisie: An Essay on the Social Imaginary, 1750–1850* (Cambridge, Mass.: Harvard University Press, 2003); and Jerrold Seigel, *Modernity and Bourgeois Life: Society, Politics, and Culture in England, France, and Germany Since 1750* (Cambridge: Cambridge University Press, 2012).

10. Daumard, *Les bourgeois de Paris au XIXe siècle*, 349.

11. See Archives Départementales du Maine-et-Loire, Angers, 2ème arrondissement, Mariages, 1810 (for the marriage of Jacques-François Foucault and Anne-Mathurine Roulet on July 18, 1810); and Archives Départementales du Maine-et-Loire, Angers, 1er, 2ème arrondissement, Naissances, 1811 (for the birth of Jacques-Symphorien Foucault on May 31, 1811). Jacques-Symphorien's father seems to have been a "farinier"—a flour merchant.

12. See Archives Départementales des Hauts-de-Seine, Recensement de la Population, Nanterre, 1841.

13. Archives de Paris, 8eme arrondissement, Mariages, 1879.

14. P. Rambaud, "Nécrologie: P. P. Malapert," *Le Poitou médical*, May 1, 1887, 116–20, at 116.

15. Daumard, *Les bourgeois de Paris au XIXe siècle*, 358.

16. Census records from 1891 to 1911 always list two female *domestiques* for the Foucault household at 8, Rue Marrier, though they seem to have come and gone with some frequency. The 1911 census specifies that one was a *"femme de chambre"* and the other a *"cuisinière."* Archives Départementales de la Seine-et-Marne, Recensement de la Population, Fontainebleau, 1891, 1896, 1901, 1906, and 1911.

17. Didier Eribon, *Michel Foucault (1926–1984)* (Paris: Flammarion, 1991), 21.

18. Archives Départementales de la Vienne, Recensement de la Population, Poitiers, 1836, 1846, and 1851. Though the 1861 census indicates that Prosper's son, Édouard, had

taken over this home as head of household, the family seems to have moved out of it at some point after his untimely death in 1876. His son Henri Paulin Malapert's marriage records list him, in 1894, as residing with his mother in Poitiers, but no address is specified.

19. See Paul Mantrant's account of a presentation on Prosper Malapert by M. A. Guillon, "Séance du 21 février 1980," *Bulletin de la Société des antiquaires de l'Ouest et des musées de Poitiers* 15, no. 1 (1980): 325–29, at 329.

20. Archives Départementales de la Vienne, Recensement de la Population, Poitiers, 1896.

21. Eribon, *Michel Foucault*, 21.

22. Archives Départementales de la Vienne, Recensement de la Population, Poitiers, 1911.

23. Louis Girard, "Premier pas en philo," interview with Jean-Luc Terradillos, *L'actualité Poitou-Charentes* 51, January–March 2001, 30–31, at 31.

24. Jeannine Cornaille, "La Rue du Docteur-Foucault, autrefois Rue du Quignon," *Bulletin: Société d'histoire de Nanterre* 12 (1997): 24–25.

25. Un travailleur, "Nécrologie," *Le journal de Nanterre*, December 26, 1897, [1].

26. See "Rue du Docteur-Foucault," in *Le journal de Nanterre*, November 10, 1898, [3]; and Cornaille, "La Rue du Docteur-Foucault."

27. The *Légion d'honneur* dossiers for Henri Paulin Prosper Malapert (*chevalier*, 1917), Paulin Louis Prosper Roger Malapert (*chevalier*, 1903; *officier*, 1916; *commandeur*, 1920), and Marie Édouard Jules Paulin Malapert (*chevalier*, 1920) can be accessed from the Archives Nationales' special database for this award, Léonore, http://www2 .culture.gouv.fr/documentation/leonore/recherche.htm.

28. Daumard, *Les bourgeois de Paris au XIXe siècle*, 353.

29. Foucault, "À propos de l'enfermement pénitentiaire" (1973), interview with Anne Krywin and F. Ringelheim, in *Dits et écrits*, vol. 2, *1970–1975*, ed. Daniel Defert, François Ewald, and Jacques Lagrange (Paris: Gallimard, 1994), 435–45, at 435–36.

30. Foucault, "Entretien sur la prison: Le livre et sa méthode" (1975), interview with J.-J. Brochier in ibid., 740–53, at 745.

31. Foucault, "Je me suis toujours intéressé aux bas-fonds," interview with Jacques Chancel, France Inter, "Radioscopie," March 10, 1975, https://www.franceinter.fr/emissions/radioscopie-par-jacques-chancel/radioscopie-par-jacques-chancel-26-juillet -2016.

32. Foucault, "Conversation avec Michel Foucault" (1971), interview with John K. Simon, translated by F. Durand-Bogaert, in *Dits et écrits*, vol. 2, *1970–1975*, 182–93, at 185–86. This interview was originally published in the *Partisan Review* 38, no. 2 (1971): 192–201.

33. Ibid., 187.

34. Foucault, "Prisons et asiles dans les mécanismes de pouvoir" (1974), interview with Marco D'Eramo, trans. A. Ghizzardi, in *Dits et écrits*, vol. 2, *1970–1975*, 521–25, *at* 525. This interview was originally published in the Italian newspaper *Avanti*, March 3, 1974, 26–27.

35. Foucault, "Table ronde" (1972), exchange with Jean-Marie Domenach, Jacques Donzelot, Jacques Julliard, P. Meyer, R. Pucheu, Paul Thibaud, J.-R. Tréanton, Paul Virilio, in *Dits et écrits*, vol. 2, *1970–1975*, *316–39, at* 336. This exchange was originally published in *Esprit*, no. 413 (1972): 678–703.

36. Foucault, "Sur la justice populaire: Débat avec les maos" (1972), interview with "Gilles" and "Victor" (Benny Lévy), in *Dits et écrits*, vol. 2, *1970–1975*, 340–69, at 351, 356. This interview originally appeared in *Les temps modernes*, no. 310 (1972): 355–66.

37. Foucault, "À propos de la prison d'Attica" (1974), interview with John K. Simon, trans. F. Durand-Bogaert, in *Dits et écrits*, vol. 2, *1970–1975*, 525–36, at 533. This interview originally appeared as "Michel Foucault on Attica" in *Telos* no. 19 (1974): 154–61.

38. "Le grand renfermement" (1972), interview with Niklaus Meienberg, trans. Jacques Chavy, in *Dits et écrits*, vol. 2, *1970–1975*, 296–306, at 303. This interview originally appeared in *Tages Anzeiger Magazin*, March 25, 1972, 15, 17, 20, and 37.

39. Foucault, "À propos de la prison d'Attica," 531, 534–35.

40. Foucault, "Conversation avec Michel Foucault," 193, 188.

41. Foucault, "À propos de la prison d'Attica," 535.

42. Foucault, "Conversation avec Michel Foucault," 193.

43. Foucault, "Entretien sur la prison," 748.

44. "Except in the eyes of the naïve, the bourgeoise is neither foolish [*bête*] nor cowardly. It is intelligent, it is brazen. It has clearly stated what it wants." Foucault, "Des supplices aux cellules" (1975), interview with Roger-Pol Droit, in *Dits et écrits*, vol. 2, *1970–1975*, 716–20, at 719 (this interview originally appeared in *Le Monde*, February 21, 1975, 16); "one must share the somewhat naïve optimism of the nineteenth-century dandies to imagine that the bourgeoisie is foolish [*bête*]." Foucault, "L'œil du pouvoir" (1977), interview with Jean-Pierre Barrou and Michelle Perrot, in *Dits et écrits*, vol. 3, *1976–1979* ed. Daniel Defert, François Ewald, and Jacques Lagrange (Paris: Gallimard, 1994), 190–207, at 203 (this exchange originally appeared in *Le panoptique* [Paris: Belfond, 1977], 9–31).

45. Though I have generally relied on my own translations, I follow here Robert Hurley's astute decision to translate *dispositif* alternately as "deployment" (when referring, consistent with Foucault's main thesis, to the emergence and dissemination of sexuality throughout society) and as "mechanism" (when referring to a system in which power, law, knowledge, and so on are combined). See Foucault, *The History of Sexuality: An Introduction*, trans. Robert Hurley (New York: Vintage, 1990 [1978]), especially part 4, chapter 3, 103–14. Though *dispositif* is a notoriously difficult term to translate, this has less to do with the difficulty or complexity inherent in Foucault's concept than with a far more elementary problem of translation: it is simply a French word for which no English term with the same range of meanings exists.

46. Foucault, *Histoire de la sexualité*, vol. 1, *La volonté de savoir* (Paris: Gallimard, 1976), 140–41.

47. Ibid., 142.

48. Ibid., 143.

49. "Mariages," *Le Figaro*, January 27, 1924, 2.

50. Martine Segalen, *Historical Anthropology of the Family*, trans. J. C. Whitehouse and Sarah Matthew (Cambridge: Cambridge University Press, 1986 [1981]), 136.

51. Ibid., 119.

52. David Macey, *Lives of Michel Foucault* (New York: Pantheon Books, 1993), 2. Eribon says that Paul Foucault practiced in two clinics. *Michel Foucault*, 21.

53. "Addendum no. III au projet de budget 1948; Traitements du personnel enseignant; Poitiers, le 20 janvier, 1948," memo by Dr. Maurice Veluet, the director of the École de Médecine et de Pharmacie de Poitiers, in "Dossier du personnel," call no. 3W35, Archives Municipales de Poitiers, Poitiers, France. Because its budget was partly funded by the Poitiers Municipal Council, some records relating to personnel and salaries are available in the city's municipal archives.

54. Christian Baudelot and Anne Lebeaupin claim that the average annual salary for a male *cadre supérieur* in 1950 was 8,144 francs, in 1967 francs. See "Les salaires de 1950 à 1975," *Économie et statistique* 113 (1979): 15–22, at 16. I was able to estimate what this and Paul Foucault's salary would be in 2022 euros thanks to a calculating engine of the French statistical agency, the Institut National de la Statistique et des Études Économiques (INSEE), "Convertisseur franc-euro," https://www.insee.fr/fr/information/2417794.

55. Macey, *Lives of Michel Foucault*, 2.

56. Archives de Paris, 13eme arrondissement, Décès, June 1984; "Avis d'obsèques," *Centre Presse*, June 28, 1984, 2.

57. Eribon, *Michel Foucault*, 21; Macey, *Lives of Michel Foucault*, 4.

58. Denys Foucault, "Nés pour apprendre," 29.

59. On Henri Fruchaud, see Paul-René Martin, *Fruchaud d'Angers (1894–1960)* (Angers: Éditions du Martinet, 2008). On the Saint-Mathurin incident, see 21–25. On his attempt to replace Paul Foucault, see 103–4.

60. R[aymond-Noël] Darget and P[aul] Foucault, "De la conduite à tenir en présence de l'impuissance sexuelle chez l'homme," *L'actualité médico-chirurgicale*, November 1938, 270–83, at 273.

61. Paul Foucault, "Les kystes du vagin," *Gazette des hôpitaux civils et militaires* 93 (November 21, 1925): 1509–11, at 1510.

62. Ibid.

63. Macey, *Lives of Michel Foucault*, 2.

64. [Daniel Defert], "Chronologie," in *Dits et écrits*, vol. 1, *1954–1969*, 13–64, at 14.

65. Ibid., 13.

66. Macey, *Lives of Michel Foucault*, 2.

67. Eribon, *Michel Foucault*, 21.

68. Voeltzel, *Vingt ans et après*, 50.

69. Ibid., 54.

70. Foucault, *La volonté de savoir*, 171.

71. Ibid., 171–73.

72. Voeltzel, *Vingt ans et après*, 57.

73. Ibid., 56.

74. Macey, *Lives of Michel Foucault*, 3.

75. Eribon, *Michel Foucault*, 22; Macey, *Lives of Michel Foucault*, 8; [Defert], "Chronologie," 13.

76. One of Francine's sons, Denis Fruchaud, worked on René Allio's 1976 film version of *Moi, Pierre Rivière* before becoming a successful set designer. Her daughter, Anne Thalamy, contributed to two edited volumes supervised by Foucault, *Politiques de l'habitat (1800-1850)* (Paris: CORDA, 1977) and *Les machines à guérir: Aux origines de l'hôpital moderne* (Brussels: Pierre Mardaga, 1979). Another son, Henri-Paul Fruchaud, is currently the family member primarily responsible for Foucault's estate.

77. Hervé Guibert, *Le mausolée des amants: Journal, 1976-1991* (Paris: Gallimard, 2001), 257.

78. Macey, *Lives of Michel Foucault*, 5.

79. Foucault, *La volonté de savoir*, 143, 144.

80. Foucault, "The Minimalist Self," 10, 9-10, emphasis added.

81. Voeltzel, *Vingt ans et après*, 49.

82. This is a rewriting of the previous quote, which comes from André Gide, *Les nourritures terrestres* (Paris: Gallimard, 1970 [1897]), book 4, 69-70.

83. Foucault, "De l'amitié comme mode de vie," in *Dits et écrits*, vol 4, *1980-1988*, 163-67, at 163-64. This interview originally appeared in the magazine *Gai pied* in April 1981, 38-39.

84. Ibid., 164.

85. Foucault, "Choix sexuel, acte sexuel," in *Dits et écrits*, vol. 4, *1980-1988*, 320-35, at 333. This interview with J. O'Higgins was originally published in *Salmagundi*, Fall-Winter 1982, 10-24.

86. Voeltzel, *Vingt ans et après*, 26-27.

87. Eribon, *Réflexions sur la question gay* (Paris: Champs-Flammarion2012 [1999]), 25-28.

88. Foucault, "Choix sexuel, acte sexuel," 323.

89. Girard, "Premier pas en philo," 31.

90. Jean Morichau-Beauchant was *doyen* (the position that replaced *directeur*) in 1971, and Michel Morichau-Beauchant was *doyen* from 2008 to 2013. I am grateful to Michel Morichau-Beauchant for his insight and the family documents he provided concerning his grandfather.

91. See *Titres et travaux scientifiques de R. Morichau-Beauchant* (Paris: G. Steinheil, 1903).

92. I owe most of this biographical information to family documents provided by Michel Morichau-Beauchant.

93. R[ené] Morichau-Beauchant, "L'inconscient, et la défense psychologique de l'individu," *L'effort* 1 (June 1910): 1-2. On *L'effort* (later renamed *L'effort libre*), see Consuelo Fernandez, "Jean-Richard Bloch, un socialiste dans la guerre, d'après sa correspondance," *Guerres mondiales et conflits contemporains* 175 (1994): 123-33.

94. Letter from Sigmund Freud to Carl Jung, December 3, 1910, in *The Freud/ Jung Letters: The Correspondence Between Sigmund Freud and C. G. Jung*, ed. William McGuire, trans. Ralph Manheim and R. F. C. Hull (Princeton, N.J.: Princeton University Press, 1974), 375–78, at 377–78.

95. Letter from Freud to Sándor Ferenczi, November 7, 1911, *The Correspondence of Sigmund Freud and Sándor Ferenczi: 1908–1914*, ed. Ernst Falzeder, Eva Brabant, Eva Brabant-Gerö, Patrizia Giampieri-Deutsch, trans. Peter T. Hoffer (Cambridge, Mass.: The Belknap Press, 1993), 314. Freud notes that Morichau-Beauchant had sent him the text that would become for "Homosexualität und Paranoia," as a submission for *Zentral- blatt für Psychanalyse* (where it would be published), as well as an offprint of "Le 'rapport affectif' dans la cure des psychonévroses," published in 1911 in the *Gazette des hôpitaux civils et militaires* (see below).

96. Letter from Ernest Jones to Freud, January 20, 1912, *The Complete Corre- spondence of Sigmund Freud and Ernest Jones, 1908–1939*, ed. R. Andrew Paskaus- kas (Cambridge, Mass.: Belknap Press, 1995), 127–29, at 127. Jones notes, most likely correctly, that Morichau-Beauchant seems to have read Freud's work in English translation.

97. Freud to Karl Abraham, Vienna, January 2, 1912, in *The Complete Correspon- dence of Sigmund Freud and Karl Abraham 1907–1925*, ed. Ernst Falzeder, trans. Caro- line Schwarzacher (New York: Routledge, 2018), 145.

98. Freud, *The History of the Psychoanalytic Movement*, trans. A. A. Brill (New York: Nervous and Mental Disease Publishing, 1917), 24.

99. Quoted in Christian Hoffmann, "La résistance française à la découverte freudi- enne: Lettre du Professeur R. Morichau-Beauchant à Sigmund Freud," *L'esprit du temps* 115 (2011–12): 13–15, at 13–14. Morichau-Beauchant was particularly distressed by the hostility of psychoanalysis on the part of Pierre Janet, whom he otherwise seemed to have admired.

100. Archives Départementales de la Vienne, État civil, naissances, Poitiers, 1905. In 1904, Morichau-Beauchant married Édith Mathilde Clémence Rambaud (1885–1962), the daughter of Pierre Eugène Rambaud (1850–1936), a prominent Poitiers pharmacist and local historian who wrote, among many other publications, the obituary of Prosper Malapert discussed in the previous chapter.

101. "Mariages," *Le Figaro*, January 27, 1924, 2.

102. P[rosper Henri] Malapert and Morichau-Beauchant, "Les angiomes du sein," *Revue de chirurgie* 29 (February 1904): 200–213. Morichau-Beauchant's *Titres et travaux* mistakenly lists this article as appearing in 1903.

103. Drs. [René Morichau-] Beauchant and [Paul] Foucault, "Le kystes du pancréas," *Revue médicale du Centre-Ouest* 9, no. 2 (February 1937): 40–46. This paper was pre- sented at the December 11, 1936, meeting of the Société de Médecine de la Vienne. Paul Foucault notes that Morichau-Beauchant, in this instance, sent him an x-ray; Morichau- Beauchant's father-in-law, Pierre Rambaud, was instrumental in establishing the x-ray clinic at the Poitiers hospital.

104. Darget and Foucault, "De la conduite à tenir en présence de l'impuissance sexuelle chez l'homme." In this piece, Foucault and Darget speak of "diminutions of the libido" (275) and of the libido being "in deficit" (278). According to the entry on "*libidineuxeuse*," in the *Dictionnaire historique de la langue française* (3rd ed., vol. 1, ed. Alain Rey [Paris: Dictionnaires Le Robert, 2000], 1206), the Latin noun "libido" entered the French language in 1913 following Freud's use of the term.

105. Defert, "Chronologie," 17. This anecdote was also passed down to Morichau-Beauchant's grandson, Michel Morichau-Beauchant, in a personal correspondence with the author, July 2018.

106. Eribon, *Michel Foucault*, 25. Eribon refers to him as "René Beauchamp" but clearly means Morichau-Beauchant.

107. Morichau-Beauchant, "Le 'rapport affectif' dans la cure des psychonévroses," *Gazette des hôpitaux civils et militaires* 84 (1911): 1845–49, at 1846.

108. Morichau-Beauchant, "L'instinct sexuel avant la puberté," *Journal médical français* 6, no. 5 (1912): 375–82, at 379.

109. Ibid., 380.

110. Ibid., 382.

111. Ibid., 376.

112. Morichau-Beauchant, "La fausse incontinence des sphincters chez l'enfant: Contribution à l'étude de l'auto-érotisme paragénital," *Paris médical*, July 22, 1922, 83–93. This seems to be the only article on a psychoanalytic theme that Morichau-Beauchant wrote after the suite of articles published between 1910 and 1912.

113. Morichau-Beauchant, "L'instinct sexuel avant la puberté," 376. In a footnote, Morichau-Beauchant referred the reader to chapter 13 of François Rabelais' *Gargantua*, because it deals with "anal eroticism" in children. Incidentally, a colleague of both Paul Foucault's and Morichau-Beauchant's at the University of Poitiers, who also married into the Malapert family, was one Jean Plattard, a literature professor and authority on Rabelais. He published, notably, *L'adolescence de Rabelais en Poitou* (Paris: Société d'édition "Les Belles Lettres," 1923).

114. Morichau-Beauchant, "Le 'rapport affectif' dans la cure des psychonévroses," 1846.

115. Morichau-Beauchant, "L'instinct sexuel avant la puberté," 379.

116. Morichau-Beauchant, "Le 'rapport affectif' dans la cure des psychonévroses," 1846.

117. Morichau-Beauchant, "L'instinct sexuel avant la puberté," 380.

118. Morichau-Beauchant, "Le 'rapport affectif' dans la cure des psychonévroses," 1846.

119. Ibid., 1147.

120. Morichau-Beauchant, "L'instinct sexuel avant la puberté," 382.

121. Freud, "Psychoanalytic Notes upon an Autobiographical Account of a Case of Paranoia (Dementia Paranoides)" (1911), in *Three Case Histories* (New York: Collier Books, 1963), 103–86.

122. Sándor Ferenczi, "On the Part Played by Homosexuality in the Pathogenesis of Paranoia" (1911), trans. Ernest Jones, in *First Contributions to Psycho-Analysis* (London: Karnac, 1994), 154–84.

123. Morichau-Beauchant, "Homosexualität und Paranoia," trans. Otto Rank, *Zentralblatt für Psychanalyse* 2, no. 4 (1912): 174–76. There is no record of the original French text of this essay. I have, however, partially drawn on a retranslation of the German text into French provided to me by Michel Morichau-Beauchant. Morichau-Beauchant refers to Monsieur X's town as "P.," but given that he refers to him as his own patient, this would seem to be a barely concealed reference to Poitiers.

124. Jean Morichau-Beauchant, quoted in Elisabeth Roudinesco, *La bataille de cent ans*, vol. 1, *Histoire de la psychanalyse en France: 1885–1939* (Paris: Seuil, 1986), 235.

125. Morichau-Beauchant, "L'inconscient, et la défense psychologique de l'individu," 2.

126. Morichau-Beauchant, "Les troubles de l'instinct sexuel chez les épileptiques," *Journal médical français* 6, no. 4 (1912): 155–61, at 161.

127. Foucault, "Débat avec Michel Foucault au Centre Culturel de l'Athénée Français: Tokyo, le 21 avril 1978," Fonds Foucault, FCL 2.13, Institut Mémoires de l'Édition Contemporaine (IMEC), Saint-Germain-la-Blanche-Herbe, France.

128. Foucault, "Je me suis toujours intéressé aux bas-fonds," interview with Jacques Chancel, March 10, 1975, "Radioscopie," https://www.franceinter.fr/emissions/radioscopie-par-jacques-chancel/radioscopie-par-jacques-chancel-26-juillet-2016.

129. Arlette Farge and Foucault, *Le désordre des familles: Lettres de cachet aux archives de la Bastille au XVIIIe siècle* (Paris: Gallimard, 1982). See, too, Foucault and Farge, "L'âge d'or de la lettre de cachet (1982)," interview with Yves Hersant, in *Dits et écrits*, vol. 4, *1980–1988*, 351–52. This interview originally appeared in *L'express*, November 26–December 3, 1982, 83, 85.

130. Foucault, "Le grand renfermement," interview with N. Meienberg, trans. Jacques Chavy, in *Dits et écrits*, vol. 2, *1970–1975*, 296–306, at 304. This interview originally appeared in German in *Tages Anzeiger Magazin*. March 25, 1972, 15, 17, 20, and 37.

131. See, for instance, his lecture course summary for 1972–73, "La société punitive," in *Dits et écrits*, vol. 2, *1970–1975*, 456–70, at 458.

132. Hervé Guibert, "Les secrets d'un homme," *Mauve le vierge* (Paris: Gallimard, 1988), 101–11, at 105, 106.

133. Denys Foucault, "Nés pour apprendre," 29. He concludes: "In the end, we spoke little about it."

134. Gallimard, Collection "Ne jugez pas," http://www.gallimard.fr/Catalogue/GALLIMARD/Ne-jugez-pas.

135. "Une femme séquestrée," *L'avenir de la Vienne*, May 25, 1901, 2 (the same title was used in a story from the following day, May 26, 1901, 2); "La séquestrée de Poitiers," *L'avenir de la Vienne*, May 28–29, 1901, 2.

136. Juge d'instruction Du Fresnel, quoted in André Gide, *La séquestrée de Poitiers* (Paris: Gallimard, 2015 [1930]), 27. Gide changed the name of Blanche Monnier to Mélanie Bastien, and of her brother Marcel Monnier to Pierre Bastien.

137. Quoted in Gide, *La séquestrée de Poitiers*, 54.

138. Quoted in ibid., 69.

139. Quoted in ibid., 54–55.

140. "La séquestrée de Poitiers," *L'avenir de la Vienne*, May 30, 1901, 2.

141. "La séquestrée de Poitiers," *L'avenir de la Vienne*, May 31, 1901, 2.

142. Gide, *La séquestrée de Poitiers*, 31–32n1.

143. See Farge and Foucault, *Le désordre des familles*.

144. Gide, *La séquestrée de Poitiers*, 82.

145. Ibid., 77.

146. Ibid., 85.

147. Quoted in ibid., 30.

148. Ibid., 34n1.

149. Foucault, *Maladie mentale et personnalité* (Paris: Presses universitaires de France, 1954), 56, 69.

150. Denys Foucault, "Nés pour apprendre," 29.

151. Louis Arnould, *Une âme en prison: Histoire de l'éducation d'une aveugle-sourde-muette de naisssance et de ses sœurs des deux mondes*, 3rd ed. (Paris: H. Oudin, 1904), 13, 15.

152. Ibid., 14.

153. Heurtin, *Mes souvenirs* (1955), http://marieheurtinetlesautres.eklablog.com/souvenirs-de-marthe-heurtin-p946274.

154. Foucault, *Surveiller et punir: Naissance de la prison* (Paris: Gallimard, 1975), 34.

155. Gérard Simmat, *L'Hôpital Pasteur de Poitiers: 300 ans au service des malades* (Poitiers: Centre hospitalier universitaire, 2011), 87–89. Most of my account of the history of Poitiers's psychiatric institutions is drawn from Simmat's book.

156. Ibid., 10.

157. In 1899, Pierre Amouroux defended a thesis entitled *Essai sur l'étiologie et la pathogénie de la maladie de Friedreich* (Paris: G. Carré et C. Naud, 1899). He had participated in the Société de Psychothérapie, d'Hynologie, et de Psychologie, notably in its June 1914 conference devoted to the "doctrine of psychoanalysis" and "the role of sexuality in the etiology of neuroses and psychoses." At this conference, Amouroux presented a paper on "states that are incompatible with psychoanalysis" ("États incompatibles avec la psychanalyse"). A tentative program for this conference was announced in the official journal of the psychoanalytic movement, *Internationale Zeitschrift für ärztliche Psychoanalyse* 2, no. 4 (1914): 400. The conference was presided by Pierre Janet, with whom Amouroux seems to have crossed paths on several occasions. In 1925, *L'évolution psychiatrique*, a major intellectual force in the reform of French psychiatry, referred to the "work of Amouroux" (and others) when discussing the impact of Freud's thought on the French medical world in an article devoted to psychoanalysis in France. See "Aperçu historique du mouvement psychanalytique en France," *L'évolution psychiatrique 1* (1925): 11–26, at 18. Amouroux died suddenly at the age of sixty in Poitiers on July 25, 1933. See "Les obsèques du Docteur Pierre Amouroux," *L'avenir de la Vienne*, July 26, 1933, [3].

158. His address was 1 bis, Boulevard de Verdun, which would seem to be next door to the Foucault household, located on the corner of that street and Rue Arthur Ranc. "Les obsèques du Docteur Pierre Amouroux."

159. Docteur [Pierre] Amouroux, "La conscience psychologique," *Revue médicale du Centre-Ouest* 2 (1929): 29–30, at 29.

160. Amouroux, "La conscience psychologique (suite)—l'activité: Excitation et dépression," *Revue médicale du Centre-Ouest* 4 (1929): 86–87, at 86.

161. Ibid.

162. Amouroux, "La névrose d'angoisse et les syndromes anxieux," *Revue médicale du Centre-Ouest* 9 (1929): 248, 251–52, at 248; Paul Hartenberg, *La névrose d'angoisse* (Paris: Alcan, 1902); Francis Heckel, *La névrose d'angoisse et les états d'émotivité anxieuse: Clinique-pathogénie-traitement* (Paris: Masson et Cie., 1917).

163. Amouroux, "La névrose d'angoisse et les syndromes anxieux," 252.

164. Simmat, *L'Hôpital Pasteur*, 101.

165. "Un drame à l'hôpital Pasteur: Une démente étrangle sa compagne de chambre," *L'avenir de la Vienne*, August 24, 1931, [3].

166. "Le drame de l'hôpital de Poitiers," *L'aliéniste français: Bulletin de l'Association Amicale des Médecins des Établissements publics d'aliénés* 12, no. 8 (1931): 334.

167. Hervé Bazin, "Ce qui arrive aux 100 000 Français que l'on a déclarés: Bons pour l'asile!," *Réalités*, January 1955, 58–67. See, too, Simmat, *Hôpital Pasteur*, 122.

Chapter 3

1. See Mark Blasius, "An Ethos of Lesbian and Gay Existence," *Political Theory* 20, no. 4 (1992): 642–71, at 667n1. Blasius explains that Foucault was his thesis adviser at the time of the philosopher's death in 1984 but does not say when Foucault assumed that role. He notes that he "spent many hours in many different places discussing gay politics and culture" with Foucault.

2. Michel Foucault, "Sexual Choice, Sexual Act: Foucault and Homosexuality" (1982), in *Politics, Philosophy, Culture: Interviews and Other Writings, 1977–1984* (New York: Routledge, Chapman, and Hall, 1988), 286–303, at 298; "Choix sexuel, acte sexuel," trans. F. Durand-Bogaert, in *Dits et écrits*, vol. 4, *1980–1988*, ed. Daniel Defert, François Ewald, and Jacques Lagrange (Paris: Gallimard 1994), 320–35, at 331.

3. Jason Fury, *The Secret of Jimmy X, and Other Stories of the Macabre* (New York: Writers' Club, 2000), 132.

4. Arnie Kantrowitz, quoted in Patrick Moore, *Beyond Shame: Reclaiming the Abandoned History of Radical Gay Sexuality* (Boston: Beacon, 2004), 21.

5. This story is drawn entirely from Edmund White, *My Lives* (New York: Harper-Collins, 2006), 197–98.

6. Death as a leitmotif of Foucault's personal and intellectual concerns is brilliantly explored in James Miller's seminal biography *The Passion of Michel Foucault* (New York: Simon and Schuster, 1993). Miller, however, begins his narrative when Foucault moved to Paris after the war, with only passing reference to his childhood.

7. Foucault, "The Minimalist Self" (1982; published 1983), interview with Stephen Riggins, in *Politics, Philosophy, Culture*, 3–16, at 7; "Une interview de Michel Foucault par Stephen Riggins," trans. F. Durand-Bogaert, in *Dits et écrits*, vol. 4, *1980–1988*, 525–38, at 528. The English transcript of the interview indicates that after making this remark, Foucault laughed.

8. Foucault, "Minimalist Self," 6.

9. Michel Foucault, "Preface," in Gilles Deleuze and Félix Guattari, *Anti-Oedipus: Schizophrenia and Capitalism*, trans. Robert Hurley, Mark Seem, and Helen R. Lane (New York: Viking Press, 1977 [1972]), xi–xiv, at xiii; Foucault, "Préface," trans. F. Durand-Bogaert, in *Dits et écrits*, vol. 3, *1976–1979* ed. Daniel Defert, François Ewald, and Jacques Lagrange (Paris: Gallimard, 1994), 133–36, at 134. Emphasis added.

10. Foucault, *Histoire de la sexualité*, vol. 1, *La volonté de savoir* (Paris: Gallimard, 1976), 125.

11. "Paul André Foucault," Document 1R1401 (1913), numéro matricule de recensement 447, Recensement militaire, subdivision militaire de Fontainebleau (Seine-et-Marne), accessed through the Grand Mémorial archive of the French Culture Ministry, https://www.culture.fr/Grand-Memorial.

12. Bernadotte E. Schmitt and Harold C. Vedeler, *The World in the Crucible, 1914–1919* (New York: Harper and Row, 1984), 97. See, too, *Historique du 45e régiment d'infanterie: 1914–1918* (Paris: Librairie Chapelot, n.d.), digitized 2012, https://www.ancestramil.fr/cms/uploads/01_doc/terre/infanterie/1914-1918/45_ri_historique _1914-1918.pdf.

13. *Légion d'honneur* dossier of Paul André Foucault, numéro de matricule 204 885, Léonore database (of *Légion d'honneur* recipients), French National Archives, https://www.leonore.archives-nationales.culture.gouv.fr/ui/.

14. *Légion d'honneur* dossier of Paulin Louis Prosper Roger Malapert, numéro de matricule 66 834, Léonore database.

15. *Campagne 1914–1918: Historique du 320e Régiment d'Infanterie* (Nancy: Imprimerie Chapelot, n.d.).

16. Ibid., 9.

17. Untitled, front-page story dedicated to the memory of Colonel Malapert in *Le combattant du Poitou*, January 1933, 1.

18. "Obsèques du Colonel Malapert," *Le combattant du Poitou*, January 1933, 1.

19. See the military records available for Prosper Jules François Roger Malapert at the Army Ministry's "Mémoire des hommes" website, https://www.memoiredeshommes.sga.defense.gouv.fr/.

20. Foucault, "De l'amitié comme mode de vie," in *Dits et écrits*, vol. 4, *1980–1988*, 163–67, at 166. This interview originally appeared in *Gai pied*, April 1981, 38–39.

21. Ibid., 167.

22. Foucault, *Histoire de la folie à l'âge classique* (Paris: Gallimard, 1972 [1961]), 26.

23. Foucault, "De l'amitié comme mode de vie," 167.

24. Foucault, "Minimalist Self," 6–7.

25. Raymond J. Sontag, *A Broken World, 1919–1939* (New York: Harper and Row, 1971), 281–82. See, too, Walter B. Maass, *Assassination in Vienna* (New York: Charles Scribner's Sons, 1972); and François Broche, *Assassinat du Chancelier Dollfuss: Vienne, le 25 juillet 1934* (Paris: Éditions Balland, 1977).

26. "Un putsch 'hitlérien' à Vienne: Le Chancelier Dollfuss est assassiné par les nazis," *L'avenir de la Vienne et de l'Ouest*, July 27, 1934, 1.

27. "Après l'assassinat de Dollfuss: Le prince Stahrenberg préside le gouvernement," *L'avenir de la Vienne et de l'Ouest*, July 28, 1934, 1.

28. "Après l'assassinat de Dollfuss: M. von Papen est nommé ministre d'Allemagne à Vienne," *L'avenir de la Vienne et de l'Ouest*, July 29, 1934, 1.

29. "Les funérailles solennelles du Chancelier Dollfuss ont été célébrées samedi matin," *L'avenir de la Vienne et de l'Ouest*, July 30, 1934, 1.

30. Foucault, "Minimalist Self," 7.

31. Foucault, *"Il faut défendre la société": Cours au Collège de France, 1976* (Paris: Gallimard/Seuil, 1997), 231.

32. "Paul André Foucault," Document 1R1401 (1913), Recensement militaire, subdivision militaire de Fontainebleau (Seine-et-Marne).

33. "Le danger aérien," *L'avenir de la Vienne et de l'Ouest*, September 4, 1939, 3.

34. "La défense passive dans la Vienne," *L'avenir de la Vienne et de l'Ouest*, September 10, 1939, 3.

35. "Alerte à Poitiers la nuit dernière," *L'avenir de la Vienne et de l'Ouest*, September 6, 1939, 3.

36. "La défense passive à Poitiers," *L'avenir de la Vienne et de l'Ouest*, October 11, 1939, 3.

37. "L'excellente organisation du centre d'accueil poitevin des réfugiés mosellans," *L'avenir de la Vienne et de l'Ouest*, September 14, 1939, 1, 3.

38. "M. Robert Schuman, député de la Moselle, nous parle des 40,000 réfugiés lorrains dont il est le chef de file," *L'avenir de la Vienne et de l'Ouest*, September 12, 1939, 3. On the same page, the newspaper had articles listing which communes in the Vienne were paired to particular communes in the Moselle, as well as one informing the public that families from the Moselle would receive priority over those from other regions when registering their students at local schools.

39. "Place d'Armes: Un regrettable incident," *L'avenir de la Vienne et de l'Ouest*, September 6, 1939, 3.

40. Foucault, "Le problème des réfugiés est un présage de la grande migration du XXIe siècle," interview with H. Uno, trans. R. Nakamura, in *Dits et écrits*, vol. 3, *1976–1979*, 798–800, at 800. This interview was published in 1979 by the Japanese magazine *Shukan Posuto*, August 17, 1979, 34–35.

41. Ibid., 798.

42. "Nos positions sont consolidées sur la Somme: Les Allemands s'efforcent de lancer des unités motorisées dans la 'Brèche de Picardie,'" *L'avenir de la Vienne et de l'Ouest*, May 25, 1940, 1.

43. "Sur le front de la Somme des actions locales ont tournées à notre avantage: Des tirs de l'artillerie française ont causé de grosses pertes aux Allemands," *L'avenir de la Vienne et de l'Ouest*, May 26, 1940, 1.

44. See *L'avenir de la Vienne et de l'Ouest*, May 24, 1940, 1, and May 25, 1940, 1.

45. Le docteur Ch[arles] Fiessinger, "Conseils aux nerveux," *L'avenir de la Vienne et de l'Ouest*, May 25, 1940, 1–2. Charles Fiessinger (1857–1942) was a prominent French doctor who embraced royalism, knew Charles Maurras, and served as his personal doctor, in addition to publishing in *L'action française*.

46. "Les moins de 20 ans ne doivent pas quitter Poitiers," *L'avenir de la Vienne et de l'Ouest*, June 19, 1940, 2. The story was reprinted the next day (June 20).

47. "Venons en aide aux réfugiés!," *L'avenir de la Vienne et de l'Ouest*, May 20, 1940, 3.

48. "Les uniformes belges," *L'avenir de la Vienne et de l'Ouest*, May 24, 1940, 3.

49. Roger Picard, *La Vienne dans la guerre, 1939–1945* (Clermont-Ferrand: Éditions Gérard Tisserand, 2001), 8.

50. "Église Saint-Porchaire, 49 rue Gambetta, " *L'avenir de la Vienne et de l'Ouest*, May 25, 1940, 3.

51. "Belges en France: Notes et communications," *L'avenir de la Vienne et de l'Ouest*, May 26, 1940, 3.

52. Gaston Dez, *Histoire de Poitiers: Mémoires de la société des Antiquaires de l'Ouest, Quatrième série, tome X* (Poitiers: Fradet et Oudin Libraires, 1969), 216. Gaston Dez taught Foucault history from 1944 to 1945 in his year in *hypokhâgne* at the Lycée of Poitiers.

53. "Bombardement de Poitiers du 19 juin 1940," VRID Mémorial (Vienne Résistance Internement Déportation), September 3, 2009, https://www.vrid-memorial.com /bombardement-de-poitiers-du-19-juin-1940/.

54. "Les combats de juin 1940 dans le nord-est du département de la Vienne," VRID Mémorial, June 27, 20211, http://www.vrid-memorial.com/afficher/rubrique/120/Com-bats/article/249/Les-combats-de-juin-1940-dans-le-nord-est-du-dpartement-de-la -Vienne.html.

55. "Avis d'obsèques," *L'avenir de la Vienne et de l'Ouest*, July 8, 1940, 2.

56. In *Discipline and Punish*, Foucault describes the Panopticon as "the diagram of a mechanism of power reduced to its ideal form." See *Discipline and Punish: The Birth of the Prison,* trans. Alan Sheridan (New York: Vintage Books, 1995), 205; *Surveiller et punir: Naissance de la prison* (Paris: Gallimard, 1975), 207.

57. On the demarcation line, see *La ligne de démarcation dans les départements de la Charente et de la Vienne, juin 1940–mars 1943*, pamphlet published by the Office national des anciens combattants et victimes de guerre (ONACVG), 2012; and Christian Richard, *La ligne de démarcation dans la Vienne 1940–1943* (La Crèche: Éditions La Geste, 2017).

58. On Hermann Herold, see Thomas Fontaine, "Policiers et agents allemands en France occupée," *Chemins de mémoire*, http://www.cheminsdememoire.gouv.fr/fr /policiers-et-agents-allemands-en-france-occupee.

59. Picard, *La Vienne dans la guerre, 1939–1945*, 66.

60. Léon Bouchet, "Appel à la population," *L'avenir de la Vienne et de l'Ouest*, June 25, 1940, 2.

61. Foucault, "De la nature humaine: Justice contre pouvoir," discussion with Noam Chomsky and Fons Elders, trans. A. Rabinovitch, in *Dits et écrits*, vol. 2, *1970–1975*, ed. Daniel Defert, François Ewald, and Jacques Lagrange (Paris: Gallimard, 1994), 471–512. The moment at which this remark occurred would be at 496, but this aside is not included in the transcription. It can be heard, however, in the filmed version. This debate took place in Eindhoven, the Netherlands, in November 1971. In his lecture course from 1973, Foucault referred to the prefects as exemplifying a new form of power based on continuous reporting, and thus of the "referral of a certain kind of knowledge by each agent of power to his superior." Foucault, lecture of March 28, 1973, in *La société punitive: Cours au Collège de France 1972–1973* (Paris: Gallimard/Seuil, 2013), 238.

62. Quoted in Jean-Henri Calmon, *Occupation, résistance, et libération dans la Vienne en 30 questions* (La Crèche: Geste Éditions, 2000), 14.

63. On Bourgain see, ibid., 14–15; and Calmon, "Louis Bourgain," VRID Mémorial, June 6, 2008,\ https://www.vrid-memorial.com/louis-bourgain/.

64. Foucault, "Les mailles du pouvoir" (1976, 1981), trans. P. W. Prado, Jr., in *Dits et écrits*, vol. 4, *1980–1988*, 182–201, at 187. This essay was originally delivered as a lecture at the University of Bahia in Brazil in 1976. The first half was published in *Barbárie* 4 (1981):23–27, and the second half in *Barbárie* 5 (1982): 34–42.

65. Calmon, *Occupation, résistance, et libération dans la Vienne*, 15.

66. Foucault, *Histoire de la sexualité*, vol. 1, *La volonté de savoir* (Paris: Gallimard, 1976), 125.

67. Ibid.

68. Foucault, "Minimalist Self," 6.

69. Foucault, *La société punitive*, 233. The other social institutions Foucault cites are religious congregations and professional organizations.

70. Ibid., 234. Foucault goes on to say in this quote that what connects the family and the state is the fact that both are invested in disciplinary power.

71. Foucault, "Débat avec Michel Foucault au Centre Culturel de l'Athénée Français: Tokyo, le 21 avril 1978," Fonds Foucault, FCL 2.13, Institut Mémoires de l'Édition Contemporaine (IMEC), Saint-Germain-la-Blanche-Herbe, France.

72. Foucault, "Minimalist Self," 7.

73. "L'exode des Catalans: 1.248 réfugiés espagnols sont arrivés à Poitiers," *L'avenir de la Vienne et de l'Ouest*, February 7, 1939, 3; *Des camps dans la Vienne, 1939–1945: Contrôler, exclure, persécuter* (catalogue for exhibition organized by the Archives Départementales de la Vienne, 2016), 18.

74. Paul Lévy, *Un camp de concentration français: Poitiers, 1939–1945* (Paris: SEDES, 1995), 17.

75. Foucault, *Histoire de la folie à l'âge classique*, 66.

76. Décret-loi du 12 novembre 1938 relatif à la situation et à la police des étrangers (law-decree of November 12, 1938 relating to the circumstances and policing of foreigners), November 12, 1938, http://pages.livresdeguerre.net/pages/sujet.php?id=docddp &su=103&np=780. See, too, *Des camps dans la Vienne*, 15.

77. *Des camps dans la Vienne, 1939–1945*, 15.

78. Lévy, *Un camp de concentration français*, 25–29; *Des camps dans la Vienne*, 21.

79. Georges Serrigny, "Poitiers, ville dépotoire," *L'avenir de la Vienne et de l'Ouest*, December 6, 1940, reproduced in *Des camps dans la Vienne*, 16.

80. Madame G. L'Huillier, "Reminisces of the Gypsy Camp at Poitiers (1941–1943)," *Journal of the Gypsy Lore Society* 27 (1948): 36–40, at 37.

81. Lévy, *Un camp de concentration français*, 42.

82. Eliezer Schilt and Joseph Robert White, "Poitiers," trans. Allison Vuillaume, in "France/Vichy," in Geoffrey P. Megargee, Joseph R. White, Mel Hecker, eds., *The United States Holocaust Memorial Museum Encyclopedia of Camps and Ghettos, 1933–1945*, vol. 3, *Camps and Ghettos Under European Regimes Aligned with Nazi Germany* (Bloomington: Indiana University Press, 2018), 202–4, at 202.

83. Quoted in Lévy, *Un camp de concentration français*, 44.

84. Marthe Cohn (with Wendy Holden), *Behind Enemy Lines: The True Story of a French Jewish Spy in Nazi Germany* (New York: Three Rivers, 2002), 25. Lévy, for his part, estimates that there were about twelve Jewish families in Poitiers in the 1930s. *Un camp de concentration français*, 31.

85. Lévy, *Un camp de concentration français*, 63–65.

86. Ibid., 69.

87. Ibid., 12.

88. Schilt and White, "Poitiers," 202.

89. Ibid.

90. Lévy, *Un camp de concentration français*, 91.

91. Ibid., 95.

92. Ibid., 92.

93. Ibid., 95–96.

94. Ibid., 169.

95. Ibid.

96. Letter of the health inspector to the Vienne prefect, December 11, 1943, unpublished typescript, Cote 109 W 71–73, Archives Départementales de la Vienne, Poitiers, France.

97. Quoted in Lévy, *Un camp de concentration français*, 183.

98. Letter of Merdsche of Feldkommandantur 677 to the Vienne prefect, March 12, 1942, unpublished typescript, Cote 109 W 150, Archives Départementales de la Vienne, Poitiers, France.

99. Letter of S. S. Untersturmführer Zwick, Der Befehlshaber der Sicherheitspolizei und des SD im Bereich des Militärbefehlshaber Frankreich (Sicherheitspolizei-SD

Kommando Poitiers) to the Vienne prefect, May 27, 1943, unpublished typescript, Cote 109 W 150, Archives Départementales de la Vienne, Poitiers, France.

100. "Décès de Jacques Quivy (1904–1965), de Poitiers, associé national," *Mémoires: Académie de chirurgie* 24, no. 91 (1965): 802–3.

101. Lévy, *Un camp de concentration français*, 186–88.

102. Foucault, "Enfermement, psychiatrie, prison" (discussion with David Cooper, Jean-Pierre Faye, M.-O. Faye, and M. Zecca) (1977), in *Dits et écrits*, vol. 3, *1976–1979*, 332–60, at 343. This exchange was originally published in *Change* 22–23 (1977): 76–110.

103. Foucault, "Attention: Danger" (1978), in ibid., 507–8, at 507. This piece was originally published in *Libération* on March 22, 1978, 9.

104. See in particular *Discipline and Punish*, 82–89; *Surveiller et punir*, 84–91.

105. Foucault, *La société punitive: Cours au Collège de France (1972–1973)* (Paris: Gallimard-Seuil, 2013), 193.

106. Lévy, *Un camp de concentration français*, 128.

107. Foucault, "Le grand renfermement" (1972) (interview with N. Meienberg), trans. J. Chavy, in *Dits et écrits*, vol. 2, *1970–1975*, 296–306, at 298–99. This interview was originally published in *Tages Anzeiger Magazin*, March 25, 1972, 15, 17, 20, and 37.

108. Foucault, "Critical Theory / Intellectual History," in Foucault, *Philosophy, Politics, Culture*, 17–46, at 40; "Structuralisme et poststructuralisme," in *Dits et écrits*, vol. 4, *1980–1988*, 431–57, at 452. This interview with Gérard Raulet was originally published as "Structuralism and Post-Structuralism: An Interview with Michel Foucault" in *Telos* 55 (1983), 195–211, translated by Jeremy Harding. The politician in question seems to have been Louis Mermaz, who at the time was president of the National Assembly.

109. Testimony by Louis Peignault, in Jean Vaudel, *Les Collèges Saint-Joseph et Saint-Stanislas de Poitiers (1607–1980)* (Poitiers: Brissaud / Librairie Ancienne "Le Bouquiniste," 1981), 382.

110. J. Coindre, "Fleurs d'héroisme: Le chanoine Georges Duret," *La croix*, March 6, 1946, 2. The Athlete's Oath declared: "I promise to take part in this sport with impartiality, discipline and loyalty, to better myself and serve my country."

111. "Hôpitaux de Poitiers," one-page typescript signed "P. Barnsby," vice président (de la Commission administrative des Hôpitaux de Poitiers), dated November 1, 1941, Cote 1536 W 80, Archives Départementales de la Vienne, Poitiers, France.

112. Denys Foucault, "Nés pour apprendre," interview with Jean-Luc Terradillos, *L'actualité Poitou-Charentes* 51 (January–March 2001): 28–29, at 29.

113. Paul V. Dutton, *Origins of the French Welfare State: The Struggle for Social Reform in France, 1914–1947* (Cambridge: Cambridge University Press, 2002), 97.

114. Donna Evleth, "The Ordre des Médecins and the Jews in Vichy France, 1940–1944," *French History* 20, no. 2 (2006): 204–24, at 208.

115. Ibid., 209–10.

116. "Syndicat Médical de la Vienne: Assemblée générale du 11 décembre 1931," *Bulletin du groupement des syndicats médicaux des Charentes et du Poitou* 9, no. 3 (March 1932): 99-108, at 99.

117. "Syndicat médicale de la Vienne: Assemblée générale du 9 décembre 1932," *Bulletin du groupement des syndicats médicaux des Charentes et du Poitou* 10, no. 3 (March 1933): 89–98, at 89; "Syndicat médicale de la Vienne: Assemblée générale du 27 novembre 1936," *Charentes et Poitou: Bulletin officiel des syndicats médicaux; Charente, Charente-Inférieur, Deux Sèvres, Vendée, Vienne* 1 (January 1937): 88–97, at 88; "Syndicat médicale de la Vienne: Assemblée générale du 24 novembre 1937," *Charentes et Poitou: Bulletin officiel des syndicats médicaux; Charente, Charente-Inférieur, Deux Sèvres, Vendée, Vienne* 6 (June 1938): 202–5, at 202; "Syndicat médicale de la Vienne: Assemblée générale du 15 mai 1938," *Charentes et Poitou: Bulletin officiel des syndicats médicaux; Charente, Charente-Inférieur, Deux Sèvres, Vendée, Vienne* (1939): 359–63, at 359.

118. "Syndicat médicale de la Vienne," *Charentes et Poitou: Bulletin officiel des syndicats médicaux; Charente, Charente-Inférieur, Deux Sèvres, Vendée, Vienne* 1 (January 1937): 1; Paul Foucault was listed as the secretary in the minutes of the meetings recorded in "Syndicat médicale de la Vienne: Assemblée générale du 27 novembre 1936," 96; and "Syndicat médicale de la Vienne: Assemblée générale du 15 mai 1938," 363.

119. "Groupement inter-syndical Charentes-Poitou: Compte rendu de la Réunion du Comité d'études du 7 novembre 1937," *Charentes et du Poitou: Bulletin officiel des syndicats médicaux; Charente, Charente-Inférieur, Deux Sèvres, Vendée, Vienne* 12 (December 1937): 373–78, at 373.

120. "Syndicat médicale de la Vienne: Assemblée générale du 11 décembre 1931," 101–2.

121. Pierre Guillaume, *Le rôle social du médecin depuis deux siècles (1800–1945)* (Paris: Association pour l'étude de l'histoire de la Sécurité sociale, 1996).

122. For an account of how the Ordre negotiated Jewish policy under Vichy, see Evleth, "The Ordre des Médecins and the Jews in Vichy France."

123. "Allocution prononcée par le Dr. Barraud, Président du Conseil de l'Ordre des Médecins de la Charente-Maritime à la première réunion de l'ordre," *Charentes et Poitou: Ordre des Médecins; Bulletin scientifique et professionnel*, (1941), 4–6, at 4.

124. Ibid., 5.

125. Ibid., 4. The quote is drawn from Alphonse Daudet's 1884 novel *Sapho*.

126. "Allocation prononcée par le Dr. Barraud," 6.

127. Foucault, *Le beau danger: Entretien avec Claude Bonnefoy* (Paris: Editions de l'École des Hautes Études en Sciences Sociales, 2011), 32. As noted in Chapter 1, Foucault referred to the doctor-priest comparison on other occasions as well.

128. J[acques] Trivas, "Le problème de l'enfance anormale," *Charentes et Poitou* 3 (March 1941): 49–57, at 49 and 57.

129. Trivas, "État actuel de l'alcoolisme en France," *Charentes et Poitou* 4 (April 1941): 85–96, at 85.

130. Trivas, "État actuel de l'alcoolisme en France (suite)," *Charentes et Poitou* 5 (May 1941): 112–20, at 118.

131. Foucault, *"Il faut défendre la société": Cours au Collège de France, 1976* (Paris: Gallimard/ Seuil, 1997), 18.

132. Trivas, "Le problème de l'enfance anormale," 49.

133. Ibid., 54, 49, 55.

134. Trivas, "État actuel de l'alcoolisme en France," 89.

135. Ibid., 91.

136. Léon Daudet, "La lutte contre l'alcoolisme," *L'action française* (Lyon edition), September 9, 1941, 1.

137. "Déclaration obligatoire des maladies vénériennes," *Charentes et Poitou* 4 (May 1941): 105–6.

138. Trivas, "État actuel de l'alcoolisme en France (suite)," 119, 120.

139. Daudet, "La lutte contre l'alcoolisme," 1.

140. Ibid.; and Trivas, "État actuel de l'alcoolisme en France," 94.

141. This account is drawn from Gilles Antonowicz, *Mort d'un collabo: 13 mai 1943* (Paris: Éditions Nicolas Éybalin / Éditions Scrineo, 2013). The account given by Maurice Garçon, the lawyer who defended Guérin's assassins, mentions that Guérin was taken to Clinique de Pont-Achard, where Paul Foucault worked (even if he does not mention the latter by name). Garçon, "Le procès des cinq étudiants de Poitiers: 10 septembre, 1943," in *Procès sombres* (Paris: Arthème Fayard, 1950), 41–81, at 46.

142. Quoted in Antonowicz, *Mort d'un collabo*, 55.

143. Pierre Chavigny [Michel Guérin], "Réflexions d'actualité," *L'avenir de la Vienne et de l'Ouest*, May 3, 1943, 1.

144. Antonowicz, *Mort d'un collabo*, 107–8.

145. Chavigny [Guérin], "Solidarité paysanne," *L'avenir de la Vienne et de l'Ouest*, May 6, 1943, 1.

146. Chavigny [Guérin], "Impressions du Zone Sud: Le règne du médiocre III," *L'avenir de la Vienne et de l'Ouest*, May 13, 1943, 1.

147. Docteur Michel Guérin, *Mariage et stérilité: Les problèmes médicaux et moraux de la continence périodique* (Paris: Legrand éditeur, [1938]), 12.

148. Ibid., 15.

149. Ibid., 16.

150. Ibid., 169.

151. Ibid., 169–70.

152. Ibid., 170.

153. This assassination is the main theme of Antonowicz's microhistory *Mort d'un collabo*. A (nearly) firsthand account of the assassination is also offered by Marthe Cohn, the *mosellane* discussed above, who, during her brief stay in Poitiers, dated Jacques Delaunay, at the very time he participated in Guérin's murder (though she was informed of it only after the fact). See Cohn, *Behind Enemy Lines*, 105–23.

154. Henri Tournier, "De tout cœur, je pardonne à tous mes ennemis," *L'avenir de la Vienne et de l'Ouest*, May 17, 1943, 1.

155. Paul Foucault and Guérin were both present (along with some other members) at the meetings of the Société Médicale de la Vienne on February 10, 1939 (at which Paul Foucault presented a paper), and March 10, 1939. See *Revue médicale du Centre-Ouest*, May 1939, 110–13, at 110; and *Revue médicale du Centre-Ouest*, June 1939, 138.

156. Foucault, *"Il faut défendre la société,"* 231.

157. Guérin, *Mariage et stérilité,* 129.

158. Foucault, *La volonté de savoir,* 196.

159. Noam Chomsky and Edward Herman cited Brazil, for instance, as an example of "Third-World Fascism." See Chomsky and Herman, *The Washington Connection and Third World Fascism* (Boston: South End, 1979).

160. Foucault, "Asiles: Sexualité; Prisons," ed. M. Almeida, R. Chneiderman, M. Faerman, R. Moreno, M. Tafferel-Faerman, with the assistance in São Paulo of C. Bojunga, trans. P. W. Prado Jr., in *Dits et écrits,* vol. 2, *1970–1975,* 771–82, at 775. First published in *Revista Versus* 1, October 1975, 30–33.

161. Ibid.

162. Foucault, *Les anormaux: Cours au Collège de France, 1974–1975* (Paris: Gallimard/Seuil, 1999), 12.

163. Ibid., 13.

164. Jean-Pierre Azéma, "La milice," *Vingtième siècle* 28 (1990), 83–106; Jacques Delperrié de Bayac, *Histoire de la Milice: 1918–1945* (Paris: Fayard, 1969).

165. Georges La Villedieu, "Les locaux de la Milice ont été inauguré hier à Poitiers," *L'avenir de la Vienne et l'Ouest,* May 24, 1944, 2.

166. Quoted in Jean-Marie Augustin, *Collaborations et épurations dans la Vienne, 1940–1948* (La Crèche: Geste éditions, 2014), 158.

167. Ibid., 167.

168. Ibid., 168.

169. Lemoine, quoted in ibid.

170. Ibid., 171–73.

171. Foucault, *Les anormaux,* 13.

172. Ibid., 14. Foucault's editors note that this anecdote is found in Joachim Fest's biography of Hitler, which had recently been translated into French: *Hitler: Eine Biographie* (Frankfurt: Ullstein, 1973); *Hitler,* vol. 1, *Jeunesse et conquête du pouvoir, 1889–1933* and *Hitler,* vol. 2, *Le Führer, 1933–1945* (Paris: Gallimard, 1973), trans. Guy Fritsch-Estrangin.

173. Foucault, "Sade, sergent du sexe" (interview with G. Dupont), in *Dits et écrits,* vol. 2, *1970–1975,* 818–22, at 820–21. This interview originally appeared in *Cinématographe* 16 (1975–76), 3–5.

174. Foucault, *"Il faut défendre la société,"* 231.

175. Ibid., 232.

176. Foucault, *La volonté de savoir,* 194.

177. Ibid., 196–97.

178. Martin Heidegger, *Being and Time,* trans. Joan Stambaugh (Albany: State University of New York Press, 1996), 303.

179. Foucault, *Leçons sur la volonté de savoir: Cours au Collège de France, 1970–1971* (Paris: Seuil/Gallimard, 2011), 82.

180. See Foucault, "La vérité et les formes juridiques," trans. J. W. Prado, Jr., in *Dits et écrits,* vol. 2, *1970–1975,* 538–646. This exchange first appeared in *Cadernos da PUC* 16 (1974): 5–122.

181. Foucault, "Preface," xiii.

182. Foucault, *La volonté de savoir*, 196.

183. Ibid., 196–197.

184. Antonowicz, *Mort d'un collabo*, 251.

185. Calmon, *Occupation, résistance, et libération dans la Vienne*, 53.

186. Antonowicz, *Mort d'un collabo*, 251–52.

187. Denys Foucault, "Nés pour apprendre," 28–29.

188. Christian Richard, *La guerre aérienne dans la Vienne, 1939–1945* (La Crèche: Geste éditions, 2009), 146–55.

189. Antonowicz, *Mort d'un collabo*, 249.

190. Richard, *La guerre aérienne dans la Vienne*, 152.

191. Testimonial of Robert Boudry (March 6, 2004), in Gérard Simmat and Jean-Marc Augustin, *Poitiers occupé, Poitiers bombardé* (Poitiers: Geste, 2013), 122.

192. "Nuit d'épouvante sur Poitiers," *L'avenir de la Vienne et de l'Ouest*, June 14, 1944, 1.

193. Richard, *La guerre aérienne dans la Vienne*, 153.

194. Bernard Guionnet, in Simmat and Guionnet, *Les bombardements de Poitiers en 1944* (La Crèche: Geste Editions, 2004), 61–62.

195. Antonowicz, *Mort d'un collabo*, 249; Calmon, *Occupation, résistance, et libération dans la Vienne*, 44 (Calmon inaccurately describes the attack as having been conducted by American planes).

196. Foucault, " Minimalist Self," 7.

197. Roger Bourdet (bailiff, or *huissier*), "PROCÈS VERBAL DE CONSTAT: L'AN MILLE NEUF CENT QUARANTE QUATRE LE VINGT ET UN JUIN, À la requête de Monsieur le Docteur Paul FOUCAULT, Chirurgien, demeurant à Poitiers, 10 rue Arthur Ranc" [June 21, 1944], unpublished typescript, Cote 92 W 43, Archives Départementales de la Vienne, Poitiers, France. This document belongs to an extensive file—consisting of over three hundred pages—that was generated by Paul Foucault's decision to apply for reconstruction funds from the new Ministry for Reconstruction and Urbanism.

198. A separate form had to be filed with the government reconstruction agency for a "completely destroyed building," like the garage, as opposed to a "partially destroyed building," like the main house. See the forms the Foucaults filled out for État Déscriptif d'un Bâtiment Partiellement Détruit" (descriptive condition of a partially destroyed building) and "État Déscriptif d'un Bâtiment Totalement Détruit" (descriptive condition of a totally destroyed building) Cote 92 W 43, Archives Départementales de la Vienne, Poitiers, France. Denys Foucault also remembers the destruction of the garage; "Nés pour apprendre," 29.

199. Anna Freud and Dorothy T. Burlingham, *War and Children* (New York: Ernst Willard, 1943), 28.

200. Foucault, "La psychologie génétique [Cours donné à l'Ecole normale]" (1953), Fonds Foucault, FCL 3.8, Institut Mémoires de l'Édition Contemporaine (IMEC), Saint-Germain-la-Blanche-Herbe, France.

201. Antonowicz, *Mort d'un collabo*, 241–42.

202. Ibid., 251.

203. Ibid., 256.

204. Jean Schuhler, *Je m'étais réservé l'espérance: 1938–1959* (Paris: Fernand Lanore, 1979), 143–44.

205. Ibid., 146, 147.

206. Antonowicz, *Mort d'un collabo*, 258.

207. "Place d'Armes. Exécutions sommaires," *La nouvelle république du Centre-Ouest*, September 20, 1944, 2. See, too, Louis-Charles Morillon, "Les troupes étrangères dans la Wehrmacht," September 3, 2009, VRID Mémorial, https://www.vrid-memorial .com/les-troupes-etrangeres-dans-la-wehrmacht/.

208. Quoted in Antonowicz, *Mort d'un collabo*, 259.

209. *Le libre Poitou*, quoted in ibid., 257.

210. Jacques Grasseau, quoted in Antonowicz, *Mort d'un collabo*, 258.

211. "Pages d'histoire. Les leçons de la Terreur," *Le patriote Poitevin*, February 4, 1945, in Louis-Charles Morillon, "Les comités départementaux de libération. Le CDL de Poitiers," January 15, 2011, VRID Mémorial, https://www.vrid-memorial.com/les -comites-departementaux-de-liberation-le-cdl-de-poitiers/.

212. Quoted in Antonowicz, *Mort d'un collabo*, 262.

213. Paul Feuilloley, *Une randonnée préfectorale* (Paris: Bordas, 1989), 30.

214. Daniel Villey, "Commentaire," in *Redevenir des hommes libres* (Paris: Librairie de Médicis, 1946): 45–49, at 48. This article was originally published in *Le libre Poitou* on December 5, 1944.

215. The main accounts of this incident are Feuilloley, *Une randonnée préfectorale*, 29–31; Villey, "Commentaire"; and Jean Péricat, in an article that appeared in *La nouvelle république* on December 2, 1974, also available at http://pourquoipaspoitiers .over-blog.fr/article-a-poitiers-le-putsch-oubie-du-2-decembre-1944-125124555 .html.

216. Foucault, with "Victor" (Benny Lévy) and "Gilles" (André Glucksmann), "Sur la justice populaire : Débat avec les maos," in *Dits et écrits*, vol 2, *1970–1975*, 340–69, at 340, 342. This exchange was first published by *Les temps modernes no. 310* (1972): 355–66.

217. Ibid., 344.

218. Ibid., 346.

219. Ibid.

220. Ibid., 350.

221. Antonowicz, *Mort d'un collabo*, 285, 292.

222. Jean-Marie Leloup, "René Savatier, un juriste dans son siècle," unpublished lecture delivered in Paris on October 16, 1996, https://savatier.com/Rene_Savatier_-_Un _Juriste_dans_son_siecle.pdf.

223. "Décès de Jacques Quivy (1904–1965), 802–3. The record on Quivy in the Mémoire des Hommes database hosted by the French Ministère des Armées lists the Renard Network as the group Quivy was affiliated with.

224. Dr. Veluet, "Avant-propos," *Revue médicale du Centre-Ouest* 1 (October 1946): 1–2, at 1.

225. Cohn, *Behind Enemy Lines*, 279.

226. René Le Blaye, "Tribune libre: Renaissances," *Revue médicale du Centre-Ouest* 2 (November 1946): 47–49. The article to which he referred is "Allocution prononcée par le Dr. Barraud."

227. "Réponse du Dr. Le Blaye," *Revue médicale du Centre-Ouest* 4 (January 1947): 119.

228. See Donna Evleth, "La bataille pour l'Ordre des médecins, 1944–1950," *Le mouvement social* 229 (2009): 61–77, at 73–74.

229. "L'Assemblée générale du Syndicat aura lieu le dimanche 8 décembre 1946 à 14h à l'École de Médecine: Cet avis tiendra lieu de convocation. Ordre du jour," *Revue médicale du Centre-Ouest* 2 (November 1946), 52.

230. Quivy, "Nos rapports avec la Sécurité sociale," *Revue médicale des Charentes et du Poitou* 3 (December 1947): 87. In 1947, the *Revue médicale du Centre-Ouest* changed its name to the *Revue médicale des Charentes et du Poitou*.

231. Ibid.

232. Quivy, "Évolution actuelle de la Sécurité Sociale," *Revue médicale du Centre-Ouest* 7 (April 1947): 229–31, at 231.

233. "Syndicat Médical de la Vienne: Assemblée générale du 8 décembre 1946," *Revue médicale du Centre-Ouest* 3 (December 1946): 66–74, at 68.

234. Patrick Hassenteufel, "Syndicalisme et médecine libérale: Le poids de l'histoire," *Les tribunes de la santé* 18, no. 1 (2008): 21–28, at 27.

235. Foucault, "Un système fini face à une demande infinie" (interview with Robert Bono) (1983), in *Dits et écrits*, vol. 4, *1980–1988*, 367–83, at 376.

236. Ibid., 372.

237. Foucault, "Sade, sergent du sexe," 821.

Chapter 4

1. Michel Foucault, "'The Minimalist Self," interview with Stephen Riggins, in *Politics, Philosophy, Culture: Interviews and Other Writings, 1977–1984* (New York: Routledge, Chapman, and Hall, 1988), 3–16, at 7. This interview, which was conducted in English, was first published as "Michel Foucault: An Interview" in *Ethos* 1, no. 2 (1983): 4–9.

2. Foucault, "Je me suis toujours intéressé aux bas-fonds," interview with Jacques Chancel, France Inter, "Radioscopie," March 10, 1975, https://www.franceinter.fr/emissions/radioscopie-par-jacques-chancel/radioscopie-par-jacques-chancel-26-juillet-2016.

3. Friedrich Nietzsche, "On Truth and Lie in the Extra-Moral Sense," trans. Walter Kaufman, in *The Portable Nietzsche*, ed. Kaufman (Harmondsworth: Penguin Books, 1976) 42–47, at 42, 43.

4. Foucault, "Leçon sur Nietzsche: Comment penser l'histoire de la verité avec Nietzsche sans s'appuyer sur la vérité" (1971), in *Leçons sur la volonté de savoir: Cours*

au Collège de France, 1970–1971 (Paris: Gallimard/Seuil, 2011), 195–213, at 197, 198, and 206.

5. Nietzsche, "On Truth and Lie in the Extra-Moral Sense," 43.

6. Denys Foucault, "Nés pour apprendre," interview with Jean-Luc Terradillos, *L'actualité Poitou-Charentes* 51 (2001): 28–29, at 29.

7. Nietzsche, "On Truth and Lie in the Extra-Moral Sense," 42–43.

8. Pierre Rivière, "À Saint-Stanislas avec Michel Foucault," interview with Pierre Pérot and Jean-Luc Terradillos, *L'actualité Poitou-Charentes* 99 (2013): 46.

9. Sébastien Charléty, "Paulin Malapert (1862–1937)," *Bulletin de l'Association amicale des anciens élèves de la Faculté des lettres de Paris*, March 1938, 21–23, at 22.

10. Henri Bergson, "La philosophie française (tableau récapitulatif destiné à l'Exposition de San Francisco)," *La revue de Paris*, May 15, 1915, 236–56, at 244 n2.

11. Malapert, *De Spinozae politica* (Paris: Félix Alcan, 1897).

12. Malapert, *Leçons de philosophie*, vol. 1, *Psychologie* (Paris: Félix Juven, 1907), 1–2.

13. Foucault, "La recherche scientifique et la psychologie," in *Dits et écrits*, ed. Daniel Defert, François Ewald, and Jacques Lagrange, vol. 1, *1954–1969* (Paris: Gallimard, 1994), 137–58, at 138 This esssay was first published in Jean-Édouard Morère, ed., *Des chercheurs français s'interrogent: Orientation et organisation du travail scientifique en France* (Paris: Privat/Presses universitaires de France, 1957), 171–201.

14. Malapert, *Leçons de philosophie*, vol. 1, *Psychologie*, 8.

15. Malapert and Madame Roy, *Psychologie appliquée à la morale et à l'éducation* (Paris: Félix Juven, 1910), 1.

16. Ibid., 2.

17. Ibid., 16.

18. Foucault, "La recherche scientifique et la psychologie," 139.

19. "Thèses de doctorat" (a report on Malapert's defense of his Latin and French theses), *Revue de métaphysique et de morale* 6, no. 1 (January 1898): 15–20.

20. Ibid., 18.

21. Malapert, *Les éléments du caractère et leurs lois de combinaison* (Paris: Félix Alcan, 1897), 300, 302.

22. Foucault, *Maladie mentale et personnalité* (Paris: Presses universitaires de France, 1954), 10, 34. In the latter quote, Foucault is referring to the school of psychiatry inspired by John Hughlings Jackson.

23. Malapert, *Leçons de philosophie*, vol. 1, *Psychologie*, 455; Malapert, *Le caractère* (Paris: Octave Doin, 1902), 36–37.

24. Malapert, *Le caractère*, 36–37, 64, and 126–27.

25. Ibid., 10n1.

26. Minutes of the Conseil de la Faculté de Lettres, Paris, June 16, 1906, quoted in Terry Nichols Clark, *Prophets and Patrons: The French University and the Emergence of the Social Sciences* (Cambridge, Mass.: Harvard University Press, 1973), 75–76n15.

27. Paulin Malapert, "Le but et la nature de l'enseignement secondaire," in *L'éducation de la démocratie: Leçons professées à l'École des hautes études sociales* (Paris: Félix Alcan, 1903), 121–55, at 143–45.

28. Malapert, *Aux jeunes gens: Quelques conseils de morale pratique*, 3rd ed. (Paris: Armand Colin, 1902), 93, 95.

29. "Avis et communications," *L'univers*, December 22, 1907, 4.

30. Malapert, "La morale sexuelle à l'école," *Médecine et pédagogie: Leçons professées à l'École des hautes études sociales* (Paris: Félix Alcan, 1910), 133–48.

31. "Séance plénière supplémentaire du 5 août, 2 heures," *IIIéme Congrès international d'hygiène scolaire, Paris 2–7 août, 1910*, vol. 3 (Paris: A. Maloine, 1910), 157–68.

32. "Séance du 28 février 1911: L'Éducation sexuelle," *Bulletin de la Société française de philosophie* 11 (1911): 29–52.

33. Malapert, "La morale sexuelle à l'école," 134–35, 133.

34. "Séance plénière supplémentaire du 5 août," 157.

35. Malapert, "La morale sexuelle à l'école," 136–37.

36. Ibid., 138.

37. Ibid., 140.

38. Ibid., 142, 145, 143.

39. Ibid., 143–44.

40. Ibid., 144.

41. Ibid., 147.

42. "La page des anciens," *Bulletin de l'Amicale des anciens élèves de l'École Saint-Stanislas et des frères de Poitiers* 13 (March 1948): 5–8, at 5–6.

43. Alexandre Dumas, *Mes mémoires*, vol. 1 (Paris: Michel Lévy Frères, 1865), 274.

44. Dumas, *My Memoirs*, vol. 1, *1802–1821*, trans. E. M. Waller (New York: Macmillan, 1907), 283–84 (I have slightly edited the original translation to adjust it to modern spelling).

45. Foucault, "Conte[sic] rendu de lecture: Dans le miel" (handwritten school essay), in Foucault's file at the Lycée des Garçons of Poitiers (also known as Lycée Henri IV), 10 T 2823, Archives Départementales de la Vienne, Poitiers, France.

46. Jacques Derrida, *Spurs: Nietzsche's Style / Éperons, les styles de Nietzsche*, trans. Barbara Harlow (Chicago: University of Chicago Press, 1979), 123.

47. Dom Marcel Pierrot, unpublished memoirs, handwritten, second entry marked "janv. [January] 1943," archive of the Saint Martin Abbey of Ligugé, Ligugé, France. I am grateful for the assistance of the monastery's archivist, Father Lucien-Jean Bord.

48. Foucault, "Foucault khâgne," unpublished handwritten manuscript, dated January 17, 1945, in Foucault's file at the Lycée des Garçons of Poitiers (also known as Lycée Henri IV), 10 T 2823, Archives Départementales de la Vienne, Poitiers, France.

49. Yvon Lamy and Guillaume Renaud, "Le 'bizutage' dans les classes préparatoires aux grandes écoles," *Genèses* 9 (1992): 138–49, at 138, 139.

50. Rivière, "À Saint-Stanislas avec Michel Foucault," 46.

51. M. le chanoine Bodet, "L'homme: Ses origines et sa formation," in *Georges Duret: Prêtre, philosophe, poète, et martyr, 1887–1943* (Paris: Éditions du Témoignage Chrétien, 1947), 1–10.

52. René-Fernand Aigrain was another priest who marked Foucault's early years. Born in Poitiers in 1886, he studied in Rome and was ordained in Poitiers, where he spent the rest of his life. Early on, he developed a fascination with early church and medieval history, solidifying his reputation as a man of great erudition. He published a book on the life of Saint Radegund, one of the best-known local saints (after whom Foucault's mother was named), followed by another on Saint Isidore of Pelusium. He became an expert on inscriptions, authoring several books on the field, including a *Manuel d'épigraphie chrétienne* (Handbook of Christian epigraphy). After he became a professor of medieval history at the Catholic University of Angers, he published books on hagiography, martyrology, and Christian archeology. He was, moreover, an accomplished organist and an expert on church music. Unlike his friend Duret, Aigrain's knowledge and scholarship received national recognition, earning him the Legion of Honor. He died in 1957. On Aigrain's significance, Eribon quotes Foucault's classmate Pierre Rivière, who emphasized the abbot's famous personal library: "Foucault was, like me, very assiduous at the abbot Aigrain's . . . and the abbot's library mattered to us because these were readings that occurred independently of any school curriculum" (Eribon, *Michel Foucault* [Paris: Flammarion, 1991], 25). In a more recent interview, Rivière notes that he and Foucault appreciated not only Aigrain's book collection, but also the man himself, who had "a good sense of humor" and "pulled everyone's leg, most of all his colleagues'" (Rivière, "À Saint-Stanislas avec Michel Foucault," 46). On Aigrain, see Charles-Edmond Perrin, "Éloge funèbre de M. René Aigrain, correspondant français de l'Académie," *Comptes rendus des séances de l'Académie des Inscriptions et Belles-Lettres* 101, no. 3 (1957): 228–31; and Paul Antin "Le chanoine René Aigrain (1886–1957)," *Cahiers de civilisation médiévale* 1, no. 2 (1958): 221–24.

53. Georges Duret, "La littérature chrétienne au Moyen âge," in *Ecclesia: Encyclopédie populaire des connaissances religieuses*, ed. René Aigrain (Paris: Libraire Bloud et Gay, 1928), 570–94.

54. Aimé Forest, "Les idées philosophiques du Chanoine Duret," *Georges Duret: Prêtre, philosophe, poète, et martyr*, 95–113, at 97.

55. Charles Péguy, *Œuvres complètes de Charles Péguy: 1873–1914*, vol. 7, *Ève* (Paris: Éditions de la Nouvelle Revue Française, 1925), 182. The idea that Duret embraced this aspect of Péguy's thought is referenced in Jean Toulat, "Un témoin de la lumière: Prêtre, philosophe, poète, 'martyr'; Georges Duret," *Eccelisa* 196 (1965): 109–15. The same passage from "Ève" is quoted by Forest in "Les idées philosophiques du Chanoine Duret," 98.

56. Péguy, *Notre jeunesse* (Paris: Cahiers de la quinzaine, 1910), 27.

57. Duret, "Quelques maximes de morale personnelle," in G 7–12 Georges Duret (Chanoine), box 2, Archives Historiques, Diocèse de Poitiers, Poitiers, France. Duret also quoted the same passage from Péguy to define his conception of a "Christian

humanism"—that is, a liberal arts education that was infused with faith's transcendent values. See Duret, "Réponse de M. Georges Duret: Idée d'un humanisme chrétien," *L'enseignement chrétien*, April 1933, 304–5, at 305.

58. Duret, "La formation chrétienne par la classe IV," *L'enseignement chrétien*, July 1931, 437–40, at 438.

59. Péguy, *Victor-Marie, comte Hugo* (Paris: Gallimard, 1934), 88–89.

60. Quoted in Joseph Coindre, "Le mouvement spirituel des *Cahiers pour les professeurs catholiques de France*," in *Georges Duret*, 185–238, at 196.

61. The titles in parentheses are the names of specific issues of the *Cahiers*.

62. Coindre, "Le mouvement spirituel des *Cahiers pour les professeurs catholiques de France*," 197.

63. René Aigrain, "Saint Polycarpe," *Série préparatoire aux cahiers pour les professeurs catholiques de France* 3, no. 5 (1920): 3–24.

64. René Aigrain, *Pour qu'on lise les pères*, vol. 1, *Les pères apostoliques* (Paris: Bloud et Gay, 1922).

65. Aigrain, "Origène et les études classiques," *Série préparatoire aux cahiers pour les professeurs catholiques de France* 4, no. 2 (1920), 3–16.

66. Duret, "Les lectures en classe de philosophie," *L'enseignement chrétien*, November 1933, 41–44, at 44.

67. The two works in which Foucault engaged most thoroughly with the Church Fathers were the 1980 lectures *Du gouvernement des vivants: Cours au Collège de France, 1979–1980* (Paris: Gallimard/Seuil, 2012); and *Histoire de la sexualité*, vol. 4, *Les aveux de la chair* (Paris: Gallimard, 2018). Augustine is particularly important to the argument Foucault makes in the latter's final two chapters.

68. Jon Kirwan, *An Avant-Garde Theological Generation: The "Nouvelle Théologie" and the French Crisis of Modernity* (Oxford: Oxford University Press, 2018), 57.

69. Sister Baptista Landry, "Étude théologique: Retour sur le Chanoine G. Duret," *D'hier à demain (alumni* newsletter for the École Saint-Stanislas) 134 (2015): 15–29, at 25.

70. Duret, "Les lectures en classe de philosophie," 42; Landry, "Étude théologique," 20.

71. Pierre Rousselot, *L'intellectualisme de Saint Thomas* (Paris: Gabriel Beauchesne, 1936 [1908]).

72. Jean Daniélou, "Les journées universitaires de Poitiers," *Études* 227 (1936): 327–35, at 327.

73. Ibid., 328.

74. Marcel Guilloteau, "Le professeur," in *Georges Duret: Prêtre, philosophe, poète, et martyr, 1897–1943*, 59–94, at 61.

75. Ibid., 61–62.

76. Duret's "Cours de culture générale" is mentioned in ibid., 70.

77. Émile Baudin, *Cours de psychologie* (Paris: de Gigord, 1917). On Baudin, see Charles Robert, "Émile Baudin (1875–1948): Enseignement à la Faculté; 1919–1942," in *Revue des sciences religieuses* 43, no. 3–4 (1969): 338–39.

78. Charles Lahr, *Éléments de philosophie scientifique et de philosophie morale, suivis de sujets de dissertations donnés aux différentes Facultés, à l'usage des classes de mathématiques A et B* (Paris: G. Beauchesne, 1908).

79. François Mauriac, *La robe prétexte* (Paris: Grasset, 2014 [1914]).

80. Duret's assigned readings are found in Guilloteau, "Le professeur," 63.

81. Quoted in ibid., 84.

82. Ibid., 78-93.

83. Quoted in ibid., 66. This passage is italicized in the original.

84. Ibid., 80.

85. Georges Duret, "La morale," typescript of lecture notes, in "Manuscrits Georges Duret, dépôt Marcel Guilloteau, 19 mai, 1998," in G 7-12 Georges Duret (Chanoine), box 2, 1. Archives historiques, Diocèse de Poitiers, Poitiers, France.

86. Ibid., 3.

87. Ibid., 12.

88. Ibid., 23.

89. Ibid., 5.

90. Quoted in Guilloteau, "Le professeur," 213-14. In this passage, Duret seems heavily influenced by Maurice Blondel, though he does not cite him.

91. Duret, "La morale,"22.

92. Toulat, "Un témoin de la lumière," 111. The quote Duret is paraphrasing from Péguy is "*Le kantisme a les mains pures*, mais il n'a pas de mains." *Victor-Marie, comte Hugo*, 223.

93. Toulat, "Un témoin de la lumière," 110.

94. Foucault knew of the Curé d'Ars and seems to have associated him with his own Catholic upbringing. In his dialogues with Thierry Voeltzel, when the latter referenced the Curé d'Ars, Foucault expressed bemused surprise that the saint was "still" discussed in Catholic circles. See Thierry Voeltzel, *Vingt ans et après* (Paris: Gallimard, 2014 [1978]), 12.

95. Coindre, "Le mouvement spirituel des *Cahiers pour les professeurs catholiques de France*," 186, 214.

96. Guilloteau, "Détachement total," in *D'hier à demain* (issue devoted to Georges Duret), November 6, 2012, 33-34, at 33.

97. Quoted in ibid., 33, 34.

98. Landry, "Étude théologique," 16, 17, 22.

99. Testimonial of Chanoine G. Papin, in Jean Vaudel, ed., *Les Collèges Saint-Joseph et Saint-Stanislas de Poitiers, 1607-1980: Notes historiques et souvenirs d'anciens* (Poitiers: Brassaud, 1982), 388-95, at 391.

100. René Savatier, "Un conducteur d'âmes: L'aumônier des universitaires et le théologien de la résistance," in *Georges Duret: Prêtre, philosophe, poète, et martyr*, 239-44, at 242-43. See, too, Landry, "Étude théologique," 24.

101. J[oseph] Coindre, "Fleurs d'héroisme: Le chanoine Georges Duret," *La croix*, March 6, 1946, 2.

102. Henri Auroux, "Le martyr," in *Georges Duret: Prêtre, philosophe, poète, et martyr, 1897–1943*, 245–56, at 247.

103. Ibid.

104. Jean-Henri Calmon, "Des ecclésiastiques dans le Réseau Renard," in *D'hier à demain* 134 (2015): 5–14, at 6–7.

105. Quoted in ibid., 7.

106. Auroux, "Le martyr," 249.

107. Ibid., 253.

108. Landry, "Étude théologique" 17.

109. Quoted in Auroux, "Le martyr," 255.

110. These accounts of Duret's prison experience are from ibid., 250–54.

111. Georges Duret, *Accents*, quoted in Paul Antin, "Georges Duret, 1887–1943," undated offprint of an essay originally published in *La revue du Bas-Poitou et des Provinces de l'Ouest* 3–4 (1968): 1–12, at 7. The original French reads: "*Mille prudences à mentir / Ne combleront jamais l'absence de martyr.*"

112. Quoted in Auroux, "Le martyr," 255.

113. Abbé Bardeau, quoted in Guilloteau, "Le sacrifice supreme," in *D'hier à demain*, November 6, 2012, 40–44, at 44.

114. In the November 6, 2012 issue of *D'hier à demain*, Guilloteau's essay includes the information and testimonials he gathered to initiate the process of Duret's beatification. At this time, the diocesan inquiry that Guilloteau requested does not seem to have been opened.

115. Eribon, *Michel Foucault (1926–1984)*, 25.

116. David Macey, *The Lives of Michel Foucault* (New York: Pantheon, 1994), 10.

117. Rivière, "À Saint-Stanislas avec Michel Foucault," 46.

118. Duret, "Qu'est-ce que la psychologie scientifique?," *L'enseignement chrétien* 89 (1940): 99–100, at 99. See, too, Duret, "Comment l'automatisme psychologique éclaire notre nature," *L'enseignement chrétien* 64 (1933): 361–64.

119. See Foucault's essay on Maurice Blanchot, "La pensée du dehors," in *Dits et écrits*, vol. 1, *1954–1969*, 518–39. This essay was originally published in *Critique* 229 (1966): 523–46.

120. Foucault, *Le courage de la vérité: Le gouvernement des soi et des autres II; Cours au Collège de France, 1984* (Paris: Gallimard/Seuil, 2009), 290.

121. Ibid., 291.

122. Quoted in Guilloteau, "Détachement total," 34.

123. Foucault, "On the Genealogy of Ethics: An Overview of Work in Progress" in Hubert L. Dreyfus and Paul Rabinow, *Michel Foucault: Beyond Structuralism and Hermeneutics* (Chicago: University of Chicago Press, 1983), 229–52, at 236; Foucault "À propos de la généalogie de l'éthique: Un aperçu du travail en cours," in *Dits et écrits*, vol. 4, *1980–1988*, ed. Daniel Defert, François Ewald, and Jacques Lagrange (Paris: Gallimard, 1994), 383–411, at 391.

124. Foucault, *Histoire de la sexualité*, vol. 4, *Les aveux de la chair* (Paris: Gallimard, 2018), 48–51 passim.

125. Foucault, *Le courage de la vérité*, 307.

126. Louis Girard, "Premier pas en philo," interview with Jean-Luc Terradillos, *L'actualité Poitou-Charentes* 51 (2001): 30–31, at 30.

127. "La page des anciens," 5–6.

128. Testimonial of Chanoine G. Papin, in *Les Collèges Saint-Joseph et Saint-Stanislas de Poitiers* 392. Eribon makes the same claim, without mentioning Bardinette by name. *Michel Foucault*, 25.

129. Denys Foucault, "Nés pour apprendre," 28. This story also seems to be the basis of the one Macey tells in *Lives of Michel Foucault*, 10–11.

130. Eribon, *Michel Foucault*, 25.

131. Denys Foucault, "Nés pour apprendre," 28; Macey, *Lives of Michel Foucault*, 11.

132. Macey, *Lives of Michel Foucault*, 11.

133. Husymans drew on his experience at Ligugé when writing his novel *L'oblat* (Paris: Stock, 1903), Claudel on his in his play *Partage de midi* (Paris: Folio, 1972 [1905]). More recently, the Saint Martin Abbey of Ligugé figures in Michel Houellebecq's novel *Soumission* (Paris: Flammarion, 2015).

134. Macey, *Lives of Michel Foucault*, 2.

135. Fr. Vincent Desprez, "Dom Marcel Pierrot (moine de Ligugé), 1903–1991," *Lettre de Ligugé* 258 (1991): 35–43, 36.

136. The information on Pierrot's life is found in ibid.

137. See Marcel Pierrot, "Relier foi et culture," interview with Patrick de Ruffray, unpublished typescript, 6, Archive of the Saint Martin Abbey of Ligugé, Ligugé, France. This extended interview seems to have been intended to be published as a book.

138. All quotes in this paragraph are from "Notre contribution personnelle au redressement de la France ((résumé de trois conférences) par le R. P. Dom Pierrot de l'Abbaye Saint-Martin de Ligugé," Offprint, Saint Martin Abbey of Ligugé, Ligugé, France. This summary of Pierrot's lectures originally appeared in *Intérêt public*, December 6 and 13, 1941 (this publication was printed in Cholet, where Pierrot gave one version of his lecture cycle).

139. Pierrot, unpublished memoirs, second page of entry for January 14, 1943.

140. Macey, *Lives of Michel Foucault*, 11. Both Macey and Eribon (*Michel Foucault*, 25) mention that Pierrot did little more than gloss the textbook.

141. Pierrot, unpublished memoirs, first entry marked "janv. [January]1943."

142. Pierrot, unpublished memoirs, untitled entry on his time at Collège Saint Stanislas.

143. Girard, "Premier pas en philo," 30–31.

144. Pierrot, unpublished memoirs, entry for "janv. [January] 1943."

145. Pierrot, unpublished memoirs, second entry marked "janv. [January] 1943."

146. Eribon, *Michel Foucault*, 26.

147. In an email from July 31, 2017, Father Lucien-Jean Bord, a librarian at the Ligugé monastery, informed me that in the library catalogue, "there is no book from Foucault that has been autographed for Father Pierrot and there is no trace in older inventories of books by Foucault that Pierrot gave to the library or coming from his personal possessions."

148. Foucault, *Histoire de la folie à l'âge classique* (Paris: Gallimard, 1972 [1961]), 58.

149. Foucault, *Les mots et les choses: Archéologie des sciences humaines* (Paris: Gallimard, 1966), 87.

150. Pierrot, "Relier foi et culture," 42–45.

151. Pierrot, unpublished memoirs, entry for "late June 1984."

152. Girard, "Premier pas en philo," 31. Macey recounts a very similar story (based on an earlier conversation with Girard) in *The Lives of Michel Foucault*, 11.

153. Eribon, *Michel Foucault*, 26.

154. Ibid. Émile Boutroux (1845–1921) was a prominent Kantian philosopher, whose work Foucault later read.

155. Girard, "Premier pas en philo," 31.

156. Audrey Levy, "Le prof de Michel Foucault se souvient," *Le point*, April 21, 2015, https://www.lepoint.fr/villes/le-prof-de-michel-foucault-se-souvient-21-04-2015-1923074_27.php.

157. On Carré, see Marcel Larnaude, "Jean-Raoul Carré (1887–1963)," offprint of essay originally published in the *Annuaire 1964 of the Amicale des anciens élèves de l'École normale supérieure*, Bibliothèque universitaire lettres et langues, University of Poitiers, Poitiers, France. See, too, Joseph Moreau, "Jean-Raoul Carré (1887–1963)," *Les études philosophiques* 20, no. 2 (1965): 211–12.

158. Carré, "Pour la centcinquantenaire de la Révolution française: La conquête de la liberté spirituelle" in *La revue de métaphysique et de morale* 46, no. 4 (1939): 627–46, 627–28. This essay was also published as *La conquête de la liberté spirituelle annonciatrice de la Révolution française* (Poitiers: Imprimerie Marc Texier, 1939), 3.

159. Carré, "Sur quelques jugements de valeur et leur réduction ou non réduction à l'unité," *Bulletin de la Société philosophique de Bordeaux* 4, no. 17 (1949): 1–13, at 7, 10.

160. Jacques d'Hondt describes how Carré, his teacher, wrote a letter introducing him to Hyppolite. See d'Hondt, "Jean Hyppolite, un homme de parole," *L'actualité Poitou-Charente* 62 (2003): 22–23, at 22. The offprint of Carré's *La conquête de la liberté spirituelle* available from the Bibliothèque des Lettres et des Langues at the University of Poitiers has a signed inscription for Wahl.

161. Girard, "Premier pas en philo," 31.

162. Ibid.; Eribon, *Michel Foucault*, 26.

163. Girard, "Premier pas en philo," 31; Levy, "Le prof de Michel Foucault se souvient."

164. After the war, Girard passed the *agrégation* in philosophy. He taught for a while at Poitiers's Lycée Henri IV—which Foucault had attended before Saint-Stanislas and where

he did his *khâgne*—before becoming a teacher, notably of *khâgne* students. Girard was also a lifelong labor activist, both locally and in the internal politics of several unions, including the teachers' union and the major Catholic union, the Confédération Française des Travailleurs Chrétiens (CFTC), which he remained with after it became the Confédération Française Démocratique du Travail (CFDT). For what it is worth Girard is one of two of Foucault's teachers (with Duret) to have an entry in Maitron's biographical dictionary of the French labor movement. After his retirement, Girard completed a doctoral thesis directed by the Poitevin philosopher Jacques d'Hondt, entitled *L'argument ontologique chez Saint Anselme et chez Hegel* (Amsterdam: Rodopi, 1995). He died in 2016.

165. Girard, "Premier pas en philo," 31. In the same interview, Girard also tells a story of how, after he got married (and was invited for the occasion to the Foucault home in Vendeuvre), he told Foucault "now it's your turn." "He went completely red," Girard recalls. "That's when I understood."

Conclusion

1. "Concours pour l'admission à l'École Normale Supérieure et pour l'obtention des bourses de licence (Lettres)" [1945] (gradebook with handwritten notes), AN 930593-62, Archives Nationales, Pierrefitte-sur-Seine, France.

2. "Concours de 1945 pour l'admission à l'École Normale Supérieure et pour l'obtention des bourses de licence (Lettres)" (typescript report, dated January 8), AN 930593-62, Archives Nationales, Pierrefitte-sur-Seine, France.

3. René Le Senne and Georges Canguilhem, "Philosophie" (typescript, report on the 1945 ENS entrance exam philosophy paper, included in a typescript consisting of reports on all the 1945 ENS exams; the philosophy report is at 9–10, quote at 9), AN 930593-62, Archives Nationales, Pierrefitte-sur-Seine, France.

4. "Concours pour l'admission à l'École Normale Supérieure et pour l'obtention des bourses de licence (Lettres)" [1946] (gradebook with handwritten notes), AN 930593-62, Archives Nationales, Pierrefitte-sur-Seine, France.

5. Foucault, *Maladie mentale et personnalité* (Paris: Presses universitaires de France, 1954); Foucault, "Introduction," in Ludwig Binswanger, *Le rêve et l'existence*, trans. Jacqueline Verdeaux (Bruges: Desclée de Brouwer, 1954), 9–128.

6. Many of these are now available in the Fonds Michel Foucault in the Manuscripts Department of the Bibliothèque Nationale de France in Paris.

7. The first topic was the subject of Foucault's 1949 thesis for his *diplôme d'études supérieures*, "La constitution du transcendantal dans la Phénoménologie de l'Esprit de Hegel," Fonds Michel Foucault, NAF 28803, Manuscripts Department, Bibliothèque Nationale de France, Paris, France; the second refers to an unpublished manuscript (presumably lecture notes), "Psychologie et phénoménologie," Fonds Michel Foucault, NAF 28803, box 46:4, Manuscripts Department, Bibliothèque Nationale de France, Paris, France; the third and fourth are listed as Foucault's research projects during his fellowship at the Fondation Thiers from 1951 to 1952; see "Rapports du directeur

au Conseil d'administration sur le travaux des pensionnaires, du 1er octobre 1946 au 30 septembre 1952," in *Annuaire de la Fondation Thiers, 1947-1952: Cinquante-troisième à cinquante-neuvième année de la Fondation* (Issoudun: Imprimerie H. Gaignault et fils, 1953), 12-42, at 40.

8. Foucault, *Maladie mentale et personnalité*, 13.

9. See, in particular, Foucault, "Cours sur la phénoménologie et Binswanger" (1952), Fonds Michel Foucault, NAF 28803, box 46:3, Manuscripts Department, Bibliothèque Nationale de France, Paris, France.

10. See Foucault, "Introduction," Binswanger, *Le rêve et l'existence*.

11. Stuart Elden, *The Early Foucault* (Cambridge: Polity, 2021).

12. These ideas are drawn largely from Foucault's 1962 complementary thesis, now published as Emmanuel Kant, *Anthropologie du point de vue pragmatique* / Michel Foucault, *Introduction à l'Anthropologie,* ed. Daniel Defert, François Ewald, and Frédéric Gros (Paris: Vrin, 2008), 11-79.

13. See Foucault's *Histoire de la folie à l'âge classique* (Paris: Gallimard, 1972 [1961]), particularly the final chapter, fittingly entitled "Le cercle anthropologique," 531-57.

14. My argument here draws on my contribution on Foucault to *The Cambridge History of French Thought,* ed. Jeremy Jennings and Michael Moriarty (Cambridge: Cambridge University Press, 2019), 456-66. I hope to return to the question of the "young Foucault" as construed above in a later work.

15. Foucault, *Les mots et les choses: Une archéologie des sciences humaines* (Paris: Gallimard, 1966), 333-46, 398.

16. For the most sophisticated and persuasive version of this argument, see Béatrice Han, *L'ontologie manquée de Michel Foucault: Entre l'historique et le transcendantal* (Paris: Éditions Jérôme Million, 1998).

17. I am paraphrasing Jean-Paul Sartre's famous comments about Paul Valéry in *Critique de la raison dialectique précédé de Question de méthode, vol. 1, Théorie des ensembles pratiques* (Paris: Gallimard, 1960), 44.

18. See, in this vein, Amy Richlin, "Foucault's *History of Sexuality*: A Useful Theory for Women?," in David H. Larmour, Paul Allen Miller, and Charles Platter, *Rethinking Sexuality: Foucault and Classical Antiquity* (Princeton, N.J.: Princeton University Press, 1998), 138-70.

19. See, notably, Ann Laura Stoler's important essay *Race and the Education of Desire: Foucault's "History of Sexuality" and the Colonial Order of Things* (Durham, N.C.: Duke University Press, 1995).

20. Foucault, "Débat avec Michel Foucault au Centre Culturel de l'Athénée Français: Tokyo, le 21 avril 1978," Fonds Foucault, FCL 2.13, Institut Mémoires de l'Édition Contemporaine (IMEC), Saint-Germain-la-Blanche-Herbe, France.

21. Foucault, "Une esthétique de l'existence" (interview with Alessandro Fontana), in ibid., 730-35, at 731. A highly edited version of this interview initially appeared in Italian in *Panorama* on May 28, 1984. A more complete version was published in *Le Monde* on July 15-16, 1984, xi.

A Note on Biography

1. Luc Ferry and Alain Renaut, *French Philosophy of the Sixties: An Essay on Anti-humanism*, trans. Mary Schnackenberg Cattani (Amherst: University of Massachusetts Press, 1990 [1985]), [vii]. The anecdote originally appeared in the French newspaper *Le Pèlerin* on September 1, 1929, 13.

2. Didier Eribon, *Michel Foucault (1926-1984)* (Paris: Flammarion, 1991), 15.

3. Ibid., 12.

4. Ibid., 44.

5. Eribon, *Réflexions sur la question gay* (Paris: Flammarion, 2012 [1999]), 379.

6. David Macey, *The Lives of Michel Foucault*, xxiii. Miller also consulted Defert for his biography.

7. Ibid., xi.

8. All these insights are found in Macey's introduction, xi–xxiii.

9. Ibid., 11–12.

10. James Miller, *The Passion of Michel Foucault* (New York: Simon and Schuster, 1993), 5. In the interest of full disclosure, I should note that I was briefly a student of James Miller at Brown University at the time he was writing his book. I assisted him in transcribing tapes of some of Foucault's lectures, in addition to discussing his ideas with him as he wrote. That said, at no point in the writing and conception of the present book was I in contact with Miller, though I continue to admire his scholarly work.

11. Ibid., 9.

12. Ibid., 19.

13. Ibid., 20.

14. Ibid., 105.

15. Ibid., 143.

16. Ibid., 251, 268.

17. Ibid., 29.

18. Ibid. Miller states this point as a question, but he clearly takes seriously this possibility.

19. The first charge is made by historian and queer theorist David Halperin, the second by Didier Eribon. For Halperin, the first problem with Miller's interpretation of Foucault's life is that it exemplifies intellectual habits that the philosopher excoriated, so that a Foucault biography becomes a singularly anti-Foucauldian book. Whatever its other qualities, Miller's book is, Halperin contends, "politically opposed" to "Foucault's project." (David M. Halperin's *Saint Foucault: Towards a Gay Historiography* [New York: Oxford University Press, 1995], 145). Halperin argues that the whole point of Foucault's analysis of the politics of discourse and knowledge was "to expose the strategic conjunction of expert knowledge and institutional power in such socially authorized practices as the narrativizing of individuality, and in order to frustrate (insofar as he could) the complex political technology to which such practices materially contribute" (130). By subjecting Foucault's private life to relentless interpretation Miller claims a "privileged access to the 'truth' of Foucault's alleged psychopathology" (165). Second,

Miller's account of Foucault's sex life is, according to Halperin, homophobic. Miller, he maintains, plays a dubious truth game in which the clues to Foucault's thought are always to be found in his personal life, and in which his personal life, in turn, is always interpreted in terms that play into straight men's exoticizing fantasies about gay life. In a scathing critique of Miller's book, Eribon takes a different approach: in his view, Miller's interpretive framework is simply implausible. He doubts that Foucault's thought can be "decrypted as an 'autobiographical allegory' in which, beyond the masks of his virtuosic prose, sado-masochistic drives and a fascination with death expressed themselves" (Eribon, *Michel Foucault et ses contemporains* [Paris: Fayard, 1994], 22). Yet Eribon also expresses frustration with Halperin's critique, which is premised on the equally totalizing claim that Foucault was motivated solely by the political project of emancipating sexual minorities from normalizing power.

ARCHIVES CONSULTED

In addition to published sources, the research in this book has also drawn on archival materials. The key archives consulted are listed below.

Archives de Paris (online). Paris, France.
Archives Départementales de la Vienne. Poitiers, France.
Archives Départementales du Maine-et-Loire (online). Angers, France.
Archives Départementales des Hauts-de-Seine (online). Nanterre, France.
Archives Historiques du Diocèse de Poitiers. Poitiers, France.
Archives Municipales de Poitiers. Poitiers, France.
Archives Nationales. Pierrefitte-sur-Seine, France.
Archives, Abbé Saint-Martin de Ligugé. Ligugé, France.
Bibliothèque de l'Académie Nationale de Médecine. Paris, France.
Bibliothèque Universitaire Lettres et Langues, University of Poitiers. Poitiers, France.
Département des Manuscrits, Bibliothéque Nationale de France. Paris, France.
Institut Mémoires de l'Édition Contemporaine (IMEC). Saint-Germain-la-Blanche-Herbe, France.

INDEX

Note: MF = Michel Foucault. PF = Paul André Foucault. Page numbers followed by "f" indicate images.

ACKNOWLEDGMENTS

This book has a meandering history, beginning as a side project of a side project. It has benefited from the insight, encouragement, and patience of those who recognized that my initial ideas had the potential to become a book and who helped me bring it to fruition. The approach taken in this book owes much to the vision of intellectual history imparted to me by the scholars I have been fortunate enough to learn from over the years. Had I not studied with Jerrold Seigel and Jim Miller, I doubt this book would have been written (though the former was only negligibly involved in this project, and the latter not at all). Though their influence is more indirect, Mark Lilla and the late Tony Judt played a crucial role in shaping my understanding of European intellectual history.

If this book exists, it is due in no small part to my colleague Ralph Lentz II. Ralph convinced me that what I believed to be one part of a much longer work was in fact a coherent book. In addition to reading early drafts, he provided me, throughout the process, with encouragement, friendship, and intellectual companionship, which have left a decisive mark on its final form.

I am indebted to Jim Goff, my department chair at Appalachian State University, who continuously pressed me to complete this book (even when it was no longer a career necessity) and who went out of his way to provide me with support in times that are hardly propitious for research in the humanities.

I have benefited enormously from colleagues who took the time to read early chapters—particularly since they are unusually long. Though I cannot do justice to the uniqueness of their insight, I can at least recognize the generosity of the individuals who provided it: Emile Chabal, Shterna Friedman, Duncan Kelly, Anthony La Vopa, Hannah Malcolm, Stephen Sawyer, Matthew Specter, Iain Stewart, and Steven Vincent.

I am also grateful to the Triangle Intellectual History Seminar, whose members read and provided valuable feedback on several chapters.

In Poitiers and its environs, I benefited greatly from the expertise and assistance of Father Lucien-Jean Bord, Doctor Michel Morichau-Beauchant, Jean-François Liandier, Gérard Simmat, and Geneviève and Jean-Michel Maudet.

Sophia Rosenfeld was instrumental in helping me to submit a proposal to the University of Pennsylvania Press. At the press, I have been fortunate to have, as my editor, Bob Lockhart, whose support, discernment, and meticulousness contributed significantly to this book. Two anonymous readers also provided valuable feedback. In the final stages of the publication process, I benefited from the invaluable editorial assistance of Noreen O'Connor-Abel. I am grateful for the thorough copyediting provided by Kathleen Kageff, as well as for the indexing skills of Elspeth Tupelo. For the final revisions, I am particularly indebted to Hannah Malcolm and her attention to detail, intelligence, and patience.

At a personal level, I am grateful for the validation provided over the years by my sister, Megan Behrent. Most importantly, this book could not have been written without the constant thoughtfulness, encouragement, and care of my wife, Cathy Cole.

www.ingramcontent.com/pod-product-compliance
Lightning Source LLC
Chambersburg PA
CBHW020335100426
42812CB00029B/3133/J